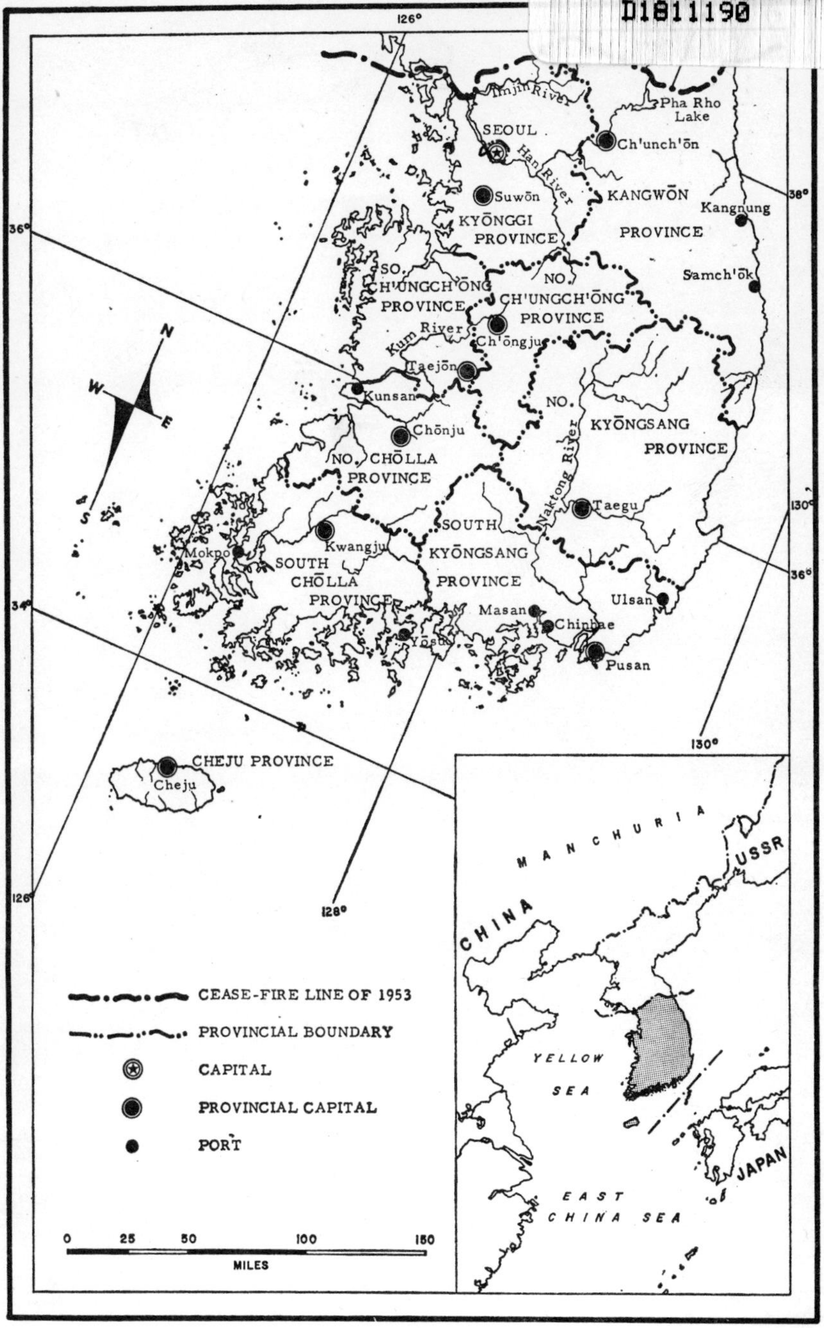

The Republic of Korea

Size: 38,175 square miles   Population: 35 million

PUBLISHED FOR THE ROYAL ASIATIC SOCIETY
KOREA BRANCH
BY THE UNIVERSITY OF WASHINGTON PRESS

KOREAN POLITICS IN TRANSITION

Edited by
EDWARD REYNOLDS WRIGHT

Contributors

Suk-choon CHO
Pyong-choon HAHM
Bae-ho HAHN
Ki-shik HAHN
Jungsae KIM
Youngnok KOO
Young-ho LEE
John P. LOVELL
Princeton LYMAN
Byung-hun OH
Edward Reynolds WRIGHT

UNIVERSITY OF WASHINGTON PRESS
SEATTLE AND LONDON
1975

Copyright © 1975 by the University of Washington Press
Printed in the Republic of Korea by Kwangmyung Printing Co.

All rights reserved. No part of this publication may be reproduced or transmitted in any form or by any means, electronic or mechanical, including photocopy, recording, or any information storage or retrieval system, without permission in writing from the publisher.

Library of Congress Cataloging in Publication Data
Main entry under title:

Korean politics in transition.

"Constitution of the Republic of Korea": p.
Bibliography: p.
Includes index.
1. Korea—Politics and government—1948–
I. Wright, Edward Reynolds, ed. II. Cho, Suk-choon, 1929–
DS917.K667   320.9'519'5043   74-34070
ISBN 0-295-95422-1

FOREWORD

This book will be welcomed by East Asian specialists and by a wide variety of scholars. There has been need for a long time for an introductory comprehensive work on the recent and contemporary politics of South Korea. Dr. Edward R. Wright has brought together an outstanding group of scholars, Korean and American, to collaborate on this successful volume which will provide a basic understanding of South Korean government and politics from standpoints of traditional culture and society, recent history, and contemporary structure, behavior, and major policy issues. Often such collaborative efforts are loose, disjointed, and of very uneven quality. The editor is to be congratulated for a well-conceived and coordinated volume. While each chapter can be read as an independent unit, each is part of a more important scholarly mosaic.

This study of South Korean politics and government should have an appeal that transcends the interests of specialists in Korean affairs. South Korea is a rapidly developing society that is seeking to establish a stable political system under great difficulties, especially the division of the Korean peninsula into two antagonistic political entities and the uncertain international context of big power politics in Northeast Asia. This situation and the long tradition of personalized authoritarian government have made it difficult, if not impossible, for South Korea to establish an effective representative and democratic system of government. At the same time, as this volume points out, there are new forces at work laying the foundation for broader and more effective popular participation in politics and government. It is to be hoped that the substantial successes of South Korea in economic and educational development and the achievement of greater regional stability in East Asia will facilitate political development in the direction of effective representative government and the strengthening of basic democratic rights and freedoms.

George M. Beckmann
Seattle, January 1975

TABLE OF CONTENTS

INTRODUCTION *by Edward Reynolds Wright*, 3

PART ONE: THE BACKGROUND, 9
    Chapter 1: The Politics of Democratic Experiment:
        1948–1974 *by Young-ho Lee*, 13

PART TWO: THE STRUCTURE AND PROCESSES OF KOREAN
    GOVERNMENT, 45
    Chapter 2: The Constitution and Governmental Structures
        by Edward Reynolds Wright, 49
    Chapter 3: The Bureaucracy *by Suk-choon Cho*, 71
    Chapter 4: Underlying Factors in Political Party
        Organization and Elections *by Ki-shik Hahn*, 85

PART THREE: MAJOR CONTRIBUTORS TO KOREAN POLITICS:
    STUDENTS AND THE MILITARY, 105
    Chapter 5: Students and Politics *by Byung-hun Oh*, 111
    Chapter 6: The Military and Politics in Postwar Korea
        by John P. Lovell, 153

PART FOUR: MAJOR POLICY FOCUSES IN CONTEMPORARY
    KOREAN POLITICS: FOREIGN AFFAIRS AND
    ECONOMIC DEVELOPMENT, 201
    Chapter 7: The Conduct of Foreign Affairs
        by Youngnok Koo, 207
    Chapter 8: Economic Development in South Korea:
        A Retrospective View of the 1960's
        by Princeton Lyman, 243
    Chapter 9: Recent Trends in the Government's Management
        of the Economy *by Jungsae Kim*, 255

PART FIVE: INTERPRETATIONS OF KOREAN POLITICS, 283
    Chapter 10: The Authority Structure of Korean Politics
        by Bae-ho Hahn, 289
    Chapter 11: Toward a New Theory of Korean Politics:
        A Reexamination of Traditional Factors
        by Pyong-choon Hahm, 321

CONSTITUTION OF THE REPUBLIC OF KOREA, 357

SELECTED BIBLIOGRAPHY OF BOOKS IN ENGLISH ON
  SOUTH KOREAN POLITICS, 385

INDEX, 393

Korean Politics In Transition

PREFACE

The essential purpose of this volume is to provide an introductory basis for understanding Korean politics. This Korean case study might also elicit meaningful comparisons for readers familiar with the politics of other developing nations.

Hopefully, the contributors have done what no single author could accomplish in preparing a balanced picture of the contemporary Korean political scene. Each author is particularly competent in the area in which he has written, and each has brought to his task a background of years of study and research. Inevitably in such a compilation there will be some repetition from chapter to chapter. Such should be looked upon as re-emphasis of significant and crucial points and not simply redundancy. While each chapter can be read as a separate entity, it is the editor's intention that the various contributions—all of which were prepared or adapted especially for this volume—constitute parts of an integrated whole. Further, the basic insights of the contributors should in no way become dated with subsequent political events, which will continue to build upon the political base explicated herein.

For the purposes of this volume, all references to "Korea" are to South Korea. This is a practical matter and in no way intended to ignore the problems of the divided Korean peninsula or the existence of its northern half, called the People's Democratic Republic of Korea. It is simply a matter of geographical focus.

Any shortcomings of the volume should be attributed to the editor and not to other contributors who have given generously of their time and scholarship. The various authors have graciously allowed the editor substantial leeway to make minor modifications and adaptations in the structure of the individual chapters. Their tolerance in this regard has been greatly appreciated. Appreciation is extended to Robert Kinney and the Seoul Branch of the

Royal Asiatic Society for inviting and encouraging the preparation of this book. Special thanks also should be given to Mrs. Cora Gatbonton whose keen eye for proofreading, editing and indexing contributed significantly to the final product. Edward Poitras gave of his time and linguistic competence to insure that spelling of Korean words and names were romanized according to the McCune-Reischauer system. This romanization system has been used for all but well-known proper names commonly spelled in other ways and for authors who have chosen the spellings and word order of their own names. Richard Rucci helped extensively in the preparation of the Bibliography. The cover design and many typographic details were done by Mrs. Sandra Mattielli. To others who read parts of the manuscript and made helpful suggestions, grateful appreciation is also expressed. This includes indispensible help by editors of the University of Washington Press. Finally, general indebtedness is acknowledged to the Korean scholars who, over the past eight years, have stimulated the editor in ways that have led to the undertaking of this first comprehensive introductory volume on contemporary Korean politics. While generous help and advice have come from many sources, final responsibility for shortcomings of this volume remains that of the editor.

Edward Reynolds Wright
Seoul, January 1975

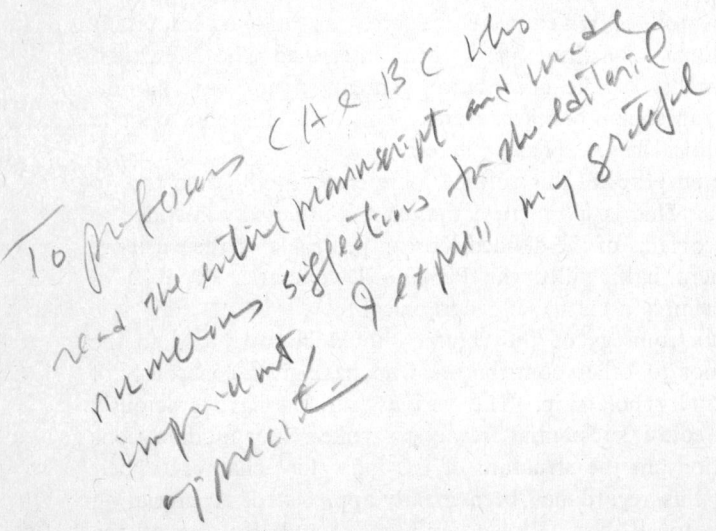

This book is gratefully dedicated to those from whom we have learned and to whom we owe so much — our parents and teachers.

INTRODUCTION

EDWARD REYNOLDS WRIGHT

By way of introduction, it can be said that the political process in Korea is highly centralized and personalized, and that the people are quite authority conscious. The nitty-gritty of political life and accomplishment is largely in terms of one's place and status in the social and political hierarchy and, relatedly, in terms of the direct personal influence one can exert on superiors and subordinates. These tactical principles seem to be operative on all levels of society and indeed can be considered to constitute the essential social fabric of the Korean people.

In Korea there are a single race, a single language, common cultural assumptions, and there is no minority group of significant size. This is in contrast to the situations in such other developing nation-states as India, Vietnam, Indonesia, and the Philippines, among others, which have populations with diverse social, cultural and/or racial compositions. Korea provides an ideal focus for a case study, not of a society which is struggling for social, cultural, economic and political identity and unity, but of one where the internal struggle for influence and power takes place on an integrative foundation already well formed.

In the years following the Second World War, western-derived liberal democratic ideas have had a phenomenal impact on the leaders of Korea, as on those of other developing nations throughout the world. Public proclamations of these leaders have spoken of a new era for their nations within a democratic political framework. At least in Korea, however, traditional elements were still strong, and these same leaders were faced with barriers to progress in the form of traditional social and political patterns. The resultant inner struggle between liberal western ideas and traditional Korean behavior has provided the basic setting for the post-war Korean political scene. To date, there has been no clear-cut resolution of this struggle. While the western democratic perspective has made inroads into the Korean political consciousness, it is equally clear that traditional factors still contribute significantly to Korean political behavior. Korea remains a transitional society—between old and new, traditional and modern.

Two crucial differences in the politics of Korea and many western nations are related to (1) the degree of centralization of power and (2) the degree of authority consciousness and dependency on the part of the masses of the people.

Politics in Korea is highly centralized and in the United States, in contrast, greatly decentralized, with perhaps the major exception being in the area of foreign policy formulation in which both have centralized decision-making systems. Korea is not overburdened with the slowness of a federal system in which political power is divided geographically, or by a structural separation of powers in which powers are delineated according to function with inbuilt institutional checks and balances.

The Korean situation provides a prime example in the non-totalitarian world of a country where public policy can be quickly and efficiently implemented. The examples are many. The Seoul-Pusan expressway was completed in little over two years, a task that would have been impossible in the United States where the carrying out of public policy is often frustrated by unenlightened public opinion and a multitude of obstacles rooted in slow and cumbersome democratic structures and procedures. In Seoul the decision to build a badly needed subway system was made rationally and effectively; construction was begun quickly, and the nine-kilometer line was completed by August 1974 in three years and four months. Resistance in the United States to the obvious need for better public transportation systems is based on irrational but traditional local government boundaries; inequitable tax burdens in neighboring governmental units; popular participation in politics, and others.

Korea has a sparkling record in comparison with other nations which are attempting to establish an industrial and technological base for society. The Koreans have flung themselves with vigor and determination into the process of economic development. Many nations classified as "developing" or "underdeveloped" are finding the task considerably more taxing and difficult. This is not necessarily to place technologically derived values above those of traditional agrarian existence; however, it is to suggest that for purely pragmatic reasons of survival in today's competitive and unstable international order, a new nation-state is compelled to progress consciously and rapidly in the transition from old to new. Without such adaptation, national entities run the considerable risk of being swallowed up or at least substantially dominated by more aggressive and powerful neighbors. Korea's economic developmental pace has been little short of phenomenal and, given the present degree of political stability and military preparedness, there seems little likelihood of imposition of outside political or military domination.

While praise for Korea is certainly in order on the above counts, we should also look at the other side of the coin. There is the danger that procedural efficiency, as evidenced in Korea, can result in arbitrarily and incautiously planned public policy. Many examples can be given. The city of Taegu was expanded many miles into the countryside in the mid-1960's before it was realized that such expansion was impractical in terms of the city government's inability to service such an enlarged area. The city limits were then summarily redrawn, roughly along the original lines. To cite another example, public apartments, called "Citizens' Apartments," were built by the Seoul city government before it was realized that in the process of sub-contracting the construction of some units turned out to be of less than the best quality. Contractors in question were then required to strengthen the undergirdings of the buildings. To give another instance, in 1972 reforestation laws were decreed to preserve and enhance the greenery in the Korean countryside; stringent penalties were to be imposed for plucking branches and small trees. The law was rescinded before it could be put into effect because it was found that villagers direly needed this source of fuel.

It seems relevant in this regard to refer to the western concept of "rule of law," a principle which westerners feel is little recognized in Korea. Stated as simply as possible, "rule of law" means that no person is exempt from the law, including public officials, and that laws are formulated in accordance with the express wishes and interests of the largest possible proportion of the citizenry. One Korean legal scholar, Hahm Pyong-choon, has pointed out that "the rule of law has never been a desirable goal of politics in Korea." This is because traditionally in Korea "Law" was seen as "an agency of rigid political regimentation.... The rule of law advocated by the Legalists, as popularly understood in the Korean political tradition, was little different from a rule of punishment or a rule by autocratic decree." The same author is quick to point out that this idea of law is a corruption of both the western view as well as the proper Korean perspective which derived from the Chinese Confucian tradition. According to the latter, the Confucian-derived concept of *Li* refers to a "moral expression of the way of the Universe." "When both the ruler and the ruled act according to *Li*, harmony prevails." So this idea of *Li*, rather than law (*Fa*), was basic to the Yi dynasty Korean political tradition. The writer continues that *Li* "is a moral expression of the way of the Universe. When both the ruler and the ruled act according to *Li*, harmony prevails. The virtuous live by it. When a society is ordered by law or by the threat of punitive sanctions, its members evade it with impunity and feel no shame. But when a society is ordered by *Li*, its members not only behave properly but also know shame. *Li* and law are thus mutually exclusive." In practice, *Li* becomes an unrealizable ideal, "more fictitiously ideal than politically real," and "the importance of countervailing forces as a prerequisite for stability was never admitted by the Confucianists.... The Confucian political theory in Korea failed to progress beyond the level of an oversimplified ideology." Further, the judicial function, which is highly institutionalized in the west for insuring that the law is equitably implemented, is hardly necessary if the ruler is "truly virtuous and benevolent." In traditional Korea "the executive or the administrative function of government ... was primary and the judicial was secondary. When the judiciary becomes predominant, it signifies a failure of government by virtue."[1]

The crucial problem is in determining when the guiding principle of *Li* is operative and when it is not. The Western tradition is inherently suspicious of rulers, and to most westerners it can never be assumed that a ruler will act with absolutely honorable intentions. Rulers have more responsibility than private citizens and therefore need more institutional and procedural checks upon their actions. Again, while being impressed by the effectiveness and efficiency with which public policy is implemented in Korea, many observers would like to see less arbitrariness and more caution and consistency in governmental procedures which culminate in concrete policy decisions.

A second major characteristic distinguishing Korean politics from that of North America and western Europe, among others, is the high degree of authority consciousness inherent in the system. Perhaps one of the most perceptive Western commentators on Asian culture is Paul Mus, who has the following to say about the social significance of Confucianism which philosophically underlies many Asian social systems:

Introduction 7

> In the Confucian society the ritual order, good direction, conformity to the past, that is to say to the cosmic structure, in the families and in the State, regulate the order of the seasons, the sun and the rain; thus understood, this society is an immense and perpetual incantation of the universe. Man does not act. He officiates. Good or evil. Certainly evil if he is not enlightened; the classical books and canons were his code: one finds in them notably the quota of ground necessary for each person to have in the collective structure so that the Empire could rest in peace.[2]

There seems to be a large degree of acceptance of events in Korean society—social, personal, political, economic—with *relatively* little questioning. In a study in 1969 related to urban transitional patterns in the city of Taegu, this writer interviewed a number of citizens concerning their perceptions of political decision-making on matters related to city development projects. In one interview a provincial government official suggested that the "intellectual level of the ordinary citizen is not so high." "The ordinary citizen has little long-range perception," and he is quite dependent on centralized authority. He concluded that "local initiative" tends to be a concept fairly alien to most Koreans. A community leader from the private sector agreed with this evaluation, giving the opinion that the people were "trained and educated in this way." They accept the Confucian dictum that "the people should follow established leadership without question, and should not be concerned about the knowledge necessary for the exercise of leadership(民可使田之, 不可使知之)." In Korea, he said, there is no real concept of the government as "servant of the people," though "lip service is paid to such an idea." In traditional terms it is "Government high, people low." A university professor suggested that most people comprehend the idea of city planning and development but feel uninvolved and do not take an active part. He pointed out that there is usually some resistance to city projects but only when a project intrudes upon some individual's or group's particular interests such as property holdings. In the same study, a professional respondent from the private sector felt that voluntary associations should be encouraged to help citizens become more participatory in local affairs. He cited as an example the desirability of strengthening mothers' clubs in schools for improvement of school facilities and programs. The people, he said, have little experience in voluntary associations and groups. He indicated a major barrier to establishment and healthy functioning of such associations—"the government is often suspicious of such groups." A government official suggested that one way to encourage more citizen participation would be to establish an elective system for city mayor and provincial governor.

In summary with regard to this survey, a substantial number of community leaders interviewed felt that the city government was largely paternalistic in its treatment of citizens. The same respondents, however, tended to agree that the masses of citizens were quite dependent on authority and as yet unaccustomed to local initiative in community development programs. From this study it was found that civic leaders' perceptions of the community power structure in Taegu point to a high degree of structural and procedural centralization, and to dependency consciousness on the part of the masses of the people.[3]

These introductory comments can be summarized by characterizing the traditional Korean political system as essentially hierarchical, personalized and authority-oriented. Subsequent chapters in this volume can be considered as variations on these themes.

FOOTNOTES

1. Hahm Pyong-choon, *The Korean Political Tradition and Law*. Seoul: Hollym Publishers and the Royal Asiatic Society, Korea Branch, pp. 15-30.
2. Paul Mus, *Viet-Nam: Sociologie d'une Guerre*. Paris: Editions du Seuil, 1952, p. 247.
3. Lee Man-Gap and Herbert Barringer, eds., *A City in Transition: Urbanization in Taegu, Korea*. Seoul: Hollym Corporation, 1971, pp. 243-266.

PART ONE: **THE BACKGROUND**

CHAPTER 1: The Politics of Democratic Experiment:
            1948–1974
            by Young-ho Lee

INTRODUCTION TO PART ONE

Young-ho Lee, in his chronological survey of Korean politics during the crucial postwar years, has taken the governmental system at its democratically based face value and examined the policies and behavioral patterns of consecutive governments in light of those governments' self-espoused democratic norms. Lee contends that the first constitutionally-based regime in Korea, that led by Syngman Rhee, betrayed its mission—that of building a foundation for democratic government in Korea. Rhee, often autocratic and arbitrary in his rule, tended to by-pass the constitutionally defined decision-making process, and allowed an atmosphere in which corruption and bribery flourished. In short, Rhee's rule was tradition-based and evidenced little understanding of democratic political procedures.

On the other hand, the succeeding Democratic Party Rule (1960–1961), following the April 1960 student revolution, failed to give the government the efficiency and coordination necessary for coping with the pressing social and economic problems of the day. The party, devoted to libertarian goals but severely factionalized and unable to suppress governmental corruption, was not able to meet its revolutionary mandate. A military coup d'etat toppled the Democratic government and retained power from 1961–1963. The military rulers were able to stabilize the chaotic political situation and, in December of 1963, discarded their military attire to run as civilians in the elections for President and the National Assembly under the new banner of the Democratic Republican Party. Since that time, the leader of the 1961 coup, Park Chung-hee, has been President. Economic development under DRP tutelage has been spectacular, and governmental administration has been improved significantly. However, because of the military threat from North Korea and because of the ever-present factionalism within Korean society, the highly centralized government remains surveillant in a way that is still somewhat removed from a democratic norm. Given the Confucian and colonial background of modern Korea, however, it can be said that her achievements in most areas have been impressive, particularly when compared with developmental progress in most other developing nations.

CHAPTER 1:

The Politics of
Democratic Experiment:
1948-1974

YOUNG-HO LEE*

As in the case of most nations, Korea during its early period —which dates back at least 3,000 years—was divided into numerous small tribal communities. As the integrative process proceeded, however, larger units replaced smaller units until Korea became a unified nation in the seventh century A.D. The country remained a well-defined, single national entity until after World War II when it was divided into two separate North and South political entities. The post-war period was marked by the failure of the Allied Powers, particularly the United States and the Soviet Union, to reach an agreement on the future of a Korea which had been liberated from a Japanese colonial rule of 35 years.[1] For nearly thirteen centuries, then, Korea's boundaries remained remarkably stable. In short, until the division following World War II, Korea was "a nation of one race, one language, one culture, and one proud past."[2]

---

*Young-Ho Lee is Director of the Policy Research Institute (Seoul) and Managing Editor of the *Koreana Quarterly*. He formerly taught political science at the University of Georgia. The author is grateful to Professors Robert E. Lane and Chitoshi Yanaga of Yale University for their comments on an earlier draft which was part of the author's Ph.D. dissertation, *The Political Culture of Modernizing Society: Political Attitudes and Democracy in Korea* (Yale 1969). He is also indebted to Professor Robert E. Clute of the University of Georgia, Professor Byung-hun Oh of Sungkyunkwan University, and Edward R. Wright, Jr. of the Korean-American Educational Commission for helpful comments and suggestions.

This long-established national identity based on an "exceptional historical continuity" makes Korea quite distinct among new nations. While most other emerging nations generally lack a strong, if any, sense of national identification, Korea does not have a national identity problem.[3] While other new nations are marked by ethnic, linguistic, religious, and/or cultural heterogeneity, and are often threatened by disintegrative forces, Korea is remarkably free from such problems. Korea too has subcultures, but the differences between them are not as pronounced as in many new nations.[4] Moreover, Korea's subcultures are defined not so much by ethnicity, language, or religion but mostly by such differences as urban-rural, regional, industrial-agricultural, modern-traditional, rich-poor, or educated-uneducated. It could even be said that one of her greatest problems has been that of excessive social-cultural homogeneity and integration.[5] Korea has few natural lines of social and political cleavage which could also be regarded as sinews of cohesion at the intermediary level. Power in Korea has thus tended to be excessively centralized in the capital with few other regional centers of power which could counterbalance central power.[6]

THE YI DYNASTY (1392–1910)

In characterizing the Korean people's historical political experiences which may be relevant to more recent developments, one need not go back beyond the Yi dynasty period. An examination of this and the subsequent Japanese colonial period (1910–1945) gives us a sufficiently broad historical perspective from which to view post-independence events.[7]

Though there were considerable variations in political experience within the Yi period, broad generalizations applicable to the entire period are not only possible but also useful. The political system during this period can be characterized as:

(1) Oligarchical in leadership recruitment;
(2) Largely despotic in ruling behavior;
(3) Absolute in state power;
(4) Highly centralized in power distribution; and
(5) Predominantly parochial-subject in political culture.

In terms of political leadership recruitment, the Yi system was highly oligarchical: only a small minority of the people, mostly members of the *yangban* (aristocratic) class, had a chance to be recruited into leadership roles. The role of the hereditary king fluctuated between reigning and ruling depending on his personality and/or the political circumstance. Surrounding the king and forming the ruling oligarchy were successful passers of the civil service examination which was patterned after the Chinese model. The number of persons who were successful in the examination throughout the Yi period was estimated at only 14,000. The base of recruitment into this ruling class was highly restricted because only descendants of the *yangban* families had the right to sit for the examination.[8]

Members of the Yi ruling oligarchy were generalists in their functions. Governmental roles were extremely undifferentiated and therefore role interchangeability was great. Such a generalist culture made few persons indispensable. Accordingly, factional strifes were widespread and intensive and engulfed the entire governmental structure. This resulted in great career insecurity.[9] Under such conditions, it was natural that there was only a weak relationship, if any, between merit and reward in public careers. This in turn encouraged the self-serving rather than public-serving tendency of Yi officials.[10]

Assisting the generalist civil servants were clerical or technical staff who were somewhat more specialized but with limited policy-making power. Serving under officials with a rapid rate of attrition, these people were highly skilled opportunists who made the best use of their superiors' inevitable unfamiliarity with local conditions.[11] The relatively amoral outlook of today's civil servants in Korea thus has a long historical tradition.

The Yi system was largely despotic in the exercise of power. Accountability of the rulers was weak. Theoretically, an official was responsible to the king, who was accountable to the Chinese emperor, who was in turn answerable to Heaven. In traditional oriental thought, Heaven was nature: Heaven's will was expressed through natural phenomena. A good harvest signified that Heaven was pleased with the ruler's performance. On the other hand, a poor harvest, a flood, or a drought meant Heaven's displeasure. Social phenomena likewise signified Heaven's mood. Thus, the old saying: "As the people feel, so does Heaven."[12] However, the enforcement of accountability was a problem, as there was no institutionalized method of proclaiming the ruler's loss of Heaven's Mandate. In practice, therefore, whether a king retained or lost Heaven's Mandate was determined by a politico-military struggle between him and his challenger(s). Accordingly, a politically resourceful ruler claimed the mandate despite apparent indications of Heaven's displeasure. On the other hand, a successful challenger could claim the shift of Heaven's Mandate in his direction regardless of the defeated (or decapitated) ruler's performance.[13] Thus originated a popular dictum: "Success makes one [challenger] King, failure makes him a traitor."[14]

At any rate, the direct recipient of Heaven's Mandate was the Chinese emperor, not the Korean king. The Chinese emperor in general was not involved in Korean affairs, leaving them largely to the Korean king. Therefore, the latter was in a sense given a *blank* mandate. As long as he showed proper respect for the Chinese emperor and managed to maintain control over the nation, Heaven was by implication quiet.[15]

There were, however, Confucian norms of behavior applying to rulership. Even the king was not supposed to be free from these. However, the application and enforcement of the norms involved power; in other words, much like in the case of Heaven's Mandate, power freed its holder from the norms, and only the powerless were made accountable for real or fabricated violations.[16]

During the Yi period, factions (or schools) developed based on different interpretations of Confucian principles. However it was not the theoretical strength of a given interpretation but the actual political resources and skills of the faction promoting it that determined whether that particular interpretation gained orthodoxy or not.[17] Yet the somewhat shared pretention that there were Confucian teachings that ought to govern human behavior moderated, if not very significantly, the despotism of the Yi rulers.

The Yi state was absolute in *extent* of power, though not totalitarian. There was almost no aspect of human life which was immune from the state's interference. There was no separation of state functions, on the one hand, and religious or moral functions, on the other, and the state assumed both functions. Thus the king was "the apex not only of the administrative but of the moral and religious system.... His bureaucrats, ruling in his name, were sanctioned with a double value: The literati were, in effect, administrators, judges, theologians."[18]

However, the Yi state operated with a relatively small bureaucracy in a predominantly agrarian society with only rudimentary systems of transportation and communication. Consequently, the state was unable to exhaust the logical limits of its theoretical authority. Theoretically, it had the right to be totalitarian; in practice it

The Politics of Democratic Experiment

remained only absolute.

Lastly, but nonetheless very importantly, the Yi political system was extremely centralized in the distribution of power. Korea under the Yi rule and Japan prior to the Meiji Restoration shared many social and cultural characteristics. One important difference was that while Japan was feudal and decentralized Korea was highly centralized.[19] As a matter of fact, Korea was non-feudal throughout most of her history.[20] What few feudalistic traits existed in earlier periods had almost completely disappeared by the time of the Yi dynasty (1392). There were few political, cultural, and/or economic centers outside of Seoul, the Yi capital. Thus, "As Paris was for France, Seoul was not simply Korea's largest town: it was Korea."[21]

The Yi political culture was highly parochial-subject.[22] The ordinary people generally were politically unaware and uninvolved. Their role was that of passive subjects. They did what state authorities told them to do. Governmental policy was something to accept and obey rather than something they could question and attempt to change. There was little opportunity for ordinary citizens to participate in the decision-making process. Political infrastructures such as parties and interest groups were absent and there were few channels of demand making. What little political participation there was basically was compliant instead of autonomous.[23] In short, the state was paternalistically authoritarian and ordinary people were submissive, except for occasional outbreaks such as peasant riots.

THE JAPANESE COLONIAL RULE (1910–1945)

The Japanese colonial rule which succeeded the Yi dynasty perpetuated and intensified the same non-democratic patterns. The colonial administration was essentially oligarchical as the Yi system had been. But the difference was that now the rulers were mostly aliens imposing on the indigenous Koreans decisions made in the interest of an alien people. The Chosen Government-General filled most of its important administrative positions with Japanese, leaving minor positions to Koreans. In 1927, thirty-five percent of all Government-General officials were Koreans, but only five out of 134 officials above the third class were Koreans.[24] By 1943, the Korean percentage in Government-General personnel rose to sixty-five percent of the total, but only fourteen percent were of the *sonin* rank—roughly equivalent of GS-9 in American federal bureaucracy—or above.[25] George M.

McCune described the situation thusly:

> ...the percentage of Koreans as against Japanese (in colonial administration) was less and less at each stage upward. Generally speaking, Japanese colonial policy called for a virtual monopoly by Japanese of administrative positions on the higher levels. Koreans were appointed to clerical and minor posts only.[26]

The colonial rule was highly despotic and arbitrary in the sense that it was not responsible to the Korean people who were directly affected by its decisions and that there were few constitutional-legal limitations on its scope of authority. The fact that the Government-General was not independent but responsible to the Japanese government[27] made the situation even worse from the Korean standpoint. It was not only an irresponsible government but one working for and directed by a foreign government.[28]

The Japanese rule was not merely absolute but also to a great extent totalitarian. With an efficient, modern bureaucracy and with well-developed, rigorously-employed control mechanisms, the colonial authority not only could, but actually did, extend government control over the totality of social life. Some scholars characterize pre-1945 Japan as Fascist. If the system was totalitarian within Japan, it was much more ruthlessly so in Korea.

In the 1930's and 1940's efforts were made to obliterate Korea not only as a political entity but also as a cultural entity distinct from Japan. Any instructions in schools and any communications in print or in public lectures which indicated that Korea was distinct from Japan historically, culturally, and racially were prohibited. Thus, Korean school children were taught that Japanese history was their own. They were penalized for uttering Korean words while in school. All Koreans were forced to adopt Japanese-style names. They were forced to worship Shintoism with particular efforts directed at Christians, many of them receiving severe punishment for refusal to obey.[29]

To implement this so-called "cultural assimilation" policy, to crush Korean independence struggles, and to maximize war-time mobilization, a vast control network was developed with some 60,000 civil and military policemen in Korea alone (as of 1941). This was one policeman for every 400 inhabitants.[30]

Power was extremely centralized. The Government-General in Seoul was the apex of not only political administration but also social, economic, moral-religious and cultural control. This highly centralized hierarchy was subordinated to another equally centralized, increasingly despotic and totalitarian hierarchy in Tokyo. The effect of centralization on colonial Korea was far more severe than during the Yi period because of the greater effectiveness with which central power was applied.

Political mobilization was considerable, largely government inspired and directed. As far as formal governmental structures were concerned, there was a high degree of differentiation. However, the development of political infrastructures was completely suppressed. Thus the centralized, well-oiled colonial machinery of extraction and regulation dealt with a helplessly unorganized population.

THE RHEE REGIME (1948-1960)

Upon liberation from Japan, Korea was divided into two zones which were placed under separate military administrations by the United States and the Soviet Union. The division into North and South Korea along the thirty-eighth parallel was supposed to be a temporary military measure but still remains in force today.[32] The Soviet authorities refused to admit a United Nations mission into the northern half of the country to supervise a nation-wide general election to form a government for united Korea, as had been called for by a United Nations General Assembly resolution. Subsequently, elections were held only in the south in May 1948 to constitute the Constituent Assembly.[33] It might be noted that this was the first opportunity for the Korean people to elect a national legislative body.[34] The Constituent Assembly subsequently drafted a constitution which featured characteristics of both American presidentialism and British parliamentarianism, with the former being the stronger of the two influences. Some features of the Weimar Constitution were also incorporated into the document, particularly in its economic provisions.[35]

South Korea became independent in August of 1948.[36] The Soviet-controlled north followed suit by establishing a Soviet-type communist regime in September.[37] Their military, economic, and even political dependence on their respective "foster-parent" countries was so great that their independence was more nominal than real. Unfortunately for South Korea, however, her foster-parent, the United States, was lacking in commitment and direction in its Korean policy, whereas the Soviet Union was certain in direction and firm in commitment in its policy of building a militarily strong and ideologically reliable communist political system in North Korea. Consequently, at the same time that North Korea's 150,000-man army—trained by Soviet military instructors, equipped with some 240 Soviet tanks, more than 200 Soviet planes, and other Soviet heavy equipment—was getting ready for an invasion of the south, the United States was executing its policy of disengagement in Korea. The defense of the country was left to a hastily assembled South Korean "army of 100,000 men with equipment for only about 65,000 men, much of it unserviceable or lacking spare parts, without any tanks, with almost no planes, and grievously deficient in other heavy equipment."[38] When Secretary of State Dean Acheson publicly announced in a National Press Club speech in January 1950, that South Korea was outside of the United States defense perimeter, the communists must have been most attentive listeners.[39] It was in effect an open invitation for them. They launched an all-out military invasion in June 1950—only five months after Acheson's speech.[40]

Confronted with North Korea's aggression which was rapidly moving southward and meeting only ineffective resistance, the United States chose to repulse the aggression. For South Korea, even this belated military commitment was fortunate because the United States, along with Korea and other allied nations, was successful in pushing back the communists who had managed to occupy most of South Korea in less than three months.[42] This was fortunate only in the sense of "better late than never." Without the United States military aid, South Korea would certainly have come under communist control. But with an earlier adoption of the same firm policy, the invasion could probably have been effectively discouraged.

South Korea did survive the aggression militarily, with a final demarcation line established, after a long truce negotiation, around the original line of partition along the thirty-eighth parallel. However, the war was an extremely painful blow to her economy which had already been severely disrupted following the liberation and subsequent division. As is often the case with wars, it made it easier for the executive to justify repressive measures in the name of emergencies. From the beginning, in his political behavior Rhee was not a democrat.[43] Apparently believing that he alone could save the country from all the difficulties engulfing it and that he alone knew what was good for the country, he allowed no one to "dare threaten or seriously contend for rule."[44] His will was the will of the Republic; he was the Republic.[45]

According to the 1948 constitution, the government was to be democratic. An extensive bill of rights was provided; the basic method of leadership selection was to be electoral; and there were provisions calling for separation of powers, and for checks and balances. Not unexpectedly, at the time the constitution was proclaimed, many seemed to believe that a genuine democratic era was to blossom on Korean soil.

This initial optimism was as naive as it was wishful. The optimists had placed too much faith in legislation as an instrument of political reform. However carefully drafted, a constitution alone cannot guarantee the fulfillment of all or even many of the goals that are set forth in it. As Almond and Powell put it, "Legal rules and ideal norms may affect [the observable] behavior, but they rarely describe it fully."[46]

Since democracy requires popular control over leaders, conditions must exist—social, economic, psycho-cultural, historical, and political —which are conducive to a relatively high level of political participation on the part of ordinary citizens. Korea lacked most of the conditions often mentioned as being prerequisite to democratic development.[47] The Korean people did not need to wait long to be disappointed with their first democratic experiment. It seemed apparent that Rhee's government, from the beginning, respected democratic norms of ruling behavior—or constitutional principles—only when doing so was not unduly inconvenient. When such norms were in the way of autocratic exercise of power, however, there seemed to be no hesitancy to violate them. Thus, under Rhee (1948–1960), democratic institutions were "disregarded, overridden, corrupted, or turned against themselves."[48] Civil rights were often disregarded, and due process of law was more often laughed at than taken seriously by the very officials who were supposed to enforce the law. The press was often censored, or its freedom of expression otherwise severely restricted. Numerous newspapers and magazines were closed down by the government, some temporarily and others permanently. Reporters, editors, and publishers were all frequent targets of government persecution. Many were arrested, interrogated, and tried. Some were punished with trumped-up charges. Terrorism through hired gangsters was resorted to not infrequently.[49]

Political opposition was in general suppressed and discouraged, with all resources at the command of the government thrown against opposition politicians and groups, sometimes legally and more often illegally or unconstitutionally. When any group became a serious threat to the Rhee rule, it was resolutely curbed.[50] Even the Constitution itself became a helpless pawn in Rhee's political game as it was unconstitutionally amended twice and violated numerous times.

According to the 1948 Constitution, the president was to be elected by the National Assembly. Though Rhee was almost unanimously elected by the Assembly for his first term, by 1951 it became apparent that his chance of being re-elected by the Assembly in 1952 was slim. Therefore, Rhee proposed a constitutional amendment which would have the president elected directly in a popular election. It was defeated by 143 votes to 19 with one abstention in January 1952. After trying various means to persuade the reluctant Assembly to reconsider it, Rhee finally took extreme measures. On May 25, emergency martial law was proclaimed in Pusan, the provisional capital, and its vicinity. The government justified martial law on grounds of national security, but it was apparently politically motivated. There followed government-mobilized demonstrations in front of the National Assembly building and elsewhere in Pusan which protested the "selfishness," the "narrow-mindedness," and the "blindness to the national interest" on the part of the Assembly members. There were wall posters throughout Pusan demanding, among other things, the assassination of certain of Rhee's opponents in the Assembly. Many representatives were arrested by the military and civil police, some for failing to carry identification cards and others for more serious-sounding charges. For reasons of personal safety and simply to avoid being arrested and detained, many representatives went into hiding. Finally, in July, the government ordered the police to round up all representatives, and "guide and escort" them to the National Assembly building, where they were confined in captivity for two days and nights. When they emerged from the confinement, it was learned that the constitutional amendment providing for popular election of the president had been passed by 163 votes to none with one abstention.[51]

In 1954, looking ahead into 1956 when his second term as president was to end, Rhee again demanded a constitutional amendment package which among other things provided that the constitutional barrier forbidding more than two consecutive terms should "not apply to the incumbent of the office of the President at the time of promulgation of this Constitution."[52] Under the constitutional provision which required the concurrence of more than two thirds of the members of the National Assembly "duly elected and seated,"[53] when the amendment bill came to a vote on November 27, 1954, it received 135 votes in favor, 60 against, and 7 abstentions (with one absentee). With an Assembly membership of 203, the total votes in favor (135) were two-thirds of one vote short of the required majority.

The presiding officer accordingly announced that the bill had been rejected. However, the following day the official government spokesman announced: "It is the position of the Government that the Constitutional amendments have been passed by the required two-thirds majority. Korea lacks precedent for the counting of fractional votes and it is the Government's feeling that the fraction must be disregarded and that the amendments therefore have been adopted."[54] The next day, in the National Assembly, the presiding officer retracted his previous announcement and declared that the bill had been passed.[55]

The meaning of the electoral process as a democratic means of selecting and holding political leaders accountable to the electorate was largely lost when election irregularities became so frequent and widespread. Interference by the police and government officials (who were by law forbidden from political activities), vote-buying, blackmail, threats, physical violence, and numerous other corrupt practices flourished. All this adversely affected the Korean people's orientation toward the electoral process in particular and toward representative democracy in general about which they were just beginning to learn.[56]

Debates and decisions in the National Assembly which was supposedly the supreme law-making body of the republic seemed increasingly empty and meaningless as more and more people came to realize that actual effective decisions took place elsewhere—in the presidential mansion or in other executive offices—and that laws passed by the Assembly were as often disregarded and violated as respected by the executive branch.[57]

The concentration of power in the executive branch made interest-promoting activities more rule-application-oriented than rule-making-oriented.[58] Widespread corruption in the government bureaucracy discouraged normal pressure tactics and encouraged bribery and other abnormal practices.

Also during the Rhee period, interest groups in general tended to become means of communication and control in the hands of the government rather than means of popular influence over the government. There were groups in Korea which in form looked much like the kinds of interest groups found in advanced democracies. However, as structures of articulating and communicating popular political demands to the government, they served a limited function. Furthermore, most groups operating at the time were non-associational or institutional rather than associational.[59] Therefore, what little interest articulation they did perform tended to be diffuse, particularistic, and affective.[60]

Political activities in general were mobilized and directed by the government. They were only very infrequently self-asserting expressions of political demands by ordinary people. Opposition activities were usually suppressed and largely without effect on policy. Under Rhee, there was something of a separation of policy from politics in the sense that government policy failed to reflect to any significant extent the freely expressed demands of the people.[61] Popular demand-making activities and parliamentary debates had limited influence on government policy.[62]

Finally, flagrant irregularities in the presidential and vice-presidential elections of March 1960 triggered violent reaction from the public, particularly high school and college students and urban-intellectual elements.[63] Spontaneous demonstrations took place over the country finally culminating in bloody encounters between demonstrators and police in Seoul in April 19–27. More than 100 demonstrators were shot to death by police fire and more than 1,000 injured. Martial law was proclaimed, troops were called in to help maintain order. Reluctant concessions were made by the government, but they were too little and too late. Demonstrations persisted; some police stations were set afire; the offices of the government organ, *The Seoul Shinmun,* and Liberal Party headquarters were sacked. Initially in protest against the conduct of the elections, the demonstrators now demanded not only new elections but the immediate resignation of Rhee and his government. It was apparent that the military was reluctant in its new role of maintaining civil order.

It was apparent too that soldiers would not fire on demonstrators as the civil police had done. The United States which had for many years endured Rhee's autocratic behavior without open criticism now publicly criticized the Rhee regime for its "repressive measures unsuited to a free democracy," insisting that it "should, in its own interest, take necessary and effective action aimed at protecting democratic rights of freedom of speech, of assembly, and of the press, as well as preserving the secrecy of the ballot."[64] Nearly two hundred professors from twelve universities in Seoul demonstrated, demanding that Rhee, the National Assembly, and the Supreme Court resign. The National Assembly, where nearly two-thirds of the members belonged to Rhee's Liberal Party, passed without debate a motion demanding Rhee's immediate resignation.[65]

Rhee finally stepped down and submitted his resignation to the National Assembly on April 27.[66] Since Vice President Chang Myŏn of the Democratic Party had resigned earlier in protest over the elections, the highest-ranking member of the administration to take over as Acting President, according to the Constitution, was Foreign Minister Hŏ Chŏng, who had been appointed to that post as a gesture of concession in the wake of the April outbreaks. Since Hŏ's identification with the Rhee regime was weak, the public accepted his caretaker government with relative readiness and good faith.

THE DEMOCRATIC PARTY RULE (1960-1961)

The April 1960 student revolution[67] was popularly viewed as a dramatic expression of the Korean people's democratic maturity. When *The Chosun Ilbo,* an independent Seoul newspaper, noted in an editorial that "The dark era of tyranny is past. The reign of the gangsters is over,"[68] its sentiment was widely shared. However, this was more wishful thinking than a realistic evaluation.

Mr. Hŏ's caretaker government carried out its limited functions relatively well. A new constitution was drafted and adopted by the National Assembly on June 15, changing the government from a presidential to a parliamentary form.[69] On July 29, elections were held, largely free from irregularities which had been so common in the past, for a bicameral legislature composed of the House of Councilors and the House of Representatives which collectively were called the National Assembly.[70] The Democratic Party emerged overwhelmingly victorious in these elections with the Liberal Party having all but vanished.[71] Chang Myŏn, the leader of "the new faction" of the Democratic Party, became Prime Minister, which was the most important post in the now parliamentary government, and Yun Po-sŏn of "the old faction" became President with ceremonial powers.[72] With the formation of the Democratic government under these two men, the Second Republic was launched.

The Democratic Party's rule, however, was beset from the beginning with many insurmountable problems. The party had a record of stubborn and courageous resistance against Rhee's "tightly run police state"[73] rule. It was also the only remaining party of any sizeable political following after the fall of the Liberal Party, which made it a logical choice for power. However, the Democratic Party still faced an acute crisis of legitimacy. The Party's right to rule was unearned: it was a gift from the students who, having anointed themselves as "the guardians of Korean democracy," were protective of their achievement. The revolution was called the Student Revolution, not the

Democratic Revolution.[74] According to the new constitution, the executive was responsible to the legislature, but the students demanded that the responsibility of the government be first of all to them. The Democratic Party was supposed to rule, but was unable to do so.[75]

Illustrative of the political situation during this period were the developments surrounding the punishment of persons held responsible for the rigging of the March elections and for the killing of demonstrators during the April uprising. Punishment that was possible under the existing laws was deemed too light by, and thus unacceptable to, "the April revolutionaries,"[76] even though the existing laws were the only laws on which justice could be based. On October 8, 1960, the Seoul District Court passed sentence on forty-eight of those Rhee officials accused of breaches of the National Security Law and the Presidential Election Law, some charged with committing capital offences. It was learned that there was only one defendant receiving a death sentence and that all others received either acquittals, probations, or fines. Apparently feeling that the revolution was being betrayed by a non- or anti-revolutionary administration of justice, many citizens, mostly students, staged angry demonstrations. On October 11, several thousand demonstrators gathered in front of the House of Representatives building and of the Seoul District Court and protested the government's lenient attitude on the matter. Some fifty demonstrators even intruded into the chamber of the House of Representatives while it was in session, occupied the Speaker's platform, and harangued the representatives about "the revolutionary spirit." Only after a government spokesman had promised an immediate preparation of special laws for the punishment of "anti-democratic criminals" and after the Speaker and other members of the House of Representatives had appeared before the demonstrators, apologized for their mistakes, and promised to take immediate steps to help "fulfill the revolutionary tasks," did the demonstrators disperse.[77]

The proper reaction of a government in such a situation should be to enforce laws by arresting violators such as those who had forcibly entered the Assembly building. The Democratic government apparently did not feel it had the moral right to do so. The situation was not normal but revolutionary. Anything that was in the way of the realization of the spirit of the revolution, as interpreted by the students and citizens who called themselves "democratic revolutionaries," lacked legitimacy. The result was mob rule.[78] It is estimated that there were approximately 2,000 separate demonstrations with a total of more than 900,000 participants during the one-year period following the student uprising.[79]

In order to punish the so-called "anti-democratic criminals" in a sufficiently harsh manner as to satisfy the demands of the revolutionaries, new laws were necessary. In order to make the new laws retroactively applicable to crimes committed before their proclamation, a constitutional amendment was necessary which would make an exception to the universally accepted judicial principle prohibiting *ex post facto* laws.

Nevertheless the Democratic government, with the support of the National Assembly, complied with the demands of the revolutionaries by speedily enacting a constitutional amendment bill and "special revolutionary laws."[80] A special court and a special prosecution office were created to conduct trials of "anti-democratic criminals." Despite the Democratic government's explanation that this should not constitute a precedent, but should be considered an exception to meet a unique situation, the precedent was established that exceptions could be made to meet "exceptional" situations. Constitutionalism, which was under constant assault under Rhee, did not enjoy a favorable climate during the Democratic period either.

These above-mentioned developments surrounding the constitutional amendment and subsequent special legislation were not out of the ordinary but rather typical of the period. The United Nations Commission for the Unification and Rehabilitation of Korea (UNCURK), one of the important duties of which was to observe Korean political developments, concluded in its 1961 report to the U.N. General Assembly that "...the ability of the Government and the National Assembly to execute and decide firmly was considerably restricted by the frequency of demonstrations and the Government's reluctance to deal severely with them."[81]

The Democratic government's loss of—or failure to secure—independence and initiative in policy-making resulted in a government of indecision and inaction which lacked firm direction and purpose, all this at a time when a strong political leadership was most critically needed.

The Democratic Party's legitimacy or claim to rule was further undermined by its internal factional strife of long standing and considerable bitterness. The "new" and "old" factions were in reality parties within a party. During the Rhee period they had remained within the framework of a single party not so much because of mutual love or shared attitudes but because of the overwhelming strength of their common foe, the Liberal Party. As Henderson put it, it was "a marriage of convenience."[82] Now that the Liberal Party was gone and the government was theirs to run, they could not agree on a mutually acceptable distribution of government power. The "old" faction, the less numerous of the two, demanded more than the smaller share of power the "new" faction was willing to give it.[83] Finally, on November 14, barely two months after the inauguration of the Democratic government, the "old" faction broke away completely and formed a separate party called the New Democratic Party to assume the role of an opposition party.[64]

This resulted in a two-party situation which may have been desirable under normal circumstances, but the actual circumstances were anything but normal.[85] The enormity of the numerous problems facing the nation at the time could have been viewed as a situation calling for a national coalition—much like that of the British government during the Second World War—rather than a factional struggle. The fact that the ruling party failed to maintain internal unity, let alone achieve an inter-party national unity, gave rise to the popular feeling that the Democrats, "new" and "old" alike, were too power-greedy and narrow-minded to place national interest above their partisan or individual interests. A neutral group (UNCURK) observed: " ... it appeared that there was more concern with immediate factional and party interests than with national problems....Both the National Assembly and the Government were hampered in dealing effectively with national problems by difficulties stemming from factional groupings and party instability."[86]

This was a great disappointment to the Korean people whose expectations vis-a-vis the new government were explosively rising after the long repression under Rhee. Many expected that with the fall of Rhee's regime a new day of freedom and prosperity would soon dawn. In other words, there had been a tendency to be preoccupied with the repression-freedom aspect of government to the neglect of other aspects and to consider the removal of the repressive aspect of the Rhee government as a political panacea.[87] However, actual developments after the fall of the Rhee regime left much to be desired. Having expected "instant democracy," the people found it difficult to accept the fact that a libertarian regime could have many shortcomings. The old saying, *"Kukwan-i myŏng-kwan-ira,"* meaning "the old official was after all better than the new one," received much currency during this period.

As a consequence of the combined effect of these and other problems from which it suffered, the Democratic rule was marked by a high degree of inefficiency.[88] "Complete freedom in all aspects of Korean life" which characterized the Democratic rule also involved many instances of abuse of freedom such as violent and disorderly demonstrations and licentious press practices.[89] Social and economic problems were left largely unattended, which meant that they grew increasingly worse. Corruption in the government continued with some cases involving members of the Chang Myŏn cabinet.[90] In the free political environment that existed at the time, corruption and inefficiency, among other things, made the Democratic government's position untenable. The cumulative effect of simultaneous demands for popular participation in politics and for welfare in the face of limited democratic institutional development and of limited human and material resources was overwhelming.

THE MILITARY JUNTA (1961-1963)

It was not the popular discontent expressed through demonstrations or elections, however, that brought an end to the Democratic government but a military coup d'etat which was carefully planned and skillfully executed by a group of young military officers. The May 16, 1961 coup met little resistance and was thus bloodless.[91] The military junta, first named as the Military Revolutionary Committee and later renamed as the Supreme Council for National Reconstruction, seemed to have few basic ideological differences with the Democratic regime it was replacing.[92] The justification for "the military revolution" was not ideological.[93] The military revolutionaries simply claimed that they were more capable of achieving the same social and economic goals than the Chang or any other leadership. In reaction to the near-anarchic situation created by abuse of freedom, the military argued that Korea was not yet fully ready for a full-fledged democracy and that a period of controlled preparation was necessary for "a new, efficient and incorruptible government which will guarantee liberty and justice under law, and provide for a better economic, social and political way of life for our people."[94] Through an "administrative democracy," it argued, steps should be taken to develop the ability for self-government,"[95] and "the foundation for new democratic institutions" established.[96]

The military junta rule lasted for two and a half years until December 1963 when the newly formed Democratic Republican Party,[97] organized and led by the military revolutionaries now in mufti, won elections and came to control the government.[98] The return to civilian government was not entirely voluntary. During early 1963, General Park Chung-hee, Chairman of the Supreme Council for National Reconstruction, pointing at "the plethora of political parties, the constant mergers and separations of political circles, their ugly feuds, and so forth," argued that return to civilian government at this time would be the same as going back to the pre-revolutionary situation and that the military government should be extended "for about four more years."[99] However, this maneuver met strong opposition from both domestic and foreign sources. Finally, the presidential and National Assembly elections took place in October and November of 1963 respectively under the new constitution adopted by a national referendum held in 1962 and the new laws governing political parties and elections.[100] The elections themselves were carried out in a relatively free, orderly, and fair manner.[101]

The military rule was remarkably successful in restoring law and order. Its performance in other functions of government, however, was far from satisfactory. Furthermore, the period of military rule was simply too brief for a fundamental social, economic, and political reconstruction of the nation.[102] What was left unfinished at the end of the junta rule was presumably to be completed by the Democratic Republican government that succeeded it.

THE DEMOCRATIC REPUBLICAN RULE:
THE FIRST ELEVEN YEARS (1963–1974)

The Democratic Republican Party (DRP) led by Park Chung-hee has been in power since 1963. As the DRP is still in office, and more than likely to be in office for some time to come, it may be too early for a definitive evaluation of its performance. What follows, therefore, must be regarded as an interim evaluation. The Democratic Republicans can be considered to have been more successful in the economic field than in any other area. The average annual rate of GNP growth during 1962–1972 was nine percent.[103] From 7.8 percent during the first five-year plan period (1962–1966), it rose to 10.5 percent during the second five-year plan period (1967–1971).[104] In 1973 it reached an all time high of 16.9 percent.[105] Similarly, per capita income rose from 75 dollars in 1962 to 255 dollars in 1972, representing a 340 percent increase over a ten-year period.[106] The volume of exports has also seen a thirty-fold growth during the period.

It grew from 55 million dollars in 1962 to 1,624 million dollars in 1972. The imports to exports ratio was 8 to 1 in 1962. There remained an imbalance in 1972, but at a much improved ratio of 3 to 2.[107]

The economy has seen a rapid rate of industrialization. The percentage of active labor force engaged in primary industry decreased from 63.2 percent in 1963 to 50.6 percent in 1972, while the percentage in secondary industry increased from 11.2 percent in 1963 to 14.2 percent in 1972.[108] There is valid criticism that industrialization has been pushed at the expense of agricultural development. Predominantly agricultural, Korea is still not self-sufficient in domestic production of agricultural commodities, and the income gap between the agricultural and the industrial sector still remains wide. The Government is placing greater emphasis on agricultural development in its third five-year economic development plan (1972–1976), but it remains to be seen how successful the Government will be in improving the lot of the farming population.

The rate of unemployment has dipped considerably, according to government statistics. Whereas it was as high as 8.1 percent in 1963, it has stood at about 4.5 percent since 1968.[109] Although these figures are somewhat misleading in that they do not reflect the extent of *underemployment*, particularly in the countryside, the fact remains that job opportunities have been on the increase. For the first time since liberation from Japanese colonial rule, wage increases have overtaken price increases.[110] For example, earnings of workers saw an increase of more than 700 percent between 1962 and 1972 in both agricultural and manufacturing industries while whole prices increased during the same period by only 322 percent, and Seoul consumer prices by only 381 percent.[111] This is not to imply that wages in general are adequate but that they are increasing not just in terms of current money value but also in purchasing power.

The government's economic goals are aptly summarized by the slogan: "Per capita income of $1,000 and exports of $10 billion by 1980." The attainment of these goals seemed much more feasible before the eruption of the energy crisis in 1973 than now. Whether such goals are reached or not will depend more on external than internal conditions—the Korean economy by necessity is marked by a high degree of external dependence. At any rate, the DRP must be credited with a high level of competence in economic areas.

The administrative performance of the DRP must also be viewed as a considerable improvement over that of either of the preceding regimes, especially in terms of regulative and extractive capabilities.

Corruption in the government, however, remains the target of constant criticism.[112] An impartial public-oriented ethos has not yet taken firm root in the Korean bureaucratic culture, though some beginnings seem in evidence. Over-centralization of authority, nepotism, politicization, and many other problems still persist and hinder the efficiency and responsiveness of the Korean bureaucracy.

In the political realm, a straight-forward evaluation is difficult since it is extremely difficult to agree on criteria to be used. In other words, there is no agreed-upon definition of good performance in political areas. In terms of liberal-democratic standards such as freedom, participation, and popular control, the DRP performance cannot be evaluated too favorably. DRP leaders themselves do not deny that some of Western democratic values have not fared well under their rule in Korea. Instead, they argue that there are other more pressing needs to be met at this stage of political development such as national security, political stability, economic development, and administrative efficiency. In short, they argue that a *Korean-style* democracy is what the Korean people must strive for. The Revitalizing Reforms launched in October 1972 and still in progress have exactly this intention.

In terms of control and stability, the DRP has fared well. Opposition forces are weak and factionalized. The government has managed to keep the problem of protest demonstrations under control. In doing so, it has of course frequently resorted to extreme measures such as martial law (1964 and 1972), garrison decree (1965), declaration of "an emergency state" (1971), closing of universities (1964, 1965, 1969, 1971, 1972, 1973), and Presidential "Emergency Measures" (1974).

The fact that it has to resort to such extreme measures seems to signify that the stability the present Government enjoys is based to an important extent on forced support. The Government can be considered to have been in power since 1961, including the period of the military junta. The critical task confronting the DRP is to transform this forced support into a voluntary support within a reasonably short span of time. Otherwise, its political future will remain quite uncertain.

CONCLUSIONS

In summary, there have been seven opportunities between 1948 and 1973 in which the Government might have been changed through constitutional means, namely the presidential elections of 1952, 1956,

1960, 1963, 1967, 1971, and 1972. On all these occasions, the incumbent was retained. However, there have actually been two changes of government—both through extra-constitutional means. The first change was the fall of the Syngman Rhee Government in 1960 in the midst of student demonstrations, and the second the toppling of the Chang Myŏn Government in 1961 in a military coup d'etat.

The establishment of a political system in which two or more parties compete for power with a more or less equal chance of gaining control of the government remains unrealized in Korea. The Korean pattern of party politics has been strongly "hegemonic," to use a term defined by Almond and Powell, a pattern not conducive to the development of a responsible party system. The fact the two actual changes of government were through extra-constitutional means may explain to an important extent the limited responsiveness and accountability of the successive Korean governments. At any given point in the post-independence period, the possibility of any opposition party's gaining power through elections has been remote. Thus the party in power has not been forced, by the competitiveness of the political situation, to "consider the interests of all important groups in making policy."

Thus the normal mechanisms for political responsiveness and responsibility—namely a competitive electoral process supported by a competitive party system, a system of active interest groups, and free and active political participation by the citizens—are lacking in Korea. In the meantime, the realization of democratic ideals of political responsiveness and responsibility must depend on the benevolence of the political leaders in power.

FOOTNOTES

1. For information on the post-liberation period, see Carl Berger, *The Korea Knot* (Philadelphia: University of Pennsylvania Press, 1957); A. Wigfall Green, *The Epic of Korea* (Washington, D.C.: Public Affairs Press, 1950); and Gregory Henderson, *Korea: The Politics of the Vortex* (Cambridge: Harvard University Press, 1968), ch. 5, pp. 113–147.
2. George M. McCune, *Korea Today* (Cambridge: Harvard University Press, 1950), p. 14.
3. According to Lucian W. Pye, the identity crisis is "the first and most fun-

damental crisis" that emerging nations must successfully deal with in the process of political development. See his *Aspects of Political Development: An Analytical Study* (Boston: Little, Brown, 1966), p. 63. Similarly Gabriel A. Almond and G. Bingham Powell, Jr. suggest four major problems of political development: state-building, nation-building, participation, and distribution. Korea can be regarded to have more or less successfully dealt with the first two. The remaining two problems are Korea's greatest challenges today. See Almond and Powell, *Comparative Politics: A Developmental Approach* (Boston and Toronto: Little, Brown, 1966), pp. 35–37, 322 ff.
4. See Almond and Powell, *op. cit.*, p. 64.
5. Since the Korean people have led a shared national life for such a long period of time, characterizing Korea as a new or emerging nation is somewhat awkward. She is one of the oldest nations. However, she is new or emerging from the democratic viewpoint.
6. Excessive social homogeneity and excessive political and economic centralization are the central themes of Henderson's analysis. (See Henderson, *op. cit.*)
7. For information on the Japanese colonial rule, see *ibid.*, pp. 72–112; Hilary Conroy, *The Japanese Seizure of Korea: 1868–1910* (Philadelphia: University of Pennsylvania Press, 1960); Chong-sik Lee, *The Politics of Korean Nationalism* (Berkeley and Los Angeles: University of California Press, 1963); C.I. Eugene Kim and Han-kyo Kim, *Korea and the Politics of Imperialism, 1876–1910* (Berkeley and Los Angeles: University of California Press, 1967).
8. The family of a civil service exam passer acquired the *yangban* status which was supposed to be effective for only three generations. However, there was some informal tendency for the claim to the status to persist long after it had officially withered. See Pak Mun-ok, *Hankuk Chŏngch'i-Ron* (A Study of Korean Politics. Seoul) (Pak Yong-sa, 1963), p. 46.
9. The generalist culture, factionalism, and career insecurity are all interrelated, one contributing to another.
10. Corruption can be considered as a function of factionalism and career insecurity. Factionalism offers channels through which officials may attempt through bribery and sycophancy to gain some job security. To do this, they need to "raise funds" either from the state revenue or from the people. That what is said here applies to the current situation in Korea only indicates the stubborn resistance of culture to change.
11. It was often these clerical assistants who actually ruled in the absence of *yangban* rulers who spent much time between posts rather than on the post or in the shadow of the latter's ignorance of local conditions.
12. In Chinese ideographs, 民心天心.
13. The concept of Heaven's Mandate is explained in Paul H. Clyde and Burton F. Beers, *The Far East: A History of the Western Impact and the Eastern Response, 1830–1965* (4th ed.; Englewood Cliffs, N. J.: Prentice-Hall, 1966), pp. 29–30. See also John K. Fairbank, *China: The People's Middle Kingdom and the U.S.A.* (Cambridge, Mass.: The Belknap Press of Harvard University Press, 1967), pp. 6–7; Thomas Welty, *The Asians: Their Heritage and Their Destiny* (Philadelphia and New York: J. B. Lip-

pincott Co., 1963), p. 154.
14. In Chinese ideographs, 成則君王 敗則逆賊. It has much in common with the Western saying: "might is right."
15. There were, however, domestic challenges to the king's mandate, some successful and others unsuccessful. These may appear to be in deviation from the theory. But it must be noted that the concept of Heaven's Mandate also equates Heaven's will with the people's will. If a king were so unpopular to be left to be dethroned, he could then be considered as having lost the mandate.
16. Henderson, *op. cit.*, pp. 247–248.
17 See Key P. Yang and Gregory Henderson, "An Outline History of Korean Confucianism," Part I, *Journal of Asian Studies,* Nov. 1958; Yang and Henderson, "An Outline History of Korean Confucianism," Part II: "The Schools of Yi Confucianism," *Journal of Asian Studies,* Feb. 1959.
18. Henderson, *op. cit.*, p. 25.
19. Japanese feudalism was a kind of *centralized feudalism* in which power was relatively more centralized than in other feudal societies. But the degree of centralization in Japan was much weaker than in Korea. See Chitoshi Yanaga, *Japanese People and Politics* (New York: John Wiley and Sons, 1958), pp.25–29; also Robert E. Ward, *Japan's Political System* (Englewood Cliffs, N. J.: Prentice-Hall, 1967), pp. 1–2, 6–7; John M. Maki, *Government and Politics in Japan: The Road to Democracy* (New York: Frederick A. Praeger, 1962), pp. 11–12; Adrath W. Burks, *The Government of Japan* (2nd ed.; NewYork: Thomas Y. Crowell, 1963), p. 9.
20. Some scholars characterize much of Korean history up to the end of the Yi dynasty as feudal. However, they appear to neglect a very important criterion: "dispersal of power in a variety of semi-independent domains." See S. Andreski, "Feudalism," in Julius Gould and William L. Kolb (eds.), *A Dictionary of the Social Sciences* (New York: The Free Press of Glencoe, 1964), p. 268. Korea during the Koryo and Yi periods showed a number of other characteristics of a feudal society such as agrarian economy, hereditary transmission of status, and lack of functional division. However, dispersal of power which is essential to political feudalism was lacking.
21. Henderson, *op. cit.*, p. 30.
22. For political culture and related concepts, see Almond and Powell, *op. cit.*, pp. 50–72; also Gabriel A. Almond and Sidney Verba, *The Civic Culture: Political Attitudes and Democracy in Five Nations* (Princeton, N. J.: Princeton University Press, 1963), pp. 3–42.
23. For a distinction between compliant and autonomous political participation, see Lester W. Milbrath, *Political Participation: How and Why Do People Get Involved in Politics?* (Chicago: Rand McNally, 1965), p. 10.
24. See Ko Ken-san, *Kindai Chosen Seiji-shi* (A Political History of Modern Korea) (Tokyo, 1930), pp. 261–262.
25. See Chong Il-hyong, "Haebang-hu ŭi Insa Haengchŏng Silchae" (Post-Liberation Practices in Public Personnel Administration), *Pŏbchŏng* (*Law and Politics,* a monthly), September 1946, p. 11.
26. George M. McCune, *op. cit.*, pp. 24–25.
27. Korea had the status of a colony until 1942 when it was "fully assimilated" into Japan and came under the administrative supervision of the Japanese

Home Ministry. Politically apart from administrative or legal considerations, however, Korea remained quite distinct from other administrative units of Japan proper due to special problems it offered to Japanese administrators as a colony of people who rejected or at least were reluctant to accept assimilation and who were never given full privileges of first-class citizenship. See Henderson, *op. cit.,* p. 105; McCune, *op. cit.,* p. 23.

28. Even though some steps toward economic development were made in Korea during the colonial years, the goal of colonial policy was not the Korean economy's self-sufficiency or balanced development. Economic policies were considered and adopted, as other policies were also, in accordance with Japan's own political, economic, and military needs. Industrialization and urbanization were pushed only to such an extent as were desirable from the Japanese standpoint. Furthermore, favored positions not only in public bureaucracy but also in private industry and commerce were given mostly to Japanese. Accordingly, as late as 1944, 95 percent of gainfully-employed Korean men and 99 percent of the women were laborers. Nearly 76 percent of employed Koreans were in primary industry. Only 11.5 percent of all Koreans lived in urban areas. See Andrew J. Grajdanzev, *Modern Korea* (New York: John Day, 1944), pp. 79–80; Irene Taeuber, *The Population of Japan* (Princeton, N. J.: Princeton University Press, 1958), p. 188.

29. See Chong-sik Lee, *op. cit.,* pp. 257–273.

30. See George M. McCune, "Korea's Postwar Political Problems" (Secretariat Paper No. 2, the Institute of Pacific Relations, 10th Conference, New York, 1947), pp. 4–5.

31. For the text of the constitution, see United Nations, *Second Part of the Report of the United Nations Temporary Commission on Korea* (hereafter referred to as the *UNTCOK Report*): *General Assembly Official Records* (hereafter referred to as *GAOR*): Third Session, Supplement No. 9 (A/575/Add. 4), pp. 23–31.

32. The present demarcation line (effective since 1953) differs somewhat from the original line. Along the eastern half of the present line a large area which originally belonged to the north now lies south of the line; an area which originally belonged to the south now lies north of the present line toward its western end. Still, North Korea has a larger total area than South Korea: 120,538 to 98,431 square kilometers. See United Nations, *Statistical Yearbook, 1966* (New York, 1967), p. 82.

33. For information on the UN decisions, activities of the UN Temporary Commission on Korea, and the general elections of May 10, 1948, see *UNTCOK Report: GAOR:* Third Session, Supplement No. 9 (A/575, Adds. 1–4).

34. The Korean people did have some limited voting experience before this. Under the Japanese, a Korean advisory body was elected on the basis of a very restricted suffrage. During American military administration, the Korean Interim Legislative Assembly had half of its membership elected on the basis of the same restricted suffrage and the other half appointed by the American military authorities. However the 1948 elections were the first experience for the Koreans to elect a supreme national lawmaking body on the basis of universal adult suffrage.

35. The President's powers were extensive but he was elected by the National Assembly. Though the Assembly did not have the power to pass a vote of non-confidence against the cabinet headed by a prime minister serving the President, it had the power to approve or disapprove the presidential nomination of a Prime Minister. The executive branch had no power to dissolve the National Assembly. See *UNTCOK Report: GAOR:* Third Session, Supplement No. 9 (A/575/Add. 4)·

36. It was independence without preparation. The shift in the U.S. policy from trusteeship to independence for South Korea was generally welcome in Korea. However, independence could have been granted along with the blessing of positive commitment on the part of the United States, economically, militarily, and politically. As it happened, independence was a function of the United States decision for hasty disengagement in Korea. The United States saw in Korea no vital interests, no hope for "progress toward a free and independent Korea," and many headaches. So why not give the Koreans the independence they demanded and get out? See Henderson, *op. cit.,* pp. 148-162.

37. See W. D. Reeve, *The Republic of Korea: A Political and Economic Study* (London: Oxford University Press, 1963), pp. 28-29.

38. Henderson, *op. cit.,* p. 149.

39. U.S. Department of State, Department of State Bulletin, January 23, 1950, p. 115.

40. See Robert T. Oliver, *Why War Came in Korea* (New York: Fordham University Press, 1950), pp. 1-22; Robert Leckie, *Conflict: The History of the Korean War, 1950-53* (New York: G. P. Putnam's Sons, 1962), where Senator Tom Connally, then Chairman of the Senate Foreign Relations Committee, is quoted as having said that Russia could seize South Korea without U.S. intervention because Korea was not "very greatly important." Leckie, combining this statement with Acheson's earlier pronouncement, concludes: "... it would have been surprising if the Communists had not taken them [Acheson's and Connally's remarks] to mean that the United States would not fight in Korea. And when the invader thinks the defender won't fight, there is always war."

41. For information concerning the United States decision to enter the Korean conflict, see Glenn D. Paige, *The Korean Decision: June 24-30, 1950* (New York: The Free Press, 1968).

42. For information concerning the course of the Korean War, see Robert Leckie, *op. cit.;* David Rees, *Korea: The Limited War* (New York: St. Martin's, 1964); I. F. Stone, *The Hidden History of the Korean War* (New York: Monthly Review Press, 1952).

43. Richard D. Allen, in *Korea's Syngman Rhee: An Unauthorized Portrait* (Rutland, Vt.: Charles E. Tuttle, 1960), p. 237, observes: "If Rhee had a single fatal flaw it was his egotism, which made it all but impossible for him to accept criticism, or to change his mind once he had made it up.... Rhee's attitude towards Korean affairs was perhaps summed up in his purported remark upon taking charge of the National Society in 1946. Observed Rhee: 'I shall take over the society and run it on a purely democratic basis. I shall appoint all the other officials.'"

44. Henderson, *op. cit.*, p. 168.
45. Allen, *op. cit.*, p. 237: "By 1945, the decades spent in the service of Korea had led him to identify himself almost totally with the future of his country." Allen also speaks of Rhee's "essentially messianic outlook" (p. 237). There seemed to be many characteristics shared between Rhee and France's Charles de Gaulle.
46. Almond and Powell, *op. cit.*, p. 22.
47. Among social and economic conditions often mentioned are a relatively high level of average wealth, education, industrialization, urbanization, mass communications development. See Seymour M. Lipset's *Political Man* (New York: Doubleday, 1959), Part I, "The Conditions of the Democratic Order," pp. 27–179; Daniel Lerner, *The Passing of Traditional Society* (Glencoe: The Free Press, 1958), Chapter III, "The Passing of Traditional Society: A Survey," pp. 76–107; Phillips Cutright, "National Political Development: Its Measurement and Social Correlates," in Nelson Polsby, Robert A. Dentler, and Paul A. Smith (eds.), *Politics and Social Life* (Boston: Houghton Mifflin, 1963), pp. 569–582.

    Korea lacks more or less all these conditions. Furthermore, the existence of a long libertarian political tradition, the opportunity to develop political institutions gradually over a long period of time without violent interruptions such as war, riot, or revolution, and the existence of strong private institutions and organizations which would tend to limit the government's tendency to monopolize power are also deemed important for democratic development. However, Korea during the post independence years faced the exact opposites of these conditions.
48. Henderson, *op. cit.*, p. 168.
49. An international inspection team sent by the International Press Institute headquartered in Zurich, Switzerland, reported after a field trip to Korea in April 1960 that there existed no freedom of the press in Korea. See *1968 Hankuk Shinmun Yŏngam* (Korean Press Yearbook: 1968) (Seoul: Korean Newspapers Association, 1968), p. 72. The same source also offers a chronology of Korean newspapers, 1945–1967, which is full of incidents where freedom of the press was suppressed. See pp. 65–85.
50. For instance, the convicted assassin of Kim Ku, Syngman Rhee's foremost rival for leadership of liberated Korea in the post-war years, was given a life sentence in 1949 but was soon found back in active duty in the Korean army as an officer with a promoted rank with more and fast promotions to follow. Even though Rhee was not formally implicated in the case, it seemed apparent that he had a hand in it, directly or indirectly. Without his permission, the convict's return to military duty would have been impossible. See Haebang Iship Nyŏn: Kirok P'yŏn (Twenty Post-Liberation Years: Records) (Seoul: Semunsa, 1965), pp. 334–340.

    In another case illustrative of Rhee's attitudes toward political opposition, Cho Pong-am, Chairman of the Progressive Party, who had also been Rhee's rival in two presidential elections, was unconvincingly convicted of engaging in activities with the intention of overthrowing the republic and was sentenced to death. Rhee could have granted him a commutation but did not. Cho was thus executed on July 31, 1959, just one day after his appeal to the Supreme Court for retrial was rejected. See *ibid.*, pp. 491–493.
51. For objective information of the events surrounding the 1952 constitutional

crisis, see United Nations, *Report of the United Nations Commission for the Unification and Rehabilitation of Korea* (hereafter referred to as *UNCURK Report*); *GAOR,* 7th Session, Supplement No. 14 (A/2187), pp. 5–11.
52. United Nations, *UNCURK Report; GAOR,* 10th Session, Supplement No. 13 (A/2947), pp. 4–5, 20; and *ibid.,* 9th Session, Supplement No. 15 (A/2711), p. 11.
53. See *Second Part of the Report of the UNTCOK; GAOR:* 3d Session, Supplement No. 9 (A/575/Add. 4), p. 30.
54. *UNCURK Report; GAOR,* 10th Session, Supplement No. 13 (A/2947), p. 5.
55. For objective information on the events surrounding the 1954 constitutional amendments, see *ibid.,* pp. 4–5.
56. During this period in Korea there was a popular saying that one could "win an election in the voting and lose it in the ballot-counting." In most cases, such an unfortunate candidate belonged to the opposition. The governing Liberal Party indulged in numerous methods which separately or together achieved such a transformation of the election results. Among the methods were ballot-box stuffing, ballot-box replacing, doctoring of valid ballots cast for an opposition candidate so that they would be declared invalid, and plain stealing of ballots for an opposition candidate.
57. Six of the acts passed by the National Assembly were not promulgated at all by Rhee during his presidency.
58. Perhaps, "rule-misapplication-oriented" is a better term to describe interest-seeking activities during this period. In reference to the bureaucratic behavior, it was often said that there was nothing that was impossible and there was nothing easy with the government officials. With enough money or the right "connections," everything including things which were forbidden by law was possible; without bribing money or the right "connections" nothing was easy including things which were perfectly legal.
59. For a classification of interest groups, see Almond and Powell, *op. cit.,* pp. 74–79.
60. For definitions of these terms, see *ibid.,* pp. 86–88; also Gabriel A. Almond, "Introduction: A Functional Approach to Comparative Politics," in Almond and James A. Coleman (eds.), *The Politics of the Developing Areas* (Princeton, N. J.: Princeton University Press, 1960), pp. 26 ff.
61. Myron Weiner talks about a similar case in reference to Indian student politics. See his *The Politics of Scarcity* (Chicago: University of Chicago Press, 1962), p.185.
62. A similar situation seems to have existed in Weimar Germany and in pre-Fascist Italy. In both cases, electoral and parliamentary activities failed to produce much responsiveness on the part of the government.
63. In these elections Rhee was unopposed since his only opponent, Dr. Cho Pyŏng-ok (Democratic Party), had died shortly before election day. Rhee's running mate, Lee Ki-pung, however faced a formidable opponent in Dr. Chang Myŏn (Democratic Party) who had defeated him in the previous vice-presidential election in 1956. When the results were announced, Lee had allegedly won an unlikely high 8,337,376 votes against Chang's inexplicably low 1,843,758. Thus the Democratic Party declared the elections

"illegal, null, and void." See United Nations, *UNCURK Report; GAOR:* 15th Session, Supplement No. 13 (A/4466 and Add.1), p. 3.
64. Quoted in Allen, *op. cit.*, p. 231.
65. At the time of the vote on the motion, the Liberal Party did not have this strong majority since the previous day 41 of its representatives had left the party. See Reeve, *op. cit.*, p. 50.
66. It must have been very difficult for Rhee to accept this since he said a few days earlier: "It is almost unbelievable that any element of the patriotic Korean people, to whom I have devoted my life, could act in such a way as the demonstrators did." His obsession with his own infallibility made it impossible for him to accept the fact that his service was no longer wanted by the Korean people and that his presidency had been a failure. See Allen, *op. cit.*, pp. 231, 12, 237–38.
67. In Korea, it is often referred to as the April–19 or 4–19 Student Revolution or Uprising.
68. Quoted in *The New York Times*, May 1, 1960, and requoted in Allen, *op. cit.*, p. 234.
69. The National Assembly decision on the constitutional amendment was 208 votes in favor to 3 against. See Reeve, *op. cit.*, pp. 143–44; *GAOR*, 15th session, *op. cit.*, p. 4; Hong Chu Mun, "The History of Korean Constitution," *Koreana Quarterly*, Vol. 7, No. 3 (Autumn 1965), pp. 11–25.
70. Even under Rhee, the constitution provided for a bicameral legislature, but Rhee refused to implement the provision—another example of his very conveniently flexible attitude toward the constitution.
71. *GAOR*, 15th Session, *op. cit.*, p. 12. The Democratic Party won 31 of 58 seats in the House of Councilors and 175 of 233 in the House of Representatives. The second largest party was the Liberal Party with four seats in the upper house and two in the lower. The Social Masses Party, the third in size, had four seats in the lower house and one in the upper.
72. See *ibid.*, pp. 3–4.
73. Allen, *op. cit.*, p. 11.
74. A nation-wide opinion poll conducted during this period found only 3.7% willing to give unreserved support to the Chang regime with 51.5% wanting to wait and see. See *The Dong-A Ilbo*, December 28, 1960.
75. For information concerning this period, see Sŏ Pyŏng-cho, *Chukwŏnja-ŭi Chŭng-ŏn: Hanguk Taeŭi Chŏngch'isa* (The Testimony of the Sovereign: A History of Korean Parliamentary Politics) (Seoul: Mo-ŭm Publishing Co., 1963), pp. 384–409. Objective observations are found in the report of the United Nations Commission for the Unification and Rehabilitation of Korea. See United Nations, *UNCURK Report; GAOR*, 16th Session, Supplement No. 13 (A/4900), pp. 3–5.
76. United Nations, *UNCURK Report; GAOR*, 16th Session, Supplement No. 13 (A/4900), p.4, paragraph 37.
77. See Sŏ, *Chukwŏnja-ŭi Chŭng-ŏn, op. cit.*, pp. 391–392; also *GAOR*: 16th Session, *op. cit.*, p. 4, paragraph 42.
78. See *GAOR*, 16th Session, *op. cit.*, p. 4, paragraph 43.
79. See Stephen Bradner, "Korea: Experiment and Instability," *Japan Quarterly*, Volume VIII, No. 4 (October-December, 1961), p. 414; quoted in John Kie-Chiang Oh, *Korea: Democracy on Trial* (Ithaca, N. Y.: Cornell University Press, 1968), p. 85.

80. On October 17, nine days after the massive demonstration in front of the House of Representatives building, a constitutional amendment bill was introduced in the lower House. On November 16, exactly thirty days from its introduction, the minimum interval required by the constitution, the parliamentary debate on the bill began. On November 23, after only a week's debate, the bill was passed by the lower House with 191 votes in favor, one against, six invalid, and two abstentions. Five days later, the House of Councilors also passed it with forty-four in favor, twelve against, two invalid, and two abstentions. The following day, November 29, the President signed and proclaimed the amendment. The amendment permitted the enactment of new laws "to punish those involved in the rigging of the presidential and vice presidential elections held on March 15, 1960, or those who had killed or wounded demonstrators protesting these illegal elections, to suspend the civil rights of those who had committed serious undemocratic acts by taking advantage of their official positions under the former regime; and to punish those who, until April 26, 1960, had amassed fortunes by using political position or power, or other illegal means." See *GAOR*, 16th Session, *op. cit.*, p. 4.
81. *Ibid.*
82. Henderson, *op. cit.*, p. 304. Henderson's comment on the Democratic Party's factionalism is in agreement with the present author's observation: "The fragile unity of the Democratic party, which was based primarily not on positive belief in democratic programs but on opposition to the Liberal Party and the governing system, began to disintegrate. With the collapse of the Liberal Party and the Rhee government, the mainspring of cohesion disappeared. Now, also the faults of the party's original construction showed: a marriage of convenience between two interest groups, not of belief and loyalty."
83. See Reeve, *op. cit.*, p. 145. On September 23, the two factions registered as separate parliamentary negotiating groups. In the House of Representatives, 95 belonged to the new and 86 to the old faction, with 14 independents.
84. See *GAOR*, 16th Session, *op. cit.*, p. 3; also Henderson *op. cit.*, p. 304.
85 See *GAOR*, 16th Session, *op. cit.*, p. 4. Party strengths in the National Assembly as of the last day of the Democratic rule (May 15, 1961) were as follows:

	House of Reps.	House of Councs.
Democratic Party	133	13
New Democratic Party	62	18
Independents	9	$6(1)^a$
Minchŏng Club	28	—
Ch'am-wu Club	—	$13(7)^a$

a. The numbers in parentheses refer to those deprived of their civil rights on April 24, 1961.
86 *GAOR*, 16th Session, *op. cit.*, p. 4, paragraph 33.
87 See Oh, *op. cit.*, p. 82.
88 See *GAOR*, 16th Session, *op. cit.*, p. 4, paragraphs 49–50.
89 *Ibid.*, paragraph 46; also *1968 Shinmun Yŏngam, op. cit.*, pp. 55, 72–73. See also Oh, *op. cit.*, p. 90: "... the great majority of the people ... enjoyed more freedom under the Chang government than at any other period in

Korean history."
90. *GAOR,* 16th Session, *op. cit.,* p. 4, paragraph 34.
91. For information on the coup, see Se Jin Kim, "Military Revolution in Korea, 1961-1963" (Unpublished doctoral dissertation, University of Massachusetts, 1966); John Kie-Chiang Oh, "The Political Role of the Military: The Making of the Third Republic," in Sidney D. Brown (ed.), *Studies on Asia, 1967* (Lincoln, Neb.: University of Nebraska Press, 1967); Walter Briggs, "The Military Revolution in Korea: On its Leader and Achievements," *Koreana Quarterly,* Vol. 5, No. 2 (Summer 1963), pp. 17-34.
92. The so-called "Revolutionary Pledges" contained the following six goals of the military revolution: (1) anti-communism, (2) pro-United Nations, pro-Western, pro-United States foreign policy, (3) elimination of government corruption, (4) economic betterment, (5) national unification through strength, and (6) preparation for an ultimate civilian democracy. See *GAOR,* 16th Session, *op. cit.,* pp. 5-6.
93. The Military's strong anti-communist stand may be viewed as an ideological departure from the Chang regime's more liberal attitudes toward leftist activities. However, it can be argued that the Chang government's such attitudes stemmed not so much from its own ideological orientation as from its general libertarian attitudes toward all political viewpoints. The Democrats themselves were also strongly anti-communist.
94. *GAOR,* 17th Session, Supplement No. 13 (A/5213), p. 7, paragraph 61.
95. *Ibid.,* paragraph 63.
96. *Ibid.,* 16th Session, *op. cit.,* p. 7, paragraph 66.
97. The Democratic Republican party was organized in secrecy before the ban on political party activities was officially lifted. Kim Chong Pil, who later became the party's chairman, is widely believed to have been the prime organizer. Accordingly, the DRP had a much earlier start than other parties as far as preparation for the 1963 elections was concerned, giving it a definite advantage in the 1963 elections.
98. For the election results of 1963, see *ibid.,* 19th Session, Supplement No. 12 (A/5812), pp. 7-10, 33-34. The Democratic Republican Party won the presidency by a narrow margin but its majority in the National Assembly was strong with 110 of 175 seats under its control.
99. *Ibid.,* 18th Session, Supplement No. 12 (A/5512), p. 11, paragraphs 125-126.
100. For the texts of the 1962 constitution and laws governing political parties and elections, see *ibid.,* pp. 29-73; for information about the constitutional referendum, see *ibid.,* p. 6.
101. The UNCURK's comments were on the presidential election: "... on the whole, procedures were carried out in a free atmosphere and in an orderly, calm and proper manner"; and for the National Assembly elections: "... they had been carried out in a peaceful, orderly and fair manner." See *GAOR,* 19th Session, *op. cit.,* pp. 8 and 10.
102. Flora Lewis, "Seoul Feels a Cold Wind from the North," *The New York Times Sunday Magazine,* February 18, 1968, p. 110; *Time,* April 26, 1968, p. 29; *The Dong-A Ilbo,* December 27, 1968, December 4, 1969, and January 13 and 30, 1970.

103. See Economic Planning Board, Republic of Korea, *Major Economic Indicators, 1962–1972* (Seoul: July 1973), p. 8, Table I–2.
104. *Ibid.*
105. *The Hankuk Ilbo*, January 16, 1974.
106. *Major Economic Indicators, op. cit.*, p. 6.
107. *Ibid.*, p. 75
108. See Economic Planning Board, Republic of Korea, *Summary of Population Statistics* (Seoul, 1968), p. 40; *Annual Report on the Economically Active Population* (Seoul, 1967), p. 68; and *Major Economic Indicators, op. cit.*, p. 97.
109. *Ibid.*, p. 96.
110. See *The New York Times*, January 19, 1968.
111. *Major Economic Indicators, op. cit.*, p. 105.
112. The anti-corruption campaign of early 1974 in which many officials of middle and high ranks were purged provides a good indication of the extent of government corruption.

PART TWO: THE STRUCTURE AND PROCESSES OF KOREAN GOVERNMENT

CHAPTER 2: The Constitution and Governmental Structures
by Edward Reynolds Wright

CHAPTER 3: The Bureaucracy
by Suk-choon Cho

CHAPTER 4: Underlying Factors in Political Party Organization and Elections
by Ki-shik Hahn

INTRODUCTION TO PART TWO

The three chapters in this section treat the Korean Constitution and formal structures of government, the Bureaucracy, and Korean political parties and elections. The first, Chapter 2, describes the constitutional and structural undergirding of the Korean political system. Though the official superstructure of Korean government is designed after western models, traditional behavior patterns are still instrumental to what happens politically. The resultant tension between tradition and modern democratic principle is reflected in many ways in the Constitution itself, as well as in governmental interpretation of Constitutional provisions. In the Constitution are provisions for a presidential system and a single-house National Assembly that is clearly subordinate to the Executive. In addition, the political party system is based upon a government or "ruling" party (the Democratic Republican Party) with the President at its helm, and a major opposition party, since 1961 the New Democratic Party. Thus far in the Republic of Korea's short history, the government party has never been turned out of office through peaceful means.

In his article, Suk-choon Cho elaborates upon certain authority patterns to be found within the Korean Bureaucracy: 1) *hierarchy* as the formal norm for governing interpersonal relations within the Bureaucracy; 2) *administrative specialization*; and 3) *personalism*. Based upon these patterns, the Bureaucracy is the principal policy formulator, and is not so inclined to look to the legislature or political parties as substantial or crucial contributors to policy formulation. Further, procedural characteristics of the Korean Bureaucracy can be identified as follows: 1) secrecy in policy formulation; 2) rationalization of politically derived decisions in terms of bureaucratic rationality; 3) inconsistency of policies over a period of time. In terms of effectiveness of policy innovation and implementation, the centralized bureaucracy is the key element in either thwarting or facilitating significant changes. And within the bureaucracy, those at the top levels are most instrumental in effecting change, while subordinates function largely in routine supervisory and clerical positions. The hierarchical nature of Korean politics reaches its peak with the highest-level personnel of the Bureaucracy and ultimately with the President. There are some signs at present, however, that "specialists" will be increasingly consulted, especially with regard to major developmental projects. At the same time, this tendency does not alter the essential hierarchical principle upon which Korean government rests. Decisions—rational or irrational—continue to be made in a highly centralized fashion.

In his general essay on political parties and elections, Ki-shik Hahn states that "party politics in South Korea has been largely a history of power struggles among conservative parties and their component factions, devoid of conflicting ideological contentions." Government parties since World War II have tended to emphasize anti-communism, national security and political stability, while opposition parties have stressed the need for greater realization of liberal democracy, respect for individual rights and freedom, and programs of mass welfare. The opposition also has lost no opportunity to point out instances of Government corruption, as well as a relatively low degree of responsiveness and responsibility to the people by the Government party. Nonetheless, Hahn concludes that party development has been rapid: "Considering the fact that Korea experienced neither self-government nor party politics before August of 1945, we may well speculate that this is perhaps one of the most rapid party developments in history." He lists three principal factors which have been contributive of South Korean party development: 1) an increasing level of political consciousness on the part of the masses as a result of experience with democratic political processes; 2) the strengthening of party leadership and organization within the government and opposition parties; 3) the increase of potential opposition supporters as a result of ongoing industrialization, urbanization and modernization.

In Hahn's view, electoral procedures have been less than ideal because of several persisting obstructions to meaningful political participation. These have included various kinds of electoral interference and manipulation by the Government, as well as problems related to the political culture and voting behavior.

Finally, Hahn identifies and discusses three factors which have been detrimental to the development of parties and other political structures: 1) primary emphasis on continuous economic growth and on political stability; 2) continuing internal schism and inveterate factional struggle within and among opposition groups; 3) international tensions affecting the Korean peninsula. The events of 1972, 1973, and 1974, including the "revitalizing reforms," the strengthening of executive authority, and increasing evidence of dissent among some elements of the populace, have prompted Hahn to conclude that "at this juncture, it is perhaps too early to be able to properly evaluate the impact of 'Koreanized democracy' on Korean political party development."

CHAPTER 2:

The Constitution and Governmental Structures

EDWARD REYNOLDS WRIGHT*

The Government of the Republic of Korea was established in 1948, three years following the culmination of World War II and the end of the 35-year Japanese colonial rule. The First Republic of Korea lasted 12 years—from 1948–1960—under the strong and autocratic rule of President Syngman Rhee. The original Constitution instituted a Presidential system which was generally used at Rhee's discretion. Student demonstrations in April of 1960, however, sparked a change in Government and Constitution. A cabinet system was substituted for the previous presidential system, and the first and only Prime Minister of the Second Republic was Chang Myŏn. Continuing unrest and demonstrations, however, did not allow the liberal Chang Government to pursue strong policies to effect social stability and economic progress. Stronger leadership came with a military coup d'etat on May 16, 1961, under the guidance of General Park Chunghee, who was installed as Chairman of the Supreme Council for National Reconstruction. He was later made Acting President. A nation-wide referendum on December 19, 1962 re-established a strong presidential system, and Park Chung-hee was elected as the first President of Korea's Third Republic in October of 1963. He was re-elected in 1967, 1971 and 1972. The 1971 election took place only after a Constitutional amendment was passed allowing a third term,

---

*The author is Executive Director of the Korean-American Educational (Fulbright) Commission in Korea and Lecturer in Political Science at Seoul National University. His Ph.D. is in Political Science from Duke University, Durham, North Carolina. He was formerly on the faculty of Midwestern University in Texas.

while the 1972 election came after extensive Constitutional changes were promulgated allowing, among other things, the indefinite tenure of an individual in the Presidential office.

On October 17, 1972, a state of martial law was declared. Under a Presidential proclamation called the "October Revitalizing Reforms," the representative National Assembly was abolished for the time being; colleges and universities were temporarily shut down, and the press placed under strict censorship. A greatly amended Constitution was approved by 91.4 percent of the vote in a November 21 national referendum. Open opposition to the new document was not allowed under martial law, therefore the result was a foregone conclusion. The rationale given for the state of martial law and imposition of the new Constitution was that the country had to be strengthened in the process toward unification of South and North.

The Park regime since 1962 has been a radical one in implementing drastic changes in Korean society—including impressive progress in economic development; building of extensive communications and transportation networks to unify the South; and modernizing of a 600,000-man military establishment. To summarize, the nation has been politically regressive from a democratic political perspective, but has accomplished in a short time a solid material and economic base for national progress which likely could not have been done on strictly democratic terms.[1]

THE PRESIDENCY

Presently, a candidate for President must be 40 years of age or more, and must have resided continuously in the country or have been serving on official duty overseas for five years or more (Article 44). He is elected by the National Conference for Unification (Article 45), a body composed of delegates numbering between 2,000 and 5,000 persons—the present number is 2,359—and elected through direct popular vote. The President is chairman of the body (Article 37). The members cannot belong to a political party, but elect the President by secret ballot, with a quorum required of more than half of those elected and voting. No debate is permitted (Article 39). The tight administrative control exercised by the Government would seem to assure a successful outcome for the Government's candidate for President. President Park Chung-hee was elected without opposition on December 24, 1972, and inaugurated on December 29.

If the office of President becomes vacant, the National Conference for Unification shall elect a successor within three months. If the remaining term of office is less than one year, however, a successor shall not be elected (Article 45). When the Presidency is vacant or when the President is unable to perform his duties, the Prime Minister and the members of the State Council shall act as President (Article 48). There is no provision for a vice-president.

Powers of the President. The powers of the President are extremely broad. He can conclude and ratify treaties, receive or dispatch diplomatic envoys, declare war and conclude peace (Article 50). He exercises supreme command of the armed forces (Article 51). He may issue ordinances on matters within the scope specifically delegated by law and required for enforcement of laws (Article 52). However, any seeming limitations on the President's ordinance-making powers are superseded through provisions of Articles 53 and 54, which give emergency powers and the power to declare martial law. In times of crisis—presumably as determined by the President—he "shall have power to take necessary emergency measures in the whole range of the State Affairs, including internal affairs, foreign affairs, national defense, economic, financial and judicial affairs" (Article 53). Further, he can "temporarily suspend the freedom and rights of the people as defined in the present Constitution, and... enforce emergency measures with regard to the rights and powers of the Executive and the Judiciary" (Article 53, paragraph 2). These emergency powers are not subject to significant restrictions by other Government agencies (Article 53, paragraphs 3,4,5,6).

The President also can, when he deems it necessary "to maintain the public safety and order by mobilization of the military forces, proclaim a state of martial law in accordance with the provisions of law" (Article 54). The only restriction on the President's power to proclaim martial law is in the provision of Article 54, paragraph 5, which states that "the President shall lift the proclaimed state of martial law" when more than one-half of the members of the National Assembly so request. However, the President, according to Article 59, may dissolve the National Assembly. In summary, the President can proclaim a state of emergency or martial law and assume all powers of Government without significant restrictions.

The Prime Minister, the State Council and the Executive Ministries fall under the President's jurisdiction in the executive branch of Government. All of these function essentially as administrative units and, insofar as policy making is concerned, serve in a deliberative and advisory capacity on matters referred or delegated by the President (Articles 66 and 69). The Prime Minister is appointed by the President with the approval of the National Assembly and cannot be an active member of the military (Article 63). The members of the State Council are appointed by the President upon recommendation by the Prime Minister, and may not be active members of the military. The State Council is composed of the President, the Prime Minister, and from fifteen to twenty-five appointive members. The President is chairman and the Prime Minister vice-chairman (Article 65). An "Emergency State Council" was established under martial law in October 1972 in order, among other things, to draft and promulgate new extensive Election, National Assembly, and Judicial Laws which went into effect in early 1973. This "emergency" body was then superseded by the duly established State Council.

The heads of Executive Ministries are appointed by the President from the membership of the State Council upon recommendation of the Prime Minister (Article 68). A National Security Council functions for the purpose of advising the President on matters related to national security. The number of members and the Council's organization and scope of powers are left to interpretation by law (Article 67).

It is evident, in conclusion, that the President is the strongest single element in the Korean political system. This stems from his constitutionally derived powers and role, including the possibility of using extensive and virtually unlimited powers under an official state of emergency or martial law; his political party leadership and control; his substantial control over the military establishment; and, most basically, historically rooted traditional factors related to extreme reliance on centralized authority in Korean society,

THE NATIONAL ASSEMBLY

Background. The National Assembly in the Republic of Korea first met on May 31, 1948. It was a weak body, and largely dominated by the executive. The second National Assembly, convened on June 19, 1950, was also restricted in its normal exercise of legislative power because of the strong executive leadership of Syngman Rhee who was unwilling to allow the legislature to threaten his powers or personal tenure in office. The situation was not helped by the outbreak of war six days after the opening of the first session. The

Assembly had to move successively southward from Seoul to Taejon to Taegu to Pusan. Elections for the third National Assembly were held on May 20, 1954, and resulted in Rhee's Liberal Party winning 114 of the 203 seats. In elections for the fourth National Assembly in 1958, the Liberal Party, increasingly controlled by Rhee, won 126 of 233 seats. This Assembly served only until the spring of 1960, when the members—as well as Rhee himself—were forced to resign as a result of the 1960 student uprising which had been triggered by the rigged presidential elections of March 15.

A fifth National Assembly was constituted on August 8, 1960, based upon a Constitutional Amendment which provided for a cabinet system and a bicameral legislature. The Democratic Party under the leadership of Chang Myŏn dominated the two Houses. The Chang Government, however, was relatively ineffectual in dealing with the nation's ills, and on May 16, 1961, a military coup d'etat easily toppled the new rulers, bringing about the dissolution of the fifth National Assembly as well as all political parties. There was no national legislature during the subsequent two and one-half years of military rule. Rather, a Supreme Council for National Reconstruction was established to perform all judicial and executive functions. In December of 1963, the Third Republic of Korea was born, bringing a return to a Presidential system and a unicameral legislature. On October 17, 1972, the National Assembly was abolished by Presidential decree under martial law; however, on February 27, 1973, the Assembly was reconstituted in nation-wide elections under the amended Constitution.

Membership and Organization. The present Assembly organization and powers are based upon Constitutional provisions, the Election Law of December 30, 1972,[2] and the National Assembly Law.[3] The latter two laws were decreed by the Extraordinary State Council appointed by the President following the martial law proclaimed in October 1973. Constitutional provisions specifically related to the National Assembly are found in Articles 75–99. The number of Assembly members is to be set by law and was proclaimed by the Emergency State Council on December 30, 1972, to be 219 representing 73 constituencies. Two-thirds, or 146 members, are chosen by universal, equal, direct and secret elections for six-year terms and one-third, or 73 members, by the presidentially responsible National Conference for Unification for three-year terms. The names of Assembly members selected by the National Conference for Unification are submitted by the President to the Conference, which is responsible to the President with regard to its duties, including selection of National Assembly membership.

The National Assembly Election Law proclaimed on December 30, 1972, greatly simplified election procedures in comparison to previous practices. Political party nominees must deposit two million won (about $5,000 U.S.) in order to run, and independent candidates three million won (about $7,500 U.S.). These deposits, minus "electioneering expenses," are returned to successful candidates and to unsuccessful candidates who receive more than one-third of the votes in their respective constituencies. In the first elections under the new regulations held on February 27, 1973, only 337 candidates entered the race for 146 seats. Election campaigns are closely circumscribed in comparison with previous practice and can be conducted only through *joint* speech rallies, distribution of campaign pamphlets and posting of campaign posters by election management committees.

Regular sessions of the Assembly are held once a year for no more than 90 days; extraordinary sessions can be called for no more than 30 days by the President or by one-third of the total membership. There is a total maximum allowable of 150 days; however, extraordinary sessions called by the President are exempt from this limitation: during Presidentially-called sessions, only bills submitted by the Executive can be considered (Article 82). For passage of bills, a quorum consists of more than half of the total membership, and concurrence is required of more than half of the members present. A tie vote constitutes rejection of a bill (Article 84). Secret sessions may be called, and the content of such sessions may not be open to public scrutiny (Article 85). Introduction of bills may be by 20 or more Assembly members affiliated with a political party or by the President (Article 87 and the 1972 Election Law). A successful bill will be promulgated within 15 days, unless the President rejects it and requests Assembly reconsideration in writing. The Assembly may override the President's veto by a two-thirds majority of those present and voting. A law generally will go into effect 20 days after promulgation (Article 88).

Procedures in the Assembly are closely circumscribed in comparison with Constitutional and Assembly Law provisions of the period before martial law was declared in October of 1972. With regard to members' floor activities, the Assembly speaker can set limits on the number of speakers on the floor and on the length of their speeches. He also must give prior permission for any member to take the floor; can determine the Assembly agenda; and can refer delinquent lawmakers to the legislation-judiciary committee for disciplinary actions. The purpose of this enhanced power of the speaker is to discourage minority deterrence of debate and passage of bills. Assemblymen's speeches are limited to 30 minutes, with possible extension of 15 additional minutes if permitted by the Speaker. Previously, there was no restriction on length of speeches or number of speakers. In standing committee debate also, the number and length of speeches may be limited by committee chairmen. Finally, there can be no debate on any bills in plenary session. In contrast, under the system before the 1972 martial law, legislative programs went through the following procedures in standing committee and plenary session: 1) explanation of the bills, 2) question-and-answer sessions, 3) general debate, and 4) vote. The new Law makes it difficult for the Assembly to query administrative officials; a majority vote in the Assembly is necessary to summon them, and questions must be presented to officials through the Assembly Speaker at least 24 hours before the question period. Further, the Assembly members cannot "insult" the President, Prime Minister, Cabinet members and their agents, or speak or write about their private lives. In the past, Cabinet members in particular were required to spend lengthy periods of interpolation on a vast range of subjects in the Assembly. Finally, the Speaker can take disciplinary action against lawmakers who violate the Assembly Law and procedural rules. Presumably, the Speaker may decide when such violations take place.

There are presently 13 standing committees, as well as special committees appointed for limited periods and for special purposes. There is no established method for appointment of standing committee members—seniority has little significance in the Korean system. Rather, the floor leaders of the parties designate the party slates for committee membership, and the National Assembly formally ratifies those nominees. The committees have from 11 to 24 members, and one Assemblyman may serve only on one committee, with the exception of the membership of the Steering (Rules) committee. The present standing committees in order of seniority are: Legislation-Judiciary; Foreign Affairs; Home Affairs; Finance; Economy-Science; National Defense; Education-Public Information; Agriculture-Forestry; Commerce-Industry; Health-Social Affairs; Transportation-Communication; Construction; House Steering.

Powers of the National Assembly. The National Assembly exercises general legislative powers except at times when the President has declared a state of national emergency or martial law. One special power of the Assembly is to deliberate and decide on the national budget, as submitted by the Executive (Article 89). However, the Assembly cannot increase the sum of any budgetary item or add items to the proposed budget—presumably it must approve or reject the budget in its entirety (Article 92). Also, the Assembly has the "right of concurrence" to treaties, and to the declaration of war, the dispatch of armed forces to foreign states, or the stationing of alien forces in Korea (Article 95). There is no indication of what might happen if the Assembly did not concur—Article 50 of the Constitution clearly states that the President can ratify treaties, declare war and conclude peace. Any limiting power by the Assembly with regard to these Presidential powers are ambiguous at least.

Another Assembly power is that of removal of the Prime Minister or an individual State Council member from office. This is done with the concurrence of more than half of the members present and voting. If such a motion is passed with regard to the Prime Minister, the President will remove all members of the State Council from office (Article 97). A final special power of the Assembly is that of impeachment of the President, the Prime Minister, Heads of Executive Ministries, members of the Constitutional Committee, Judges, members of the Central Election Management Committee, members of the Board of Audit and Inspection and "other public officials" deemed to have "violated the Constitution or other laws in the exercise of their duties." A proposal for impeachment is by at least one-third of the total Assembly members, and a subsequent vote of at least one-half is necessary to institute impeachment. In the case of the President, however, proposal is by more than one-half and impeachment by at least two-thirds. The penalty for impeachment is simply dismissal from public office, though subsequent charges may be brought for civil or criminal liability (Article 99). Before October 1972 the Assembly had the right of parliamentary inspection of the administration; however, this has been abolished.

It should be reiterated that all Assembly powers may be overridden by the Executive when a crisis requires implementation of emergency powers or martial law. The Korean National Assembly is directly subject to the greater weight of executive authority and cannot exercise significant powers not condoned by that authority.

THE JUDICIARY

Background. The Korean legal system, established in 1895, was modeled after the German system of the nineteenth century. The Court Organization Act of that year provided for five types of courts: local courts, harbor courts, circuit courts, a high court, and a special court. The local courts were those of first jurisdiction in criminal and civil cases, along with the harbor courts which had jurisdiction over cases involving aliens, among others. The circuit courts were courts of appeal for decisions from the local courts, and the high court heard appeals from the harbor courts. The special court was set up to adjudicate criminal cases related to acts committed by the royal family. In 1899 the high court became the court of final appeal from all other courts. There was a Court Reorganization Law of 1907 which provided two levels of appeal from an original lower court decision.

With Japan's annexation of Korea in 1911 came a complete reorganization of the system. A Japanese decree established three court levels: district courts, appellate courts, and a high court. Sharing the work of the district courts as courts of first jurisdiction over criminal and civil cases were branch courts. The appellate courts heard appeals from the lower courts, while the high court was the court of last appeal.

The present system is based essentially on the Court Organization Act of 1948 which established four kinds of courts: summary courts, district courts, appellate courts, and a Supreme Court. The summary courts, however, were never created, and the court level of original jurisdiction in all cases became that of the district courts. Only minor modifications in the system have been made in the years from 1948 to 1973. In the capital city of Seoul, the district court was divided into two parts on June 18, 1963—a Seoul Civil District Court and a Seoul Criminal District Court. On July 31, 1963, a Family Court system was established for settlement of cases related to domestic relations. On December 17, 1963, the Supreme Court was given the power of judicial review over laws of the National Assembly, however this power was given in December 1972 to a special Constitution Committee of nine members.

On February 1, 1973, significant procedural changes went into effect as decreed by the Extraordinary State Council. The right of habeas corpus, technically in effect from 1948, was abolished—the provision of the Code of Criminal Procedure was eliminated which had previously upheld the right to ask a court to re-examine the legality of a prosecution's arrest or detention of a suspect. Public prosecutors and judicial police officials now may apprehend a suspect without an arrest warrant if he is suspected of having committed an offense punishable by imprisonment or a severer penalty; previously this could be done only in instances punishable by more than a three-year imprisonment. Also, public prosecutors and judicial police officials were newly empowered to re-arrest a person who had already been arrested and released if important new evidence were discovered. A public prosecutor also may now immediately appeal to a higher court against a court ruling granting release on bail or suspending arrest or detention; formerly no such prosecution appeal was possible. Finally with regard to criminal procedures, there can be no appeal to the Supreme Court by the prosecution against an appellate court ruling except when important new evidence for the prosecution is found.

Structure and Powers of the Courts. The two bases of the judicial system are found in Articles 100-108 of the Constitution and in the Court Organization Act of 1948, as amended. Concerning the structure of the court system, the Constitution in Article 100 states simply that there will be a Supreme Court and other courts at specified levels. It further stipulates that the qualifications of judges shall be determined by law. The present court structure can be described as follows:

1. *The Constitution Committee.* A special Constitution Committee with nine members is empowered to judge the following matters: the constitutionality of a law at the request of the Supreme Court; impeachment; and dissolution of a political party. Decisions must be by at least seven affirmative votes. Three members are selected by the National Assembly; three by the Chief Justice of the Supreme Court; and three by the President. Their term of office is six years, and members cannot join a political party or participate in political activities (Articles 109-111).

2. *The Supreme Court.* The Supreme Court may hear appeals from decisions of appellate courts, appellate divisions of district and family courts, and military courts in cases of courts martial. Under Article 105 of the Constitution, "when the constitutionality of a law is involved in a trial, the [Supreme] Court shall request of the Constitution Committee a decision, and shall judge according to the decision thereof." The Supreme Court also has the "ultimate power to decide the constitutionality or legality of administrative decrees,

The Constitution and Governmental Structures

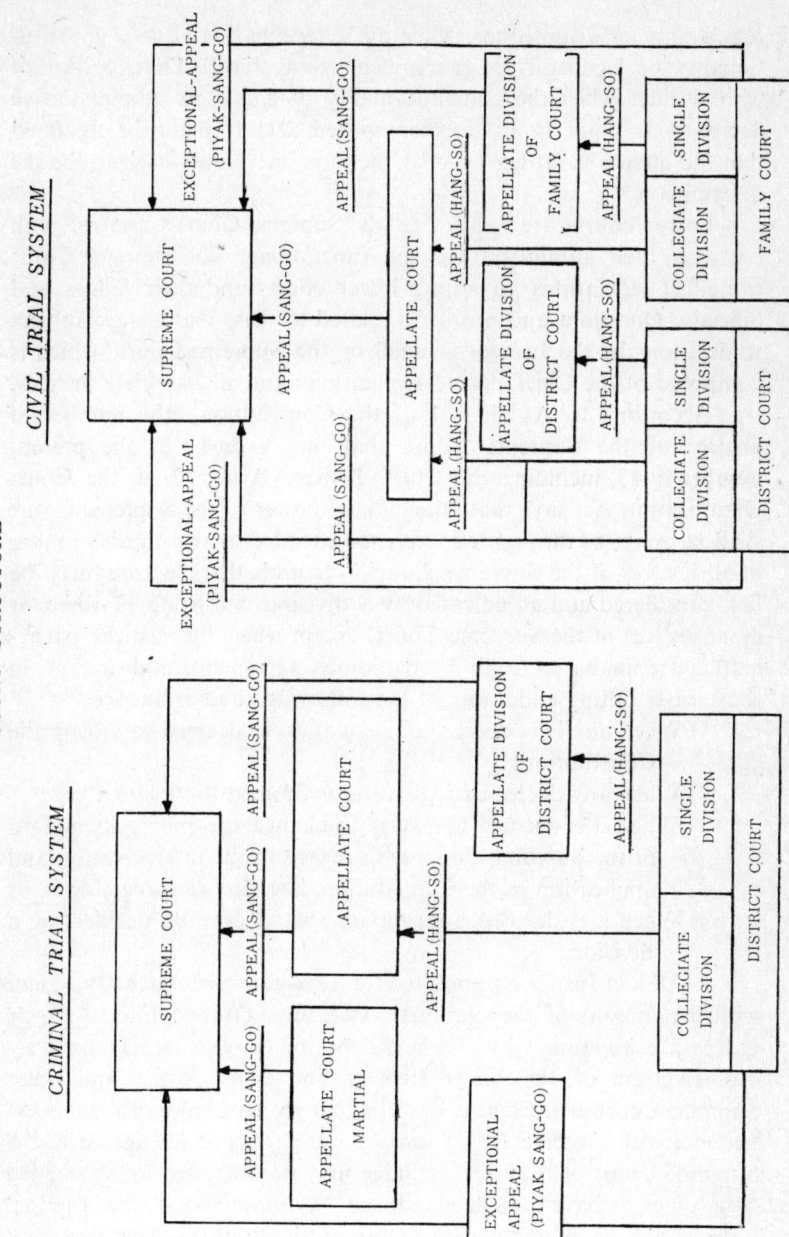

regulations, or dispositions, when the determination of their constitutionality or legality is a prerequisite to a trial." The question of who decides when the constitutionality of a law or administrative decree is at point is not further spelled out. It might be assumed that the intention, at least, is for the Supreme Court itself to be the determinant.

Lower courts are subject to the Supreme Court's control with regard to their administration and functioning. The Supreme Court can effect regulations governing lower courts and their judges and officials. Questions and problems related to these matters are subject to decisions by the Justices Council of the Supreme Court, which is composed of the Chief Justice as chairman and all associate justices.

According to Article 101 of the Constitution, the number of justices of the Supreme Court shall not exceed 16; the present number is 13, including the Chief Justice. Article 7 of the Court Organization Act says that "the judicial power of the Supreme Court shall be exercised through a conference attended by two-thirds or more of all justices of the Supreme Court." It adds that "a case may be first considered and adjudicated by a division consisting of three or more justices of the Supreme Court, except when the justices participating are unable to reach a unanimous agreement, and except in those cases falling under any of the following circumstances:

1) When any law, decree, or regulation is deemed to violate the Constitution;
2) When any decree or regulation is deemed to violate a law;
3) When it is deemed necessary to change the previous opinion of the Supreme Court with regard to the interpretation and application of the Constitution, law, decree or regulation, or
4) When it is deemed appropriate that a case be decided by a division."

The Chief Justice is appointed for a six-year term by the President with the consent of the National Assembly. Other Supreme Court judges are appointed by the President for ten-year terms upon recommondation of the Chief Justice. The Chief Justice and other Supreme Court justices must have had 20 years or more of judicial experience. All Supreme Court justices must retire at the age of 65. A Supreme Court or lower court judge may be dismissed or suspended from office or have his salary reduced by impeachment, by criminal punishment, or by disciplinary action by the President. The President was not so empowered before 1973. Article 104 of the Constitution is vague about "suspension," as contrasted with "dismissal." A judge may not be "dismissed from office, nor shall he be suspended from office or have his salary reduced, or suffer from other unfavorable measures, except through disciplinary measures." These provisions seem sufficiently vague as to allow for great flexibility, at least potentially, in application. Furthermore, Article 104 provides that "in the event that a judge is unable to perform his duty because of mental or physical deficiencies, he can be removed from office in accordance with the provisions of law."

3. *Appellate Courts.* Korea's three Appellate Courts are located in the cities of Seoul, Taegu and Kwangju, and have civil and criminal divisions. They have jurisdiction over appeals from judgements and rulings of District Courts and Family Courts, as well as any other cases in which jurisdiction may have been granted to the Appellate Courts by law. Each Appellate Court has a Chief Judge who is assigned from the already-appointed judges, and who administers the affairs of the court in accordance with Supreme Court regulations. The Chief Judge of an Appellate Court must have the same qualifications as those for a Supreme Court Justice, except that his previous period of service need have been only 15 years rather than 20. An Appellate Court judge must retire at age 62.

4. *District Courts.* District Courts are located in Seoul and in eight provincial capitals. They have both criminal and civil jurisdiction. Only in Seoul are there separate divisions for civil and criminal cases. Usually a single judge presides over a District Court trial. There is no right in this or other Korean courts to a trial by jury. All cases are decided by a judge or judges.

In certain categories of cases, however, three judges, collectively called a collegiate court, are required to sit as a court of original jurisdiction. These types of cases are as follows:
1) Cases which the collegiate divisions decide to adjudicate by themselves;
2) Civil cases in which the amount in controversy exceeds 300,000 won except cases demanding payments of money involving checks and promissory notes;
3) Criminal cases in which the defendant can be punished by death, penal servitude for life, or penal servitude and imprisonment exceeding one year, except the cases covered by certain articles of the Criminal Code and crimes against the Military Service Law;
4) Accessory cases which are to be tried simultaneously with cases mentioned in the preceding paragraph;

5) Adjudication of a party's challenge of a District Court judge;
6) Other cases in which jurisdiction is granted to the collegiate division by law.

The District Courts, sitting collectively and apart from the collegiate division, also have appellate jurisdiction in cases of appeal from judgements, decisions, or rulings of a single judge of the District Courts.

A Chief Judge of a District Court must have the same qualifications as those of a Supreme Court justice, except that the service time requirement is stated as only seven years. A presiding judge of a District Court must have five prior years of service. Finally, judges of District Courts must have passed the National Judicial Examination and successfully passed the full course of instruction at a state-administered graduate school of law, as of 1971 conducted directly under the jurisdiction of the Ministry of Justice. This school until 1970 was administered by Seoul National University. The alternative to completion of the graduate school of law is to have the qualifications of a prosecutor or lawyer. A District Court judge must retire at age 60.

5. *Family Court.* At present there is a Family Court only in Seoul. Matters related to domestic, or family, affairs outside of Seoul are handled by District Courts. There is a Chief Judge and an unstipulated number of other judges, as needed. The Chief Judge must have the same qualifications as those of the Chief Judge of a District Court, and other Family Court judges the same as those of District Court judges.

6. *Courts-Martial.* These courts have jurisdiction over offenses committed by members of the armed forces and civil employees. Such offenses include treason, disobedience, desertion and other crimes as defined in the Military Penal Law. Civilians may also fall under court-martial jurisdiction if they are found to be involved in cases of military espionage, interference in the execution of military duties, the provision of harmful foods to the military, giving aid and comfort to the enemy, and other specified offenses. Decisions of the Courts-Martial may be appealed to the Supreme Court.

In summary, though the court system has regular judicial functions, it offers little political balance to offset the dominant role of the executive in governmental decision-making.

THE BACKGROUND AND STRUCTURE OF
LOCAL GOVERNMENT

The Local Autonomy Law of 1949 provided the basis for a local autonomy system that was implemented in 1952. In that year elections were held for membership in local councils and for heads of local administrative offices. However, in 1958 under Syngman Rhee's Liberal Party Government, constitutional changes were made in the system which allowed direct central government control of key local officials. In 1960 the Democratic Party under Chang Myŏn passed new legislation to allow popular election of mayors of the "special" cities of Seoul and Pusan, provincial governors, heads of local autonomous bodies, and members of various local councils. This situation was short-lived, however, as the Revolutionary military regime which displaced the Chang government in 1961 reverted to a totally appointive system for local government officials. Also, local councils were dissolved. These actions were taken under a law promulgated by the military government and entitled, "Provisional measures for local administration." This ruling has remained in effect since, and local administration is under the direct control and supervision of the central government. The central government today appoints the mayors of the *special cities* of Seoul and Pusan and of the city of Taegu; the nine provincial governors; and heads of certain other local Administrative agencies. The Constitution, in Articles 114–115, provides for a local assembly; however, it has no decision-making power but only the power to advise.

The present structure of the territorial districts for local administration can be broken down as indicated in the chart on page 64. Cities are defined as urban areas of 50,000 population or more; counties (Kun) supervise the smaller administrative units of towns (Eup), which have between 20,000 and 50,000 people, and townships (Myŏn), which have less than 20,000 population. The city's smaller administrative units of wards (Ku) in turn are broken down into precincts (Dong). Towns and townships are divided into either of two smaller administrative precincts, called Dong and Ri. The functional organization of provincial administration in general can be outlined as follows:[4]

TERRITORIAL DISTRICTS FOR LOCAL ADMINISTRATION

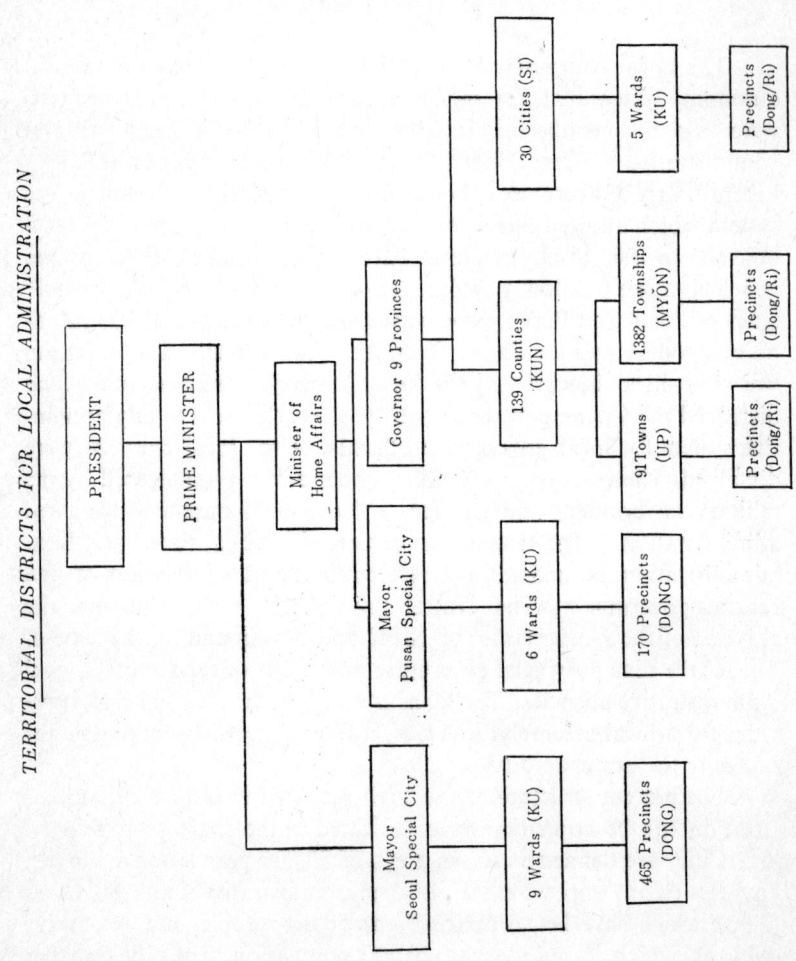

ORGANIZATION OF PROVINCIAL GOVERNMENTS

1. Governor
2. Deputy Governor
3. Public Information Office
4. Planning and Inspection Office
5. Home Affairs Bureau
   1) General Affairs Section
   2) Local Affairs Section
   3) Surveys and Statistics Section
   4) Finance Section
   5) Accounting Section
6. Public Health and Social Affairs Bureau
   1) Social Affairs Section
   2) Public Health Section
   3) Medicine Section
   4) Women's Affairs Section (Kyŏnggi-to only)
   5) Sanitation Section (Ch'ungch'ŏng-Namdo only)
   6) Child & Maternal Health Section (Ch'ungch'ŏng-Namdo only)
7. Agriculture & Forestry Bureau
   1) Agriculture Administration Section
   2) Agriculture Production Section
   3) Farmland Improvement Section
   4) Farmland Reclamation Section (except Ch'ungch'ŏng-Pukto and Kangwŏn-Do)
   5) Forestry Section
8. Production Bureau
   1) Commerce & Industry Section (except Kyŏngsang-Pukto and Kyŏngsang-Namdo)
   2) Food Administration Section
   3) Livestock Section
   4) Fishery Section (except Chŏlla-Namdo and Kyŏngsang-Namdo)
   5) Sericulture Section
9. Commerce & Industry Bureau (Kyŏngsang-Pukto and Kyŏngsang-Namdo only)
   1) Commerce Section
   2) Industry Section
10. Fishery Bureau (Chŏlla-Namdo & Kyŏngsang-Namdo only)

1) Fishery Administration Section
2) Production Section
3) Facilities Section
11. Construction Bureau
1) Regional Planning Section
2) Construction Section (Kyŏnggi-to & Chungchŏng-Pukto only)
3) Highway Section (except Chungchŏng-Pukto & Kyŏnggi-to)
4) Flood Control Section (except Chungchŏng-Pukto & Kyŏnggi-to)
5) Tourism & Transportation Section
6) City Planning Section (Kyŏnggi-to & Kyŏngsang-Namdo only)
12. Police Bureau
1) Police Administration Section
2) Public Safety Section
3) Security & Communications Section
4) Criminal Investigation Section
5) Intelligence Section

There are two specified categories of local administrative organs: ordinary and special. The former refers to general administrative offices related to provincial and county governments; the latter to specialized organs such as local tax bureaus and construction offices. Overall administration in a given province is the general responsibility of the province governor; however, there are two cities designated as special cities, Seoul—Korea's capital and largest city with six million population—and Pusan, in which the mayors are directly responsible to the central government. The Taegu mayor's responsibility with regard to matters of city development is also directly to the central government, though Taegu has not yet been designated as a special city. The mayor of the special city of Seoul reports directly to the Prime Minister, while the mayor of the special city of Pusan and the nine provincial governors report directly to the Home Affairs Minister. The Ministry of Home Affairs contains one Office and two Bureaus: a Planning and Management Office; a Local Administration Bureau, and a Police Bureau.

The functions of the Home Ministry can be succinctly described as follows:

> The Planning and Management Office is responsible for establishment, consolidation, and coordination of guidelines for the Ministry's basic operation programs; formulation and execution of the budget; and personnel management and management improvement programs. The Police Bureau is responsible for all police and fire activities in the nation and ... exercises direct supervision over police and fire personnel wherever stationed. The Local Administration Bureau consists of five Divisions: Administration; Guidance; Planning and Inspection; Finance, and Local Tax. The Local Administration Bureau provides the staff arm for the Minister of Home Affairs.[5]

On the local level, the structure and personnel of government is largely oriented toward the central organs. When appointment and lines of responsibility are centrally oriented as in Korea, there is little room for independent local initiative in policies and programs.

Provincial governors and selected mayors, because of their direct relationship to the central government, can take administrative actions within the framework of established law, and can issue municipal or provincial regulations without reference to local organs. Most provincial and municipal governments have bureaus for home affairs, finance, industry, education, social affairs and police. Provincial governors *recommend* the appointment of county chiefs; however, final appointment is by the President of the Republic. Cities of 500,000 or more are broken down territorially into wards, and ward chiefs are appointed by the President on recommendation of the city mayors.

In any political situation, there must be formal or informal provisions on the local level for administrative continuity. Particularly in Korea, where top-level personnel are centrally appointed, it is imperative that such a lower echelon of administrative personnel function on a more stable and permanent basis. During the Yi dynasty, those lower officials were called achŏns. Writing in 1906, Homer B. Hulbert observed that, "Comparatively low though the position of achŏn may be, it can truthfully be said that he is the most important man in the administration of the Korean government. The achŏns...held the ship of state to her moorings in spite of tides which periodically sweep back and forth and threaten to carry her upon the rocks."[6] This point can be said to have some relevance today. While lower level personnel are not in a position to instigate significant innovation or to make high-level policy decisions, they do however function as a stabilizing force to provide administrative continuity during times of crisis or of change in higher level personnel who may or may not be well acquainted with local circumstances.

SUMMARY

In summary, the structure and operation of Korean government are highly centralized, both in formal constitutional terms and in a more basic behavioral sense. Status and hierarchy are generally determinants of *what* is done and virtually always determinants of *how* things are done. The chapters that follow will reiterate and substantiate these points, not simply in terms of the present-day formalistic structures of Korean government but primarily in terms of basic and largely tradition-rooted behavior patterns.

FOOTNOTES

1. English-language materials on matters of Korean constitutional development and governmental structure are listed below. Much of the purely descriptive material included in this chapter is derived largely from these sources:
    a) *Structure of Government* (Seoul: Ministry of Public Information, Republic of Korea, 1968).
    b) *Local Administration System in Korea: Organization and Functions of the Local Government* (Seoul: Public Services Division, U. S. Agency for International Development/Korea, November 1968).
    c) *The Constitution of the Republic of Korea* (Seoul: The Office of Legislation, Government of the Republic of Korea, 1970).
    d) *Draft Amendments to the Constitution of the Republic of Korea* (Seoul: Korean Overseas Information Service, October 1972).
    e) *Korean Legal System* (Seoul: Supreme Court of Republic of Korea, 1970).
2. The previous Election Law, which went into effect in 1971, stipulated that all organizations other than the electioneering committees of the political parties were forbidden to campaign for a candidate or party in any election. This interpretation was made by the Central Election Management Committee (CEMC) on February 2, 1971. The Federation of Korean Trade Unions (FKTU) had announced a "political activity committee" which would have included in its activities the active supporting of candidates for public office. After the CEMC ruling, the FKTU changed the name of the committee to "political education committee," indicating that it would function to cultivate a political sense among union members. See *The Korea Times*, February 3, 1971, p. 1; and February 4, 1971, p. 1.
3. The organization and procedures of the National Assembly are given in "The National Assembly Law," as promulgated November 26, 1963, and as amended

September 11, 1964 and February 2, 1973. The 1973 amendment constituted virtually a complete rewriting.
4. All provinces except that of Cheju Island are similar in organizational structure. Cheju, being an offshore island with a relatively small population, has a greatly simplified administrative structure.
5. *Local Administration System in Korea: Organization and Functions of the Local Government* (Seoul: Public Services Division, U.S. Agency for International Development/Korea, November 1968).
6. Homer B. Hulbert, *The Passing of Korea* (Seoul: Yonsei University Press, reprinted in 1969, originally published in 1906), pp. 52–53.

CHAPTER 3:

The Bureaucracy

Suk-choon CHO*

INTRODUCTION: THE STRUCTURE OF THE KOREAN BUREAUCRACY

Major agencies belonging directly to and performing staff functions for the Korean President are the Board of Inspection and Audit, the National Security Council, the Council on Economics and Science, the Administrative Reform and Investigation Commission, and the Central Intelligence Agency.

In the chain of command between the President and his ministers, there is the Prime Minister who has his own staff agencies such as the Offices of Planning and Coordination, Legislation, and Veterans' Affairs; the Ministries of Government Administration, Science and Technology, and National Unification; and the Economic Planning Board. There are thirteen functional ministries also under the Prime Minister. These are the Ministries of Foreign Affairs, Home Affairs, Finance, Justice, National Defense, Education, Agriculture and Forestry, Commerce and Industry, Construction, Public Health and Social Affairs, Transportation, Communications, and Public Information and Cultural Affairs.

Within each ministry there is a vice-minister and under the latter is a Planning and Management Office and General Affairs Section in

---

* Suk-choon Cho is Associate Professor in the Graduate School of Public Administration, Seoul National University. His Ph.D. is in Political Science from the University of Minnesota.

addition to various functional bureaus. The bureaus are divided into sections which in turn are composed of sub-sections.

The local governments are organized into provinces, cities and counties. The internal administrative machinery of each of these local government units is subdivided into bureaus, sections and sub-sections as in the ministries of the central government.

The jurisdictional areas of the field agencies of the central government usually correspond with the geographical boundaries of the local governments concerned. On the average, around twenty such field offices are located at the sites of county governments and medium-sized cities.

As of May 1, 1968, the total number of government employees in Korea was 369,079. (Following figures in this introduction are cited from this same source.) Around ten percent of this number are working in the central offices. Those belonging to the local government service, which is subject to the direction of the central offices, number 55,456. Most of the supervisory and executive posts on the local government levels are filled by those from the national civil service.

The national service itself is broken down into the categories of general service, educational service, police, foreign service, and judicial service. The educational service has the largest proportion numbering 132,579, with the teachers of schools of various levels comprising 117,663 of the total.

Each of the above services operates on the basis of a rank system. For example, the general service, which is the second largest in number of employees, is graded into nine ranks. Those above the rank III-B are regarded as members of the higher civil service possessing supervisory responsibilities and the rest are regarded as within the operative level. There are 2,339 persons in the higher civil service— that is, whose rank is above that of III-B. The ranks of the higher civil service generally correspond to the following positions in a central government ministry.

Ranks	Positions
I	Director, Planning and Management Office
II-A	Bureau Director
II-B	Bureau Director
III-A	Section Chief
III-B	Sub-Section Chief

SOCIAL BACKGROUNDS OF KOREAN BUREAUCRATS

In terms of social and political backgrounds, the Korean government bureaucracy contains three layers of higher civil servants. The first is composed of former Japanese colonial government civil servants with legal backgrounds who quickly ascended to higher positions following Japanese withdrawal from Korea. Most of these officials finished their college education during the Japanese rule. Secondly are those somewhat younger who finished grade or high school under the Japanese and college after the liberation either in Korea or in Anglo-American countries. A survey shows that 11.7 percent of Korean higher civil servants were educated in Anglo-American countries and that there is a tendency for the percentage to increase in the upper ranks.[2] Those belonging to the third category are ex-military men who entered the higher civil service after the military coup d'etat of 1961. Some 14.08 percent of higher civil servants had been in the military immediately before joining the civil service. This percentage increases in the higher ranks; in 1965, 56.12 percent of the age group of 36 to 40 were ex-military men.

Some 50.4 percent of all higher civil servants were born in rural areas and 42.1 percent had their fathers' occupations in agricultural pursuits. Those who had fathers in professions such as civil service, medicine, teaching, law, and business management comprise 35.5 percent of the total number of higher civil servants. Of the 30 percent who have declared religious affiliation, around 15 percent are Christians, and the rest are divided between Confucianism and Buddhism.

It can be concluded that the socialization processes among Korean higher civil servants were quite diverse. Of particular significance is the fact that around half were raised in rural areas where the change in traditional values is bound to be slow. Also significant is the contrast in formal educational backgrounds. Some were educated through high school and college under the pre-World War II Japanese colonial regime. Some received part of their education under the Japanese and part in independent Korean schools after the liberation. Still others received part Japanese and part Anglo-American educations. And others received military training and education. Those in the younger age category of 30 to 35 received all of their education after World War II.

This heterogeneity of backgrounds among Korean higher civil

servants has resulted in sharply different value orientations within the Korean bureaucracy.

AUTHORITY PATTERNS IN THE KOREAN BUREAUCRACY

In spite of the heterogeneity of values which are frequently in conflict, there are commonly accepted authority patterns which bind the men of the Korean bureaucracy together. It is because of these threads that the bureaucracy has been able since World War II to survive two revolutions and ensuing changes in regimes. These characteristic patterns of Korean bureaucratic behavior can be summarized as follows: *hierarchy* as the formal norm for governing interpersonal relations within the bureaucracy; *administrative specialization*; and *personalism*.

Hierarchical Norm for Interpersonal Relations within the Bureaucracy. In Korea a dominant value governing bureaucratic behavior is that of hierarchical order which tends to be regarded as the natural form of human relations. Confucianism was the traditional system which was instrumental in the formulation of this view of the bureaucracy, and the Japanese colonial government reinforced it. Egalitarian norms introduced after World War II have not significantly influenced the traditional behavior patterns of bureaucrats. As of June 1, 1966, 84 percent of higher civil servants were over the age of 36,[3] and most underwent primary school education under the pre-war Japanese colonial government. The formative years in their personality development were spent in traditional family structures which did not inculcate egalitarian norms. New democratic norms introduced after the liberation in high schools, colleges or in foreign travels and study remain peripheral to the main value orientation.

Consequently the basic norm governing human relations in the bureaucratic framework remains one's hierarchical role. A superior is expected to govern the behavior of subordinates, not only in the areas of legal jurisdiction and task performance, but also in the area of personal affairs. Subordinates are likely to obey the superior even when their judgement of the task requirement does not agree with that of the superior.

This emphasis on hierarchy is expressed in the formal structure of the Korean bureaucracy, at the apex of which the President dominates the structure through gradual scaling of responsibilities down to the field workers. There are no agencies which are structurally independent and which enjoy autonomous status vis-a-vis the President. The lack of horizontal coordination at the middle and lower levels of the structure is also largely due to the hierarchical norm. Responsibility for coordination is likely to reside with one man whose accountability to a superior is supposed to be explicit and without conditions. Committees and conferences without the participation of a hierarchical superior will easily fall into chaos and result in no decisions. Meetings in which a superior presides will be dominated by him, because subordinates will not dare raise different opinions. The consequence is eventually and usually dissolution of the committees.

Contrary to administrative principle and practice in the United States where the quality norm is strong, subordinates in the Korean bureaucracy are not likely to experience substantial frustration when faced with an authoritarian style of supervision. In Korean administration, delegation of authority is not viewed as an attempt to enhance the well-being of subordinates and to encourage democratic management. The attitude of administrators toward the clientele is also governed by the hierarchical norm. Administrators are supposed to rule and, at best, to teach and guide the people. Governmental action is generally regarded as a favor rather than as an obligation. Consequently the clientele are in the position of begging for special favors rather than requesting the government's abidance with legal provisions. At best, governmental favors are handed out because of sympathy toward the people, and at worst, because of paybacks by clients to particular administrators.

Those with superior bureaucratic roles generally coerce and threaten subordinates, thereby depriving the latter of incentives normally associated with bureaucratic career advancement. Though not always regarded legitimate, coercion exercised for the achievement of legitimate tasks does not invite criticism within the bureaucracy.

Administrative Specialization. Though the Korean bureaucracy is fast being filled with college graduates,[4] this cannot be interpreted as a consequence of the importance placed upon the role of specialization. It is rather a reflection of the population structure which shows enormous increase in the number of college graduates in recent years, as well as of the administrators' attainment motivations. Except in the case of positions requiring knowledge of the natural sciences, no particular correlation exists between one's educational background and his administrative position.

Staff positions dealing with personnel, finance, accounting, purchasing, organization and methods, planning and programming are likely to be filled with those who are not specialists in these fields. Those upper posts in the hierarchical ladder which are directly responsible to and strongly supported by the head of an agency are more likely to wield influence on policy decisions than those lower echelon offices filled with persons possessing a high degree of specialized knowledge. Most administrators belong to no professional associations and generally are out of touch with current developments in their administrative specializations. However, regardless of their educational backgrounds and professional interests, Korean bureaucrats are specialized at least in the formal sense of being placed within the framework of vertical and horizontal divisions of work essential for the operation of large scale enterprise. Those in subordinate positions are given duties related mainly to vertical contacts with superiors and subordinates. Responsibility for coordination is always placed at the top management level, and those in supervisory positions between top management and the rank and file are usually and primarily occupied with relaying documents up and down the hierarchy. By the time an administrator accumulates a degree of knowledge about his position, he is transferred to an entirely different position, where he will start this learning process all over again.

In the Korean bureaucracy when an administrator is absent from his duties his subordinates, superiors and clients generally have to wait until he appears again in order to resume the processing of documents; it is he who knows best the matter in question and who is accountable for the specific step involved. It is in such a situation, however, that a subordinate may have the opportunity to exert some influence based upon his specialized training and knowledge. It can be concluded, however, that when the elements of hierarchical position and specialized knowledge are in conflict, disputes are generally resolved in favor of the former.

Personalism. In Korean public administration, there is substantial value placed on mutual confidence among bureaucratic personnel. Such confidence is generally built up only after long periods of interaction. The ideal supervisors are those who are paternalistic toward their subordinates. Thus, deeply rooted personal relationships undergird the formalistic lines of administrative authority.

In the recruitment process, there are relatively few who have entered the higher civil service solely through objective and universally applied criteria. Most are recruited rather through the channel of so called "special appointment" which has more lenient criteria for selection. Promotions are also most likely to be made through the "special appointment" process.[5] This means that an individual so selected or promoted had a patron, sponsor or go-between either at the time of joining the civil service or on the occasion of his promotion. Such particularistic human ties serve as the bases on which various informal groups are subsequently formed. The functions of these groups are diffuse in that they provide members with banking functions, recreational activities, and traditional rituals for festivity and condolence; they also protect and advance the members' interests within the bureaucracy. The structure of such informal groups, then, is characterized by their extension beyond the boundaries of formal organizational units.[6] This is certainly the case within the Korean bureaucracy where a formal organizational head may have difficulty controlling these tightly knit groups unless his formal authority is supplemented by provision of similar functions to his own subordinates or by his capacity to mobilize an alternative and more powerful informal group.

With the prevalence of these factions and cliques within the bureaucracy, every administrator is likely to seek ties with others who have similar attachments in order to protect and advance his own particular interests. Such informal personal ties constitute the principal modification of the hierarchical values underlying the formal bureaucratic structure. Only a subordinate who has won the personal confidence of the higher echelon through this process can actually exercise any discretion, even to the extent of being able to disregard procedural regulations and to exercise coercive power over his subordinates. Those who do not enjoy such confidence, however, will faithfully abide by formal legal provisions, even to the extent of adopting extremely formalistic interpretations of the law in order to avoid the possibility of later review of and punishment for bureaucratic actions which might be construed as irregular or illegal.

BUREAUCRACY AND POLICY FORMULATION

The president and prime minister have tended to rely on the bureaucracy as the major policy formulating and implementing apparatus in the country. In fact, the bureaucracy has served as a major channel for supply of major political appointees such as ministers and vice-ministers.[7] The feeling of identification by higher civil servants with political appointees of bureaucratic backgrounds has served to strengthen the hierarchical orientations of the former.

Though most of the higher civil servants are brought into the bureaucracy through the expedient and relatively lenient channel of "special appointment" as mentioned above, it does not neccessarily mean that all appointees are the beneficiaries of party patronage. Yet the bureaucracy is frequently deeply involved in exercising its influence for the benefit of the government, or so-called "ruling" party. This function is especially evident at the time of general elections for the nation's president and representatives for the National Assembly. Examples of governmental agencies which are actively involved in support of the ruling party are: the national police; local governmental units which actually serve as administrative field offices for the central government; the national broadcast system; government publications, and some government-created interest groups such as agricultural and fishery cooperatives.[8] Those agencies which have a large business clientele are most likely to serve as major channels for providing funds for the government party through their power to grant or withhold government favors.[9] The only agencies which do not involve themselves in such behavior are those central management agencies whose clients are other government agencies or those whose civilian clients are small in number and relatively unorganized.

Since the bureaucracy is hierarchically oriented and since its democratic undergirding is not strong, it is disinclined to regard the legislature and political parties as significant in the process of policy formulation. Members of the National Assembly are strongly motivated to seek appointment in the higher echelons of the executive branch. However, the likelihood of their becoming ministers and vice-ministers is slight; therefore, higher civil servants have not been inclined to pay substantial attention to the wishes of individual legislators. The only exception to this in post-war Korea was in the late nineteen-fifties during the Syngman Rhee presidency when a group of ex-government ministers formed an oligarchically-structured governing group which overlapped the legislature and the government party. The relatively higher degree of loyalty shown by senior civil servants to legislative leadership during that brief period was due primarily to the latter's personal attachments which had been previously formed in the bureaucracy. Other related factors included their intimate working knowledge of the bureaucracy and the personal confidence placed in them by President Rhee.[10]

Korean higher civil servants may show loyalty to individual members of the National Assembly, but are not inclined to act on the basis of the principle of democratic responsibility to the Assembly as a whole or to a wider electoral constituency. Their legislative affinities are rather based on personal relations with individual legislators. In Korea's hierarchical culture the legislator's power is largely determined by the degree of confidence displayed in him by the president of the nation. Thus those directly part of the power structure of the ruling government party—in comparison with those in lesser ruling party positions or those in the opposition party—are likely to get relatively greater attention from the senior civil servants in the policy formulation process.

With regard to specialization, ex-bureaucrat legislators are likely to command more respect from the bureaucracy than accorded their legislative colleagues. Principles of specialization and division of work have been widely introduced into the bureaucratic structure in recent years. Especially since the advent of military rule in 1961, advanced techniques of military management imported from the American military have been extensively adopted in the civil bureaucracy. However, legislators have been relatively slow in accepting the idea of specialized knowledge as an essential criterion of job competence and selection. The degree of legislative unfamiliarity with governmental programs has been increasing in recent years. As a result, new managerial techniques introduced into the bureaucracy for the sake of efficiency have tended to minimize the legislature's ability to control the bureaucracy. As a result of the above factors, the influence of the National Assembly has been greatly minimized, a situation which has tended to reinforce the attitude of the bureaucracy which views the National Assembly as relatively insignificant in policy formation. Policy staffs of both the legislature and the two major parties generally possess less specialized knowledge than their counterparts in the government bureaucracy. Most party and legislative personnel at one time or another seek to join the career civil service at various levels. One side effect of such aspiration is the lesser amount of prestige which they enjoy within the bureaucracy vis-a-vis career civil servants. For the first time in modern Korean history, the ruling Democratic Republican Party in the 1960's under President Park has adopted in principle the institution of a professional policy staff within the government bureaucracy.

It is because of the above factors that the legislature and the parties are unable to influence significantly the process of governmental policy formulation. A sense of failure and frustration drives legislators and party members to adopt various alternative methods of exerting political influence. For example, Assembly members are likely to request favors of the bureaucracy on behalf of particular constituent interests or to raise extremist and agitative demands which are predictably unlikely to be honored. Legislators' begging for bureaucratic favors tends to reinforce the bureaucratic selfperception of superiority relative to the legislature, and of the bureaucracy as the only significant policy-making body.

The bureaucracy is the main focal point of interest group activity, rather than the legislature or political parties. Most interest groups are concentrated in urban areas, and it is rare to find competing groups in one functional area. Therefore, the possibility that an interest group will criticize government actions is minimized, and consequently a bureaucrat's interpretation of the public interest is likely to be uni-dimensional. With the exception of some strong interest groups based on middle class professions, interest groups generally deal secretly with civil servants.

A single most important pressure group in the eyes of most higher civil servants is the press. This is mainly due to the control function the press exercises over bureaucrats. The press serves as a watchdog of the administration and because of its relative independence is likely to criticize various government actions. In the bureaucracy where formal communication is restricted, the press serves as an informal alternative channel of upward communication. Subordinates within the bureaucracy generally can enlighten their superiors only indirectly by divulging information to newspapers and journals which will be read by higher civil servants and political leaders, including the President. Thus the degree of influence of the press on the bureaucracy is based largely on its upward communication function, which in turn is based upon the hierarchical orientations of the bureaucrats themselves.[11]

It can be concluded that the arena for policy formulation in the Korean government is largely limited to the bureaucracy, restricted only by the limited functions performed by outside groups and institutions as delineated above.

PROCEDURAL CHARACTERISTICS OF THE KOREAN BUREAUCRACY

Three basic procedural characteristics of the Korean bureaucracy can be identified as follows: secrecy in policy formulation; rationalization of politically derived decisions in terms of bureaucratic rationality; and inconsistency of policies over a period of time. The first, secrecy, is valued not only because of the need for national security but more particularly because of the desire to avoid criticism by the press and opposition parties. Secrecy is also valued because of intra-bureaucratic politics. Whenever a policy issue might induce opposition from other agencies in the bureaucracy, the originating agency is likely to approach a common hierarchical superior in secrecy in order to get his prior commitment. Once approval is acquired in this way, there is little chance that the matter will be either negated or significantly changed.[12]

Thus, the policy formulation process is not governed by widespread participation and consensus building either within or without the bureaucracy. Relevant agencies and persons in a horizontal relationship are generally neglected in the process, and "consensus" is attained through vertical and authoritarian means.

A second characteristic relates to bureaucratic rationalization of policies formed at the upper political echelon of government. Since bargaining and conciliation are not instrumental in the process of public policy formulation, the content of the policy formed appears rational in the sense that the specialized knowledge of the sponsoring agency is well reflected. Such seeming bureaucratic rationality appears to have governed the policy formulation process more dominantly when the presidents of the nation were more technocratically oriented, as in the latter part of the nineteen-fifties under Syngman Rhee and in recent years under President Park. In truth, however, policies are not so rationally arrived at. The search for information by the civil servants is not extensive and what information they gather is frequently removed from the facts. Also, information stored in the official files for later reference is usually neglected. As implied previously, the most important premise for policy formulation is what is ordered by hierarchical superiors. This premise simply cannot be revised significantly, consequently facts gathered and analysis undertaken are usually governed by the degree of need for rationalization of the premise.

There is also a high degree of inconsistency in the policies formulated within the bureaucracy. A newly appointed head of an agency is expected to be an innovator and to undertake new policies. It is therefore highly likely that changes of ministers and other agency heads will result in abdication of the previous policies and proclamation of sharply contrasting new policies. The shorter the terms of office of succeeding top-level bureaucratic officials, the greater is the tendency for inconsistencies in policies pursued over a period of time. During the period from August 1948 to March 1963, the average term of office of ministers was 11 months.[13] This figure, however, has increased somewhat since then. Other causes of inconsistency in policy formulation are attributable firstly to particularistic influences related to personal ties in and out of the bureaucracy, and, secondly, to rapid environmental changes surrounding the bureaucracy, which do not generally permit a long-range forecast and which can quickly deteriorate the value of previous policies.

BUREAUCRACY AND INNOVATION

The hierarchical orientation of the Korean bureaucracy is the key to implementation of innovative policies. Those at the apex of the bureaucratic structure usually serve as originators, advocates and legitimators and sometimes initial adopters of new ideas. Such diffusion of innovative functions at the apex of the hierarchy means that there is virtually no opportunity for civil servants at subordinate levels to perform other than routine supervisory and clerical work. The source of ideas for most top management personnel is their prior experience. Those rare top-level individuals who provide a continual flow of new ideas over an extended period seem to rely on sources of inspiration which cannot be easily identified.

It should be pointed out, too, that innovative ideas originating from the top levels of the bureaucratic hierarchy frequently receive only half-hearted support from subordinate civil servants because of their lack of feasibility from the specialists' viewpoint.

Policy innovations capable of attracting substantial support by higher civil servants are usually successful only in a certain set of circumstances. First, there should be an enclave of specialists with a strong professional orientation. Such an enclave may pre-exist the appointment of a new political elite, or perhaps the latter may bring in its own new group of specialists. Secondly, the political elite should be task-oriented and recognize its dependence upon the enclave for specialized knowledge which the elite itself may not possess. Such a situation existed in Korea's economic development planning beginning in the late 1950's. Within the Ministry of Reconstruction there was established an Economic Development Council (EDC) composed of a substantial number of foreign-educated young intellectuals. Since then the EDC together with the Research Department of the Bank of Korea and similarly oriented intellectuals in various governmental ministries have served as a bureaucratic enclave in efforts to formulate long range economic development programs. It was under the military government that the top bureaucratic management who were strongly motivated toward task achievements seriously relied upon specialists. The first successful economic development plan (1962–1965) was the outcome of such a situation in which the political elite was heavily reliant on the expertise of specialists.[14]

Besides economic planning, another instance of bureaucratic openness to innovation is that of reforms in management techniques introduced since the inception of the military government. Young majors and colonels who had been trained through American military assistance programs in the development of managerial techniques in the Korean army were placed in 1961 and 1962 in the Ministry of Government Administration, especially in and around its Administrative Management Bureau newly established by the military government. This enclave of specialists had strong support from the political elite and was able to implement innovative programs with the full support of the top echelons of nonspecialists which served largely a legitimizing function.

In the Korean administrative context in which hierarchical authority is instrumental in decision-making, changes in political regimes and top echelon personnel have been important leverage points for bureaucratic innovation, especially when the new political elites were strongly task-achievement-motivated and had a high regard for administrative specialization. Higher civil servants with such motivations and usually with some awareness of what is going on in more developed countries will tend to seek out colleagues of similar outlook. Through the forming of groups of like-minded persons, they may have a chance to survive within an administrative context in which various informal groups actively compete against one another. The chances for a greater degree of openness and innovative outlook within the Korean bureaucracy depend largely upon the increased encouragement of and support for enclaves of specialists by the political elite.

FOOTNOTES

1. *Haengjŏng Kwalli,* Vol. 7, No. 1, p. 107.
2. Yu Hoon (Yu Hun), "The Social Background of Korean Higher Civil Servants," *Korean Journal of Public Administration,* Vol. IV, No. 2, p. 256.
3. *Ibid.,* p. 245.
4. *Ibid.,* p. 253. Yu Hoon's survey shows that 46.4 percent of higher civil servants are college graduates.
5. Bark Dong-suh (Pak Tong-sŏ), *Historical Development of the Bureaucracy in Korea* (Seoul: The Korean Research Center, 1961), p. 197.
6. For an elaboration of this point, see Sidney Verba, *Small Groups and Political Behavior* (Princeton: Princeton University Press, 1961), pp. 45–49.
7. Bark Dong-suh, "A Study of the Qualifications of the Korean Administrative Executive," *Korean Journal of Public Administration,* Vol. VI, No. 2, p. 85.
8. Cho Suk-choon (Cho Sŏk-jun), "A Study of the Changes in Central Government Structures in the American Military Government and the First Republic of Korea," *Korean Journal of Public Administration,* Vol. V, No. 1, pp. 134–152.
9. Suh Il-soo (Sŏ Il-su), *Election Irregularities Involving Public Officials* (Thesis for the Master of Public Administration degree, Graduate School of Public Administration, Seoul National University, 1968), pp. 14–33.
10. For a description of the orientations and behavior of this oligarchical group, see Lee Hahn-been, *Korea: Time, Change and Administration* (Honolulu: East-West Center Press, 1968), pp. 92–96.
11. For a description of police response to the press with regard to press criticism of police corruption, see Jo Kyu-sang (Cho Kyu-sang), *The Discipline of Police Personnel* (Unpublished Thesis for the Master of Public Administration degree, Tongguk University, 1968.)
12. For a typical case, see Huh Bom (Hŏ Pŏm), *A Case Study on the Decision-Making Process,* Unpublished Thesis for the Master of Public Administration degree, Graduate School of Public Administration, Seoul National University, 1967.)
13. Pak Mun-ok, *The Korean Government* (Seoul: Pak Yong Sa, 1963), p. 435.
14. For a more detailed analysis of the formulation process of the first five-year economic development plan, see Cho Suk-choon, "A Comparative Analysis of Two Reforms under the Military Regime in Korea," a paper presented at the Development Administration Group/EROPA Seminar on Administrative Reform and Innovation in Asia, held in Kuala Lumpur, Malaysia, June 20–27, 1968. This paper will be included in a forthcoming volume, *Administrative Reforms in Asia,* edited by LeeH ahn-been and Abelardo Samonte. Also see the chapters below in this volume by Princeton Lyman and Kim Jung-sae.

CHAPTER 4:

Underlying Factors in Political Party Organization and Elections

Kɪ-sʜɪᴋ HAHN*

INTRODUCTION

Immediately following Korea's national liberation from Japanese control in 1945, a fierce and bloody ideological power struggle began between left wing forces spearheaded by the Korean Communist Party and rightist forces under the leadership of Syngman Rhee. In the meantime, the Cold War conflict was being intensified, and suppressive measures were undertaken against the internal Communist organization. The Communists and their followers were wiped out or driven underground, and the conservative parties emerged as the major power force. The foundation of the Republic of Korea was the result of the victory of anti-communism in South Korea. Since then, communism has become absolutely taboo. Even identification with socialism is a serious political liability for aspiring officeholders.

Party politics in South Korea has been largely a history of power struggles among conservative parties and component factions, devoid of conflicting ideological contentions. This is certainly true of government parties and major opposition parties in the 1950's, 1960's and early 1970's: the Liberal Party and Democratic Party during the Rhee era; the Democratic Party and New Democratic Party under the Chang administration; and the Democratic Republican Party and New Democratic Party under the Park government. There has been a pattern, on the one hand, of government parties tending to stress the importance of anti-communism, national security and

---

*Ki-shik Hahn is Professor of Political Science at Korea University, Seoul. His Ph.D. is from the University of California, Berkeley.

political stability and, on the other hand, opposition parties tending to demand greater realization of liberal democracy, respect for individual rights and freedom, and achievement of mass welfare. In practice, opposition parties have denounced government parties for alleged violations of constitutional law and democratic principles. Government parties, on the other hand, defend their rule in terms of anti-communism. Opposition party leaders attack government party leaders as "corrupt" and "despotic," while government party leaders allude to the opposition as irresponsible and even bordering on the subversive.

Anti-communist slogans having been excessively used and abused by the Rhee government, the Democratic Republican Party (DRP) initiated the use of new slogans in the latter half of the 1960's, such as "modernization of the fatherland," "economic reconstruction" and the sort. In the early 1970's the DRP has stressed "increasing national strength for the materialization of territorial unification." The government party seems to command infinite resources which it can deploy against the claims of opposition parties that it rules with a high degree of "authoritarian" domination.

On the other hand, the opposition parties did not have new symbolic weapons capable of coping with the government party's propaganda offensive in the 1960's. Instead, they attacked the government party for "pervasive corruption," "anti-democratic" government, and "CIA" politics. But in the 1971 election, the presidential candidate from the New Democratic Party, Kim Tae-jung, used slogans such as "taejung minjujuui" (mass democracy), "taejung kyongjae" (mass economy), and "taejung bokchi" (mass welfare), pronouncing "taejung" after his first name.[1] Thus, he pointedly attacked the gaps between the elite and the masses, the urban and the rural, and the rich and the poor—gaps which the opposition claims have become more conspicuous and serious under the development policies of the Park Government.

As in many other non-western countries, in Korea government political parties have been characterized by a relatively low degree of responsiveness and responsibility to the people. They have tended to represent some particular sector of the political stratum, and have responded primarily to the wishes of a limited interest grouping or faction. On the other hand, opposition parties have rather tended to represent and respond to a wider sector of the population—the number of the dissatisfied and alienated has been larger than those whose aspirations and demands have been partially or fully fulfilled.

Korean politics has been highly factional. Therefore, matters of national interest are usually secondary to those of factional, or limited, concern. Thus, it is usually difficult to distinguish public interest from private interest. Within the Korean political culture there has been little experience among the masses in organizing and institutionalizing group interests for the purpose of representing those interests strongly to the government. Political leaders, on the other hand, have shown little inclination to represent other than their own narrow groupings or constituencies. As a result, the Korean people in general have had little success in impressing their feelings and views upon party politicians. Though Korean political parties have been fairly instrumental in the political elites' efforts in vote gathering, they have been little effective in conveying mass demands and concerns to the government and in influencing decision-making by the political leaders. They rather have tended to represent more their personal or group interests and to place greater importance on the fulfillment of obligations to partisan or factional groupings than to the nation at large. The low level of representativeness and responsiveness of Korean political parties to the general populace can be ascribed largely to the past pattern of one party dominance, i.e., to the lack of a *tradition* of peaceful transfer of power. The opposition parties have little hope of being able to represent the people, simply because there is almost no prospect of gaining political power through peaceful means.

POLITICAL PARTY DEVELOPMENT IN POST-WAR KOREA: AN EVALUATION

Two months after Korea's liberation from Japan in 1945, there were 54 political parties registered in Seoul alone. One observer pointed out: "By January 1946, there were 61 important political organizations, and in June the total of registered national parties was 107."[2] A year later, there were known to be over 344 such organizations in the American zone of military occupation.

If we examine the results of National Assembly elections between 1948 and 1971, we can find a decrease of independents: there were 85 in 1948, 126 in 1950, 67 in 1958, 49 in 1960 and none after 1963. When the development of party politics shows an inverse relationship to the number of independents who have no party affiliation, rapid party development is normally indicated. We can also detect a striking decrease in the number of splinter political parties participating in

National Assembly elections since 1948: there were 49 in 1948, 38 in 1950, 28 in 1954, 15 in 1958, 12 in 1963, 11 in 1967, and 6 in 1971. On the other hand, we can observe an increasing concentration of votes for the major government and opposition parties: 48.5 percent in 1948, 29.6 percent in 1950, 48.3 percent in 1954, 76.9 percent in 1958, 88.5 percent in 1960, 67.2 percent in 1963, 83.3 percent in 1967 and 93.15 percent in 1971.

The above figures reveal an increasingly high degree of integrative capability. Since like-minded political forces are being gradually absorbed or amalgamated into the ranks of major government or opposition parties, we can say that Korean party politics at least has been approaching the model of a two-party system. Considering the fact that Korea experienced neither self-government nor party politics before August of 1945, we may well speculate that this has been perhaps one of the most rapid party developments in history.

If we acknowledge the intervention and pressure which the Government exercises during every major election, this development is all the more impressive. If it can be agreed that a growing power balance between government and opposition groups increases the possibility of popular control over the government, then the striking increase in opposition power in recent years can be interpreted as an indication of growing democratic strength in South Korea. The major opposition party vote has been as follows: 14.5 percent in 1948, 11.4 percent in 1950, 7.4 percent in 1954, 33.9 percent in 1958, 3.4 percent in 1960 (until the old faction within the Democratic Party seceded from the Party to form a new opposition, called the New Democratic Party), 32.0 percent in 1963, 25.7 percent in 1967 and 44.6 percent in 1971.

We see the same tendency in presidential elections. While the number of presidential candidates has not decreased, the popular vote has become concentrated on the government and major opposition candidates. The first President was elected in the Constitutional Assembly, and Syngman Rhee is unique in Korean presidential history in having been chosen by a nearly unanimous vote of the Assembly. In the Presidential election of 1952, Rhee received 74.6 percent of the votes, while Cho Bong-am (an ex-Communist) and the senile, infirmed Yi Si-yŏng received relatively insignificant percentages. In 1956, Rhee received 70 percent and Cho 30 percent. In 1960, Syngman Rhee was the only candidate left after the sudden death of the opposition candidate Cho Byŏng-ok. In 1963, when the head of the military junta, Park Chung-hee, ran for President, he received only

46.6 percent of the votes; the major opposition candidate, Yun Po-sŏn, received 45.1 percent. Park apparently would not have won the election had the opposition been united against the military leadership. In 1967, Park and Yun were opponents again, and this time Park won the election by a wider margin: 51.6 percent versus 40.9 percent. In the 1971 presidential election, however, the contest between Park Chung-hee and the young opposition candidate, Kim Tae-jung, was closer: 54 percent to 46 percent.

FACTORS CONTRIBUTING TO PARTY DEVELOPMENT

There are three principal factors which, from this writer's perspective, have been contributive to party development in South Korea since World War II: (1) an increasing level of political consciousness on the part of the masses as a result of experience with democratic political processes; (2) the strengthening of party leadership and organization within the government and opposition parties; (3) the increase of potential opposition supporters as a result of ongoing industrialization, urbanization and modernization.

(1) *An Increasing Political Consciousness on the Part of the Masses.* It has been said that after World War I, there were some Germans who regretted not having had poor rulers on the assumption that inept leadership might have occasioned the development of democratic institutions and social forces. Not having had such rulers, the German people never felt an acute necessity for the development of democratic ideas and institutions. Based upon this thesis, it may be a blessing that the Korean people did not have genuinely satisfactory and completely dependable political leaders in the years immediately following the foundation of the Republic. Under the arbitrary and inefficient government of Syngman Rhee, they developed a great suspicion of the ruling elite and a strong desire to control governmental power.

Popular oppositionist support often became so overwhelming that prominent opposition candidates might have defeated the charismatic Syngman Rhee, had they not in every instance died just before the elections. Shin Ik-hŭi who died in 1956 is an example. Ex-Communist Cho Bong-am's influence grew greatly during the 1950's; however, he was executed on charges of Communist conspiracy in 1958. Cho Byŏng-ok might have won the presidential election of 1960 had he not died two months earlier. In each election, government techniques for election manipulation improved—the Liberal Party government knew that it could not maintain power through fair elections.

The majority of Korean intellectuals and middle-class citizens seem to be aware of the functional necessity for an opposition party, and most of them hope to see it strengthened to a point of influencing the behavior of the government party and of paving the way for a peaceful, electorally-based change of power. An increasing number of the electorate has tended to vote for the opposition in recent years, not so much because the voters trust and support the opposition but because they view support for the opposition as the only way to balance the two parties, thereby exercising more effective control over the ruling party. There is no doubt but that this heightened level of political consciousness on the part of the masses has thus far contributed to the development of party politics.

(2) *The Strengthening of Party Leadership and Organization.* As stated above, the Republic of Korea was founded in 1948 after conservative forces succeeded in eliminating left-wing, middle-of-the-road and moderate right-wing forces from the South Korean political scene. The most potent conservative force aiding and supporting Syngman Rhee's nation-building efforts was the Korean Democratic Party. This party was a grouping of indigenous social and political notables—landlords, business elites, professionals and former high-ranking civil servants.

As the major political force in South Korea the Korean Democratic Party anticipated that the government formed under Syngman Rhee would naturally be a KDP government. But Syngman Rhee thought this political group already too strong and felt that its strength should somehow be curtailed. Thus, he did not recruit many KDP leaders for Cabinet posts. Strongly disappointed, the KDP became the core opposition force to the Rhee regime.

In an attempt to curtail the indomitable power of Rhee's charisma, the KDP tried to enact a series of constitutional amendments which would change the government from a presidential to a British-style cabinet system. It also tried to absorb or amalgamate all conservative opposition forces into the KDP ranks. In 1949 the KDP joined with the National Party, led by Shin Ik-hŭi, to form the Democratic National Party. In 1954 the Democratic National Party became the Democratic Party after absorbing other independent political forces. Despite these developments, the basic nature of the opposition party remained largely unchanged, i.e., a grouping of indigenous sociopolitical elites.

On the other hand, the Liberal Party was founded at the instigation of Syngman Rhee, who felt an acute need for a strong supportive political party capable of blocking pressures from the opposition. In contrast to the Korean Democratic Party—proud of its high status and social influence—the Liberal Party leadership was staffed by lesser figures who showed unconditional loyalty to President Rhee and his hand-picked second man, Yi Ki-bung. Other than these top two figures, the Liberal Party leaders were relatively young, modernized and functionalized in comparison with the older, semi-feudalistic and faction-oriented opposition elites.

Through constant competition between government and opposition parties, the quality of party leadership and organization improved a great deal even under the Rhee regime. This relationship between government and opposition parties has been carried over into the Park era. The leaders and organization of the Democratic Republican Party tend to be younger, more modernized and functionalized than those of the New Democratic Party. During the 1960's the opposition party was led by older social and political notables who were in their late fifties, while most government party leaders were in their middle forties. In broad terms, we may say that the older age group has tended to be more authoritarian, personalistic, factionalistic and even romantic in their disposition and behavior, whereas the younger age group has tended to be more organization-minded, professionally trained, and realistically oriented. This difference in perspective constituted a definite disadvantage for the opposition party in the 1960's.

The necessity for rejuvenating the New Democratic Party leadership was especially discussed following the defeat of the constitutional amendment of 1969, which eliminated the limitation on the number of terms that a president may serve. As a result, a 45-year-old presidential candidate, Kim Tae-jung, was nominated for the 1971 election. The manner in which Kim Tae-jung won the nomination is itself highly significant. Contrary to the conventional party practice of negotiating and maneuvering behind the scenes with party bigwigs, Kim won his nomination by appealing directly and openly to delegates at the National Convention. This approach was completely new to the traditional, faction-ridden caucus party.

(3) *The Increase of Potential Opposition Supporters.* Another factor conducive to the development of two-party politics has been rapid socio-economic and cultural change. Several voting studies have

disclosed that the urbanized, better-educated, younger and upper-income voters have tended to vote differently than the rural, less-educated, older and lower-income voters. The latter—proven government party supporters—constituted a much larger proportion of the populace in the 1950's, as compared to those who can be characterized as potential opposition supporters. Considering the socio-economic changes of the 1950's, the ratio of potential government party supporters vis-a-vis potential opposition party supporters shifted roughly from an 8:2 to a 7:3 ratio. In the 1960's, however, the ratio shifted from approximately 7:3 to 6:4, on the basis of available statistical data.

In particular, nearly 80 percent of the electorate lived in rural areas at the outset of the 1950's. By the end of the 1960's, however, the urban population had increased to 45 percent. Agewise, about 50 percent of the electorate was under 35 years of age in 1969. This means that half of the electorate belongs to an age group exposed to a more or less democratic culture and experienced in democratic methods of decision-making.

With regard to educational level, approximately 26 percent of the electorate has a secondary or higher education and 65 percent a primary education. This is indeed an extraordinarily high educational level for a "developing" country. As long as this sociocultural evolution continues, we can speculate that a relatively modern and democratic political culture will prevail in South Korea by the end of the 1970's, overshadowing the hitherto prevalent pre-modern political culture.

ELECTION PRACTICES

In the present section, we will deal with the workings of the Korean electoral system and consider to what extent election practices have helped people to convey their opinions and sentiments regarding the choice of party policies and candidates. In a way, Korean party politics hitherto described and analyzed have been intimately connected with the election practices which are described below.

In this writer's view, two factors have hindered the effective working of the electoral system in Korea: (1) deliberate interference and election maneuvering by the Government, and (2) the political culture and voting behavior.

(*1*) *Election Interference and Manipulation by the Government.* The element of electoral interference and manipulation has involved (a) government favoritism; (b) police hindrance and maneuvering; (c) occasional use of hoodlums, and (d) ballot rigging. In general, these extraordinary measures have been used overtly or covertly whenever and wherever necessary to win elections.

(*a*) *Government Favoritism.* As in any other country, in Korea the leaders of the government party are always mindful of maintaining power. Therefore, they are generally preoccupied with winning the support and goodwill of the largest possible numbers of the electorate. As election time approaches, government relations with the people become remarkably lenient, generous and considerate. Increased contacts are made with opinion leaders in local districts, followed by a rash of promises and hospitality. Many "inducements" are offered. For example, fertilizers are often supplied to farmers without the usual demand of immediate payment, and rations are passed out to the destitute. The enforcement of those rules and regulations which may incur widespread discontent or protest is delayed or temporarily loosened. Group picnics or social meetings are unofficially subsidized or officially sponsored. Thus, government party officials project an image as benign friends and reliable protectors.[3]

Should voters in a particular district support opposition candidates, the residents in the area must be prepared to suffer substantial disadvantages, probably for a prolonged period. Government supply of goods is curtailed or suspended; roads and bridges are not repaired; police chiefs often are replaced by stronger and harsher personalities. Thus, local villagers have learned well the pitfalls of supporting opposition candidates.

(*b*) *Police Hindrance and Maneuvering.* In the Republic's third Presidential campaign in 1956, a police lieutenant of Kyŏnggi province submitted his resignation because of disagreement with the following directive from his superiors:

(i) Police should not hesitate in assisting the election of Liberal Party candidates;
(ii) The campaign activities of opposition party workers must be hindered, and they should be arrested for any plausible reason;
(iii) The general electorate should be segregated from opposition party campaigners as much as possible;
(iv) In dominantly opposition areas, police should work for electing Liberal Party candidates after midnight curfew hours.[4]

Taking an extraordinary example from the 1960 Presidential election, Minister of Interior Ch'oe In-kyu told a group of local government chiefs: "As you may recall, opposition party candidates such as Shin Ik-hŭi and Cho Bong-am have collected a remarkable number of votes in past presidential elections. The Liberal Party candidates may not win this election without resorting to extraordinary measures. We must face this. Have you people ever heard of any single instance of a presidential election being disputed in courts at any time in the history of the world? Never mind about laws and rules. If anybody is to be punished for these deeds, I will be the one who takes the whole responsibility."[5]

Following is the blueprint prepared by the Rhee regime for the 1960 Presidential election: "(a) Buy up or obtain 40 percent of the ballots beforehand and insert them into the ballot boxes before the voting takes place; (b) group our Party voters together into nine- or three-man units for the purpose of mutual supervision; (c) all-out party supporters must wear identifiable arm bands in order to exert psychological pressure upon opposition voters; (d) election supervisors of the opposition party should be kept out of balloting places by means of threat or bribery...."[6]

In addition, a Chief of the Security Bureau issued a number of detailed instructions on election rigging including means for "revising" the number of votes at the time of announcement of election results. With the aid of such schemes, the government party polled more than 83 percent of the total vote, as planned before the election.

(c) *The occasional use of hoodlums*. The Rhee regime also counted on the use of hoodlums, who often worked in collaboration with the police. Hoodlums were mobilized to threaten or attack opposition party candidates, election workers, and even opposition voters. Sometimes they disturbed the election campaign rallies of opposition parties, or were strategically placed to thwart anti-government demonstrations. The 1960 student uprising erupted after government-controlled hoodlums attacked a peaceful student demonstration protesting the presidential election, and the Liberal Party regime collapsed following subsequent mass demonstrations.

(d) *Ballot rigging*. There are a number of quaint byproducts of Korean democratic processes, such as the "relay" ballot, "piano" ballot and "owl" ballot, among others.[7] Although these particular methods of ballot rigging seemed to have disappeared with Rhee's downfall, similar kinds of ingenious electoral invention have allegedly persisted even since the Rhee regime.

Along with the low level of political consciousness on the part of the electorate, these election practices could cast serious doubt upon the viability of a young democracy like South Korea. Complaints of "rigged" elections have been endemic to this day, even though there is no way to adequately substantiate such contentions.[8]

(2) The Political Culture and Voting Behavior. The success of democratic institutions depends most basically on the level of political consciousness shown in the voting behavior of the people. According to several studies on Korean voting behavior, the level of political awareness is still too low to expect a successful working of a truly democratic government. In this regard, we should examine briefly the following considerations: (a) the level of political awareness; (b) motivations for political participation; (c) sources and uses of Party Finance and Election Outlays, and (d) the people's attitudes toward political parties and toward the electoral system in general.

(a) The Level of Political Awareness. Voter turnout in terms of percentages is quite high. It does not follow, however, that there is a high level of political consciousness on the part of the electorate. The turnout of Seoul voters is lower than that of predominately rural voters, though Seoulites are more politically aware. For example, in the 1954 general election, voter participation in Seoul was 88.3 percent, while that in rural Kangwon province was 98.3 percent. In the 1958 general election, the voter turnout in Seoul was 80.4 percent and that of Kangwon province 93.3 percent. On the other hand, we can detect a decrease in voter turnout when voting experience increases. The following table, based on a study by Kim Kyu-taik reflects voter turnout in the general elections of 1958, 1960 and 1963.[9]

	Seoul	Large city	Small city	Town	Rural area
1958 general election	80.4	85.9	88.4	90.7	93.3
1960 general election	75.4	78.3	84.6	83.4	87.1
1963 general election	62.9	63.5	75.2	73.6	76.1

Kim's study also indicated that the more urban the district is, the stronger the opposition; and the more rural the district is, the stronger the government party. Another study has revealed that the higher a person's educational level, the more he tends to vote for the opposition.[10] This would indicate that the less informed and less educated voters have a much higher participation rate than their more sophisticated counter-parts. Therefore, a higher voting turnout implies a lower quality of voting, which is more susceptible to the possibility of government manipulation.

(*b*) *Motivations for Political Participation.* Yoon Chon-ju, in a survey related to voter motivations, asked respondents: "What are you voting for? Are you voting for the benefit of the nation and state, or for individuals, or for a particular political group?" Of those polled, those who responded the "nation and state" numbered 166; individuals, 118; party or group, 45. Yoon interpreted his findings as follows: [11]

> A breakdown of 96.8 percent of those polled shows the motivating factors in voting as follows: 42.8 percent voted on the basis of patriotism; 29.8 percent, candidate orientation; 11.1 percent, party and group identification. Approximately 45 percent indicated their vote would be based on knowledge and understanding of the facts of the election. Thus, about 55 percent of the respondents had only some vague notion of the purpose or motive on the basis of which they would vote. This latter group, then, was especially susceptible to pressures and last-minute changes of mind.

In his survey, Yoon also raised this question: "Do you think that votes of rural village people went to one candidate in bloc or were scattered among several candidates?" 165, or 40.8 percent, of the respondents answered that they thought villagers had voted in bloc for one candidate; 105, or 26 percent, thought villagers had voted for several candidates; and 101, or 25 percent, said they did not know. To a follow-up question concerning why village people tend to vote in bloc, 66.7 percent of the 165 attributed the voting practice to external pressures.[12]

According to Oh Byung-hun's survey research on the 1960 general election, 72.7 percent of his respondents said they voted on the basis of individual personality of candidates, 14.7 percent on the basis of party, while the rest had no clear-cut response.[13] In Yoon's survey mentioned above, the following question was posed: "Why did you vote for particular candidates?" Some 68.8 percent indicated the individual personality of candidates; 5.9 percent, the party; 18.3 percent said both candidate and party. His survey further revealed that there had been little consistency in voter party allegiance over the three previous general elections. To the question, "How many times have you voted for the same party through the last three general elections?", only 6.9 percent said they had voted for the same party; 11.1 percent had voted only twice; and 38.0 percent had voted for a different party in each election.[14]

(c) *Sources and Uses of Party Finance and Election Outlays.* For better or worse, democracy can be a costly business. Accordingly, money talks a great deal and perhaps more so in a country that is inexperienced in the management of democratic government. It is a matter of common knowledge that one can hardly understand the real dynamics of party politics without tracing the sources and uses of party finance and election outlays. This is particularly true in a situation such as that in South Korea where the behavioral and institutional anomalies in party politics and elections are closely linked to anomalies in party financing and election outlays.

Like parties in other democratic polities, those in Korea maintain a high degree of secrecy about their finances; therefore, reliable data on the subject is limited. According to the financial report of the Central Election Management Committee, the annual expenditures of the major political parties for 1963, 1964 and 1965 were as follows:[15]

	1963 in won*	1964 in won*	1965 in won*
Democratic Republican	5,700,000,000	4,300,000,000	4,800,000,000
Minjung (Mass) Party	1,600,000,000	1,800,000,000	1,600,000,000
Democratic	780,000,000	1,200,000,000	
Liberal Democratic	670,000		

*At that time 130 won equalled one U.S. dollar.

In 1968, the Democratic Republican Party reported that its monthly party expenses amounted to four million won. Yet, few would accept these figures as reliable. Some knowledgeable sources have estimated DRP expenses as follows: The Central Party Headquarters, approximately 15 million won per month (280 won equalled one U.S. dollar), including 4.5 million won for the salaries of 480 party staff workers; three million won for office maintenance; and seven to eight million won for organizational, propaganda and parliamentary activities. In addition, it has also been said that the DRP has subsidized its members in the National Assembly to the extent of 100,000 won each per month.[16] This means that the DRP headquarters alone likely spent more than three billion won in 1968 on the above-stated areas.

Party finance is primarily from three sources: party membership fees; Government contributions; political funds raised by the party. The party membership fee is the most insignificant and negligible part of funding. DRP regulations stipulate that party members are to pay a membership fee of at least ten won (about three cents in U. S. currency) every three months; this regulation, however, has not been stringently enforced.[17] The New Democratic Party has no requirement for a party membership fee.

Regarding contributions, the Party Law stipulates that the Central Election Management Committee raises contributions and distributes political funds to major political parties according to the ratio of votes cast for each party in the last general election.[18]

"Political funds" raised by the parties actually constitute the main source of party finance. In raising political funds the government party has a distinct advantage in attracting large contributions, particularly from large-scale business interests which tend to court the party in power for special favors.

On the other hand, opposition parties have little opportunity to raise political funds through bartering special privileges. In order to raise campaign funds at election time, the opposition New Democratic Party has been known to sell National Assembly nominations. The buyers of higher priority (relatively "safe") seats are virtually assured of being elected to the National Assembly.[19] Yet, the number of priority seats available to the NDP is limited. Therefore the opposition sometimes has to look to the government party for financial aid. The government party thus stands in a position of uncontested superiority by virtue of being able to exercise substantial control over the opposition. In effect, the government allows the opposition to function only to the point of not constituting a serious threat to the party in power.

In both government and opposition parties, persons who can draw upon large sums of political funds generally are able to exert a greater amount of political influence with the party. In a government party, the President, having a monopoly of power, can direct and control the behavior of party members from his unequivocal position of authority. In opposition parties, however, the locus of power and the shape of the power structure is bound to be more amorphous and fluid, because the opposition leader has relatively little control over the sources of money. Thus, the government party can exert considerable influence upon the make-up of the opposition party leadership by deliberately and selectively subsidizing one opposition factional group or another. National Assemblymen belonging to the opposition party therefore are extremely vulnerable to governmental pressures. Under these circumstances, it becomes virtually impossible for opposition parties to compete on equal terms with a government party. Even so, opposition parties have remained active and determined through the 1950's and 1960's. The fact remains, however, that as long as the present pattern of party funding continues, a system of one-party dominance is inevitable.

SUMMARY AND CONCLUSIONS

In general, we can identify three factors in the Korean environment which have been detrimental to the development of parties and other political structures: 1. Primary emphasis on continuous economic growth and on political stability; 2. Continuing internal schism and inveterate factional struggle within and among opposition groups; 3. International tensions affecting the Korean peninsula.

1. *Primary Emphasis on Continuous Economic Growth and on Political Stability.* The favorite slogan used by the DRP Government at election times has been: "Political stability is the indispensable requisite of economic growth." This implies that political stability can be assured by political continuity and the extension of governmental power. The rapid economic growth of the 1960's actually has tended to widen the gap between the Government and the people, the rich and the poor, the urban and rural. At times of rapid social and economic change, those who are basically content are relatively few, while most of the people tend to become increasingly discontented, frustrated and alienated. This sentiment of alienation and frustration was fully capitalized upon in the 1971 presidential election by the opposition candidate, Kim Tae-jung. His forthright criticism of Government policy aroused a substantial grassroots following.

In reaction to the opposition's success in gaining support, one Government party leader stated that for the sake of political stability a person capable of controlling the military should be president. The implication was that President Park was uniquely qualified to fill that role. A further implication was that any government without the support of the military may be overthrown by the military. Kim Tae-jung contended that the DRP regime wished to impose a perpetual rule in the style of Franco's Spain or Chiang Kai-shek's Taiwan.

On the last day of the campaign, President Park pledged not to run again for the Presidency. He would step down from his office after cleaning up government corruption and promoting mass welfare, areas in which—by his own self-admission—his policies had not been totally successful in the past. As indicated in the introductory chapter of this volume, the Constitution was subsequently amended to allow the President to run for an indefinite number of terms.

2. *Continuing Internal Schism and Inveterate Factional Strife within the Opposition.* Following the 1971 elections, factional strife and animosity with the NDP leadership flourished between factions led by Yu Chin-san and Kim Tae-jung, respectively. Yu Chin-san, the most influential old-guard member of the NDP, and two younger members, Yi Ch'ŏl-sŏng and Kim Young-sam, united their supporters in order to stop Kim Tae-jung's rise. In a compromise move, ex-General Kim Hong-il, an independence fighter under the Japanese colonial regime, was made NDP party leader as a temporary caretaker. However, Yu Chin-san reassumed the party reins in May of 1973.

3. *International Tensions Affecting the Korean Peninsula.* The October 1972 "Revitalizing Reforms" were justified by the President in terms of an acute necessity to strengthen the Government's hand in order to cope with the new international situation surrounding the Korean peninsula. The sudden mood of detente in the Far East, occasioned by the Nixon visit to Peking and the subsequent normalization of Japan-China relations, has weakened the staunch anti-communist positions of governments in the Republic of Korea, the Republic of China in Taiwan, and the Republic of Vietnam.

It can be concluded that the South Korean party system was definitely weakened by events of 1972 and 1973. The Government party is now actually two—one is the Yujŏnghoe (the Political Association for Revitalization), a grouping of National Assembly membership appointed by the President through the National Conference of Unification; the other is the regular party organization and membership. The opposition party, in early 1974, was divided into pro-Yu Chin-san and anti-Yu Chin-san factions. Yu's death in April 1974 left the party in considerable disarray with regard to leadership. A new NDP President, Kim Young-sam, was elected only on August 23, 1974. The NDP split and leadership vacuum was capitalized on by the government and contributed in no small way to strengthening President Park's authority.

The President, himself, has succinctly given a rationale for weakening the structures and powers of Korean political parties: "All the activities of political parties must be oriented toward the strengthening of national power. Representative institutions should likewise be operated in such a way as to accelerate the strengthening of national power. Insofar as party activities contribute to this cause, we can achieve the identity of a party with the nation and guarantee the national consensus, providing the conditions of social stability and national happiness. This is a shortcut to the development of democracy suitable to our political environment.... The DRP must be a policy party, steadily pursuing long-term national objectives; an organization party, equipped with a fully disciplined structure of leadership; a service party based on the principles of efficiency and productivity...."[21]

American Scholar Edward A. Shils has maintained: "No new state can modernize itself and remain or become liberal and democratic without an elite of force of character, intelligence, and high moral qualities."[22] He has said further: "If democracy can be understood in a partial sense ... it is entirely possible that some form of democracy has, in the long run, the best chance to survive among the alternative models. But even then it will be able to survive only if the elite has a very powerful will to be democratic—only, i.e., if the elite is willing to be the teacher and parent of democracy in a society which by its nature does not incline in that direction."[23]

The political development of South Korea since World War II has been largely shaped by political elites centering on two central figures and these two most influential leaders had in common a distaste for party politics. They found party give-and-take more or less uneconomical, controversial and undisciplined.[24] They maintained a Government party in order to contain opposition groups, but did not encourage party development for its own sake. The "Koreanized democracy" advocated by President Park in 1972 has been characterized by strong executive and administrative leadership and subsidiary party and representative institutions.[25] At this juncture, it is perhaps too early to be able to properly evaluate the impact of this "Koreanized democracy" on Korean political party development.

FOOTNOTES

1. Kim Tae-jung, "Taejung Minju Ch'eje eui Kil" ("Path toward a Mass Democratic System"), *Jungang,* November 1970, pp. 92–95.
2. Edward G. Meade, *American Military Government in Korea* (New York: The King Crown Press, 1951), pp. 54–55.
3. Park Kwŏn-hŭn, "Yŏlp'ung Chonya eui Sŏnggo P'ungsokto" ("A Variety of Election Practices and Manners before the Hot Election Contest"), *Sedae,* September 1970, pp. 170–179.
4. Min Kwan-sik, *Kangoku Seijishi (Korean Political History)* (Tokyo: Sekai Shisosha, 1967), pp. 35–105.
5. *Sawŏl Hyŏngmyŏng Ch'ŏngsa Py'ŏngch'anhoe (The History of the April Revolution)* (Seoul: Songgonsa, 1960), p. 470.
6. *Ibid.,* pp. 471–473.
7. The "relay ballot" was used in the 1958 general election. The first voter would enter the balloting place and mark his ballot. Instead of inserting it into the box, he handed it to the person next in line in order to make sure that the latter would vote for the government party candidates. This second person would enter the balloting place and insert the preceding person's ballot into the box and hand his own ballot to the third person for inspection. In the "piano ballot" a voter would stain, and thereby effectively void opposition votes by rubbing the ballots with stamp ink from his fingers. This was done in case the opposition seemed to be winning over the government party. The "owl votes" were so named because the ballots were counted in darkness, thereby giving election officers ample opportunity to increase the number of government candidates' votes. In such cases there had been a convenient failure of electric power, usually when the opposition seemed to be winning.
8. *Yukp'al Ch'ongsŏngŏ Paeksŏ (The White Paper of the June 8 General Election)* (Seoul: Shinmindang, 1964). See also *Osam Songo eui Pujuŏng Pulbŏp Chinsangŭn Irŏt'a (These are the True Facts About the Illicit and Illegal May 3 Elections)* (Seoul: Shinmindang, 1964); and *Ikŏsi Yukp'al Sŏngŏda (This is the True Story of the June 8 General Elections)* (Seoul: Minjukonghwadang, 1968).
9. Kim Kyu-t'aik, "Yŏkdae Sŏngŏ eui T'ongejŏk Punsŏk" ("Statistical Analysis of the Korean Elections"), *Sahoe Kwakak,* September 1967, pp. 63–65.
10. *Ibid.*
11. Yoon Chon-ju, "Voting Behavior of Eup Inhabitants," *Journal of Asiatic Studies,* IV, June 1961, p. 57.
12. *Ibid.,* p. 58.
13. Oh Byung-hun, "Analysis of the July 4th General Election, "*Journal of Asiatic Studies, III* (December, 1960), p. 76.
14. Yoon, *op. cit.,* pp. 57–58.
15. Nam Jae-hŭi, "Chŏngdang Unyŏng kwa Tang Chaejŏng" ("Party Manage-

ment and Party Finance"), *Chŏnggyŏng Yŏngu* (*Politics and Economics*), No. 25, Seoul, February 1967, pp. 132–137.
16. Kim Kyŏng-nae, "Chŏngch'i Chagŭm kwa Chaebŏl" ("Political Funding and Financial Groups"), *Sedae,* No. 35, Seoul, June 1966, pp. 86–92.
17. Cho Il-mun, "Chŏngch'i Chagŭm eui Yiron kwa Hyŏngsil Koch'al" ("On the Theory and Practice of Political Funding"), *Sasangge,* Seoul, February 1970, pp. 45–72.
18. *Ibid.*
19. Nam Jae-hŭi and Cho Il-mun, *op. cit.*
20. This is an excerpt from the congratulatory statement presented at the thirteenth anniversary of the founding of the Democratic Republican Party on April 28, 1973.
21. Edward A. Shils, *Political Development in the New States* (Hague: Mouton and Co., 1966), p. 86.
22. *Ibid.,* p. 90.
23. Huntington exposited their mentality as follows: "The party necessarily reflects the logic of politics, not the logic of efficiency. A bureaucracy... is by the latter logic a more modern institution than a political party which operates on patronage, influence and compromise. Consequently, the promoters of modernization, like the defenders of tradition, often reject and denigrate political parties. They attempt to modernize their society politically without establishing the institution that will make their society politically stable. They pursue modernity at the expense of politics and in the process fail to achieve the one because of their neglect of the other." Samuel P. Huntington, *Political Order in Changing Societies* (New Haven: Yale University Press, 1968), pp. 91–92.
24. In this context, Apter's description of a "neomercantilist regime" seems suggestive: "If a modernizing country began as a reconciliation system, it will move, as it modernizes, toward a neomercantilist society by increasing coercion... (a neomercantilist system) will be more efficient for a long period of time than a mobilization system and more stable than a reconciliation system. The neomercantilist societies can become dynastic. A small group of people around a presidential monarch may become the equivalent of a royal lineage. They may choose incumbents of political office by conflict between themselves and their supporters."

PART THREE: MAJOR CONTRIBUTORS
TO KOREAN POLITICS:
STUDENTS AND THE MILITARY

CHAPTER 5: Students and Politics
by *Byung-hun Oh*

CHAPTER 6: The Military and Politics
in Postwar Korea
by *John P. Lovell*

INTRODUCTION TO PART THREE

Two elements of Korean society that have most profoundly influenced postwar Korean politics have been the students and the military establishment. Byung-hun Oh, in his article on "Students and Politics in Korea," traces the historical background of Korean students and student attitudes. The Korean educational system rests largely on a Confucian base, in that education is the most essential element on the road to power, status and wealth. The overwhelming desire of Korean families and Korean youth for optimum education can be attributed largely to the Confucian inheritance, engendered during the more than 500 years of the Yi dynasty (1392–1910).

An American educational model was superimposed on a combination Japanese-traditional system after World War II. The consequent encouragement of mass education was readily accepted by a population that was education-starved following the lean years of Japanese colonial occupation (1910–1945). However, the postwar Korean governments did not impose strong controls on educational expansion, and the result was an unplanned and rather unwieldy system, generally lacking in quality of curriculum and instruction. A related problem was the mass production of high school and college graduates into an economy where there were too few jobs to accommodate their newly-earned skills.

During the American Military Government period (1945–1948), there were two main divisions of students in terms of political orientation—the left and the right. The left had for its leadership a small group of communist students, while the right was factional and badly organized. Those on the left were suppressed and disappeared from open activity near the close of the American military occupation. They had completely disbanded by the beginning of the Syngman Rhee regime in 1948. Students were quiet during the early Rhee years; however their dissatisfaction with Rhee's autocratic leadership and the corruption that was rampant under his rule brought open opposition to governmental policies in the middle and late 1950's, erupting in widespread student demonstrations in the spring of 1960. In the face of student and other opposition, Rhee resigned the presidency in April of that year.

The ensuing short period of the Chang Myŏn Government found the student movement factionalized. There was little general agreement among the factions concerning a next step, now that there had been a change of governments. When the bloodless military revolt took place in

May of 1961, all student organizations were disbanded. The change to civilian attire by the military rulers in the autumn of 1963 resulted in more freedom for the students, who proceeded to mount demonstrations in the spring of 1964 in opposition to the proposed terms of normalization of relations with Japan. Students felt that the Korean government was taking a "humiliating posture" toward Japan in the normalization negotiations. The demonstrations became so intense that martial law was proclaimed and schools were temporarily closed. Demonstrations occurred again on the same issue during the spring of 1965. These were forcefully and effectively put down by the government, and the normalization treaty was signed in the late summer of 1965.

There were no major student political activities in 1966; however, new demonstrations were sparked by irregularities in the National Assembly elections of June 8, 1967. As in 1964, schools were closed before the end of the term—this time by the school authorities rather than the Government. The next large-scale student uprising was in the fall of 1969 in protest against a proposed Constitutional amendment to allow the nation's president to run for a third consecutive four-year term. The demonstrations were effectively put down by the Government, and the amendment was approved in a nationwide referendum by a large majority. Major student disturbances occurred again in 1970, 1971, 1973 and 1974—all related in one way or another to the cry for greater democratization of the political system.

There are a number of contributing factors related to the nature and extent of Korean student political involvement. One is the centralization of higher educational institutions and students in Seoul. About 70 percent of the nation's college and university students are in the capital city. They tend to be highly politicized, living as they do in the centralized seat of control of Korean society. A related consideration is that the most prestigious universities—Seoul National, Korea, and Yonsei—tend to produce the leadership for student protest movements. Students at these institutions feel that they constitute an intellectual elite among the nation's student population and therefore must assume a leadership role on issues of national import. Within that "elite," students living away from home tend to be more activistic, due in large part to the fact that they are removed from family sanctions and supervision. Also, students from the provinces attending school in Seoul are mostly from traditionally upper class families which, however, have become relatively disadvantaged economically since the Korean War and the introduction of a business and industrially based society. Their grievances were at least partially reflective of the more traditional attitudes derived from their family backgrounds.

With regard to the rationale of the students themselves, there have been at least five kinds of student motivations which can be identified with student uprisings during the 1960's. Firstly, Korean students tend to be more value-oriented than issue-oriented. Their essential arguments are usually related to the *principle* underlying an issue. They are secondarily, if at all, concerned with limited and pragmatic goals. Secondly, and relatedly, their concerns are largely political and nationwide in scope. Social, cultural, and economic matters have not provided primary incentives for large-scale student demonstrations. Thirdly, student political uprisings have all been anti-government in character. Throughout Korean history, there has been no peacefully achievable alternative to control by a particular regime, and this has remained true of the period since World War II—there has yet to occur a peaceful transfer of governmental power. A fourth consideration is that Korean students tend to be idealistic and messianic in their sense of mission to take collective action for the righting of wrongs and upholding of principles. This is reflective of a traditional emphasis in the Korean socialization and educational process on abstract and general knowledge and understanding; consequently students have a tendency to think and reason in vague terms, and to overgeneralize and look for all-encompassing solutions to problems. Fifthly, and finally, Korean students are strongly nationalistic. They are aware of the nation's historical legacy of periodic subservience to Japan and China, and of the strong influence by and dependence on the United States of America. They are also wary of potential Japanese economic influence in Korea. Students have been quite concerned with the adoption of an independent stance in the international community, and with the unification of their divided nation.

The students of Korea have been effective in making their collective voice heard in opposing what they consider to have been the misuse of power by successive postwar regimes. They have not, however, been able or inclined to consolidate their positions to pursue more positive and practical programs and goals. Pursuit of more constructive policies has rather been the role of the Korean military which, among other things, has been instrumental since 1961 in creating a high degree of political stability and economic progress in the southern half of the Korean peninsula.

Until the beginning of the Korean War in 1950, the South Korean military establishment was in an embryonic stage and was not a major military or political force. However, with firm American support, the structure and organization of the military were consolidated during the war and further developed during the 1950's. Syngman Rhee was successful in channeling the power of the military to support his regime. However, after Rhee was toppled as a result of the 1960 student demonstrations, the military took little time before seizing power from the weaker successor regime of Chang Myŏn. The coup d'etat took place on May 16, 1961, with no resistance. The military had now become not simply an element in Korean politics, but the controlling factor.

The military rulers based their regime on pledges of anti-communism; industrialization and economic betterment; "spiritual regeneration", and "social reconstruction." They contrasted these policies with what they considered to be an antithetical Confucian tradition. President Park Chung-hee particularly pointed to the political and economic example of West Germany in the years following World War II and expressed his determination to create a "miracle on the Han River" in emulation of Germany's "miracle on the Rhine."

The military revolutionary elite was composed of various factions. One included at least six members of the eighth graduating class of the Korea Military Academy in 1949. Many, too, had been American trained during and immediately after the Korean War. A key figure in the military government, though not ostensibly part of the ruling elite, was Kim Chong-p'il, who headed the Central Intelligence Agency under the military regime and who was instrumental in establishing the Democratic Republican Party which was led by key figures from the military regime, now in mufti. Kim has been in and out of key leadership roles since that time. Most recently he was named vice-president of the Democratic Republican Party in March of 1971 and actively campaigned for Park Chung-hee's re-election in the winter and spring of 1971. After Park's victorious third term election on April 27, 1971, Kim was named Prime Minister.

In 1963 President Park and his military associates were elected to head the new civilian government, which has remained in power since. The military establishment remains instrumental in the apparatus and politics of government. All able-bodied Korean men must serve in the military, which numbers more than 600,000 in the active forces. This military service requirement has had one effect, among others, of providing technical training for hundreds of thousands of Koreans who might otherwise not have been so exposed. The military also has engendered a "civic action" program, which utilizes the military for developmental activities throughout the nation. Projects have included those related to agricultural development; construction of dams, roads and schools; and distribution of various materials and supplies to villages, among others. In effect, the military maintains close ties between the Government and the people. It can be concluded that the high degree of political cohesion and economic development in Korea during the 1960's would not have been possible to such an extent without close and overlapping links between the Korean government and military establishment.

CHAPTER 5:

Students and Politics

BYUNG-HUN OH*

In the process of rapid transformation, Korea, like other underdeveloped countries, is being challenged by political instability, economic privation, social tensions and cultural change. There exist, however, additional afflictions unique to the Korean scene which demand constant attention from the government and the people. For example, there is the division of the country into two parts which imposes attendant burdens on national resources and development. Then there was the Communist invasion of 1950 which placed the country on the verge of total collapse. As a result there exist the ever-present fear of another invasion and the need to maintain armed forces of an enormous size to guard against it. In addition to these factors are unplanned and therefore uneven changes juxtaposed with lingering traditions throughout various sectors of the society; heterogeneous foreign influences permeating social life; and the precarious dependence of national fortune on international power politics. The unusually strong power of the government may also be added to the list. Finally, one might well name the educational structure as one of the most serious current problems. The latter originally grew out of

---

*Byung-hun Oh is Professor of Political Science at Sung-Kyun-Kwan University, Seoul. His M.A. degree is in Political Science from Harvard University. This article is a revised version of his paper presented at the Conference on Students and Politics, sponsored by the Center for International Affairs of Harvard University and the University of Puerto Rico, and held in San Juan, Puerto Rico, March 27-March 31, 1967. The original paper was published in *Koreana Quarterly*, Volume 9, No. 4 (Seoul, International Research Center, Winter 1967).

the social vacuum created after independence, and a lack of planning has meant unstructured growth and serious difficulties.

These unique features of Korean society are mentioned at the outset because they seem the have wielded a peculiar influence on the minds and activities of students in one way or another, though there are many other conditions which Korea shares with other countries that influence student activities in general. The purpose of this paper is to clarify the nature and extent of political activity by Korean students, first by following the history of the Korean student movement, next by depicting campus life, and lastly by clarifying and explicating political implications of student activism.

KOREAN SOCIETY AND EDUCATION

Historical Background. Though Korea has maintained political independence throughout most of her history and has developed a distinct culture, her geographical location has destined the country to live under the varying influences of foreign cultures. Thus, Korean education was affected directly or indirectly by Indian Buddhism imported through China during the period of Silla (57 B.C.-916 A.D.) and Koryo (917-1392); by Chinese Confucianism during the Chosun period or Yi dynasty (1393-1910); by Japanese imperialistic ideas and western ideology, especially those of Germany through Japan, during the Japanese colonial rule (1910-1945); and by western democratic ideas from the United States since the liberation in 1945. Presently, it may be said, the educational system is oriented toward the American model, but is severely plagued by the remnants of Confucian and Japanese influences.

The Korean people have suffered from autocratic government throughout their history. Authoritarian government always searches for some ideology to maintain stability, and Confucianism served this purpose well. Originally a conglomeration of moral teachings but elevated almost to the status of a national religion, Confucianism taught the people absolute obedience to the ruler, veneration of elders, excessive ancestral worship and ceremonialism, development of individual personality, disregard for material comfort, cautious moderation "in every word and step," and the importance of education for attaining these objectives. The last point, i.e., stress on education, calls for close examination here in view of its widespread and lasting influence on educational policy. During the five hundred years of the Yi dynasty, the main task of all schools was to teach Confucianism, directing the students to memorize faithfully and interpret properly its teachings and to imitate its canonical texts beautifully in writing prose and poetry. The final goal of education was to produce a man of virtue who was modest, righteous, and altruistic. The educational system was closely interwoven with the social structure and political system of the day. Completely centralized autocracy left little sphere for private economic activities, and higher government officials, appointed through strict national examinations, wielded enormous economic power as well as in other areas. Since government appointment meant not only honor and power but also wealth, the system of national examinations was the gateway to both power and wealth, which stimulated a strong desire for education among the young men. Traditional Confucianism maintained itself until the beginning of the present century and has continued to wield its influence even now on ethics textbooks in elementary schools.

Another legacy derives from the Japanese colonial rule which, despite its comparatively short duration of 36 years, left a strong imprint. Education, especially higher education, was not strongly encouraged by the colonial government, and general education in humanities and social sciences was discouraged in view of its nourishment of nationalistic sentiment. Emphasis was placed on technical education at the high school level, and about half of 17 junior colleges were vocational, devoted to such subjects as agriculture, engineering and medicine. There was only one university in the country (Keijo Imperial University), and even there the ratio of enrollment of Koreans to Japanese was strictly kept at 40 to 60 percent. The Koreans' traditionally high aspiration for education was thus frustrated. Some students went to schools in Japan and abroad, but their number was limited. The colonial authorities were afraid of and guarded against the strong nationalism of Koreans, especially of the intellectuals. The policy was understandable because anti-Japanese uprising—notably the March 1 Movement of 1919, June 10 Movement of 1926, and the Kwangju Uprising of 1929—had been led by students. After these incidents, especially the last, the colonial authorities employed extreme measures to subdue the nationalism of Korean students. Students suspected of anti-Japanese sentiments were kept under constant surveillance by security police, and the espousing of nationalistic ideas was punished if discovered. Teaching of Korean history and language was banned, and speaking the mother tongue was discouraged even at home. But Confucian teachings were skillfully taken into the curriculum because of their doctrines of obedience to power and of moderate conduct. Those who could not stand the suffocating atmosphere quit schools to join underground independence movements in and out of Korea.

The stifling of the traditional aspiration for education, especially for higher general education, the suppression of nationalistic sentiments, and the proclivity of students for "patriotic" actions during the Japanese rule brought about explosive events in the educational system and student movement after liberation in 1945.

Divided occupation of the country by the Allied Forces in 1945 and the subsequent American military government in the southern half for three years caused tremendous changes in Korean society even before the establishment of an independent government in 1948. One of the revolutionary changes occurred in the field of education. The whole educational system was remodeled after the American pattern, and Korean history and language were enthusiastically revived, while Japanese history and language vanished from the curriculum. But little more than this was done during this period. Unplanned and unchecked by the government, the traditional aspiration for education resulted in the establishment of new schools at all levels. Among the new schools, those of general education and humanities were much larger in number than those offering vocational training and natural sciences, and many of the already existing vocational schools broadened their curricula. A strong desire for higher education was satisfied by the emergence of numerous colleges and universities. The new schools had inadequate facilities, poor teaching staffs, and meager funding. Many were founded primarily for pecuniary motives.

Shortly after the outbreak of the Korean war in 1950, an occasion arose which gave a prodigious spur to this tendency. The government had already replaced the volunteer system of army recruitment with a conscription system, so all students of colleges and universities went into the military. But when the front lines became gradually stabilized, the all but empty classrooms of universities caused grave concern for those who worried about the future of the country. Heeding a resolution of the National Assembly, the government decided to defer the conscription of college and university students, and furthermore to shorten the ordinary three-year term of military service by half for students and graduates of colleges and universities. Naturally, many high school graduates flocked to enter a college—any college—in order to take advantage of the privilege. Since existing college facilities were unable to accommodate this demand, so-called "school mongers" took full advantage of the easy terms for establishing or expanding colleges. New colleges mushroomed, some high schools were upgraded to colleges, and existing colleges did their best to increase enrollments. Because institutions concentrating on natural sciences or vocational training were time-consuming to build and expensive to operate, "school mongers" preferred to found or expand colleges and curricula in humanities and social sciences. Like department stores pressed to stock a variety of goods, colleges in a haphazard fashion became universities. Professors were in short supply, and many were forced to teach too many students, sometimes at several universities at the same time.

Belated government measures to curb these maladies were inadequate to undo what already had been done. The privilege of shorter military service was discontinued, the deferment system was applied only to students under 24 years old, and a government-determined ceiling was set on the enrollment in each department of each university. But these measures proved unsuccessful in diminishing the overexpanded number of students. Once founded, universities sought to maintain themselves by evading government supervision, by illegal extra enrollment, and by ignoring public criticism. One result was the concentration of large numbers of universities and students in the capital city of Seoul, without which the 1960 student uprising could never have succeeded. The military government, right after the coup of 1961, tried to reduce the number of universities and students. But pressures put on the military government by the universities succeeded in making the authorities discard the plan. In the following year, the military government held national examinations for last-year students in high school before they could qualify for graduation. But this also proved unsuccessful after it was tried once. Universities and colleges were finally allowed to exist and operate without substantial government restrictions on enrollment, that is until 1969 when a government-drafted examination system was implemented whereby a prospective college student has to pass a government exam qualifying him to apply for the entrance examination to the college or university of his choice. This greatly affected the total number of students allowed to take entrance examinations to colleges and universities and, by 1970, many institutions of relatively low prestige and status could not fill their student quotas. Some smaller ones were struggling for their lives.

The rapid expansion of universities and colleges is shown in the following tables which compare the situation in 1945 and that in 1964.

Table 1 shows the differing rates of increase in a number of schools at various levels. (Independent colleges, junior colleges and colleges within universities are counted as colleges in this table and hereafter.)

TABLE 1
INCREASE IN NUMBER OF SCHOOLS AT VARIOUS LEVELS

	1945 number	1964 number	Annual rate of increase
Elementary schools	2,834	5,004	1.77
High schools	165	1,857	11.25
Colleges	19	189	9.95

While normal growth might be considered to be at even rates among various levels or at slightly higher rates at higher levels considering the suppression of higher education before the liberation, the actual growth rate is the highest at high school level with colleges following closely. Since the increase of elementary schools, lowest in rates, is far from catching up with the population increase, the increase of colleges is more lopsided in comparison with other educational levels than appears to be the case in the table.

The preponderance of higher education expansion is more clearly understood when the rates of increase of students are considered, as seen in Table 2.

TABLE 2
INCREASE IN NUMBERS OF STUDENTS AT VARIOUS LEVELS

	1945 number	1964 number	rate of increase
Elementary schools	1,366,024	4,726,297	3.46
High schools	84,572	1,066,247	12.61
Colleges	7,819	142,629	18.24

Since the enrollment ratio of school age children in 1964 was 95 percent, the rate of increase in numbers of pupils, 3.46, seems reasonable when one disregards the poor learning environment. The growth of high schools seems healthy, since the rate of increase in the number of students, 12.61, was followed by the similar rate of increase in number of schools, 11.25. But when the situation of colleges is considered, one is struck by the disparity between the increase in facilities and in students. While the number of colleges increased about ten times, itself an abnormally high expansion, the number of students increased 18 times. In addition to reasons mentioned above, there was another reason for this abnormal increase, namely the unemployment situation among college graduates. With an enormous number of college graduates pouring into the society which, at its low stage of economic development, could not accommodate their demands for employment, common sense seemed to dictate that high school graduates refrain from entering college. But actually just the opposite occurred. While some college graduates were lamenting about the society which would not pay due regard to their intellectual ability, many others braved to take jobs formerly taken by graduates of lower schools, such as clerks and policemen. Since employers tended to prefer the abundant supply of college graduates, more high school graduates were forced to go to college and elementary school graduates to high school. The more graduates coming out of colleges and taking jobs of various kinds, the more the hard pressed high school graduates went to college. This vicious circle is still in evidence, mass-producing unemployed college graduates. The situation has been somewhat but not entirely relieved with the upsurge in the economy in recent years.

The problem becomes more serious when the quality of those graduates is examined. It is possible to get an idea of teaching quality by comparing the number of faculty members in relation to students. Comparative increase of number of teachers at various levels is shown in Table 3.

TABLE 3
RATE OF INCREASE IN NUMBER OF TEACHERS AT VARIOUS LEVELS

	1945 number	1964 number	rate of increase
Elementary schools	19,729	75,455	3.83
High schools	3,219	30,375	9.44
Colleges	1,490	5,351	3.59

By comparing Tables 2 and 3, one can see that the growth of teachers kept pace with the increase of pupils at elementary schools, with rates of increase being 3.83 and 3.46 respectively, though the number of pupils per teacher was and still is too big, as shown in Table 4. The picture on the high school and college levels is much more disparate. While the numbers of high school and college students increased 12.6 times and 18.2 times respectively, that of teachers increased 9.4 times in high schools and only 3.6 times in the colleges. The picture becomes clearer when the number of students per teacher is compared.

TABLE 4
NUMBER OF STUDENTS PER TEACHER AT
VARIOUS LEVELS

	1945	1964
Elementary schools	69.7	62.6
High schools	26.3	35.1
Colleges	5.2	26.7

In high schools the rate of increase in school facilities, 11.25, kept an even pace with the rate of increase in number of students, 12.61, during the twenty-year period under consideration. Though the elementary schools have improved somewhat in terms of pupil-teacher ratio, the ratio is still unfavorable, and there is also a drastic shortage of classrooms. The situation is particularly difficult in the colleges, however. In humanities and social science departments the student-teacher ratio is 50:1 or more in some instances. In any event, it can be concluded that Korean educational institutions on all levels are over-crowded, understaffed, and drastically lacking in adequate physical facilities and equipment.

Intellectuals and the University in a Changing Society. Thanks to the widespread aspiration for education, the literacy rate in Korea is comparatively high. Twenty-two percent of the total population is in school, and the literacy rate is officially estimated at over 90 percent, although those who can both read and write with ease constitute about 70 percent. The ratio of university students to the whole population is 0.5 percent, and the ratio of university students in the capital to its population is 3 percent. The existence of a multitude of underpaid college graduates certainly engenders a variety of social and political problems, but equally undeniable is the fact that they play the role of educating the people and serving as a catalyst when circumstances permit. In Korea, the traditional veneration the common people hold for the intellectuals' persuasion and reasoning permits them to wield substantial influence on the general public. Political power, however, comes into the process inevitably in this highly centralized and overwhelmingly political society. Hence there is, in turn, a political flavor to the intellectuals' activities. The degree and nature of political assistance and hindrance are independent variables in the intellectual's position and role in Korean society.

With no serious regional difference, no religious rift, no clear class cleavages, and only a single language, Korean society seemed to have a smooth way ahead when liberal democracy was proclaimed as the underlying principle of the newly independent government in 1948. But, in addition to other conditions unfavorable to rapid modernization, the government could not eliminate the traditional trait of authoritarianism, especially under the autocratic first president, Syngman Rhee. The people, too, did not change their traditionally ambivalent attitudes toward government. They admired, followed and relied on the powerful central government, but at the same time they hated, despised and tried to avoid it. Because too much depended on the government, the intellectuals naturally tended to be critical of government policy. For its part, the government simply tended to ignore their criticisms. When they became a nuisance, the government suspended newspapers or harassed professors by the use of police surveillance, a legacy from the colonial period. Fields of academic research were restricted and articles had to be written with extreme caution. The Rhee government failed not only in providing and utilizing academic resources but also in according academic freedom to the university. It is no wonder, then, that one of the slogans in the 1960 student uprising concerned freedom for the university.

After the downfall of the Rhee regime, there were substantial changes in the academic situation. There was a one year interlude between the student uprising of April 1960 and the military coup of May 1961, during which professors swarmed to government organizations and agencies, and flooded newspapers and magazines with articles on a scale never seen before. However, the weak Chang Myŏn government proved to be incapable of effectively utilizing this academic assistance. Immediately after the 1961 coup, the military regime felt compelled to draft academic resources in helping to organize and operate an entirely new government from scratch. Large numbers of professors were called on to serve in various fields of government for advice and consultation. But these professors came to be disillusioned by their limited influence; and the government was disappointed in the professors who, in its view, were ignorant of reality, involved only in idealistic and irrelevant arguments. In effect, each expected too much of the other. Though some professors still helped the government in one way or another, the university community was now back to its previous state of confinement and isolation on the campus.

Student Activism. Korean society has experienced various kinds of student activities during the past 22 years. Important events are explained below by categorizing them into periods by particular regimes, since student activities were defined to a substantial degree by the attitude of the government as well as the existing social environment.

1. *American Military Government (1945-1948).* The liberation threw the whole of the small student community into the political arena. The student community was divided ideologically into left and right wings. The left wing was led by a small nucleus of communist students who had survived underground during the Japanese period, and who functioned as a student league of the communist party. The right wing was less cohesive and was torn into several factions. Unable to take unified action, they individually joined the rightist parties and organizations. Since no election was held and no participation in the governing process was allowed under the military administration, the students came back to wage a fratricidal fight on the campus. Meetings of the student association were the scene of constant scuffles between the left and the right on ideological issues, but the initiative was always taken by the left which was more aggressive and sophisticated in its arguments. The leftist students focused on the boycotting of "reactionary" professors, protesting against the dismissal of leftist professors, and demanding a voice in the management of the university. The consolidation of one strongly leftist college and more rightist colleges into a national university in 1946 touched off a general student strike which lasted for several months.

These incidents took place amid tremendous social upheaval and in the absence of any restraint by the military government. Despite the apparent campus issues, the underlying issues were for or against the American military government, for liberal democracy or Marxism, and other issues of an ideological and nationalistic character. As the leftist parties began to go underground, leftist students slowed down their campus activities, agitating sporadically for "democratic" education. They were either converted or went to North Korea in 1950. The rightist students, on the other hand, accepted the existing political and social order, and saw no reason to advocate political activities on the campus after the underground left had ceased to take the initiative. Campus issues as such were considered too minor for serious dispute. Active rightist leaders simply joined the existing political parties and ran for public elective offices after graduation, although they maintained close ties with their personal followers on the campus.

2. *The Syngman Rhee Regime (1948–1960)*. The first half of the Rhee period saw no student activity. Students were satisfied with the establishment of a sovereign government (though limited to the south), respected the national leader, President Rhee, and hopefully waited for the vigorous development of the country. Furthermore, the Communist invasion of 1950 and the resulting chaos simply did not allow students to engage in independent activity since many of them were in the army and the rest were living in a social environment which made student action impossible. Students, however, were mobilized on various occasions by the government to show their support of government policies. Students on every campus were grouped by the government into a Student Defense Corps, which replaced the student associations for the purpose of regimentation. The number of university students was not as large at that time as it was to become later; therefore the government's control function was not so difficult. The Rhee regime's authoritarian character began to show its signs gradually, but the students, along with their elders, were resigned to think of it as an unavoidable evil when the nation itself was in danger.

With the start of the latter half of Rhee period, the picture gradually changed. The armistice had been signed and the strains were slowly fading away from everyday life. At the same time, Rhee's oppressive measures against opposition parties and the press grew more evident. These actions began to stir the university students who were especially sensitive to the political climate based upon their value-oriented and strongly idealistic inclinations. In addition, the number of students was rapidly expanding, but was not as large as it was to become by 1960. The constitutional amendment to allow Rhee a third term presidency intensified the popular and student support for the opposition. Many students privately helped the opposition party in the presidential campaign of 1956. When the opposition candidate suddenly died of a heart attack during the campaign, hundreds of students participated in a spontaneous demonstration by carrying the casket to the gate of the presidential palace to show their anger at the government. The next year when the adopted son of Rhee was admitted to a law college through the back door, students of that college went on strike both to protest against the college administration and to show their dislike for Rhee. The strike was suppressed but succeeded in fact because the son dared not remain at the institution, though he had attended classes for a brief period.

The intensified oppression and apparent corruption of the Rhee regime finally induced an explosion on Korean campuses in 1960. Rhee's authoritarian and patriarchal posture was still unchallengeable, but difficulty arose when he tried to get his running mate for the vice-presidency elected. Illegal electioneering by the ruling party and suppression of the opposition party's campaign became known to the students. Small groups of university and high school students, ranging from a few hundred to one thousand, participated in sporadic and spontaneous street demonstrations in provincial cities. On March 15, the day of the presidential election, demonstrations on a large scale were mounted by citizens and high school students in a provincial town, Masan, where election irregularities were so flagrant that many citizens were not allowed to vote. Police suppression by clubs, tear gas and bullets seemed to calm demonstrations by high school students in other provincial towns. Unfortunately for the government, the abandoned corpse of a high school boy with a tear gas shell stuck in his eye was found by a fisherman three weeks later in Masan. Angry demonstrations by high school students followed and spread to other provincial towns.

In the meantime, university students in Seoul had been secretly discussing possible protest actions. Since there was no national association of university students, and the staff of the Student Defense Corps was considered to be a stool-pigeon for the government, unofficial and self-appointed individuals in various universities took over the student protest leadership. Students of Korea University staged a street demonstration on April 18. Starting from the university campus, more than three thousand students marched in columns to break through police defense lines and finally succeeded in holding a sit-in rally in front of the National Assembly building. In the beginning the police thought it would be wiser to let students march peacefully than to restrain and anger them. When flocks of citizens poured out on the street to cheer the students, however, the police thought otherwise and ordered underworld hooligans to assault the students on their way back to the campus. The resulting bloodshed provided added impetus to the students.

April 19 saw a large majority of students of most Seoul universities and colleges stream onto the narrow streets of Seoul, medical students in white gowns, girl students in high heels, joined in no time by high school students. Once on the streets, the students were virtually uncontrollable. Foremost in the student outcry were demands for new elections and academic freedom, as well as protests against police brutality and corruption within the ruling party. The police finally fired into the columns of students, resulting in several hundred casualties. Martial law was proclaimed, and Seoul came under army control.

A crisis situation remained for several days while the government tried to appease the students by reorganizing the cabinet. Then, after a series of secret meetings, more than two hundred university professors gathered on April 25 to react to the challenge and filed out on the street for a demonstration to demand Rhee's resignation. The next day students from many schools, including pupils of an elementary school led by their teachers, demonstrated in the streets of Seoul, joined by ordinary citizens. The city was thrown into complete chaos. The troops did not fire on the students but rather let them ride on their tanks around the city. On April 27, Rhee resigned his presidency after a twelve-year reign. A caretaker government was set up to operate until the establishment of a new government.

The outcome surprised everybody, most of all the students themselves who never thought of actually toppling the government by their own initiative. The success of the student uprising was actually to be credited, not only to the students themselves, but also to the long struggle by the opposition party, the persistent resistance put up by the press, the neutrality of the army, the support given by professors, the discreet encouragement of American officials, the people's enthusiastic support of protest movements, the incurable corruption of the bureaucracy under Rhee, and Rhee's own undemocratic behavior. What the students fervently desired was the realization of their collective strength which had been dormant so long under iron-tight governmental surveillance and suppression.

Why the students rose up not earlier but in the particular year of 1960 is a subject for further research. Suffice it to say here that the rigged elections of March that year served as a crucial catalyst for the eruption of general disgust for the accumulated corruptions and injustices of the Rhee regime, and that only the students were in a position to rise *en masse* against the government. Organized labor, businessmen, farmers, and other socio-economic organizations were too dependent on the government for their existence to raise a strong voice against it. The army generals had been skillfully and meticulously manipulated by Syngman Rhee to avert a possible coup. Thus, the students remained the only disinterested group at that time. Furthermore, 1960 was the sixteenth year after the liberation from Japanese rule, which means that most of the college students belonged to the first crop of youth to be immersed in democratic ideas from elementary school. The uprising was by-and-large spontaneous with little preparation and coordination on the part of the students. Precisely because the students were poorly organized, their successful movement was able to take the unguarded government by surprise.

3. *The Caretaker Government and the Chang Myŏn Regime (April 1960–May 1961).* Now that the victory had been won, the students wanted to do something with the power they had gained. A national federation of student associations was formed, and various elements of Korean society including political parties, mass communications media, interest groups and other social and cultural groups solicited student opinion and cooperation. But students now found little or nothing in common with these groups. Political parties were, in their minds, groups of politicians led only by notable personalities with no ideological base; such organizations had little attraction for the students. In addition, the student federation became factionalized.

Unable to agree on a common objective, the students were divided into various groups for specific goals. Leftist students formed their own cliques. Others agitated for severe punishment of high officials of the previous regime, and still others protested the exile of Syngman Rhee to Hawaii. Those who were dismayed by the chaotic political situation formed a student service group to educate farmers during the summer vacation period, only to come back to the campus with bitter disappointment over the farmers' general failure to respond to their efforts. The activities of students during this period resulted in some changes in attitude and tactics. Recognizing the difficulty of pursuing vague principles, some student groups turned to more visible and pragmatic goals. They stopped official cars on the streets to see if they were being used for private purposes. They stopped pedestrians to search for illegal foreign goods. Some of the more ambitious students ran for legislative seats in the National Assembly elections— twelve university students and 33 recent graduates ran to constitute 33 percent of the total number of candidates. None were elected.

With the opening of the second semester in September of 1960, students gathered on campuses and were stimulated to further action by the politicized atmosphere. Two contradictory courses were taken, one practical and toward limited goals, the other more general and value-oriented. With regard to the practical approach, students of some universities rallied and agitated in protest against the raising of tuition and miscellaneous fees and refused in some cases to register. Students of one university staged a sit-in to make the same sort of protest and threw the disliked president of the university out a window (he miraculously suffered only slight injury). Students at another university went on strike, asking for the resignation of the board of trustees. These incidents were all confined to particular universities, but similar events continued to occur on various campuses until the spring of the following year.

The situation was different with those students who were more idealistic and value-oriented. They took up the issue of Korean unification. Unification at any cost was their nationalistic aspiration. They disregarded the danger of Communist infiltration into their ranks and went so far as to demand a meeting with North Korean students. An uncoordinated but visible alliance of student organizations began to form, led by nationalistic students and perhaps by some leftist students. They began to demand that the Chang government take concrete action toward quick unification. Ceaseless and restless agitation continued in the spring of 1961, until the military coup took place on May 16.

Eleven months of turbulent student activity have been dealt with at some length because events of those months typify what university students might do collectively in the absence of self-restraint. The 1960 student uprising aroused the political consciousness of Korean students and made them aware of their potential and actual strength. The causes for which they fought were justifiable ones, in the general view of other elements of Korean society. Their motivations were idealistic and value-oriented. Their uprising was spontaneous and widespread. Their activities were political in nature but voluntary and unrelated to alliances with political parties. And most importantly, their major objective was realized: the deposition of the Rhee regime.

At the same time, some critical assessments can be made. While their political actions were most effective, the students were too inexperienced to have a clear and definite plan of action after their initial success. Student leaders ignited the demonstrations, but were unable to guide them afterwards. The students became an amorphous mass rather than a disciplined movement. And, as mentioned above, the success of the uprising must be credited not only to the students but to other elements in Korean society, especially the army and the general public whose nation-wide support was the final blow to the Rhee government. The students became disorganized and divided, and proved incapable of sustaining a coherent movement. Once given the free atmosphere of the weak Chang government, they tended to become irresponsible. Groping for an ideological common tie but unable to find one, their easiest recourse was to nationalism—a nationalism that was sentimental and only vaguely defined.

4. *The Park Chung-hee Regime (May 1961-   ).* Some young army officers had planned a revolt against the Rhee regime after the March elections and before the student uprising of April of the previous year, either alone or in alliance with the students. Failing in this and after waiting for another year, the young officers mounted a successful coup on May 16, 1961. The military junta immediately disbanded all student organizations. At the same time, alarmed by the large size of the university student population, the military government planned to reduce the number of universities and colleges and at the same time to decrease the total number of students to 50,000, less than half of the then existing number. This failed to materialize as planned due to subtle manipulation and pressure from the universities, whose organic desire for survival and growth knew no obstacle.

After the 1963 general elections of October and November for the presidency and the National Assembly respectively, the military government changed into mufti, and the new civilian government, composed of the same top leadership, took office in December. The first thing it had to worry about was the students. With the coming of spring, and April in particular, the police and the government began to feel uneasy, since the season of student demonstrations, or at least of student rallies on the campus, generally starts then. The season opens not only because the freezing winter wind is replaced by the soothing April breeze, but also because the memory of the great student uprising of 1960 tends to stir the young student generation. One demonstration even occurred under the strict military rule in June of 1962. On that occasion students of two universities, one thousand from each, demonstrated near their respective college gates, unable to push onto the streets because of a police cordon. The demonstration was prompted by rumors that American soldiers were lynching Korean nationals. The students demanded a status of forces agreement which the Americans were hesitant to agree to. There was one widespread rumor that the demonstrations were instigated by the Korean government to expedite negotiation toward such an agreement. In any event, the issue was a highly technical one, and the student demonstration failed to have any impact. It became apparent, however, that the students could easily be stirred by nationalistic feeling.

Three relatively quiet springs passed under the military regime. However, the spring of 1964, the first after the return to civilian rule, was due to be a noisy one. Nationalism was again the prime mover. The particular issue was the "humiliating" posture of the government in negotiating the normalization of diplomatic relations with Japan— a process which had been going on for some time. Rallies were organized on every campus; later students filed out onto the streets, to be clubbed and tear-gassed by the police. Thousands of students, braving the tear gas, participated in street demonstrations. A week later, the government decided it would be better to persuade the students than to suppress them. The President met eleven student representatives to try to explain the normalization situation. The next day cabinet ministers tried to clarify to more student representatives that the government was not taking a humiliating posture to Japan. Student leaders called off the demonstrations, hoping that more favorable signs would appear in the negotiations. The government seemed at that point to want to make use of the student demonstrations to elicit from the Japanese more favorable terms in the final agreement. But diplomatic negotiation on such a sensitive issue could not be made in the open, nor could it be concluded in a short time. The students became dissatisfied and rose up again in May, only to face stern treatment by the government this time. Unable to break through police lines which were now reinforced by a provincial police force called to Seoul, the students went on a sit-in and hunger strike on the campus. Provincial students then followed the example of Seoul students. Momentum reached a point whereby several thousand students succeeded in swarming into the central district of Seoul. Martial law was proclaimed and schools were closed, thereby forcing the students to take vacations, both academic and political.

Demonstrations of the same nature on the same issue occurred the next spring while normalization talks were still going on. Troops were again called to Seoul, and schools were closed for another enforced vacation. The only difference was that 52 leading students and 18 "political" professors were expelled from the universities by order of the government. Demand for their reinstatement was made by students in September when the campuses were opened again. However, demonstrations were crushed. Troops pursued students into at least two university campuses, hitherto sanctuaries for the students, and the lesson was learned. Nobody dared to plan rallies on campus, not to speak of street demonstrations. With the signing of the Korean-Japanese normalization treaty in December, the students decided to focus their activities on specific issues rather than on vague and general questions. However, with bitter memories of the harsh measures applied to professors and fellow students and under the iron-tight surveillance of the university administration and police, the students let the spring and summer of 1966 pass without rallies or demonstrations. When September came, however, there was a report of smuggling of consumer commodities by Korea's largest private enterprise company with the tacit collaboration of the government. Students felt compelled to protest against the alleged smuggling and against the alleged government corruption. A few small-scale student rallies were held on the campuses, but were quickly quelled by the university administrations. Student leaders of the rallies were severely punished, and no further demonstrations were attempted.

In the spring of 1967 campuses remained calm. With the Presidential and National Assembly elections coming up in May, the government was in an embarrassing position vis-a-vis possible student demonstrations. The government felt compelled to quiet any demonstrations which might occur, but not so harshly as to diminish the government's reputation. By this time two major issues had been resolved with the normalization treaty with Japan and a status-of-forces agreement with the United States, concluded in February 1967. The issue of unification of the northern and southern halves of the country was still too vague to grapple with. Another alternative was to concentrate on the university authorities and campus affairs. The spring wind in Korea always seems to decide the path of the students.

The May 3, 1967, presidential election caused little stir among the students, but the succeeding National Assembly general election of June 8 again touched off angry demonstrations by a small number of secretly but well-organized students at universities in Seoul and the provinces. Election irregularities, which the government admitted in part, reminded the students of the April Uprising of 1960, the direct cause of which had been the preceding government-rigged elections. After a series of scuffles between students and police, the universities and colleges went "voluntarily" into early summer vacation, barring the students from chances and places for gathering. Campuses reopened in September under relatively normal conditions.

Almost two years went by before the students were aroused again by political issues. The incumbent president was prohibited by constitutional provisions to run again after his second term which was to end in the summer of 1971. After considerable speculation in the spring of that year, the government announced the draft of a constitutional amendment which would be voted on by the National Assembly in September and put to a national referendum thereafter. The amendment would allow a third four-year term for President Park. University students started the usual pattern of spring rallies, street demonstrations, and ready acceptance of punishment by university authorities as well as by the police. Most universities and colleges again went into early summer vacation.

This time, however, the reopening of campuses was accompanied by more troubles. During the night of September 14, the government party convened secretly to vote for the constitutional amendment in a hall across the street from the National Assembly building which at that time was being besieged by members of the opposition party. Schools were again thrown into a state of confusion with the continuation of rallies, demonstrations and hunger strikes. After overwhelming ratification of the amendment by a national referendum on October 17, students reluctantly returned to classes, though they let it be known they were doing so under protest. During the spring of 1970 renewed student protests were based upon a demand for readmission of fellow students who had been expelled from school because of their participation in various sorts of student protest during the previous year, as well as against a newly implemented compulsory military policy for all able-bodied students. The demonstrations died down in time for final examinations in June and early July.

The May 1971 election for the presidency prompted only intermittent disturbances by the students; however, the June National Assembly elections provided the focal point for students who criticized not only alleged election irregularities and compulsory military drill but also alleged severe corruption in the higher echelons of government. Campus rallies and street demonstrations accompanied by police tear gas, student stone throwing, and student punishment were followed again by an early summer vacation. After universities reconvened in the fall, students demanded reinstatement of purged fellow students as well as a cleanup of corruption in government circles and the abolishing of compulsory military drill on campuses. The culmination of volatile confrontations between police and students was direct military intervention which closed down the eight most troubled universities. Armed soldiers camped on these campuses for more than two weeks. Subsequently reopened colleges and universities remained calm during the fall of 1971, probably due to cold weather and the need for students to prepare for final examination.

Two years went by, much to the chagrin and disappointment of student radicals, without any campus disturbance. In the fall of 1973, however, class boycotts, rallies and demonstrations unexpectedly erupted on several major university campuses. The usual pattern was followed by authorities in dealing with the situation: early winter vacation, punishment of student leaders and subsequently, backing down from the punitive measures. Causes of the student unrest this time were twofold: firstly, a voicing of concern to the government against possible economic servitude of Korea to Japan; secondly, demand for democratization of government policies along with criticism of the mode of operation of the government's intelligence network. This situation continued through the winter of 1974.

In conclusion, it can be projected that there will be no end to student activism in Korea in the coming years, though its extent and nature may vary from time to time. Neither the students nor the government can be the final winner in their periodic altercations: the students obviously are not the ultimate holder of power in Korea, while the government, even with its monopoly of power, cannot pursue any anti-student policy beyond a temporary show of strength. Student activities serve the function of calling attention to crucial social, economic and political problems, though student activists can never succeed in pushing the government into hurried remedial measures in response to student demands. Student rallies and demonstrations undoubtedly will remain as an ongoing phenomenon though they cannot have substantial impact on the main currents of Korean society.

KOREAN STUDENT UNIVERSITY LIFE

Student Career Patterns. The prestige of a student is generally determined by the social reputation of the university which he attends, regardless of his academic achievement or field of study. The general reputation of a particular university is, therefore, the main determining factor when a high school graduate chooses a university. Among the colleges and universities with programs of four years or more, there are ten which stand above others in the quality of students, faculty and facilities; three in particular—Seoul National University, Korea University and Yonsei University—belong to the uppermost bracket, at least in the public image. Students of these three have consistently been leaders in student demonstrations and political activity. Korea University was instrumental in the 1960 uprising. Seoul National University, especially its College of Arts and Sciences, played a leading role in the 1964 demonstrations. Yonsei acted as a crucial helper in both instances.

Students in other universities and colleges seemed to wait for cues from these three institutions before and during the demonstrations.

It is significant that these three universities, along with half a dozen universities on the next level in reputation and/or quality, are located in Seoul. In terms of both quantity and quality, universities are concentrated in Seoul. More than two-thirds of the universities and colleges in Korea with programs of four years or more, that is, 37 out of 74, are in the capital city. Furthermore, the student population is heavily concentrated in Seoul. Over 70 percent of the students in higher education—about 100,000 out of 140,000—live in Seoul. The reason for this concentration is manifold. Traditionally, all sorts of social and cultural activities and institutions have been concentrated in Seoul. Education is no exception to this rule. Graduates of provincial high schools who can afford to do so invariably go to universities in Seoul regardless of their quality. Nearly 60 percent of students in Seoul are from the provinces. Secondly, Japanese policy brought about a reaction after the liberation. The Japanese had built a small number of universities and colleges in Seoul and only vocational colleges in the provinces. Thus, provincial youths wishing to study social sciences and humanities, which had been suppressed and discouraged during the Japanese period, naturally tried to go to Seoul. Also, many (prestigious) high schools are located in Seoul. Few graduates of Seoul high schools apply to provincial universities or colleges, though graduates of good provincial high schools are most eager to go to Seoul.

The heavy concentration of university students in Seoul was an important contributing factor in the frequent demonstrations in the capital. There is also a heavy concentration of population in Seoul, which contains nearly six million people, about 16 percent of the entire country's population. The dense population provides a setting for a potentially explosive situation, and student demonstrations contain the potential for sparking more widespread demonstrations.

In recent years, however, students have tended to be preoccupied with their ordinary career aspirations. They are haunted by the thought of examinations, not simply one-hour exams or term exams but primarily college or university entrance examinations. College students are also worried about employment examinations long before graduation. College graduates in Korea are interested not only in employment in the government bureaucracy, as is the case in some countries, but also in various other fields of employment including private enterprise. Many go to the army after graduation. Still, chances of employment are very limited for many college graduates. Limited openings force the employees to hold employment examinations for the applicants, in spite of, or because of, the prevailing nepotism. Sometimes the ratio of competition goes as high as 100 to 1 for choice positions. College students are, therefore, obliged to prepare for them for one or two years prior to graduation by studying sample questions. However, with economic improvement in the past few years, jobs for qualified aspirants have become more generally available and the situation has become somewhat relieved as of 1971.

The same nightmare tends to haunt high school students. High schools are, in fact, preparatory schools for colleges. Both teachers and students stress preparation for the all-important entrance examinations, the average ratio of competition in this case being about 3 to 1 or 4 to 1 at universities of the highest reputation. In 1971 the ratio was 4.3:1 at Korea University; 2.5:1 at Yonsei University; 3.7:1 at Seoul National University; and 2.3:1 at Ewha Womans University. The ratio has fallen dramatically from the situation in the mid-1960's when prestige universities sometimes had as many as 18 applicants for every student slot available. In 1969, the government instituted a preliminary qualifying examination which students were required to take in order to apply at particular universities. This automatically cut down the number of applicants to colleges and universities. The same gloomy situation governs the middle schools. Gates to high schools and some good elementary schools used to be as narrow as those at higher levels. But open admission was adopted nationally for elementary schools in 1967 and for middle schools in 1969, thus freeing pupils from strenuous preparation for entrance exams.

To realize his high aspiration for education a student thus must overcome various stages of examinations. The ratio of graduates going to higher school levels decreases as the level of education becomes higher, but the rate and degree of competition never decreases. Sixty-seven percent of middle school graduates go to high schools, and 32 percent of high school graduates go to colleges. However, since entrance to college is the last stage in the educational career, the competition at that stage is more intensive than at lower stages. And many of those who fail in the entrance examinations to the most prestigious universities try again the following year at the same universities instead of downgrading their choices. Competition has become so severe and the obsession to succeed has grown so strong that, in the case of entrance examinations to the most prestigious universities held in February of 1969, over 60 percent of those who passed the examinations and were admitted to the universities are known to have tried the second time, some for the third or fourth times.

This pattern of student recruitment has varied effects on the behavior of university students. When they enter the universities after so many years of continuous preparation for entrance examinations, they suddenly feel a sense of liberation. Except for those majoring in medicine and some fields of natural sciences, most students do not study so diligently. This tendency is most evident in cases of students majoring in social sciences and humanities; they are usually given very few assignments and therefore any study that they undertake is largely voluntary. This situation is apt to turn students' interests to things other than study. Lack of adequate pocket money to spend for recreation and restrictions on free association between the sexes create discontent and frustration. Departments in social sciences and humanities have produced more leaders and participants in demonstrations and rallies than those in the natural sciences. Most leaders in student demonstrations have been those majoring in political science. Students in colleges of medicine and natural sciences have not generally participated in demonstrations except in the case of the 1960 uprising.

Also, students of the first-class universities tend to feel responsible for guiding the student movement. This was the case with the students of Korea University in 1960, and with those of Seoul National University in 1964. Another reason for this centralized leadership may be that these students are actually wiser and more effective than those of less eminent universities in planning, organizing, and directing the demonstrations.

But there are, on the other hand, elements inherent in the present system of student recruitment which tend to discourage an active student movement. Students tend to be cautious in order to maintain their prestigious institutional relationships and finish their student careers without interruption. Also, since a degree from a first class university means better employment opportunities, students in those universities tend not to take hasty and reckless actions. Once a student is expelled from a university for political reasons, he cannot normally be enrolled in any other university, by order of the government.

In the same vein, a high percentage of students admitted to the universities, tend to be those who in recent years have become less predisposed than before to student activism. Many years of hard study since childhood make the students relatively docile and nonactivistic. This tendency has become more apparent in the past few years as the entrance examinations have become more competitive and harder to pass.

Students in the military ROTC program are particularly in a position requiring cautious behavior. They are allowed into the program at the beginning of the junior year if they have acquired average grades of B and if they have a record of good conduct. Therefore, students hoping to be recruited and to stay in the ROTC try to remain aloof from politics; otherwise they could be ruled ineligible for ROTC participation.

All these factors combine to make students in the upper division classes cautious, even those who might wish to participate in politics. The tendency since 1964 has been for students in the junior and senior classes to hesitate to become openly involved, and instead remain behind the scene, agitating and encouraging the freshmen, who are not yet so restrained and cautious.

There is also the problem of employment of graduates. Hiring organizations usually impose an age limit on applicants in order to get the best of a new crop. And questions asked in the employment examinations are based on the content of the present university curricula, and also on topics related to recent domestic and world events. All students, therefore, tend to neglect their college courses when they are trying to prepare for employment examinations. Students know that many applicants do not successfully pass these employment examinations before their second or third attempts, and do not want to "waste" time on the university campus when they can be preparing for the all-important exams.

Many students serve in the army during their university years. Since two years and a half of military service after graduation means that students forget much of what they learned and that they have to study anew to prepare for employment examinations, most students prefer to fulfill their military service obligation during their school years. The prevailing tendency is to go into the army at the end of the sophomore year in order to have two more years at the university after discharge. This is an ideal plan in terms of employment opportunities, because larger hiring organizations require the fulfillment of military service as a prerequisite to employment and at the same time want to employ the latest graduates. Slightly less than half of the junior and senior students belong to this category, and they are usually more mature after their military experiences. They, together with the ROTC students, constitute more than half of the junior and senior students, thus producing a more restrained atmosphere on the campus.

On the whole, it may be said that the changing character of student experience in recent years has made the students take a more cautious attitude toward their collective activities than did their predecessors.

Problems of Student Life. The students' difficulties begin with initial registration. University entrance fees for beginning first-year students plus tuition and miscellaneous fees for the first semester amount to nearly U.S. $300 at private universities and about $75 at national universities. Thereafter, tuition and fees at private institutions average about $200 per term, and at national universities about $60. (The enrollment in national universities is about one-fourth of the total college enrollment.) That means that students in private universities pay about U.S. $400 for one academic year in a country where the per capita gross national product is slightly less than U.S. $400. Therefore, registration fees are a considerable burden for students and their parents. It is estimated that the total amount of those fees for universities, high schools, middle and elementary schools constitutes about one tenth of the total amount of currency circulating in the nation at the beginning of any given semester.

Living expenses are an additional problem for the students, especially for those not living with their parents. Lack of dormitory facilities is characteristic of most universities, and this forces all students living away from home to take rooms in boarding houses. Shortage of housing in general and the scarcity of money make it convenient for several students to share a small room. The result is usually a continual bull session, sometimes leading to the planning of political actions and the improvisation of a "factory" for printing handbills and posters for distribution during student rallies and street demonstrations. Many students living away from home prefer to live in houses where they receive room and board and some money by tutoring sons or daughters in the family who are attending high school, middle school, or elementary school. The luckiest students are those who live with their families, especially if those families earn more than a modest income.

Little study has been made concerning the way in which students' life styles affect their roles in student activities. However, one can generalize as follows: upper middle class students living with their families are least likely to get involved in rallies or demonstrations, since their conservative family backgrounds and their parents' daily supervision function as a brake on any hasty judgment or action; those students who are tutoring are in the second most difficult position to participate in risky political activities, since the ubiquitous and continuous examinations at various levels of schools force them not to miss their tutoring duties too often, and since rallies and especially demonstrations usually entail the possibility of getting arrested or detained by the police. Moreover, the knowledge of their active participation by the parents may endanger the tutoring job itself. Students in the remaining category, those who are away from home but do not need to have tutoring jobs or other kinds of part-time employment, are the most susceptible to political involvement. One survey of the 1960 uprising seems to support this hypothesis in part. During that upheaval, in which almost all students seem to have participated, many surprisingly avoided the turmoil. The ratios of participants against nonparticipants were: 25 percent to 75 percent in cases of students studying and living with their families in Seoul; and 44 percent to 56 percent in cases of those studying and living by themselves in Seoul, away from their families. Sanction and supervision by families seem to wield no little effect on student activism.

Students who belong to the last category seem to have come from middle-class families of Seoul, from the upper middle class of provincial cities and towns, and the upper class of rural areas. The middle class in Korea reflects some noteworthy characteristics. Its members are above the average intellectual level and often have a good educational background. Socially they still receive due respect for their intellectual ability or social status, though not as much as they might wish. On the economic scale, however, they are below the middle point. Mainly salaried men and lacking substantial means, they are the most affected by rising inflation and frequently harassed by increasing debts. Political change, social upheaval, and economic metamorphosis have been so abrupt, enormous, and frequent in Korea in recent years that the salaried middle class has become relatively poorer while wealth has been accumulated largely in the hands of the relatively few *nouveau riche*. The provincial upper class, composed mostly of landlords, holds the same disadvantageous position vis-a-vis the more dynamic *nouveau riche* business interests concentrated in the cities. This kind of family background is strongly reflected in the way of thinking and attitude of those students who come from these more economically depressed strata of Korean society.

In summary, the most politically active students are neither the more wealthy nor the poorer students, but those of middle-class backgrounds. They bring an idealistic and value-oriented perspective to their academic environment. A qualification to be made here is that the collective activities of these students from middle-class backgrounds tend to be relatively moderate. In the 1964 and 1965 demonstrations more radical behavior was noticed primarily among a limited number of students from extremely poorer family backgrounds. More recent demonstrations have required more adamant and radical attitudes on the part of activist students due to the need for more secrecy, planning and persistence, since surveillance has become more effective and the average student has become less outspoken and demonstrative. The most politically activistic students are said to come from relatively poor families in rural villages, and are prone to resent the growing poverty of the farming areas.

Once he enters the university, the student is required to take an excessive number of class hours. A student, whether in a national or a private university, is required by law to acquire a minimum of 160 credit points for graduation. In addition, eight more credit points are required for military training. Therefore, a student has to take at least 20 credit hours for each semester during his four years. However, most students want to take more than the required number of points during their first two years of college, so that they can have more free time to prepare for employment examinations later. Since one credit point denotes one fifty-minute class a week for one semester, 20 points mean that students have to sit 20 hours a week in class-rooms for an average of eight different courses. Two hours a week are counted as one point for some courses, such as laboratory work or physical training, thus increasing the actual number of class hours. Since classes cannot be arranged to make all students happy, class hours are scattered throughout the day, which means that students have to spend almost all day on campus.

This system of course scheduling derives from the aftermath of the Korean war. University facilities were devastated by the war, and there was no hope of quickly recovering from the damage. Shortage of textbooks and lack of library facilities, in addition to other general inadequacies, made the assignment of homework or required reading almost impossible. Under the circumstances government officials felt that the only way to make students learn anything was to let them stay on the campus for as many hours as possible to listen to lectures. The minimum requirement of class hours was set at 180 points at first, and reduced to 160 points later. The consequence of this system has been laborious and tedious for professors as well as students. Attendance was not and could not be enforced, and the minimum requirement of the students was, in actual fact, to take a one-hour examination for each course at the end of the semester on the basis of notes taken during lectures.

The "school mongers" who mushroomed in this period exploited the situation, simply providing classrooms to hold as many students as possible. The student-teacher ratio was most unfavorable. Expulsion of a student was unthinkable even if his academic record was extremely poor because it meant instantaneous military conscription for the student and a loss of registration fees for the university. This state of affairs lasted for several years and its effects were felt even longer.

The 160-point system makes it virtually impossible for students to find much time for independent reading. Textbooks are now being published in larger quantities than in the past, but the prices are prohibitively high for many students. Library facilities are poor, too. There is no single university with a library which can seat more than one-tenth of the students enrolled. Assignments have been difficult to give for various reasons, including a shortage of accessible reference books and the students' lack of time for homework. Outside studying is usually left to the students' own initiative and ingenuity. In July of 1972 the Ministry of Education announced an experimental program in five universities to reduce the required four-year courseload to 140 hours. If successful, implementation throughout the system of higher education would not be made for several years.

It was said during the 1964 and 1965 demonstrations that the obligation to attend many and frequently tedious classes was one factor which made some students welcome demonstrations, though they themselves did not necessarily participate. The government has been somewhat uneasy about the large numbers of students who feel little obligation to attend classes or carry out independent studies. The Ministry of Education in recent years has encouraged universities to enforce students' attendance at classes, to impose more reading and written assignments, to expel students with poor academic records, and to give more scholarships to students with good marks. However these measures have been only partially executed, largely because of the inertia of both professors and students and a shortage of funds and facilities at most institutions. In partial pursuance of this policy, Seoul National University in 1970 expelled two students for academic reasons and kept 140 more from moving to the next class. The figures were 12 and 130 respectively in 1971. Those expelled had had below C averages for the second or third successive years.

The kind of campus life mentioned above is not true of all students. The prime exceptions are to be found among those majoring in natural sciences including medicine and pharmacy. And in the most prestigious universities some students in the departments of humanities and social science are also an exception to the rule. Science students are loaded with heavy assignments in addition to clinical and experimental work. In the cases of medicine and pharmacy, students have to pass national qualifying examinations before graduation. Entrance examinations to various departments of natural sciences are harder to pass in most cases, and those of the natural science departments of the first class universities are the most difficult of all.

Mainly to promote the natural sciences hitherto neglected, to train more technicians needed for economic development, and partly to see that the number of "troublesome" students majoring in social sciences and humanities is reduced, the government has been endeavoring to reverse the present ratio of students in humanities and social sciences to those in the natural sciences. This ratio now stands at 6 to 4. Thanks to the movement toward modernization and the increasing need for technicians at the growing number of factories, some parents and students have quickly discarded former prejudices with regard to traditional fields of study. The universities, too, are busy increasing the departments of natural sciences and technology in order to attract better students and to receive subsidies from the government. If this tendency continues, the time will come when more students than now will hold relatively apolitical attitudes. A case in point is that of the College of Engineering of Seoul National University. Thanks to recent trends and due to excellent employment prospects for its graduates, the best high school graduates in the nation apply for admission to this College, making the entrance examination perhaps the most difficult in the country to pass. Study after admission is also quite rigorous, forcing some students to do extra work under private tutors. The College is located on the outskirts of the capital, far away from the town center. The isolated location of the College, the nature of the courses, the necessity of strenuous study, and the superior academic quality of its students might have contributed in recent years to the apolitical attitude of these students who were stirred to participate in demonstrations in 1964, but not since.

If it is true that a dedicated student with the promise of a secure future is not likely to be distracted from his studies, the opposite, too, may be true. This is evidenced by students in humanities and social sciences. There are those who originally intended to study engineering, pharmacy, law, economics, or commerce, but enrolled in other departments of lesser interest to them because they gave up applying to departments of their first choice due to the severe competition, or enrolled in departments of their second choice as a result of their poor grades on the entrance examinations. Many students, then, become frustrated after entrance and become more disappointed when they find that their majors will not guarantee employment after graduation. The frequency of producing leaders in past student movements has been greater among students and departments which nurture less promise for the future, such as political science, sociology, and literature.

If one cannot hope to enter a department of his choice in a certain top-class university, the natural choice should be the same department of a second-class university. But there the incurable malady of Korea is in evidence: the mania for the so-called first class school. For example, the results of entrance examinations at Seoul National University held in February of 1967, show that 68 percent of those who passed successfully came from 28 so-called first-class high schools of the nation. Since the three universities known as first-class institutions—Seoul National, Korea and Yonsei—consist of students of generally superior qualifications, more high school graduates want to go to those universities, shunning those of lower reputation. In this process, many are forced to go to departments of their second or third choice, though still in the university of their first choice. Those who are discontented with their majors and would like to shift departments constitute around 30 percent of the university students, a rather high percentage. Dislike of a major field which one does not really want to study, as well as worry about adequate employment after graduation, tends to make students frustrated and restless during their school years.

The relationship between students and professors is generally most cordial. Professors usually stand *in loco parentis*. Students consciously or unconsciously follow the traditional custom of venerating their teachers as second only to their parents. They never smoke in front of professors and few, if any, openly resist their teachers' advice. Professors are often asked for opinions on the students' personal problems. Professors are, thus, in a position to wield a great influence on the students' collective activity, though they are prohibited by law to join political parties or take actions of a political nature. Since the government and university authorities interpret the professors' expression of opinion on student demonstrations as political action, most professors maintain a neutral position, though students usually take the silence of professors as tacit approval of their actions. Though students would like to have more time for consultation with their professors, the latter tend to have little time for this. Student-professor relationships are cordial but not intimate.

The university administrative authorities, consisting of the president, deans of colleges, and officers of various administrative divisions, take a different position from that of the professors. Since any student disturbance means trouble to them, they do their best to discourage student demonstrations. Administrative officials usually end up having to make apologies to the Government and having to rescue detained students from police stations. University authorities thus have tried to urge the students to confine themselves to the campus by letting them demonstrate freely in campus rallies. When students begin to break through police lines in front of university gates, the university authorities seek to discourage them, some times punishing the ringleaders. Relations between students and university authorities are thus, at most, cool.

Realizing that they cannot elicit any overt encouragement from professors and having to face stern opposition from the university authorities, students have tended not to consult with their elders in the planning of rallies or demonstrations. This has been the case particularly since 18 professors were expelled from universities in 1965 because of their articles in newspapers and magazines, and their speeches in and out of campuses which criticized government policies and indirectly supported the students' cause—at that time opposition to the terms of diplomatic normalization with Japan. Immature in their judgment of various issues, especially complicated foreign policy issues, students naturally sought advice from outside, thus opening a channel through which political parties could infiltrate into the campus. The usual pattern has been that the government party accuses the opposition parties of supplying money to the student leaders, while the opposition parties criticize the ruling party for disrupting student activities. This situation could be alleviated by the amendment of existing laws to allow the organization of political clubs on the campus so that the students could dispute, discuss and hold meetings within the confines of the campus, but both ruling and opposition parties oppose the suggestion. The ruling party fears the building up of the organizational strength of opposition parties among the students while the opposition parties suspect that the ruling party would exploit its position by distributing funds and other benefits to the students.

Student Organizations and Extracurricular Activities. Every university has a student association which is similar in organization and is recognized officially by each university administration. Students of every department participate in two elections, one to choose a chairman of the department study club and the other to choose a department "deputy." Department deputies in turn take part in two elections: one to choose the president of the college student association, and the other to choose the president of the university student association. At every election, candidates make speeches stating their views on many subjects ranging from the state of the department, college and the university to the state of the country and world affairs. They also make various promises concerning their future actions if elected to office. Unfortunately, what really matters most seems to be the amount of money individual candidates can afford to spend. It is generally accepted that many candidates buy drinks, give presents, and even distribute cash to students, a phenomenon common to nearly all universities now.

The reasons for the severe campus electoral competition are manifold. Though the department deputies and the presidents of college student associations are little more than honorary positions, the chairmen of department study clubs and the president of the university student association enjoy more than honor and prestige. Originally the study clubs were to promote the voluntary academic study activities of students outside classes by holding discussion groups, inviting guest speakers, and providing funds and facilities for other related functions. But money is necessarily involved in this process, and the study club chairmen have control over the expenditure of funds. The president of the university student association has the same kind of fiscal power on matters pertaining to the university as a whole, as well as to inter-university activities. (There is no permanent body for inter-university activity but occasions arise which require coordination.) The presidency of the university student association is also regarded as a good stepping stone to national politics.

Funds needed for campus election campaigns vary in amount according to the number of students involved and the degree of competition, but they are usually far beyond the resources of individual candidates. The result is that candidates, both for the presidency and the club chairmanship, have to rely on outside sources, i.e., individual politicians, political parties and other agencies which are willing to supply the money in order to gain influence in the university. The ruling party has access to far greater funds than the opposition. It has been suggested that in recent years the comparative inactivity of students in protesting and resisting government policies might be attributed to the fiscal influence of the ruling Democratic Republican Party.

The aim of the study club or student association is largely to promote friendship among students. It organizes various sorts of student seminars, mock parliaments, and other conferences, as well as social events such as festivals and sightseeing trips. Students are not allowed to participate in collective activities of a political nature or those which might conceivably have any relation with current national politics. Since the students' interest in public affairs has traditionally been in politics, it is difficult for students to restrain themselves, when major issues emerge on the national political scene. The usual pattern is for the president of the university student association to act voluntarily or under student pressure and on the advice and consent of his staff to call student rallies on the campus and stage demonstrations in the street, if possible. He is also responsible for coordinating actions with the presidents of other university student associations. This coordination is imperative because street demonstration by students from a single university is certain to be crushed immediately by the police. When the president of a university student association opposes or hesitates to call student rallies for one reason or another, as has often occurred in the past few years, presidents of college student associations may attempt to round up the students of their college. When presidents of college associations choose to remain inactive, the chairmen of department study clubs, alone or in alliance with other departmental clubs, may start the movement. When all students in official positions take negative attitudes, a group of ordinary students may try to assume leadership, but their unofficial position and lack of backing usually makes such a movement short-lived.

A student can run as a candidate for deputy, representing his department in the student council, or for the chairmanship of a department study club only if he has finished a minimum number of required courses with a B grade average or better. This automatically excludes students who fail to achieve a B average for one reason or another. This rule has been rigidly applied in the recent past with the effect of visibly reducing the number of action-oriented student leaders. This situation is reputed by students to be one cause of comparative political inactivity in the student movement in recent years. It would also seem to explain why students with no official position try to take action when student officials show a negative or passive attitude.

Apart from the official student association, there are various sorts of extracurricular student groups including athletic clubs; high school alumni clubs; county friendship clubs composed of students coming from the same locale; study groups; and fraternities. These groups have to have the formal approval of university authorities in order to organize, as well as each time they wish to hold meetings on the campus. Fraternity organizations are sometimes composed of students of several universities but are usually small and only for the purpose of promoting friendship. Of special interest are the county friendship clubs. Since provincial students studying in Seoul generally come from the upper social classes in their respective counties, they attract the attention of politicians from their localities, particularly incumbent or aspiring National Assemblymen who provide the students with favors, benefits, and even money in the form of private scholarships. Since politicians of each party have easy access to the campuses, the students are subjected to various shades of political influence.

In short, the campus is not organized so as to facilitate unified student action and a single movement. Exceptions have been those occasional cases of truly spontaneous and widespread uprisings which lead naturally to an alliance of student groups. The student uprisings of 1960 and 1964 were cases in which students organized spontaneously with little prior planning. Since 1965, however, there has been no such formation of instantaneous organization.

There have been some efforts by the university authorities to promote recreational and other extracurricular activities to curb the students' interest in politics. However, since the political orientation of Korean students is deeply rooted, recreation and extracurricular activities do not seem to be realistic alternatives to the political consciousness and interest of the students.

STUDENT VALUES AND POLITICAL INVOLVEMENT

Value Orientations of University Students. Opinions of university students on political affairs are not known precisely—the political environment is not as conducive as it might be to objective questioning on matters bearing directly on political situations. However, several sociological surveys plus general observations enable one to assemble the known views of the students in order to attempt to gauge their value orientations. Generally speaking, Korean students hold a moderate attitude towards their society. Traditional bonds still restrain them both individually and collectively and prevent total acceptance of radicalism, though they are quick to accept new ideas and modes of life. The idealistic younger generation gropes for new principles and ideas, but the undercurrent always has a strongly nationalistic flavor. They do not usually raise their voices for the redress of individual grievances, but they protest when they think that general values and principles are in danger. Students were asked in one survey if it was wiser to keep quiet on public affairs and thereby stay away from trouble. (See bibliography, Hong, Sung Chick, "Political Diagnosis of Korean Society Through a Survey of the Values of the Military and Non-Military Groups.") While 29.8 percent of those interviewed answered in the affirmative, 61.8 percent said no. The conclusion must be that the larger portion of the students are public spirited. However, this does not mean that they always want to play an active role in public engagement, such as student rallies or demonstrations. Answering another question, 76 percent of the students expressed a desire for some sort of socially rewarding participatory activity during their school years as a preparation for their future, and yet most were not eager to go beyond debating, participating in enlightenment missions in the rural areas, and such. Most were not willing to brave the hazards of street demonstrations which could entail punishment both on and off campus.

As to traditional values, students tend to keep some traditions and reject others. Another survey has shown that one-third of students questioned disapproved of the burdensome tradition of ritualistic ancestor worship, though veneration of the elders is still faithfully observed. (See bibliography, Hong, Sung Chick, "Values of Korean Students.") Concerning marriage, 36 percent of the respondents insisted that the choice of a marriage partner is one's own concern.

The remaining 63 percent thought that the selection of a marriage partner is a cooperative task for parents and children. Of these, one-half thought that children should choose their partners first and ask for their parents' consent afterwards.

Korean students' individual concerns have tended to be closely related with the state of society. The above-cited survey showed that 63 percent of the respondents regard uncertainty about their future life plans as a source of anxiety, reflecting the instability of the society. Twenty-eight percent believe the world is a hazardous place where vicious people live, while 43 percent think otherwise, and the remaining 25 percent see both sides. They generally reflect a substantial sense of idealism and moralism with regard to life goals. Fifty-six percent expressed the desire to be men of integrity and of good character; 12 percent wished to render service to the development of the nation; 9 percent wanted to do philanthropic work; while 10 percent wished to become national leaders. These tendencies reflect, to a considerable degree, the legacy of traditional Confucian education and many years of student nationalistic aspirations and activity.

Values held by the students seem to be strongly influenced by Confucianism and nationalism, and to an extent by democracy. A background of Confucian education and the teaching of ethics courses at the elementary and middle schools still influence the students on such matters as disregard for material comfort, moralism and idealism. Nationalism, too, survives and nationalistic sentiments seem to be increasing despite national independence. The necessity of arousing a national consciousness for modernization and the prevalence of foreign influences in Korean society are continuing concerns of the students. Thus, most of the surveys thus far conducted suggest that the majority of respondents believe that the personality traits most desired for national leaders should be honesty, modesty, and patriotism. And more than half of the student respondents have given the nation as their primary object of geographical, social, and political concern; following were the local community and the world in that order.

Though the students are divided almost equally between those who see Western democracy as suitable for Korea and those who think it unsuitable, and many express hope for the appearance of some new and unique ideological system for Korea, they hold no strong wish for the abrupt and complete overthrow of the fundamental system of the existing society. It is perhaps only natural that students should hold more progressive attitudes than the less educated and most adults, but in Korea students still hold relatively conservative attitudes. A study made on radicalism among Korean students using the Eysenck measure indicates that the average weight of the radical character of Korean students is 5.7. This compares with British political party figures of 5.7 for members of the Conservative Party; 10.3 for those of the Labour Party; and 12.7 for Communist Party members. Student rallies and demonstrations in the past produced more radical and more concrete slogans during the event than those planned and conceived at the start, but they never aimed at the overthrow of the government or the reformation of the social system. Even during the 1960 uprising, most of the slogans were aimed at condemning corruption in government, election rigging, police brutality, and sometimes at demanding freedom of the press and academic research. Only at a later stage were requests made for the resignation of higher government officials and ultimately of the President himself. But never was there a demand for the abolition of the existing political, social, and economic system. If there are students sympathetic to a drastic change in the social system, their number and influence have been negligible.

Conclusions. Korean society experienced a series of large-scale student political activities during the 1960's and the beginning of the 1970's. Some succeeded but most failed in fulfilling their original aims, though undoubtedly these activities have constituted indirect influences on Korean policymakers. Being political, the activities tended to spread and to last in inverse proportion to the ability and determination of the government to subdue them with police and military force.

It is never easy for Korean students to make themselves heard in the nation's political life. Government and university authorities are most reluctant to allow students to express their views freely on matters concerning government policies and actions.

By way of summary, five general traits of Korean student political involvement can be delineated, as follows:

Firstly, students tend to be more value-oriented than issue-oriented in spite of economic hardship and other environmental difficulties. Remnants of traditional socialization and education still influence student behavior in public affairs. Legacies of Confucianism have led the students to ameliorate or negate creature comforts, to take strongly moralistic views on public matters, and to take action only on the basis of universal norms or causes. Protests against specific injustices, such as police brutality and severe punishment of students, have been secondary events which occurred in a series of chain reactions subsequent to the original incidents. Korean students have not tended to demonstrate so much for limited or narrowly selfish aims as for broader goals relating to society as a whole or to correction of social, economic or political injustices.

Secondly, the causes and goals of student collective action are basically political in nature. Election irregularities angered the students in 1960. Alleged lynching of Koreans by American soldiers hurt the students' national pride, and their aim became the earliest conclusion of an agreement on the status of American forces stationed in Korea. Demonstrations of 1964 and 1965 sought double political objectives: to force the government to take firmer attitudes in negotiating with Japan and to give vent to nationalist pride and hatred of Japan. Again in 1966, sporadic student rallies were overtly directed toward the smuggling of consumer goods by a large business firm, but the students' real intention was to criticize the allegedly tacit collaboration of the government in the smuggling business. Demonstrations of 1967, too, were sparked by alleged irregularities in the National Assembly elections in June of that year. Social, economic, or cultural affairs lie outside the students' interest when it involves collective action, unless these affairs have a direct bearing on politics.

Thirdly, all demonstrations and rallies have been and will be anti-government in character. Traditional ambivalence of the people toward officialdom is reflected in the negative attitudes of intellectuals toward the government. The intellectuals, who generally take a more independent stance than the common people, tend to reflect attitudes more of resentment and criticism than of fear and reliance vis-a-vis the government. Their grievances relate basically to the high degree of government centralization and control and to the overwhelming supremacy of the executive. In a sense, the intellectuals have always been anti-government. And the students are by no means an exception to this rule. They are well aware of western-derived democratic principles, including those of academic freedom and university autonomy. They are most sensitive to the intrusion of governmental authority into the campus, though they often tolerate the suppressive measures taken by university authorities. Confucian ethics based on the "trinity" of king, teacher, and father has long disappeared, and the highly centralized government has become an object of bitter criticism by the students, though teachers are still held in some veneration.

Fourthly, student activities are motivated by an idealistic and almost messianic sense of mission. Traditional emphasis on abstract and general knowledge in education is being slowly modified by the increasing tendency toward scientism, but it will take a long time before the students refrain from the habit of making hasty over-generalizations and seeking all-encompassing solutions. Leaders and participants in student political involvements often find difficulty when asked to justify their actions. Young university intellectuals, most of whom are in the 19–23 age group, sometimes consciously overlook the defects inherent in their idealistic positions, believing that their elders are bound too closely to details and practical obligations to be able to act boldly regarding public issues. The prevailing desire of the students for a new "ideological" system more suitable to Korean reality is only another evidence of their idealistic perspective. Styling themselves as the "conscience of the nation and the incarnation of the sovereign people," the students have a tendency to think that the future of the nation rests on their shoulders. To them, elders are too reticent and old-fashioned to adapt to new developments; they feel that the masses of the people are susceptible to being led by an intellectual elite which might be stimulated by or even come out of the student movement. Hence, the student leaders maintain their messianic sense of duty to initiate actions for democracy and modernization in the face of immediate barriers.

Finally, the students are strongly nationalistic. Varying degrees of dependence on China for so many years and, ultimately, complete submission to Japan aroused the strong aspiration for independence in the past. In the students' view, liberation from Japan still did not bring about real independence, because the nation was divided into two parts and varying degrees of foreign influence wield enormous, but not always obvious, power in Korea today. Unification of the two Koreas is a major goal of Korean students and an issue which is bound to continue to arouse student emotions. The United States and Japan, which are the two prevailing foreign influences today, receive both the envy and the resentment of the students. The resentment reveals itself especially when they think that national pride is hurt and the national interest is in danger. Feelings of this kind inevitably result in criticism of the Korean government, which, the students will maintain, must be responsible for allowing an undue degree of foreign influence to infiltrate into Korea.

These observations are not intended to convey the impression that Korean students are strong in organizational terms or that they have a particularly great impact on everyday concerns of their society. Lacking a sustained organization for political purposes and having no desire to participate constructively in the governmental process, the students are considered primarily only as a potential force in Korean politics. Furthermore, their relatively frustrating experiences since the 1964 demonstrations seem to have taught them to be more cautious before taking any collective actions. Various factors, such as the legal prohibition of student political activities, severe punishment of active participants, and factionalism among student leaders, act as major deterrents to the appearance of any coherent student political movement.

Student generations in Korea, past and present, may be grouped roughly into four main categories in accordance with their ages and value orientations: (1) those over 45 years old, (2) those between 35 and 44, (3) those between 25 and 34, and (4) the current student generation, most of whom are under 24. The first group consists of those who spent their high school and college days before 1945 under Japanese rule; they tend to be more nationalistic and patriotic than the other groups. The second group includes those whose high school and college years spanned the late period of Japanese rule and the early years of the independent republic. These personally experienced the 1950 communist invasion; they are essentially nationalistic and anti-communist in their attitudes. The third group includes those who started elementary school under relatively democratic conditions immediately after the 1945 liberation, but grew up under the autocratic practices of the Rhee regime. Members of this group constituted the main force in the 1960 student uprising. The immediate past and current student generation consists of those who started their higher education during the 1960's and who have experienced the apolitical atmosphere of the military regime and its successor civil government. These years under President Park Chung-hee have strongly emphasized economic development and "cultural life," especially since 1965.

The fourth group, consisting of current students and recent graduates, evidences a more drastic departure from the traditional way of student life and thinking than do the members of the third group. Emphasis by the government on economic growth rather than on democratization and political modernization has succeeded in diverting the interest of the general public from political to economic and cultural matters. Most students seem to care mainly for good course grades while in college and opportunities for secure and well-paid employment after graduation. They tend to try to avoid any trouble during college years by disclaiming active interest in politics and other public affairs. At the same time, the possibility of general student uprisings over important questions in coming years must not be discounted. If the tendencies of recent years offer any guidelines for future prognostication, then it seems clear that protests in coming years will be issue-oriented and will arise only when there is an issue of such import as to justify demonstrations.

College and university students who, along with the professors, are more knowledgeable and objective in their scrutiny of public actions and issues than other social groups, could and should be encouraged to contribute more to the development of their changing society. The principle of academic freedom, a tradition established in the West for so many centuries, seems to be the real answer to the problem of politically conscious students in Korea. More academic freedom, genuine and untinged with political motivation, could induce more responsible and relevant attitudes and actions from the students, and from the professors. It can be concluded that, in Korea, widespread social and political disturbances are generally caused more by lack of genuine freedom than by its abundance.

BIBLIOGRAPHY

Bureau of Higher Education, Ministry of Education, *Current Status of Higher Education* (Seoul: Ministry of Education, Republic of Korea, September 10, 1971).

Chung, Bŏm-mo: "Individual Problems of College Students," (unpublished manuscript, College of Education, Seoul National University, 1959).

Douglas, William A.: "Korean Students and Politics," *Asian Survey* (December, 1963), pp. 584–595.

Hong, Sung Chick: "Values of Korean College Students," *The Journal of Asiatic Studies* (Korea University, May, 1963).

Hong, Sung Chick: "Political Diagnosis of Korean Society Through a Survey of the Values of the Military and Non-Military Groups" (A paper presented at the Sixth World Congress of Sociology at Evian, France, September, 1966).

Kim, C.I. Eugene, and Kim, Ke Soo: "The April 1960 Korean Student Movement," *The Western Political Quarterly*, 17 (March, 1964).

Kim, Kyŭng-dong: "Measurement of Confucian Values," *The Korean Journal of Sociology*, 2 (1964).

Kim, Sung Tai: "A Study on the Motivating Factors of the April 19th Student Upheaval in Seoul," *Sung Kyun Kwan University Journal*, 5 (1960).

Lee, Chong Sik: *The Politics of Korean Nationalism* (Berkeley: University of California Press, 1953).

Lyman, Princeton N.: "Students and Politics in Indonesia and Korea," *Pacific Affairs*, Vol. XXXVIII, Nos. 3 and 4 (Fall-Winter 1965-66), University of British Columbia.

Oh, Byung-hun: "Political Attitudes of Korean Voters," *The Journal of Asiatic Studies* (Korea University), 3 (December, 1960).

"Social Participation of Students," *Research Review of the Student Guidance Center, Seoul National University* (Supplementary Issue), Vol. 5, No. 1 (July 1966), pp. 93–138.

"A Survey on the Transfer Problem of Seoul National University Students" and "Freshman Survey in 1965," Vol. 4, No. 1 (August 1967). Also see Vol. 5, No. 1 instead of Vol. 4, No. 1 for the Supplementary Issue (1966–1967) of the *Research Review of the Student Guidance Center, SNU* (the title of the article is "Social Participation of Students").

CHAPTER 6:

The Military and Politics in
Postwar Korea

JOHN P. LOVELL*

The erosion of civil authority and the rise of the military to political dominance in Korea during the period since World War II present a pattern that in many respects is familiar to all who have observed the political dynamics of developing nations in recent decades. In other respects, however, the changing political role of the military in Korea during the period represents a combination of historical circumstances and cultural ingredients that make the Korean case highly distinctive. The case holds interest, therefore, for persons concerned broadly with the study of comparative politics as well as for persons concerned exclusively or primarily with Korean events.

The purpose of the present study is that of analyzing the pattern, including some generally unfamiliar as well as familiar facets, of involvement by the military in Korean politics since 1945. In order to analyze, however, the pattern must be described. Description of political activity of the military in turn requires a rather detailed description of the growth and development of the Korean military establishment. Although the Army has been the most politically significant arm of service in Korea, as in most nation-states, the study focuses on all arms of service—Army, Air Force, Navy (initially termed the "Coast Guard"), and Marines—with some attention also to the police and to paramilitary youth movements, as groups posses-

---

*John P. Lovell is Associate Professor of Political Science, Indiana University. His Ph.D. is from the University of Wisconsin.

sing; many important political resources that are similar to those of military elites.

The following questions are central to our analytical concern. What structural conditions in Korea at various periods of time since 1945 have made the political system susceptible to various forms of political involvement by the military (or by particular factions or components of the military)? To what extent have resources possessed by the military at various periods facilitated or inhibited various forms of political involvement? What values and beliefs of military men have conditioned their behavior in the political arena?

Space limitations preclude a detailed comparison of our findings with comparable data on the role of the military in politics in other nation-states. However, organization of our analysis around these central questions, with discussion proceeding chronologically in order to highlight the dynamics of the relationship of the military to politics, should provide a useful framework for viewing the findings here in comparative perspective.[1]

The task of analyzing in detail the involvement of the military in politics during the period included for review in this volume is a formidable one, the more so because accurate analysis of the role of the military in politics hinges upon a comprehension of the intricate, tumultuous, and elusive phenomena that comprise Korean politics as a whole during this period. To that formidable task, we now turn. The discussion that follows should be read in the context of a more complete account of political events provided elsewhere in this volume.[2] Selected aspects of the political situation will be alluded to here only by way of providing reference points, linking this chapter to others.

AN EMBRYONIC KOREAN MILITARY ESTABLISHMENT

Although the problems confronting the United States Armed Forces in Korea (USAFIK) upon their arrival in September 1945 to occupy the territory south of the 38th parallel were many and complex, the paramount problem was necessarily the maintenance of order. In the three weeks since World War II had ended and before the first American troops had arrived from Okinawa, a semblance of order had been maintained by a variety of self-appointed groups throughout Korea. These included the so-called Peace Preservation Corps of the Committee of Preparation for Korean Independence, which claimed to be the legitimate provisional government of all Korea; a variety of armed political factions; and remnants of the police force which had served under the Japanese (composition of which had been roughly 30 percent Korean). To have attempted to disband various groups and assume full responsibility for the maintenance of order themselves no doubt would have taxed the meager resources of USAFIK beyond capacity.[3] The strategy of the USAFIK command, therefore (after an initial fiasco of reinstating the Japanese authorities and then hurriedly ousting them again), was to assert USAFIK authority throughout South Korea, but to rely heavily upon existing groups to maintain order, assimilating them gradually into a national police force and constabulary.[4]

Police. In October 1945, the former Japanese police academy in Seoul was reopened, and a one-month training course given to new recruits. The core cadre for a police force was provided by those who had had prior experience under the Japanese. Thus three years later, on the eve of the founding of the Republic of Korea, the Director of National Police admitted that 53 percent of all police posts above the rank of lieutenant were held by officers trained by the Japanese, including 9 out of 10 commanders of the Seoul Metropolitan Police. He further acknowledged that many of the Japanese trained policemen were resistant to police methods being introduced under the guidance of Americans.[5]

Constabulary. Early in the occupation, USAFIK postulated the need for supplementing the police force with a formal military establishment of some sort. Thus, in November 1945 a Headquarters of National Defense was established within USAFIK. The headquarters was assigned the mission of organizing a Korean army and coast guard, and training them in the maintenance of peace and order and in making a contribution to national development. Since the police and military roles were largely undifferentiated initially, the headquarters originally embraced both a Bureau of Military Affairs and a Bureau of Police Affairs. However, in April 1946 the latter was given a status independent of the Headquarters of National Defense.

Recruitment into the embryonic military establishment was relatively unsystematic. As in the case of recruitment into the police force, USAFIK depended heavily upon those who had had prior experience under the Japanese or (in the case of the military, but not the police) the Chinese. With a change of Japanese policy in 1937, all physically fit young Korean men had been forced to serve in the Japanese armed forces. Between 300,000 and 400,000 Koreans had served by 1945. Consequently, the postwar pool of men with some prior military experience was relatively large. A relatively small number of those who comprised the pool had served as officers, the most prestigious as graduates of the Imperial Defense College in Tokyo or of the Manchurian Military Academy of the Japanese Army.

In December 1945, the first school for training South Korean military officers was established in Seoul, on the campus of a Methodist seminary. Referred to as the Military English Language Institute, the school actually was the forerunner of the Korean Military Academy. The first students at the Institute consisted entirely of veterans of the Japanese, Chinese, or Japanese-Manchurian armies, and were selected largely from candidates nominated by six of the leading private armed political factions in South Korea. The 200 men who were admitted to the school were given limited training in the English language; but also they were trained in military subjects. At the end of April 1946, after producing 110 graduates, the Institute was closed, being replaced by the South Korean National Defense Officers Training Academy, located in the outskirts of Seoul.[6]

By this time, a constabulary force of 2,406 was in existence. Korean officers to command the first units of the constabulary were selected on the advice of Yi Hyŏng-kŭn, who had been one of the highest ranking Korean officers in the Japanese Army. Support for the constabulary was poor, both in terms of resources (arms, clothing, equipment, funds) and in terms of advice and supervision. On the average, between 1946 and 1948, no more than six American military advisors were available to the constabulary at any one time. These men had to cover such a stretch of territory that their visits to any given unit were necessarily infrequent; furthermore, the advisors were dependent upon interpreters for communicating with Korean officers. One consequence of the lack of adequate American supervision during this period was a heavy reliance by Koreans upon knowledge and methods that had been acquired in previous service with the Chinese, Japanese, or Manchurian armies. Training during the period was limited in scope as well as quality, consisting primarily of drill and instruction in small arms, although some training in mortars and machine guns was provided in spite of regulations by the Department of Internal Security to the contrary.

Coast Guard and Marines. Flourishing smuggling and piracy along the Korean coasts made the creation of a Coast Guard a matter of some urgency. The Coast Guard faced problems of resources and training, however, which perhaps surmounted even those of the constabulary. In the first place, there were practically no vessels available to the Coast Guard. By April 1946, the Coast Guard had commissioned only 33 officers, and had a total strength of 1,011. Until September 1946, when a contingent of fifteen U.S. Coast Guard officers and enlisted men arrived, the South Korean Coast Guard depended for advice primarily upon a handful of junior officers from the American Army. In order to meet long-range needs for a corps of well-trained indigenous officers, a Korean Coast Guard Academy was formally opened at Chinhae in February 1947. In May of that year, a Marine Academy was opened, with 312 students in the entering class.

Korean National Youth Movement. It is interesting to note that in addition to conventional police and constabulary forces established to help maintain order, the U. S. Army Military Government in Korea (USAMGIK) also supported the establishment of a Korean National Youth movement. The KNY movement is of interest, first of all, as a precursor of the "civic action" concept, in which the United States has supported the utilization of indigenous military forces in developing nations to perform activities such as education, construction, sanitation, and other activities designed to further economic and social development. The rationale of "civic action" has hinged especially upon the assumption that military units, with a nation-wide base of recruitment, with discipline, and with technical skills, were ideally suited to provide the impetus for economic and social development.[7] Similarly, the KNY organization was seen by American officials as a vehicle for instilling "character, patriotism, and citizenship" in the Korean people through a trained cadre of indigenous personnel, who would provide training and indoctrination at the village level.[8] As with many subsequent American-sponsored "civic action" programs, however, the political utilization of the KNY by its leaders as a force for politicization and influence largely made a mockery of the official USAMGIK claim that the group was "strictly non-political and non-military."[9]

The fact is that the KNY movement was an officially sponsored rival to a large number (estimated at more than 120 by 1948) of other youth groups that had sprung up in South Korea after World War II, nearly all serving as instruments of various political factions. ("Youth" is a term used broadly to refer to an age span from adolescence to middle age, somewhat in the manner of the composition of "Young Democrat" and "Young Republican" groups in the United States.) The leader of the KNY organization, Yi Pŏm-sŏk, had had long military experience in China, and had worked with American military intelligence forces in underground activity during World War II. With financial support and guidance from USAMGIK, General Yi worked actively to make the KNY movement a major anti-Communist organization in Korea. By the end of May 1948, membership in the KNY was listed at 859,208. In the same month, 33 members of the movement were elected to the first National Assembly of the Republic of Korea.[10]

The Politics of Survival. For virtually the entire period of American military government in Korea (September 1945–August 1948), the existence of nearly all who lived in the American zone of occupation was dominated and circumscribed by the following harsh realities. War, the sudden departure of skilled Japanese technicians and managers, and the division of the nation-state into two zones of occupation had badly disrupted key economic institutions of the nation. The fishing industry had virtually collapsed; trade, which for decades had been largely a bilateral exchange with Japan, was almost at a standstill; fertilizers, which had come primarily from the north, were in short supply; rice production was far below prewar levels; many mines were flooded and inoperable; power and mineral resources, which came mainly from the north, were scarce—and in early 1948, power from the north was shut off completely. The population flow was incessant and chaotic. Hundreds of thousands of Japanese who had resided in Korea were leaving; an even greater number of Koreans from abroad or from north of the 38th parallel were streaming into the American zone of occupation. Within slightly over two years after liberation, more than two million Koreans had migrated to South Korea, roughly half of whom had been living in Japan. Over 800,000 Japanese had left South Korea to return to their native land. Unemployment was widespread, aggravated by the refugee flow. Fuel, which also came largely from the north, was in short supply. Housing was inadequate in view of the growing pressures of population growth. In the summer of 1946, the most severe flood in twenty years destroyed more than 13,000 homes and did severe crop damage. Inflation was rampant.

As it became increasingly apparent to the Korean populace that expectations as to the benefits to be enjoyed from liberation from Japanese rule were not being realized, popular disillusionment mounted, feeding the anxieties and frustrations that had been generated from conditions such as those identified above. Although issues such as trusteeship and elections provided subjects of widespread political controversy and debate, the dominant motivating force behind most political activity under conditions that existed at the time may be accurately described as that of sheer survival. Political struggle at such a fundamental level, taking place in a context of turbulence, placed a premium on skill in manipulating or avoiding formal laws and institutions, and on the command of force and coercion as instruments of political power. Blackmarketeers flourished. Thieves in great numbers roamed city streets and the countryside. Armed bands, political youth groups, policemen, and others with access to instruments of coercion extorted payments of money or food from those unable to resist. Civic disorder and official repression fed upon one another.

The conditions of the time were analogous to those which, in other places at other times, have stimulated an indigenous military elite to employ its force to seize control of government. However, in South Korea at this time, the embryonic military establishment (and all important elements within it) lacked the cohesion, the sense of common political aims and grievances, and above all the political resources, to gain political dominance. In each of these respects, the police, and probably the Korean National Youth movement as well, represented far more potent sources of political influence. The constabulary and Coast Guard combined numbered less than 7,000 at the beginning of 1947, in contrast to a police force of over 25,000, growing rapidly. The police had the added political advantage in many instances of prior experience, and thus familiarity, with the instruments of political control utilized by the Japanese in various Korean localities. Especially advantageous was access to intelligence files that the Japanese had used to keep track of the activities and backgrounds of the local populace. The military, in contrast to the police, remained a relatively unskilled and insignificant group in Korean politics until well after the establishment of the Republic of Korea.

FROM FOUNDING OF THE REPUBLIC TO WAR

Reduction of American military force levels in Korea was part and parcel of the U.S. policy that led to the establishment of an independent Republic of Korea in 1948. Appeals were made by the ROK National Assembly and President that the withdrawal of U.S. troops be delayed until the ROK military could be established on a firm footing. However, pressure upon the United States to accelerate rather than decelerate withdrawal was exerted by an announcement by the Soviet Union of its intention to withdraw all of its forces from Korea by the end of 1948, followed by a resolution of the UN General Assembly asking for the complete withdrawal of all foreign troops from Korean soil. At the end of June 1949, American forces having been withdrawn almost completely from Korea, Headquarters USAF-IK was deactivated. Through an agreement between the American and ROK governments, an advisory function, which American military personnel had performed from the beginnings of the ROK military establishment, was retained. A provisional Military Advisory Group was renamed, in mid-1949, the United States Military Advisory Group to the Republic of Korea (KMAG). However, the number of advisory personnel provided by authorizations for the group was too few to implement the postulated goal of assigning an advisor to every ROK military unit down to battalion size. The number of advisors available to the ROK Navy, Air Force, and National Police was even fewer, proportionately as well as absolutely, than that available to the ROK Army. During the year from the formal founding of KMAG to the outbreak of the Korean War, there were rarely more than a dozen American advisors with the ROK Navy, nor more than half a dozen each with the ROK Air Force and National Police at any one time.

Diluted as the American influence was by factors such as the small number of advisors, their short tour of duty, and their characteristic inability to speak Korean, the influence was still of importance, particularly upon the ROK Army. The year and a half from the founding of the Republic of Korea to the outbreak of the Korean War were a seminal period for the ROK armed forces; the direction and form of development during the period largely were determined by American influence.

Foundations of the ROK Army. Within a year from the founding of the Republic of Korea, thirteen separate educational institutions had been established within the ROK Army. Those that were founded after KMAG began its operations were organized under the direction of KMAG personnel; those that were already in existence were reorganized under KMAG supervision. Particular effort was devoted by KMAG personnel to the Infantry School and to the Command and General Staff College, both of which were founded in September 1949. Instruction at the latter, which at the time was the top level educational institution within the ROK armed forces, at first was given entirely by American advisory personnel.

Another important institution that was reorganized during the period was the Korean Military Academy (KMA). Plans were underway until disrupted by the outbreak of war to move to a four-year program of instruction along the lines of the program at West Point; full implementation of the plans was resumed in 1952. The war also disrupted plans for a more comprehensive program of instruction at various career levels for military professionals. However, by the time of the outbreak of war, more than 9,000 Korean officers and 11,000 enlisted men had graduated from various ROK military educational institutions; the first handful of officers to be sent to the United States for training had also completed their courses of instruction.[11]

Air, Navy, Reserve, and Paramilitary Forces. One might say that a ROK Air Force was created in spite of, rather than because of, the advice of KMAG. American officials feared that the ROK economy could not sustain a separate air force; furthermore, KMAG was not equipped to provide such a force with professional assistance. Nevertheless, after functioning for several months as a branch of the ROK Army, with fourteen aircraft provided by the U. S. Army on the assumption that the craft would be used for routine army liaison tasks only, a separate ROK Air Force was established by Presidential decree in October 1949. An Air Academy, forerunner of the ROK Air Force Academy, had been established at Kimpo Airfield the previous January.

The cadre of the new Air Force was composed primarily of personnel who had had experience with the Japanese Air Force during World War II. For example, Col. Kim Chŏng-yŏl, who was appointed as the first Chief of Staff of the ROK Air Force (later Minister of Defense under Syngman Rhee, and Ambassador to the United States under Park Chung-hee), was a graduate of the Japanese Military Academy and of the Japanese Army Air Force Flying School. He had served both as a squadron commander and as a group commander with the Japanese during World War II.

Just as the United States government disapproved of the creation of the ROK Air Force, it did not look favorably upon the aspirations of the ROK government to expand its coast guard into an operational navy. Consequently, even after the Coast Guard was redesignated the ROK Navy in August 1948, American officials and advisors continued to refer to the organization as the Coast Guard. In May 1949, the naval college which had been in existence since 1946 was redesignated the ROK Naval Academy, and a four-year course of study was instituted. In addition, during 1948 and 1949 a number of training schools for warrant officers, non-commissioned officers, and seamen were established. Simultaneous with the order instituting the ROK Naval Academy, a Presidential decree was issued creating a ROK Marine Corps, under the jurisdiction of the Chief of Staff of the Navy.

In the case of the Navy, its leading figure initially had received his early training under the Chinese rather than the Japanese. Rear Admiral Son Wŏn-il, first Chief of Staff of the ROK Navy and the man usually credited with having organized the Korean Coast Guard during the American occupation (and later Minister of Defense under Syngman Rhee, as in the pattern of the first Army Chief of Staff), had served for a number of years with the Chinese Coast Guard.

To complete the discussion of the early efforts to organize a military establishment in the Republic of Korea, some mention must be made of reserve and paramilitary forces. The law of November 1948, which set forth the basic organization of the armed services, provided for a reserve force for the Army and the Navy in the form of a National Protectors Corps. A conscription law passed in August 1949 stipulated that the reserves should be placed under the direct control of Army and Navy Headquarters.

In November 1949, an organization to provide young men with military training prior to their induction in formal military service received official status under the title, Youth Protector Corps. Local Units of the Corps were provided with advisors from the ROK Army; within the Army, a Bureau of Youth Defense was established. The Youth Protector Corps, with an estimated 1,250,000 members, was an offshoot of the Korean National Youth movement, whose leader, Yi Pŏm-sŏk, was retained as head of the new organization. The political potential of the Corps is suggested by the fact that General Yi served concurrently as the first Premier of the Republic of Korea and as the first Minister of Defense. Initially this relationship, and the power of the Youth Protector Corps, worked to enhance the political strength of Syngman Rhee. Within a few years, however, Rhee worked systematically to undermine the political strength of Yi and the Youth Corps, which had become a threat to Rhee's own position. In April 1950, the Youth Corps was abolished as an official organization; but it continued to function informally for some time thereafter.

Continued Political Impotence of the Military. Although the years from the founding of the Republic to the beginning of the Korean War were seminal ones for the ROK military establishment, the political role of the military remained limited during this period. Or to state the matter more accurately, if paradoxically, the political *influence* of the military on policy during the period was limited by the relatively small size, inexperience, and lack of organizational cohesion of the military, as well as by the conflicting demands that were made upon ROK military leaders. However, the *activity* of the military during the period was, except for training, *almost exclusively political*. The paradox of a relatively impotent military establishment being actively engaged in political activity is explicable in terms of the intensity of political struggle and intrigue of the times.

The political arena had become sharply and bitterly polarized, with individuals and groups gravitating either to the right-wing leadership of Syngman Rhee or, if opposed to Rhee or his policies or authoritarian tactics, to the left-wing leadership of indigenous Communists. Problems such as those of inadequate housing, monetary inflation, unemployment, and food shortages, which had plagued Korea during the occupation period continued in dire form during the first years of the Republic. Communist efforts to promote insurgency fed other sources of agitation and discontent, and represented the most important political threat to the Rhee regime. Rhee attempted to deploy military units as well as police to quell dissident elements within the society, and thereby to cope with the threat. However, dissidence reached far up the ranks of military units; thus, mobilization of the military in a counter-guerrilla role nearly backfired.

For example, a rebellion led by Communists had broken out on the island of Cheju in April 1948, suppression of which had required the services over a period of months of large numbers of the constabulary, the Coast Guard, and the police. In October of the same year, when the newly-installed Rhee regime ordered elements of the 14th Regiment at Yosu to assist in the suppression of guerrilla forces that continued to hold out on Cheju, a mutiny resulted. The Yosu mutiny, in which Communist members of the 14th Regiment played a prominent role, was followed by a number of other uprisings, and by still more mutinies in the armed forces, including the defection of two Army battalions and the crew of a Navy minesweeper to North Korea. A widespread purge of the ROK armed forces followed, with an estimated 180 officers and over 1,000 enlisted men arrested, executed, or dismissed. Nonetheless, Rhee continued to deploy "purged" elements of the military in an effort to enforce the stringent National Security Law of 1948, and to suppress potential or actual rebellion. According to one estimate, 60 percent of the ROK national budget of 1949 was devoted to such activity; during the final six months of the year, the ROK Army mounted 542 separate counterguerrilla actions.[12] Such actions provided at least some semblance of training for the combat that began in 1950; however, the purges and internal strife had badly weakened an organizational apparatus that was yet in the embryonic stage.

CONSEQUENCES OF WAR

The history of the Korean War has been reported in voluminous detail and need not be recounted here. Rather, brief attention will be focused on those effects of the war that are relevant to our study of the role of the ROK military in politics. Ultimately, such effects included a considerable increase in the political capability of the military, and some increase in inclinations among the military toward political activism. But the initial impact of the first several weeks of war upon the ROK military was that of near-disaster.

Within a week from the time North Korean troops moved south of the 38th parallel, ROK Army Headquarters could account for approximately 20,000 troops, or roughly one-fifth of the estimated strength of the Army a week earlier. The rest were dead, wounded, prisoners of the North Koreans, or deserters, in some cases abandoning their units to flee southward as civilians. ROK equipment at first was no match for the Soviet armor and weapons employed by the North Koreans. Morale was low, and some ROK military leaders seemed to be acting impulsively to the detriment of whatever effectiveness might have been mustered among their units.

To compensate for its loss of manpower, the ROK Army literally combed the streets and countryside conscripting men into the ranks. A ten-day training program was instituted during which, according to an American advisor on the scene, the trainees were expected to learn how to dig foxholes and how to care for their weapons; but the real training ground was the battlefield. A ten-day training program could not produce officers and non-commissioned officers, however; consequently, thousands of Korean conscripts who could not be absorbed into the Army, which lacked the officer and non-com strength to supervise them, were assigned to American Eighth Army units, which could provide the requisite officers and NCOs. Although some Koreans served in American units as soldiers at the squad level, many more were employed by American unit commanders as laborers in the KATUSA program (Korean Augmentation to U.S. Army).

Rebuilding and Expanding the Military. The strength of the ROK Army had been built back up to 82,000 by August 1950. After another setback when the Chinese entered the war in November, the ROK Army rose by February 1951 to its initial strength as of the outbreak of the war of 100,000 (not including KATUSAs).

When General Mark Clark replaced General Matthew Ridgway as Commander of UN Forces in Korea in May 1952, General Clark indicated a desire to have the ROK Army expanded "to its maximum capability," and to have the ROK Navy and Air Force expanded as much "as technical skills of the Koreans permitted and as equipment became available."[13] Previously, as Chief of U.S. Army Field Forces, General Clark had arranged to permit Korean officers to attend the U. S. Army Infantry School, Artillery School, and General Staff College. This program was continued, and indigenous training programs were augmented under the guidance of KMAG during General Clark's tour in Korea, which lasted through the armistice of 1953. Two-hundred-fifty ROK officers went to the United States as the first contingent of the program; upon their graduation in 1952 a second contingent of equal size was sent. By the middle of 1952, most of the indigenous training facilities which had been in existence prior to the war also had been reopened. Thus a full-scale training program in the ROK armed forces had been resumed in the final year of the war.[14]

By the time Dwight D. Eisenhower was elected President of the United States on a platform that included a famous pledge to go to Korea to see for himself what could be done to bring the now-unpopular war to a conclusion, the size of the ROK Army had risen to over 400,000. One of Eisenhower's early acts as President was to authorize the organization of two new ROK divisions, bringing the ROK Army to a size of 14 divisions and approximately 525,000 troops.[15]

Thus by the end of the Korean War, the ROK Army was one of the largest in the world in absolute numbers. Furthermore, its officers had acquired combat and non-combat (for example, managerial and governmental) experience; military personnel at all levels had been exposed to modern equipment and techniques; military units had developed increased effectiveness and cohesion. Finally, the military were relatively and absolutely more important to the society than they had been previously. A broad measure of importance was provided by governmental expenditures—nearly 80 percent of the budget for fiscal year 1953-54 was committed to military purposes.[16]

At a level more specific to the daily lives of most Koreans, the increased importance of the military was evident in the scope and magnitude of military control over activity and property under the warrant of martial law, which was extensively imposed throughout the war.

Sources of Discontent. Within the military establishment, however, there were numerous sources of discontent—including, but not restricted to, poor food, inadequate clothing and equipment, and low pay. During the Korean War, the pay scale in the ROK military ranged from about 3,000 won per month for a private to about 60,000 won per month for a general officer, at a rate of exchange of 4,000–6,000 won to the U.S. dollar.[17] As General Clark observed:

> Pay was so low in the ROK Army that it was not only a morale factor but forced whole ROK units to take time for extracurricular activities to make a living for families of their troops. Two divisions stationed on the fairly active East Coast, for instance, operated their own fishing fleets. These divisions were renowned in the ROK Army as wealthy divisions. They sold their fish to their own division mess halls and also to the civilian population. The divisions had an edge over their civilian competitors in the fishing business, of course, for the ROK troops had American Army trucks and gasoline to help them transport their catch.[18]

Contact with the relatively affluent American Army, especially in contrast to the paltry pay and resources with which Korean soldiers were provided, served to raise the threshold of expectations of the latter—collectively on behalf of their society, and individually—and thus to aggravate their grievances. Although the evidence suggests no large, organized plots among Korean military men at this time to seize the reins of government, it is not surprising that signs of increasing politicization of attitudes among the military were detectable. The authoritarian tactics of Syngman Rhee, in particular, aroused discontent among many Korean military men. The use of military units for blatantly partisan purposes, as in the employment of military force against recalcitrant Assemblymen opposed to constitutional amendments that would greatly enhance Rhee's power, highlighted the hypocrisy of his democratic pretensions. A retired ROK Army general has told the author that during the war several young officers came to him and asked, "'Is this democracy?'" Although the senior officer agreed with his younger colleagues that democratic practices had been severely compromised, he successfully dissuaded them from the view that the military should "do something about it."[19] However, it is clear from this and reports of others who were in military service during the period that the barracks increasingly became a forum for political discussion, if not for conspiracy.

A prominent example of friction between Rhee and elements of the military included the dismissal of Lt. Gen. Yi Chong-chan as Army Chief of Staff in 1952 when General Yi refused to be a party to the arrest of Assemblymen. Further evidence of increased political activism among the military was provided by the request of 41 officers for discharge at the end of the war in order to compete for National Assembly seats in the forthcoming elections. Of equal interest, however, was Rhee's response to the request; a decree was issued ruling that all officers must remain in service for a minimum of five years.[20]

THE AFTERMATH OF WAR: ORGANIZATIONAL DEVELOPMENT AND POLITICIZATION

No doubt the continued dependence of Korea upon U.S. financial, technical, and military aid during the period of reconstruction after the Korean War strengthened the hand of Rhee in domestic politics. For although frictions between Rhee and members of the American government often reached heated proportions, he nevertheless had a bevy of supporters in America. Moreover, Rhee's access to the coffers of American aid appeared greater than that of any other prominent Korean, a fact which Rhee and his followers did not let the voters of South Korea forget.[21]

The American government made a number of promises to Rhee in return for his eventual agreement to abide by the armistice. Those most relevant to the present study included the promise of a U.S.-ROK Mutual Security Pact, the promise of long-term economic aid including a first installment of 100 million dollars and immediate distribution of emergency relief, and support for the increase of the ROK Army to twenty divisions, with appropriate increases also in the size of the Navy and Air Force. The Mutual Defense Treaty between the two countries went into effect late in 1954, initial drafts modified only to the extent of the insertion by the United States of a proviso which guarded against the commitment of American forces to any ROK-instigated effort (frequently threatened by Rhee) to reunify

Korea by force.[22]

Continued Military Organizational Development. The strength of the ROK Army was increased to twenty divisions in 1954, plus an additional ten reserve divisions. A special ten-week military training program for all male college students was put into effect. In 1955, a Command and Staff College for Naval officers was opened; in addition, provision was made to send a small group of senior officers annually to the U. S. Naval War College. An arsenal was established for the Army; construction of a drydock for naval vessels, begun during the war, was completed. Two seaplanes were provided for the Navy; jet aircraft for the Air Force were obtained.

In 1956, Offices of Psychological Warfare and Public Information and a National Defense College were established within the Army. The Naval Recruit Training Center and Service School Command were integrated into a Naval Training Center for recruits and for petty officers. At the Army Replacement Training Center near Nonsan, some 600 men per day were being admitted for training by 1956. By the end of the year, more than 600,000 men were on active duty with the ROK Army, making it the fourth largest army in the world.[23]

One of the consequences of the rapid growth of the military, however, when accompanied by political manipulation of appointment and promotion to top ranks, was that officers at the middle grades (field grade especially), having experienced rapid promotion during the period of wartime growth of the military, now found a situation in which future promotion appeared thwarted. Top positions in the military were occupied by men young enough, in most cases, to be many years from retirement; furthermore, although in a number of instances their own general education and military training were inferior to that of their immediate subordinates, political loyalty rather than competence seemed to be the criterion for their continuation in positions of authority.

Thus important sources of discontent existed within the ROK military establishment. Signs of political activism were becoming more apparent as the tendency for the Liberal Party to manipulate the military for political purposes increased. Moreover, the military hierarchy itself had become an important arena of intra-group politics, with important economic benefits (far beyond those accruing from meager salaries) and power commanded by those in top leadership posts, most notably at the level of Chief of Staff and, at least until the murder of Lt. General Kim Ch'ang-yong ("Snake" Kim), who had held the post, of the Commander of the Counter-Intelligence Corps. Factionalism and "politicking" within a subsystem rife with intrigue and corruption were but a step away from taking political action at the broader level of the political system itself. Furthermore, elsewhere in the world military men had vented their grievances by seizing control of the government. Coups in Egypt, Argentina, Burma, and Pakistan in the 1950s were later cited by some of those who executed the military coup in Korea in 1961 as having influenced their own thinking by suggesting action by military men "aimed at recovering national integrity by eliminating political corruption."[24]

The Student Revolution. Yet it is interesting that in spite of growing discontent, and in spite of the possession of substantial political resources, the ROK military did not follow the Egyptian, Argentine, Burmese, or Pakistani example until *after* Syngman Rhee had yielded power to an interim government in the aftermath of widespread popular demonstrations. To the end of his tenure in office, Rhee demonstrated time and again impressive skill in warding off potential threats from the military, managing instead frequently to utilize the military to his own political advantage.

Many potential rivals to Rhee among military officers no doubt were kept at bay by a grudging respect or fear of his skill and power. Similar attitudes were common among the civilian populace. When Cho Pyŏng-ok, rival candidate to the aged Rhee for President in 1960, died on the eve of the election, the event was enough to convince some Koreans that "Syngman Rhee's ancestors will not let him be defeated."[25] Surely the fate of Rhee's key opponents over the years had been wretched. Kim Ku, rival for the Presidency in 1948, had been assassinated in 1949. Cho Pong-am, leading opposition candidate in 1952 and 1956, was subsequently convicted of treason and hanged. Shin Ik-hŭi, the contender in 1956, had died of a heart attack less than two weeks prior to the balloting that year.

However, as details of the events leading up to the 1960 elections began to emerge it became obvious to nearly all observers that more than the spirit of his ancestors had intervened on Rhee's behalf. Both Syngman Rhee and Yi Ki-bung, his running mate, were elected by substantial margins. Evidence became widespread that the Liberal Party had resorted to fraud, intimidation by police, suppression of opposition publications, and other means of securing an electoral victory. Disclosures of election corruption resulted in widespread popular demonstrations culminating in the so-called "Student Revolution" of April 1960.

By this time, although dissident elements within the military still did not openly move to seize power, Rhee's ability to manipulate the military effectively on behalf of his own political fortunes had ceased. Evidence of the changed attitudes of military professionals toward the Rhee regime by this time is provided first of all by the inaction of the military toward those who were demonstrating in protest of election corruption. Although martial law had been declared as an effort to quell the protests, military units charged with the responsibility of maintaining order took little action against the demonstrators. Indeed, there is evidence that General Song Yo-ch'an, Army Chief of Staff, personally exerted pressure upon Rhee to resign (as did Defense Minister Kim Chŏng-yŏl, a former Lt. General), and that General Song permitted a student delegation to visit Rhee to present a similar request.[26]

Further evidence of the increased resentment of groups within the military toward the Rhee regime is provided by retrospective accounts by those who executed the military coup of May 1961 of their views in the spring of 1960. As General Park Chung-hee has emphasized: ... this military revolution did not take place on May 16 all of a sudden and by chance, but had been already in the making since the notorious rigged mid-March elections a year ago when youthful officers of the Korean armed forces were resolved to take the initiative to chastise the Liberal Party for its rotten practices and irregularities.... When they were just about to touch off the coup, the April revolution took place and the Liberal Party regime was overthrown. Accordingly, they suspended the coup and engrossed themselves in their assigned military duties, eagerly looking forward to a better future for this country.[27]

SEIZURE OF POWER

In August 1960, the government of Chang Myŏn replaced the interim government of Hŏ Chŏng, which in turn had governed since the Student Revolution. The difficulties experienced by the Chang regime, including economic distress, a split between the "old faction" and the "new faction" in the Democratic Party, and continuing student protest demonstrations, are described elsewhere in this volume. The Chang regime, generally permissive anyway in its attitudes toward demonstrations, was hindered in the modest efforts that were made to maintain order by the weakness of the police. Ironically, efforts by the Chang government to purge the police of corrupt or otherwise undesirable elements, coupled with post-Rhee antipathy to the police throughout Korean society, rendered the police virtually impotent for several months. Although college graduates were hired, for the first time, to fill police posts, demoralization of the police force was so thorough and persistent demonstrations were such a trial that many of the college graduates resigned from the force along with hundreds of other policemen who resigned voluntarily. In addition, by early December 1960 the Chang regime had relieved over 2,000 policemen, including 81 police chiefs.[28]

Capability and Motivation of the Military. Almost by default, the military emerged during this period as the most important group in South Korean politics. The purge and discrediting of the police had eliminated from competition the only other major group with a substantial means for organized violence at its disposal. Among the two major political parties, the Liberal Party had been discredited, and the Democratic Party was faction-ridden and suffered in the minds of many Koreans from being virtually indistinguishable ideologically and in terms of upper-class base from the Liberal Party. The students, like the military, represented an important modernizing force in Korean society; they had gained political stature in the April Revolution. However, all efforts to develop an effective national student organization failed. Consequently, student activity continued to be organized around relatively small, highly personalized cliques.

The military, on the other hand, had acquired increased stature through their refusal to employ violence against the students in the April Revolution. They were a huge, disciplined, hierarchically organized group, with modern communications and weapons at their disposal. Shortly after Hŏ Chŏng had taken over from Rhee, an observer in Seoul noted not only the strong possibility of a military coup, but that the interim government would certainly "*ask* the army to take over should a new crisis develop."[29]

The removal of Syngman Rhee meant the departure from the scene of a man who had demonstrated great skill at retaining control of the military. However, during Chang Myŏn's service in the key post of government, to add to his other difficulties, he not only showed little capacity for enlisting the positive allegiance of the military, but also his government took a number of actions which severely threatened important elements of the military.

During his election campaign, Chang Myŏn had urged the reduction of the ROK armed forces from nearly 700,000 men to a force of 400,000. In the final stages of the campaign, a statement was issued pledging a reduction of 100,000 in the armed forces if the Democrats were made the ruling party. This pledge was reiterated by the new Minister of Defense shortly after the Chang government came to power.[30]

Almost immediately, however, the new government found itself caught in cross-pressures. On the one hand, elements within the ROK military complained that a thorough and rapid purge of corrupt elements in the officer corps, especially at the highest levels, must be carried out. On the other hand, others within the military exerted pressures to retain their jobs. Furthermore, representatives of the American government expressed fear that a reduction of 100,000 in the ROK armed forces was excessive, and warned that toleration of the efforts by junior officers to have their seniors removed was the kind of insubordination which would undermine the discipline of the entire ROK military structure.[31]

It is true that talk of a "purge" of high-ranking officers had been the apparent stimulus to a number of widely publicized incidents in which subordinates defied or openly repudiated the authority of their superiors. For example, the Fleet Commander of the Navy made public allegations of malfeasance on the part of his superior, the Chief of Naval Operations. In the Army, the most well-known incident was one in which five colonels and eleven lieutenant colonels, purporting to represent the 8th Graduating Class of the Korean Military Academy and two other classes, called upon the Chairman of the Joint Chiefs of Staff, General Ch'oe Yŏng-hŭi, and recommended that he retire "for the sake of purification of the Army."[32]

Although American officials had made it clear that aid in the modernization of the ROK armed forces was dependent upon demonstration that the ROK government was determined to maintain discipline within its military establishment, the initial reaction of the Chang government to such pressures was to express resentment of U. S. interference in Korean affairs, and to claim that the "purification" of the armed forces would continue. However, the Chang regime soon came in line with American proposals. The announced figure for reduction of the armed forces was trimmed from 100,000 to 50,000, then to 30,000 men, limited to Army units in rear areas, excluding the Navy, Marines, Air Force, and frontline Army units. In November 1960, at a meeting with ROK service chiefs and other top-ranking officers, Premier Chang announced that the purge of high-ranking military officers had been completed. He emphasized that henceforth, criticism of superior officers by subordinates should not be tolerated.³³

Abortion of the plans for a sweeping purge of top military leadership left in power general officers who continued in key positions so as to block the promotion of subordinates, and who also held power over the careers of their subordinates by virtue of their being members of promotion screening committees. Distrust and resentment of such power among many officers in the middle grades led to bitterness at the failure of the Chang government to implement its "purification" plan—bitterness which became an additional precipitant for implementation of a military coup.

Numerous signs of friction within the armed services were visible, including a reshuffling of key staff and command assignments to place dissident officers in less critical positions, the court martial of the sixteen officers who had requested that the Chairman of the Joint Chiefs of Staff resign, and the retirement to reserve status of officers (Lt. Colonels Kim Chong-p'il and Sŏk Chŏng-sŏn), believed to have been influential in instigating the visit to the Chairman.

Beneath the surface, plans for execution of a military coup d'etat moved from the level of abstract speculation to detailed planning. Leading figures in planning the coup included: Maj. General Park Chung-hee, who commanded the Army Logistical Command at Pusan until a few months before the coup, when he was transferred to Second Army Headquarters; Maj. General Kim Tong-ha, commander of a Marine division at Pohang; Lt. Colonel Kim Chong-p'il, nephew by marriage of General Park; and a number of other officers who, like Lt. Colonel Kim, were members of the 8th Graduating Class of the Korean Military Academy in 1949.

Cohesion among members of the so-called 8th Graduating Class³⁴ proved to be an ingredient important to the success of the coup. The basis of cohesion of the class is difficult to pinpoint. The following common experiences seem particularly relevant. First, this was the initial class to enter the Academy after its formal designation as the ROK Military Academy. Second, almost precisely one year after graduation, members of the class were thrown into battle in positions of leadership at the company level. The chaotic state of affairs after the initial attack by North Korean forces, and later after the entry into the war of the Chinese, made company-level leadership of enormous importance. Many members of the class were killed in battle; those who lived could share a feeling of pride at the contribution that they had made to the survival of the nation. Third, during and after the war, members of the class served in command and staff positions under the authority of officers who had had, in many cases, training inferior to that of the 8th Graduating Class and yet who blocked the aspirations of members of the class to rise to top leadership positions. Action taken by members of the class to rectify the endeavor provided a final stimulus to a number of them to undertake a coup.

In anticipation of a possible crisis on April 19, 1961, the first anniversary of the Student Revolution, the Chang government had instituted riot control training in the armed forces, including plans for troop mobilization. Those officers planning a coup therefore decided to use anti-riot measures on that date as a cover under which seizure of the government could be effected. However, no riot occurred, and troops therefore were not mobilized. A new date, May 12, was selected for a coup; but again plans miscarried, this time because an informant leaked plans to authorities. Finally, in the early hours of May 16, approximately 5,000 soldiers and marines were committed in successful execution of a virtually bloodless coup d'etat. At 5 a.m., Seoul time, the nation was told by radio that the government had changed hands.

Ideology of the Military Revolution. The analyst of a revolution or coup d'etat[35] invariably must confront the all but impossible task of disentangling the private motives of those who effect the overthrow of a government from their public efforts to justify the act. Frequently, critics of a particular revolutionary movement take the position that publicly espoused ideals of the movement are nothing more than ideological whitewash, functioning solely to conceal underlying opportunistic motives of the revolutionary leaders. Admirers of a particular revolutionary movement, on the other hand, often are inclined to accept public revolutionary pronouncements, manifestoes, and "white papers" at face value, as sufficient explanation of the behavior and motives of the revolutionaries. The truth in the case of most revolutionary movements, and specifically in the case of the one that led to the Military Revolution of May 1961 in Korea, would seem to lie somewhere between the cynical verdict of critics and the idealistic conclusions of admirers. For reasons described in preceding paragraphs, those who led the overthrow of the Chang government had various personal grievances against that regime. Yet as also indicated previously, the ills which beset the Chang regime were many. Thus the ideological justification of the Military Revolution represented a statement of grievances and aspirations for Korean society with which a substantial part of the civilian sector agreed.

At the very least, the formal ideology of a revolution is of considerable interest as a reflection of the self-image that leaders of a movement have of themselves as revolutionaries and of the doctrine that they believe to be most palatable in justification of a forcible overthrow of government. Virtually every revolutionary ideology is composed of two elements: a derogatory image to be conveyed of the situation prior to the revolution (that is, a list of grievances), and an image of the favorable situation to be created as a result of the revolution (that is, a list of promises).

In Figure 1, the recurrent themes that are found in the various tracts issued during and following the takeover of the ROK government

FIGURE 1. IDEOLOGICAL JUSTIFICATION OF THE MILITARY TAKEOVER

Problem Area	Image of the Past (Under Civilian Rule)	Image of the Future (To Be Developed by Military Rule)
National Security	Nation weakened against external threat through factional strife, and inadequate leadership; susceptible to Communism.	Nation strong before its enemies.
Economy	Subsistence economy, heavily dependent upon the U.S., oriented to lavish consumption items.	Self-sufficient economy providing for the welfare of all, attained through planning, emphasis on primary industry, expanded base of trade.
Social Values and Ideals	Continued prevalence of decadent Confucian ideas and customs. Rampant hedonism and corruption, even among the young.	Prevalence of modern ideas; achievement-oriented society. Cultivation of a new morality, based upon austerity. Rejuvenation of the ideals of the young.
Social and Political Structure	Factions, parties, and cliques feuding with one another and pursuing their own self-interest under the guise of democracy.	National solidarity; "Administrative Democracy."
Governmental Leadership	Those in power committed to self-aggrandisement, profiteering at the expense of the people. Rulers incapable as well as irresponsible.	Those in power committed selflessly o building the nation and promoting the welfare of the people. Rulers wise and efficient.

by the military in May 1961 are summarized. The student of comparative politics will find it interesting to compare the themes with those expressed by leaders of military coups elsewhere—for example, in Turkey, Egypt, Pakistan, or Indonesia.

A statement issued by the Military Revolutionary Committee on May 16, the day the Chang government was overthrown, contained six pledges to the Korean people. The first of these was that the military revolutionary government would "uphold anti-Communism as our foremost national policy...."[36] In subsequent justification of the revolution, military leaders contended that under the Chang regime, a "political and ideological vacuum" had been created, stimulating increased Communist subversion and generating domestic unrest to the point that it might have exploded in a form susceptible to Communist takeover.[37] Thus military men found themselves in a dilemma, according to those who led the coup. "Was it their duty to maintain their constitutional posture, aloof from politics, while the nation drifted slowly through chaos toward Communism? Or was it their real duty to take swift and positive action to save the country before it was too late?"[38] To this rhetorical question, the military revolutionaries "most reluctantly concluded that it was their duty to take action to save the country, and to lay a solid foundation for real democracy after their revolutionary task (has) been completed."[39]

A second problem area about which the revolutionaries expressed concern was that of economics. Indeed, the theme of the economic plight of the nation was given greatest emphasis in revolutionary doctrine. Revolutionary leader General Park Chung-hee wrote, for example:

> ...I want to emphasize and re-emphasize, that the key factor of the May 16th Military Revolution was to effect an industrial revolution in Korea. Since the primary objective of the revolution was to achieve a national renaissance, the revolution envisaged political, social and cultural reforms as well. My chief concern, however, was economic revolution.[40]

Economic conditions under the Chang government were described not only as generally bad, but also as contributing to the enjoyment of the wealthy few to the detriment of the poverty-stricken many, and leading to the construction of "tea shops, billiard halls, and bars" while construction in primary industry remained neglected.[41] The military revolutionaries proposed to remedy these economic ills, and to attain economic self-sufficiency for Korea, through "establishment of a planned economy,"[42] emphasis on the development of primary industry and acceptance of austerity in consumer goods, and expansion of trade and stimulation of foreign investment (for example, through normalization of relations with Japan).[43]

A third tenet of revolutionary ideology of the military was to promote "a spiritual regeneration of the people."[44] According to Yi Su-Yŏng, who served as Ambassador to the United Nations for the military government, this was the most basic objective of the revolution and "the need for it is the ultimate justification of the Military Revolution."[45] The continued prevalence of traditional ways of thinking, rooted in Confucian teachings, was described by General Park Chung-hee and other revolutionary leaders as a fundamental barrier to progress which had to be overcome through "social reconstruction" and the cultivation of a new sense of personal dignity and identity among the Korean people. The traditional perspective of the Korean, Park contended, was one in which there was no established ego.

> Where there is no established ego but only father-son, master-slave and adult-child relationships, there can be no equality, and no human rights.... Establishment of the ego is, first of all, to know oneself. Only after understanding himself will one understand others and understand the national entity to which he belongs. And only when one trusts himself will he trust others. *Trust of others and reliance upon others are essentially different things. The difference between the two is as great as the difference between the feudal age and the modern age.* Only when we trust others and understand others can there be cooperation and compromise.[46]

The problems which Korea had inherited from its traditional past were aggravated, the military revolutionaries maintained, by corruption and privilege consciousness among the Democratic Party, which had proved to be little more than the "twin" of the Liberal Party. The old system under the Rhee and Chang regimes was the more insidious, leaders of the military government maintained, because "it disguised itself under the cloak of democracy," whereas in fact "...it was no more than an oligarchy bolstered by monetary influence."[47]

It is important to note that the leaders of the military revolution did not claim that their own rule could be called "democratic," nor did they believe that Western-style democracy was appropriate to Korea at that stage in her history. Rather, the contention was that disease of the body politic had reached such an acute stage that major surgery was required in order to create the healthy conditions under which democracy could flourish. As General Park observed, the Military Revolution was "not intended to strangle democracy in this country but to suspend it temporarily while it is undergoing medical treatment. In other words, the military revolution assumes a nature of *controlled or remedial democracy*."[48]

The entire rationale justifying the military seizure of government in Korea was of course predicated on the assumption that civil rule had been a total failure. The April 1960 student uprising had been a genuine revolution, according to General Park and his colleagues. However, the April Revolution had failed, because "in spite of the righteousness of its ideals... it did not have any real power. It could destroy a government, but did not have enough strength to prevent the emergence of a corrupt government similar to one it had superseded."[49] Rather, those entrusted with carrying out the April Revolution turned out to be a "faithless mob, completely betraying the hopes of the people."[50]

What had happened essentially, military revolutionaries claimed, was that the Student Revolution had failed to uproot the old generation of power holders. "The power and money held by the established generations were too great and too well entrenched."[51] Therefore a new force was needed that would be willing to carry on the spirit of the Student Revolution and would have the power to do so. The Military Revolution was designed to meet the need. "It was to enable a new elite... to take over the nation and the State. In this light, this revolution is a national, common people's revolution, a revolution of national consciousness, and a turnover of generations."[52]

As a final comment on the ideology of the Military Revolution, it is interesting to note the influence of earlier revolutionary models on the perspectives of Korean military revolutionaries. Park Chunghee has cited five revolutions or periods of revolutionary development as providing lessons which Korean military revolutionaries sought to emulate: the modernization movement of Yat-sen Sun in China; the Meiji Restoration in Japan; the revolution of the "Young Turks," led by Mustafa Kemal; the Egyptian Revolution, led by Nasser and the Free Officers Corps; and post-World War II reconstruction in West Germany.[53]

The first four movements had in common the fact that they were modernizing as well as nationalistic movements, directed against internal despotism and backwardness as well as against foreign oppression. The fifth, which Park has termed the "miracle on the Rhine," was one in which a nation physically divided and economically in ruins, and "subjected to persecution, hatred and a cold reception by the whole world," rose to become one of the top economic powers in the world in a matter of fifteen years. Although Park has acknowledged that the currency reform of 1948, American aid, a large influx of labor from East Germany, and other such factors contributed to the West German economic recovery, he has placed major emphasis upon the importance which German "national character" played in achieving "the miracle," and upon the guidance provided by strong leadership. German diligence and respect for order are unsurpassed, and the key to their success, Park has said. Of German leadership, he had contended that "it is a fact that even Bismarck and Hitler were men who could do 'something' for their people." In the period after their defeat in World War II, Park has observed, the Germans were fortunate enough to have a strong leader like Adenauer to help them on their road to recovery. Following the German example, Park has advised his people, the Koreans can create their own "miracle on the Han River."[54]

STRUGGLE FOR SURVIVAL: REVOLUTIONARY POLITICS

Every regime that comes to power by extraconstitutional means faces the threat, often especially great immediately after acting to seize power, that it will lose control of the government by means similar to those which it employed to gain control. If a society has grown accustomed to civil rule, a military junta faces the additional problem of being under pressure to relinquish the position of dominance at some point in the near future. Such a problem might be viewed as but a species of the generic problem of legitimation which all revolutionary regimes must face. Physical control of the reins of government is not enough. Sooner or later (depending upon the distribution and intensity of political values and beliefs within the society), a regime must attempt to legitimize its power—through elections, real or rigged; through propaganda and the cultivation of myths favorable to the perpetuation of the rule of the regime; through performance and acts which win public favor (or which elicit the support of important sectors of the public). The problem of maintaining political control is especially delicate because most revolutionary regimes contain within them disintegrative tendencies virtually from the moment of seizure of power. Factions within the ruling group become dissatisfied with their representation in the power structure; junta members become jealous of one another's prerogatives; persons originally inspired by revolutionary rhetoric become disillusioned by the failure of the regime to live up to pledges or goals.

The problem of maintaining political control and the concomitant problems of legitimacy and ruling-group cohesion were present in acute form in the case of the Military Revolution in Korea. Indeed, the coup might have been thwarted in the first place if the ROK First Army, the key front-line army whose commanding general (Lt. General Yi Han-lim) initially was hostile to the idea of a coup, had taken decisive action to suppress it. UN Commander-in-Chief General Carter B. Magruder had issued a public statement the morning that coup forces moved into action, calling upon "all military personnel in his command to support the duly recognized Government of the Republic of Korea headed by Prime Minister Chang Myŏn."[55] He had further urged President Yun Po-sŏn (key representative of the government since Chang had gone into hiding) to permit Magruder to mobilize 40,000 troops to suppress the coup. The American Charge d'affaires, Marshall Green, agreed with Magruder's plan; Green also had made a public statement backing the Chang Myŏn government. But President Yun refused to endorse a countercoup, arguing that revolution was inevitable and to forcibly oppose it might lead to civil war.[56]

Throughout the period of military government, ROK leaders repeatedly were faced with American distrust, criticism, or outright opposition (as in the first days after the coup). The new leaders were not, for the most part, men with whom American officials and military officers had been on first-name and golfing-companion terms. As one American put it when the military junta took over, "The 'golf link Charlies' are out and the hairshirt boys are in."[57] For their part, the new regime expressed dissatisfaction with the extent of Korean dependence upon the United States as one of the tenets of revolutionary ideology. On the other hand, the need for continuing American aid was a fact of life which the ROK military leaders had to recognize, and did. Thus various steps were taken to alleviate tensions with the United States, and to seek support abroad and at home.

A number of such steps might be cited by way of illustration. First, President Yun Po-sŏn was persuaded to remain in office (although without any real power), thereby permitting the revolutionary regime to avoid the problem of seeking diplomatic recognition from the United States and other nations. Second, the Army Chief of Staff, Lt. General Chang To-yŏng, was made Chairman of the Military Revolutionary Committee, and then Chairman of the Supreme Council for National Reconstruction (SCNR), the principal decision-making authority under the military government. (The committee's original title was perhaps patterned after the Revolutionary Command Council of the Egyptian military revolution; the name was changed to SCNR three days after the coup.) General Chang was a man well known to and apparently liked by American officials and officers. Although it was known by American officials in Seoul that he had not been a member of the "core group" of the junta, his statements on behalf of the regime that Korea would continue to cooperate closely with the United States somewhat relieved anxieties in Washington as to the nature of the new regime. When Chang To-yŏng was removed from his key positions (he held the positions of SCNR Chairman, Premier, Minister of Defense, Army Chief of Staff, and Martial Law Commander concurrently), another American "favorite," General Song Yo-ch'an (nicknamed "Tiger" by Americans during the Korean War), was installed as Premier.[58]

Controversy Over Restoration of Civil Rule. Another step taken by the military regime to legitimate the seizure of power was the promise to restore civil rule—the question, however, was, when? The sixth of the pledges promulgated the day of the military takeover had been a vague commitment to transfer governmental authority back to civilians "as soon as revolutionary tasks have been completed."[59] As SCNR Chairman, General Chang To-yŏng had given further assurances that military rule was to be temporary. In August 1961, General Park Chung-hee, now Chairman of the SCNR, set forth more explicitly the details of how and when the transfer of government to civilian rule was to be accomplished. A new constitution would be established prior to March 1963, and political activities would resume early that year in preparation for general elections to be held in May 1963.[60]

However, subsequent to General Park's explicit pledge of a return to civil rule, a "political purification law" was enacted by the SCNR, banning from further political activity all former politicians except those successfully screened by the military government. Some persons feared that the law was designed to thwart a genuine return to civil rule by rendering able civilian politicians impotent. Kim

Chong-p'il, Director of the ROK CIA, pointed out during a visit to the United States that the "civilian" government to be established in 1963 would be, in fact, a "transitional" government. The military revolutionary elite would "also participate in the civilian government to consummate the nation's revolutionary tasks."[61] To help *ensure* that the military would continue to participate in governing the country, a group of military officers, led by Brig. General Kim Chong-p'il, in January 1963 announced the formation of a new political party, the Democratic-Republican Party (DRP), which would spearhead the drive to enlist popular support at the polls for those sympathetic to the revolution.

SCNR Chairman Park Chung-hee's position from this point for a period of weeks was a difficult one, and one which led to considerable vacillation. In an oath-taking ceremony in February, Park made a public pledge ("tearfully" it was said) not to take part in the civilian government that would be formed on the basis of elections later in the year. Prior to Chairman Park's speech, 53 political and military leaders had sworn to uphold a nine-point "political stabilization proposal" as the fundamental basis for transition to civil rule. Point number one was a pledge that "the armed forces would maintain political neutrality and support a popularly elected government."[62] Points two through nine outlined the guarantees that the military would expect in return. Especially relevant for mention here were guarantees of freedom for members of the military government to return to active military duty *or* to retire and run for elective office (point 3); that the new government would carry on the spirit of the revolution of 1960 and 1961; that there would be no political reprisals or arbitrary dismissal of civil servants legitimately hired by the military government (points 2, 4, and 5); that military veterans would be given priority in filling vacancies in government positions (point 6); and that "all political parties" would "stop factional strife" (point 7).[63]

In March, however, following bitter in-fighting and turbulence within the ruling junta itself (some details of which are presented in subsequent pages), Park proposed that military rule be extended for four years, and that a national referendum be held to endorse the extension. One-hundred-sixty military commanders, mostly of general officer rank, submitted a resolution to Park supporting the extension of military rule. However, under considerable pressure both at home and abroad to reverse himself again, Park agreed to compromise to the extent that a coalition of civil and military leaders would rule for two years in preparation for a transfer to full civil control. Finally, in early April, Park announced that the plan for holding elections had been revived; elections would be held in the autumn. In late May, Park Chung-hee, who had pledged in February to take no part in the next government, was named Presidential candidate of the Democratic-Republican Party.[64]

The initial promises of the military government to pave the way for an early return to civilian rule, rather than serving to help legitimate the Military Revolution, had come to serve as a symbol of illegitimacy in the minds of many whose support the regime had hoped to enlist. The U. S. State Department announced, in response to the expressed intention of the ROK government to extend military rule, that such extension of military rule would produce instability; U.S. President Kennedy urged Korean military leaders to effect an early transfer of power to civilian rule. When the resumption of political activity in Korea finally came in 1963, the first prominent party formed in opposition to the DRP called itself the "Civil Rule Party," and made restoration of civilian rule its *cause célèbre*.

Factional Strife Within the Junta. Furthermore, the issue of whether or not to extend military rule was one, more than any other during the period of military government, that generated disintegrative forces within the ruling junta itself (much as the proposed constitutional amendment to permit President Park Chung-hee to seek a third term caused a sharp rift within the ruling DRP in 1969). A review of the composition of the SCNR during the period of its existence from June 1961 (the SCNR was formed in May but did not achieve a relatively stable membership until June) to December 1963, when the Council was formally disbanded, highlights some of the factional strife which occurred within the ruling military elite, and sheds some light on the characteristics of those who executed the Military Revolution of 1961.

The Basic Law which established the SCNR provided that the Council was to consist of not more than 32 nor less than 20 members.[65] The military regime saw fit to preserve the illusion of constitutionality by maintaining the formal structure of government virtually intact. The Basic Law which they proclaimed was declared to have precedence over any provision of the Constitution with which it conflicted (there were many such provisions); but ostensibly the Basic Law merely amended the Constitution, rather than superseded it as did the new Constitution endorsed by public referendum in December 1962. The SCNR did not replace the various ministries of government; rather, the Council served as the supreme decision-making authority, with supervisory and policy-making responsibilities over each of the ministries and the judiciary as well.

Given the concentration of authority in the SCNR, it is not surprising that its membership consisted largely of those who had been chiefly responsible for planning and executing the overthrow of the Chang Myŏn regime. However, the coup had been a combined Army-Marine operation. Air Force and Navy leaders had not made a commitment for or against the coup until its success seemed apparent. Nevertheless, when the Air Force and Navy Chiefs of Staff, Lt. General Kim Sin and Vice Admiral Yi Sŏng-ho, respectively, did announce their support of the revolution, a united front of the armed services was created. The reward for this belated gesture would seem to have been a place on the SCNR, although it is doubtful that either General Kim or Admiral Yi ever played more than a nominal role during his relatively brief tenure on the Council.

The core SCNR membership consisted of men who had been young generals or colonels in the Army or Marines at the time of the coup. By early 1963, there were but nineteen left of those who had served on the SCNR in June 1961—all of the nineteen were Army or Marine generals and colonels. The oldest, Chairman Park Chung-hee, had been 44 the year of the coup; the youngest, Marine Colonel O Chŏng-kŭn, had been 32 that year. At no time did members under the age of 40 comprise less than 70 percent of SCNR membership, although 37 percent of those with continuous membership on the Council from June 1961 to December 1963 were between the ages of 40 and 44.

The youth of leadership under the military government is particularly striking in contrast to the age distribution of leadership under the Syngman Rhee and Chang Myŏn governments (Table 1). The contrast between the military government and its predecessors is somewhat exaggerated by the figures in Table 1, since those for the Rhee and Chang periods are based upon the ages of cabinet ministers, bureau chiefs, governors, key ambassadors, and key Assemblymen, whereas those for the military government period include only SCNR members.[66] Nevertheless, there is no doubt that the Military Revolution had effected a "changeover of generations" as the revolutionary leadership claimed.

The Military Revolution also represented a shift away from political dominance by those born in what is now South Korea to a representation on the SCNR of those born in northern provinces in

TABLE 1. PERCENT DISTRIBUTION OF SCNR MEMBERS BY AGE COMPARED WITH LEADERSHIP DURING THE RHEE AND CHANG REGIMES

	Age					
	Over 80	70–79	60–69	50–59	40–49	30–39
Leadership,[a] Rhee regime (Age as of 1959)	1.4	4.7	29.1	38.5	24.3	2.0
Leadership,[a] Chang regime (Age as of 1960)	0	0	27.9	36.1	32.5	3.5
Members, SCNR,[b] June 61, Jan. 62, Dec. 62, or Dec. 63 (Age as of 1961)	0	0	0	0	22.5	77.5

a. Adapted from Hahn Bae-ho and Kim Kyu-taik, "Korean Political Leaders (1952–1962): Their Social Origins and Skills," *Asian Survey*, Vol. 3 (July 1963), p. 314. Composition of the leadership groups is described in the text of the present study and in the study cited.

b. Percentages computed with N:40. Data on date of birth were unavailable for 8 SCNR members.

approximately equal numbers with those born in the south (Table 2). Regional backgrounds take on significance in terms of the factional pattern of Korean politics. Although by no means the only relevant explanatory factor, common "hometown" or common provincial background (usually implying common kinship ties as well) has been an important basis of political association in Korea. Indeed, provincial ties proved to be one source of factionalism within the military regime itself.

Probably a more important common denominator for factional groupings among military men, however (certainly more important in the past few years), has been shared career experiences. In this regard, it is of interest to note that several of the SCNR members had graduated from the Manchurian Military Academy (of the Japanese Army) and had remained close friends subsequently. These included General Park Chung-hee; General Yi Chu-il, Vice-Chairman throughout most of the existence of the SCNR; General Kim Tong-ha, chairman of key committees within the SCNR and leading representative of the Marines on the SCNR; General Pak Im-hang; General Ch'oe Chu-chong; and General Kim Yun-hŭn. Nearly all of the 15 Army members on the SCNR who served continuously from June 1961 to early 1963 had in common the fact that they had graduated from the Korean Military Academy prior to the outbreak of the Korean War. The central role in the coup of members of the 8th Graduating Class was noted earlier; at least half a dozen of the SCNR members were graduates of this class.

TABLE 2. PROVINCE OF BIRTH: LEADERSHIP OF
SYNGMAN RHEE, CHANG MYŎN, AND
MILITARY GOVERNMENT PERIODS COMPARED

	Province of Birth								
	NE[a]	NW[b]	Hwng[c]	Kang[d]	Kyng[e]	Chng[f]	SW[g]	SE[h]	Foreign
Leadership,[i] Rhee regime	4.8	8.8	4.2	5.4	22.4	13.6	13.6	25.8	1.4
Leadership,[i] Chang regime	5.8	11.6	3.5	2.3	13.9	12.8	26.8	22.1	1.2
SCNR Members,[j] June 61, Jan. 62, Dec. 62 or Dec. 63	18.4	15.8	13.2	0	15.8	13.2	5.3	18.4	0

a North and South Hamgyŏng.
b North and South P'yŏngan.
c Hwanghae.
d Kangwŏn.
e Kyŏnggi and Seoul.
f North and South Ch'ungch'ŏng.
g North and South Ch'ŏlla.
h North and South Kyŏngsang.
i Adapted from Hahn Bae-ho and Kim Kyu-taik, "Korean Political Leaders (1952–1962): Their Social Origins and Skills," *Asian Survey*, Vol. 3 (July 1963), p. 315.
j Percentages are computed using N: 38; data on province of birth were unavailable for 10 members.

Graduation from the ROK War College in the post-Korean War years was another experience that many SCNR members had in common. Many of them also had been among the early group of officers sent by the ROK government to the United States for training during or just after the Korean War.

One must look beyond the composition of the SCNR, however, to identify fully the composition of factions within the military revolutionary elite, for one of the most powerful factions centered on Kim Chong-p'il, who was not a member of the Council. Kim is a close friend of Park Chung-hee and his nephew by marriage. As indicated previously, he was a member of the KMA 8th Graduating Class, from which many of his political associates had come. Kim's experience in Army intelligence had served him well in his central role in planning and organizing the overthrow of the Chang regime. Subsequently, these same talents were put to use in heading the ROK Central Intelligence Agency, an organization which became the key instrument of political control by the new regime. Late in 1962 and early in 1963, Kim utilized the organizational apparatus of the CIA as a base from which to oversee the planning and management of the new Democratic-Republican Party.

As mentioned previously, it was with the creation of the DRP that a particularly severe rift within the ruling junta occurred, primarily between a group rallying to the banner of Kim Chong-p'il and those opposed to Kim. The key points at issue were not only whether or not it was desirable to make a transition to civil rule, but also whether the party should follow the leadership of Kim, or whether the party should seek alternative or perhaps multiple leadership.

Early in January, General Song Yo-ch'an, former Premier of the military government, and once Park Chung-hee's commanding officer, charged that the proposed extension of military rule was a betrayal of public pledges, and that excessive power had been concentrated in Park's hands. A week later, Brig. General Yu Wŏn-sik, a former SCNR member, made similar charges. Less than a week after that, Marine Lt. General Kim Tong-ha resigned from the SCNR, asserting that the regime was "betraying the people's confidence" and that the DRP, of which he had been a charter member, had become simply a faction of Kim Chong-p'il and his followers.[67]

During the next six weeks, nine more Councillors left the SCNR. Five of these resigned to devote full time to the DRP. Four were relieved of their positions, including Kim Tong-ha's Marine associates, Chŏng Se-ung and Kim Yun-kŭn, and Army Colonels O Ch'i-sŏng and Pak Wŏn-bin. In March, the ROK CIA announced that it had uncovered a plot to overthrow the government. Twenty-one military and civilian suspects were arrested, including Kim Tong-ha, Kim Yun-kŭn, and former SCNR member Pak Im-hang. Earlier in March, Brig. General Yu Wŏn-sik and others had been arrested on charges of involvement in various financial scandals. In August, Song Yo-ch'an was arrested after publishing an open letter urging Park Chung-hee not to run for the Presidency.

Kim Chong-p'il and his followers were ostensibly the political beneficiaries of the above purges. However, the political situation was turbulent and complicated, with the Kim forces experiencing "downs" as well as "ups." Under pressure from those critical of Kim's increasing power, Chairman Park had persuaded Kim to resign from the DRP in February 1963, and to go into temporary exile as an "ambassador-at-large." Direction of the CIA was turned over to new leadership, and several CIA men identified with Kim were removed. It was rumored that the DRP would be disbanded; a separate party, led by anti-Kim forces in the military, was organized. By July, however, the Kim forces had regained dominance in the junta. Kim Hyŏng-uk, classmate and confederate of Kim Chong-p'il, took control of the CIA. The former director went into exile. The DRP remained in existence, with Park Chung-hee as its Presidential candidate. In the autumn of 1963, Kim Chong-p'il returned to Korea to win a seat in the National Assembly and to regain his central position in DRP leadership—only to quit both again in mid-1968.[68]

QUASI-CIVILIANIZATION

The phase of Korean politics that was ushered in with the 1963 elections can be described aptly by Finer's concept of "quasi-civilianization."[69] Most of the ruling junta resigned their mililitary commissions, but after the elections moved into key elective or appointive positions as "civilian" officials. The base of power was broadened through assimilation of civilian politicians and civil servants into the governmental structure. This process of "quasi-civilianization" was continued, with reliance on civilian institutions strengthened somewhat by the recurrence of elections in 1967. However, the Presidency and several cabinet positions have continued to be occupied by former high-ranking military officers. Moreover, Lee Hu-rak, for years Secretary-General to the President, later head of the Korean Central Intelligence Agency and now (1974) in retirement; Kil Chae-ho, former Secretary-General of the ruling DRP; Kim Hyŏng-uk, former Director of the CIA; and many other leading figures in the political arena are retired military officers.

Although former military experience remains salient as a basis of factional grouping and of reference group identification among retired military men, the fact that a process of quasi-civilianization has occurred makes it important analytically to make a distinction between those who have left military service, however much sentimental attachment they may retain for the military, and those who are still in uniform. The relevance of the distinction can be suggested by observing that it has become in the interest of those among the former group of individuals who now occupy influential "civilian" positions in government to depoliticize the latter group, or at least to neutralize any political ambitions that the latter may entertain. In subsequent discussion, the term "military" will be used to refer to those who remain formally in the armed services; those who have resigned or retired will be described as "ex-military" men.

Since the process of quasi-civilianization began, political power has been anchored in the group of ex-military leaders. However, the present military establishment possesses impressive political resources in its own right, the utilization of which could sharply alter or affect the course of Korean politics in coming years. Space limitations preclude a detailed enumeration of such resources here. We shall comment briefly only on (1) the scope and variety of roles which the military performs in Korea, (2) some politically relevant consequences of the ROK military commitment in Vietnam, (3) the salience of the primary role of the ROK armed forces at home in the light of renewed tensions with North Korea, and (4) some differences in attitudes that are evident between the current generation of young officers and those who came to power in the coup of 1961.

Scope and Variety of Military Roles in Korea. Over the past twenty-five years, every city, town, and village in Korea has sent young men into the armed forces. As of 1969, the number of men serving in the various arms of the ROK military establishment was as follows: Army, 560,000; Air Force, 15,000; Navy, 15,000; Marines, 25,000. In addition to the more than half a million men in uniform on active duty, hundreds of thousands now in civil life have had two or more years of military experience. Around 2,270,000 are reported to be getting continued exposure to the military through service in the militia, which is led primarily by retired officers.[70]

It is difficult fully to comprehend and impossible fully to document the cumulative impact of the process by which millions of Koreans have been exposed to military institutions and military ideas. One may safely suggest, however, that quite apart from the institutional changes effected by the 1961 coup, the social, economic, and political changes stimulated directly or indirectly by the military have been more far-reaching and significant than those generated by any other single group within the society. The development of modern skills, the transmission of knowledge and beliefs that undercut or replace traditional outlooks, the cultivation of new aspirations and altered values, all have been by-products of direct or indirect military experience (that is, experience of those who have themselves served in the armed forces, and of those in local communities whose lives have been changed by the presence of military units or by the return of military veterans).

Like all rapid social change, the process of change generated by the military in Korean society has had negative as well as positive consequences. The "how're-you-gonna-keep-'em-down-on-the-farm" effects of travel and contacts made during military service have produced a stream of thousands of young men from rural backgrounds to the cities (especially Seoul) upon completion of their service, thereby aggravating the problems of housing, congestion, and unemployment that characterize urban areas of Korea, as well as depriving farms and villages of potential skills. The awareness acquired through contact with the military of what technology can produce has stimulated a spiral of demands upon local and national governments which they seldom are able to satisfy. Moreover, the power and material benefits which those of high rank within the military sometimes enjoy have not only fired the imagination of ambitious subordinates (and in fact military careers have been an important avenue of upward social mobility in Korea), but also have fed a structure of patronage and favor.

Nonetheless, from the acquisition of primary education to the comprehension of the intricacies of highly complex modern equipment, the skill level of hundreds of thousands of Koreans has been increased through exposure to military training. Most skilled Korean technicians in fields such as electronics, auto and aircraft mechanics, shipbuilding, heavy construction, civil engineering, ordnance, and sanitation received their initial instruction in the military.

Moreover, the ROK military continues to perform a variety of roles that depart from a conventional combat orientation but nonetheless have important effects on the lives of fellow Koreans. The so-called "civic action" concept, which many American military and some civilian leaders regard as a promising means of fostering modernization in developing nations, had its original application in the Korean context and is still practised there. "Civic action" denotes the utilization of military units in a wide variety of developmental activities in a society. In Korea, ROK military men have assisted farmers in rice planting and harvesting as well as in the development of new and more effective means of production; military men have built dams, roads, and schools; they have distributed food, medical supplies, machinery and equipment to needy civilians; they have brought transistor radios to villages previously without any of the mass media; they have entertained and educated villagers and have provided them with medical treatment; military units have established fraternal relationships with civilian communities and schools, and have organized youth groups.[71]

The Korean Commitment in Vietnam. In September 1964, Korea took the first step in a military commitment to the Republic of Vietnam with the dispatch of one medical company. The commitment was greatly expanded in 1965 with the dispatch of an Army infantry division and a marine brigade to Vietnam, shortly after the major American combat commitment in Vietnam had begun.[72] By 1969, more than 50,000 Koreans were on active military duty in Vietnam. In addition, some 15,500 Korean technicians and about 1,500 Korean civilians in various categories ranging from business to diplomacy were in Vietnam by 1969. The Vietnam commitment was providing Korea with revenues (mostly from the American government) of over $165 million for fiscal year 1968 (as compared to approximately $135 million in FY67, and $18 million in FY65).[73]

For the ROK military themselves, the Vietnamese experience has had a number of consequences in addition to the increase in size and improvement of equipment that have been made possible through agreement with the United States. An across-the-board pay increase became possible, as well as combat allowances which, relative to regular pay scales in the ROK armed forces, were lavish. A ROK private serving in Vietnam made the equivalent of $38.40 in U. S. currency per month, for example, whereas if he remained in Korea he would be paid the equivalent of less than $2 per month. A second consequence of the Vietnamese commitment was that ROK military units acquired valuable combat experience and training that in many instances they would have been unable even to simulate in Korea. For instance, Lt. General Chae Myŏng-sin, who served for nearly three years as commander of ROK forces in Vietnam, has observed that Korean artillery troops had nearly unlimited supplies of ammunition to fire as the situation dictated in Vietnam, whereas in Korea they are limited to one practice-firing per year. A further consequence of the Vietnamese experience was that the impressive performance of Korean troops enhanced the prestige of the military.[74]

HEIGHTENED TENSIONS ALONG THE 38TH PARALLEL

The importance of the ROK military to the civilian sector in Korea has been increased not only through benefits derived and prestige accrued from the Vietnam commitment, but also by virtue of anxieties generated from the series of armed clashes along the 38th parallel and from the sharp rise since 1966 in provocative incidents by North Korean forces operating in South Korea. The incidents include an attempted assassination of President Park Chung-hee in January 1968, the seizure of the American *S.S. Pueblo* two days later, an ambush of a United Nations command truck, the shooting down of an American reconnaissance plane in April 1969, the hi-jacking to North Korea of a Korean Airlines passenger plane in December 1969, and various guerrilla landings along the South Korean coast, including one landing of about 130 North Korean commandos. The imminent possibility of a renewed outbreak of war with North Korea strengthens the voice of ROK military leaders in the councils of government, and provides a major incentive for all politicians to advocate maintenance of the armed forces at top levels of strength and readiness. At the same time, the credentials of politicians who are ex-military men, such as President Park, are enhanced to the extent that people believe that those with military backgrounds and connections are peculiarly able to keep those presently on active duty in the military under control. Those of the ruling Democratic-Republican Party who have favored a constitutional amendment paving the way for a third term of office for President Park Chung-hee have cited his proven ability to control the armed forces as a distinctive qualification for continuation in the Presidency.

The New Professionals. Although President Park and most of the other key figures who executed the military coup of 1961 are still relatively young, the gap in values and perspectives between them and those who are now moving into important middle level positions (such as those held by various participants in the 1961 coup) in the armed forces may be greater than the difference in years suggests. For instance, results of an attitude survey conducted at all of the leading military educational institutions in the Republic of Korea in 1966 have shown striking differences between respondents age 30 and above, and those under 30. Most of the older officers held views on policy issues (such as that of Korea-Japan normalization) that were highly congruent with policy views articulated by the Park Chung-hee administration. Among younger officers, cadets, and midshipmen, there was a much lower degree of congruence with administration views. Indeed, the divergence from official views among young military professionals resembled a similar divergence among a civilian college sample.[75]

The first of those who have had a full four-year education in the Korean service academies are now beginning to assume important responsibilities in the ROK military establishment. It is not surprising that their attitudes and outlooks differ from those who comprised the officer corps at the time of the constabulary and during the early years of the ROK military establishment. The four-year academy graduates have had other career experiences sharply different from most of those who planned and executed the coup of 1961 and who now hold top positions in the civilian government. Few officers with prior experience in the Japanese army remain on active duty. Indeed, the bulk of the officer corps now consists of men who were too young to have served during the Korean War; many instead saw combat in Vietnam. This is, in short, a "new breed" of ROK military professionals. By and large they are better trained than any group of their predecessors, and have received more and better-quality education. Given the important responsibilities that they will be undertaking and the vast political resources that they will command, it seems inescapable that the new professionals will exert an important influence on Korean policies and politics in the years ahead. The probable nature and direction of that influence remain important but largely unanswered questions.

FOOTNOTES

1. I began the research that led to the present analysis several years ago from documentary, biographical, and periodical sources publicly available in the United States; the early research was supported by the Center for Research in Social Systems. In the summer of 1965, I was able to travel to Korea, where I met with faculty members at most of the leading ROK military educational institutions and engaged in discussions with a number of civilian politicians and with several Korean social scientists. The field research in Korea was supported by Indiana University through Ford Foundation grant funds. Subsequently, I have probed further into the complex events of the early post-World War II years in documentary materials in the custody of the Modern Military Records Division, U.S. National Archives; Miss Hannah M. Zeidlik, Office of the Chief of Military History, has greatly helped me in searching through available sources. In both early and recent phases of research, I have profited enormously from the assistance and advice of Key P. Yang, Head of the Korean Section, U. S. Library of Congress, and of his assistant, Young H. Yoo. At Indiana University, I have had valuable assistance at various stages of research from Young Bae Kim, Peter Lee, and

Tong Won Kim. My analysis has benefited from criticisms and comments by Gregory Henderson, Bae-ho Hahn, William Henthorn, J. Mark Mobius, and Ilpyong J. Kim on an early draft of the manuscript. Collaboration on a related research project with Mun Hui Sok and Young-ho Lee, and on another with C. I. Eugene Kim also has directly enhanced the analysis reported here. Finally, there are many other persons to whom I am deeply grateful for sharing ideas with me or for recounting personal experiences relevant to the analysis, but whom it is inappropriate to identify personally. These include a former Premier of the Republic of Korea, two former Ministers of Defense, three persons who have served as ROK Army Chiefs of Staff, several ROK officers who participated in the coup of 1961 as well as some who did not, and a number of other persons currently or previously engaged in politics in Korea. If, in spite of the abundant assistance herein noted, errors of fact remain in the analysis, these are to be laid at my feet, not at the feet of those who have helped or encouraged me. Likewise, the interpretation of events is exclusively my responsibility; help or encouragement to me in no way suggests endorsement of my findings or conclusions.

2. The present analysis also should be viewed in the context of the historical pattern of Korean politics. For a synthesis of the old and the new in Korean politics, see Gregory Henderson, *Korea: The Politics of the Vortex* (Cambridge, Mass.: Harvard University Press, 1968). In a trenchant and compelling manner, Henderson relates the pattern of recent Korean politics to structural constraints and patterns of political behavior that had become entrenched hundreds of years before, especially by the administrative centralization and state Confucianism of the Yi dynasty.

3. The paucity of resources of USAFIK included not only a relatively small contingent of personnel, but more importantly a woeful lack of preparation for occupation duties in Korea. The dearth of American policy preparation for the Korean occupation, and the extent to which problems in Korea were compounded rather than alleviated by the American occupying forces due to ignorance of the Korean situation are subjects worthy of extended analysis and discussion; unfortunately, space limitations preclude such analysis here. Pertinent data are available at the U.S. National Archives (see note 1). Also, see E. Grant Meade, *American Military Government in Korea* (New York: King's Crown Press of Columbia University, 1951); Soon Sung Cho, *Korea in World Politics, 1940-1950: An Evaluation of American Responsibility* (Berkeley: University of California Press, 1967); Robert Sawyer, with Walter G. Hermes, ed., *Military Advisors in Korea: KMAG in Peace and War*, U.S. Army Historical Series (Washington: U.S. Government Printing Office, 1962).

4. Meade, pp. 54-56; Sawyer, pp. 8-9; *The Voice of Korea*, III (Feb. 25, 1946), 86.

5. *The Voice of Korea*, V (May 15, 1948), 284.

6. Republic of Korea, Department of Army, Office of Military History, *Yukkun Palchŏn-sa* (History of the Development of the Army; Seoul, 1955), I; Sawyer, p. 12.

7. A detailed statement of the American governmental rationale in support of "civic action" programs, with numerous examples of the application of the concept, is found in a special issue of *Army* (July 1963). An analysis providing a systematic framework for critically evaluating civic action programs is that of Davis B. Bobrow, "The Civic Role of the Military: Some Critical Hypotheses,"

Components of Defense Policy, ed. D. B. Bobrow (Chicago: Rand McNally, 1965), pp. 272-283. Civic action programs in a variety of nation-states have been assessed by Jess P. Unger, *The Military Role in Nation Building and Economic Development* (Comparative Administrative Group Occasional Papers; Bloomington, Indiana: International Development Research Center, Indiana University, 1963).

8. U. S., Army, U. S. Army Forces in Korea, *South Korean Interim Government Activities,* No. 25 (National Economic Board of Korea, October 1947), p. 165.

9. *Ibid.*

10. *South Korean Interim Government Activities,* No. 32 (May 1948), p. 185.

11. Republic of Korea, Ministry of Defense, Bureau of Troop Information and Education, *Kukpangbu-sa* (History of the Ministry of Defense; Seoul, 1954), I, 22. See also Sawyer, pp. 79-87.

12. U. S., Department of the Army, *U. S. Army Handbook for Korea,* prepared by the Foreign Area Studies Division, Special Operations Research Office, The American University (1964 ed. rev.; Washington: GPO), pp. 562-563. The purge in the ROK armed forces also is described in a letter from Brig. General William L. Roberts, first chief of KMAG, cited in Sawyer, p. 40.

13. Mark W. Clark, *From the Danube to the Yalu* (New York: Harper and Brothers, 1954), p. 171.

14. The ROK Air Force, like the Army, had expanded its training program. For details, see William Green and John Fricker, "The Republic of Korea Air Force," *The Air Forces of the World* (1958), p. 192.

15. Dwight D. Eisenhower, *Mandate for Change* (New York: Signet, 1965), p. 229.

16. United Nations Korean Reconstruction Agency (UNKRA), *Report of the Agent General of the United Nations Reconstruction Agency for the Period 1 October 1953 to 1 September 1954* (General Assembly, 9th sess., official records, supp. No. 29, A. 2750, 1954).

17. T. R. Fehrenbach, *This Kind of War* (New York: Macmillian, 1963), pp. 65-76.

18. Clark, p. 179.

19. Interview by the author with a retired ROK general, Dec. 1964.

20. *New York Times,* July 24, 1952, p. 3. *The Voice of Korea,* XI (Feb. 19, 1954), 719. It is of interest that subsequent to his dismissal as Chief of Staff, Lt. General Yi became Superintendent of the Army Command and Staff College, which during his tenure became an important forum for political discussion among military professionals.

21. For example, with Presidential elections forthcoming, the Korean Ambassador to the U. S. issued a statement in 1956, published also in Korea, warning that there was a "danger that the present program of American aid to the Republic of Korea would not be continued if anyone other than President Syngman Rhee became President of the Republic of Korea." Quoted in the *Korean Republic,* Jan. 28, 1956, and cited in *The Voice of Korea,* XIII (Mar. 1, 1956), 815.

22. The text of the treaty is in *U.S. Treaties and other International Agreements,* Dept. of State, TIAS 3097, V, part 3, 2372-2375.

23. Figures on ROK Army strength at the time vary somewhat. Official ROK Army sources put the total at 600,000. See Hq. ROK Army, Office of Information, *Republic of Korea Army 1957* (Yearbook, 1957), p. 106. A former Korean advisor to the U.S. Military Governor in Korea during 1948-1949 estimates that

by 1956 the ROK Army had a strength of three-quarters of a million men. Channing Liem, "Korea: Partner for Freedom," *Current History*, XXXI (1956), 20. Another specialist on Korea puts the figure at 700,000. Shannon McCune, "The United States and Korea," *The United States and the Far East*, ed. Willard L. Thorp (The American Assembly, 1956), p. 39.

24. "Military Purification Movement Leads to 1961 May Revolution," *Korean Report* (May 1962), pp. 10–12.

25. An "old Seoul gentleman" (quoted by Edward Neilan, "Rhee Ad Infinitum," *The New Republic* (March 1960), pp. 8–9.

26. Kyung-cho Chung, *New Korea: New Land of the Morning Calm* (New York: Macmillan, 1962), p. 71

27. Park Chung-hee, "What Made Revolution Succeed," *Koreana Quarterly*, as reprinted in the *Korean Republic* (Aug. 15, 1961), p. D.

28. Richard C. Allen, "South Korea: The New Regime," in the "Notes and Comment" Section of *Pacific Affairs* (Spring 1961), p. 55.

29. Edward Neilan, "South Korea Poised on Uneasy Edge," *Christian Science Monitor* (June 8, 1960), p. 9. Italics are added.

30. "Defense Minister Emphasizes for Neutrality of Armed Forces," *Hankuk Ilbo*, as translated in *Korean Daily Press Translation Service* (Aug. 25, 1960), p. 10.

31. For example, see "General Palmer Opposes Drastic Disarmament," *Hankuk Ilbo;* "Gen. White Urges Prudence in Cleaning of Armed Forces," *The Dong-A Ilbo*; "Army Chief of Staff Refutes Gen. Palmer's Statement," *Minkuk Ilbo*; and "On Conflict of Opinion Concerning the Purge of Military Leaders," *Chosun Ilbo;* as translated in *K.D.P.T.S.*, (Sept. 21, 1960), p. 6; (Sept. 22, 1960), p. 34; (Sept. 22, 1960). p. 31; and (Sept. 24, 1960), p. 21, respectively.

32. "16 Leading Army Officers Visit Joint Chief of Staff Chairman to Make Some Important Recommendations on Purge of Generals," and "16 Army Officers Referred to Disciplinary Committee for Recommending Resignation of Former JCS Chairman," *Seoul Il'il Shinmun*, as translated in *K.D.P.T.S.* (Sept. 25, 1960), p. 41, and (Oct. 9, 1960), p. 32, respectively.

33. "Gov't to Reduce 30,000 Instead of 50,000 Servicemen Next Year," *Hankuk Ilbo*, as translated in *K.D.P.T.S.* (Sept. 29, 1960). "Key Armed Forces Commanding Generals' Conference Convenes: Premier Chang Announces Completion of Purge Among Military Personnel," *Dong-A Ilbo*, as translated in *K.D.P. T.S.* (Nov. 15, 1960), p. 42. "Chang Addresses Meeting of Service Chiefs," *The Republic News Service* (Nov. 14, 1960), p. 2.

34. Actually, three different programs of instruction were given to various members of the group known as the "8th graduating class." Only those who had had no prior military experience entered the academy in December 1948; their instruction was of six months duration. Those who had had prior military experience joined the class after three months. One group of those with prior military experience was drawn from the ranks of the ROK Army, and given a three-months program of instruction. Another group, known as the "special squad," was drawn from among those who had served in the Japanese, Manchurian, or Chinese Army. The "special squad" received only a couple of weeks of training at KMA prior to being commissioned; because of their short stay at the academy, they are sometimes excluded from descriptions of the composition of the 8th graduating class. Kang In-sŏp, "The 8th Graduating Class of the Military Academy," *Sin Tong-a*

(Sept. 1964). See also *Korean Report* (May 1962), p.11.

35. I am conforming to the practice prevalent in writings about Korean politics in describing the events of April 1960 and of May 1961 as the "Student Revolution" and the "Military Revolution," respectively. Whether either, or both, of these events effected a "revolution" in a rigorous analytical sense is debatable. From a broader historical perspective, the two events were but important landmarks in a period of rapid social and political change that had begun decades earlier, and that had been accelerated by the turbulence of the occupation period and of the Korean War. However, it is convenient for present purposes to set terminological issues aside, using the terms "revolution" and "coup d'etat" almost interchangeably. More important for our purposes than a definitive labelling of the events is the fact that the military elite that came to power in 1961 *called themselves revolutionaries,* even though they subsequently expressed some ambivalence as to whether their actions had effected a genuine and lasting revolution.

36. Other pledges included: (2) continuation of adherence to the UN Charter, fulfillment of international agreements, and restrengthening of ties with the U.S. and other free nations; (3) eradication of corruption and rejuvenation of the national spirit; (4) relief of economic misery and the establishment of a self-sustaining economy; (5) development of the strength needed for ultimate realization of reunification; (6) transference of the government to civilian control and the return of the military to their original duties—upon completion of the other pledges. With some variations in wording, English translations of the six pledges are found in the following sources. Republic of Korea, Military Revolutionary Committee, *A Statement by the Military Revolutionary Committee* (May 16, 1961), P. I. Park Chung-hee, *The Country, The Revolution and I,* Leon Sinder, ed. (Publisher not indicated, 1963), pp. 55–56, Park, *Korean Republic* (Aug. 15, 1961), p. D.

37. "The Military Revolution in Korea," *Korean Report* (Oct. 1961), p. 6.

38. Republic of Korea, Ministry of Foreign Affairs, *Republic of Korea* (July 1, 1961), 15 pp., p. 11.

39. *Korean Report* (Oct. 1961), p. 6.

40. Park, *The Country, The Revolution and I,* p. 177.

41. Park, *Korean Republic* (Aug. 15, 1961), p. D.

42. Park Chung-hee, *People's Path to the Fulfillment of Revolutionary Tasks* (Seoul: ROK Ministry of Public Information, n. d.), 12 pp.

43. Song Yo-ch'an, "Revolution's First 2 Months' Achievement," *Korean Republic* (Aug. 15, 1961), p. E.

44. Lee Soo-young, *The Revolution in Korea: A Report to Our Friends Around the World,* foreword by Oh Chae-kyŏng, ROK Minister of Information (Seoul, Jan. 1962), 12 pp., pp. 7–8.

45. Lee Soo-young, pp. 7–8.

46. Park Chung-hee, *Our Nation's Path: Ideology of Social Reconstruction* (Seoul: Tong-a Publishing Co., 1962), pp. 14–15. Italics are added.

47. Park, *Korean Republic* (Aug. 15, 1961), p. D.

48. Park, *Korean Republic* (Aug. 15, 1961), p. D. Italics are added.

49. Park, *Our Nation's Path,* p. 106.

50. Park, *Our Nation's Path,* p. 47.

51. Park, *Our Nation's Path,* pp. 106–107.

52. Park, *Our Nation's Path,* p. 105.

53. Park, *The Country, The Revolution and I,* pp. 109–153.

54. Park, *The Country, The Revolution and I*, pp. 145-153, 181.

55. Walter Briggs, "The Military Revolution in Korea: On Its Leader and Achievements," *Koreana Quarterly*, V (Summer 1963), 17-34. Magruder is quoted on p. 30. Briggs served as consultant to the ROK Mission to the UN. It is of interest to note that Lt. Gen. Han-lim Yi was imprisoned during the military government period for his failure actively to support the coup. However, subsequently he became head of a government-owned fertilizer factory, and in 1969 was brought into the cabinet as Minister of Construction.

56. Briggs, *Koreana Quarterly*, V (Summer 1963), pp. 17-34. There was some criticism of the Magruder and Green statements in Washington, since they were made without consultation with the State Department or the President. *New York Times*, May 19, 1961, p. 1.

57. Quoted by A.M. Rosenthal, "Men of New Type Run Seoul Regime," *New York Times*, July 14, 1961, p. 1.

58. The fall of General Chang came in stages. See *New York Times*, June 4, 1961, p. 9; June 6, 1961, p. 3; July 4, 1961, pp. 1, 18.

59. *Korean Report* (Oct. 1961), p. 7.

60. Republic of Korea, SCNR, Chairman, *Statement Concerning the Turnover of the Government to Civilian Control* (Aug. 12, 1961), p. 1.

61. Kim Chong-p'il, as quoted in Kim Kwang-sŏp, *Korean Report* (Jan. 1963), p. 12.

62. An English translation of the nine-point proposal and an account of key events relevant to the decision to go ahead with elections in 1963 (especially detailed for the period January-March 1963) are contained in *Korean Report*, III (Feb.-Mar. 1963), 3-6.

63. *Korean Report*, III (Feb.-Mar. 1963), 3-6.

64. This confusing sequence of events was followed quite closely by the *New York Times*, January-May 1963.

65. Republic of Korea, SCNR, "New Law Concerning Extraordinary Measures for National Reconstruction" (sometimes called the Basic Law of the Military Government) signed and promulgated June 6, 1961, English translation in Chung, *New Korea*, pp. 224-230.

66. Fragmentary data collected by the author on 279 persons holding ambassadorships, gubernatorial posts, or top civil service positions during the period since 1961 reveal that 5 percent were over 60 years of age as of 1960, 23 percent were between 51 and 60 years, 35 percent were between the ages of 41 and 50, 35 percent between 31 and 40, and 2 percent 30 or younger.

67. *Korean Report*, III (Feb.-Mar. 1963), 5. The Song Yo-ch'an, Yu Wŏn-sik, and Kim Tong-ha episodes and their relationship to the 1963 elections are described in Chong-sik Lee, "Korea: In Search of Stability," *Asian Survey*, IV (Jan. 1964), 656-665.

68. A more detailed, albeit concise, description of key political events of 1963 is found in William A. Douglas, "South Korea's Search for Leadership," *Pacific Affairs*, XXXVII (Spring 1964), 20-36. A biographical sketch of Kim Chong-p'il, describing some of the key events of the period is found in "Ambitious Korean," *New York Times*, June 6, 1964, p. 4. It should be noted that Kim Chong-ik, brother of Kim Chong-p'il, was elected in 1968 to the Assembly seat which the latter had vacated.

69. As Finer notes, the transition from direct military rule to "quasi-civilian-

ization" is a common one. S.E. Finer, *The Man on Horseback* (New York: Praeger, 1962), pp. 176–190.

70. *Korea Week,* April 30, 1969, p. 1.

71. In addition to information derived from interviews of ROK officers and of American officers who have served in Korea, *Yukkun Sinmun* (Army Times), a weekly publication of the ROK Army Bureau of Information and Education intended for distribution to military personnel, provided the basic source of information utilized by the author in investigating ROK civic action programs. The author is grateful to Tong Won Kim for assistance in selectively translating the periodical over a two-year period.

72. One can identify a causal relationship between the American decision to escalate the U. S. commitment in Vietnam and the ROK military commitment in Vietnam. The major Korean commitment came only after the U. S. government had agreed to support (that is, equip and supply) an increase in ROK forces remaining in Korea equal to 50% of the number committed to Vietnam. The United States also agreed to provide logistical support to all allied forces in Vietnam, and through a contract with the Korean government provided two out of three of the daily meals to ROK servicemen in Vietnam. A chronology of the Korean commitment to Vietnam is provided in *Korea Week,* May 15, 1968, p. 1. A brief description of the American-Korean quid pro quo is provided in *Korea Week,* June 15, 1969, p. 2.

73. *Korea Week,* June 15, 1969, p. 2.

74. *Korea Week,* July 15, 1969, p. 2.

75. John P. Lovell, Mun Hui Sok, Young Ho Lee, "Professional Orientation and Policy Perspectives of Military Professionals in the Republic of Korea," *Midwest Journal of Political Science,* XIII (August 1969).

PART FOUR:　　MAJOR POLICY FOCUSES
IN CONTEMPORARY KOREAN POLITICS:
FOREIGN AFFAIRS AND
ECONOMIC DEVELOPMENT

CHAPTER 7: The Conduct of Foreign Affairs
　　　　　　by Youngnok Koo

CHAPTER 8: Economic Development in South Korea:
　　　　　　A Retrospective View of the 1960's
　　　　　　by Princeton Lyman

CHAPTER 9: Recent Trends in the Government's
　　　　　　Management of the Economy
　　　　　　by Jungsae Kim

INTRODUCTION TO PART FOUR

Two major focuses of governmental attention in Korea in recent years have been foreign relations and the economy. Both areas have seen dramatic changes, particularly in the past ten years. In the following section Youngnok Koo has written about foreign relations, and Princeton Lyman and Jungsae Kim about economic planning and development.

In the realm of foreign affairs, Korea's stance has ranged from staunch anti-communism of all shades and varieties during the 1950's and until the mid-1960's, to a current policy of rapprochement with any nation, other than North Korea, willing to establish friendly relations. The basis rationale behind this modified approach to foreign policy is economic—any nation which can enhance Korea's export volume has become worthy of attention. It is also intended to further isolate North Korea from the international community.

Historically, Korea's role in international relations has been passive, in reaction to the vicissitudes of larger Far Eastern powers, including China, Japan, Russia and, more lately, the United States and other western nations. During the Yi dynasty China wielded the greatest influence on Korea—culturally, politically and socially. In general, Korea accepted her subordinate role and at least remained an independent entity. This ended, however, with Japanese colonization in 1910. The colonial period, in turn, ended with the defeat of Japan in 1945, when the nation was divided into north and south, supposedly for temporary military occupation purposes. The two occupying powers, the United States and the Soviet Union, supported a continuing division of the nation, basically because the northern regime would not allow free United Nations movement and observation which might have led to open elections for unification under a single government. This division was maintained during and after the stalemated Korean War (1950–1953) and remains true today.

South Korea up to the present has espoused adherence to the Hallstein Doctrine, which refuses to recognize the North Korean state, and to exchange ambassadors with any nation that recognizes North Korea. Even so, South Korea has embassies in Indonesia, India and the United Arab Republic where North Korea also maintains diplomatic relations on the ambassadorial level. And, as indicated above, economic relations are welcome with all "friendly" nations. South Korea's present attitude toward the North is that a communist regime exists north of the demarcation line; however, this does not constitute recognition of North Korea as a separate and sovereign state. Just how consistent the Korean Government can be in maintaining the Hallstein Doctrine remains to be seen. The Government presently holds to the idea of "One Nation, One State, Two Governments." The total application and significance of this stance remains to be clarified at some future date.

Two major foreign policy issues during the 1960's were the normalization of relations with Japan in 1965 and the sending of Korean troops to Vietnam beginning in 1964. Both decisions were objects of nationwide debate and even street demonstrations. In the United Nations, South Korea in 1969 suspended its twenty-year policy of automatic annual debate on the Korean question and decided to present the issue to the General Assembly only when the need might arise. In 1971 and 1972 the General Assembly resolved to postpone the debate for another year. In 1973, however, South Korea proposed a dual representation system for Korea in the U.N., and acquiesced to the dissolution of UNCURK. The General Assembly then adopted a consensus statement saying that reunification should be achieved by peaceful means without outside force or interference. South Korea's position is that the Koreans themselves should deal with the reunification issue directly rather than in an international forum such as the U.N. The creation of the Asian and Pacific Council (ASPAC) in 1966 was an attempt by the Republic of Korea to establish closer relations with other non-communist Asian nations. Instigated by South Korea, ASPAC maintains a cultural and social center in Seoul and a registry of experts' services in Canberra. Most member-nations have seen ASPAC as properly concentrating on economic, technical, social and cultural programs, while Korea in ASPAC's initial years seemed alone in favoring a future extension of functions of the organization to include a regional collective defense system. However, Korea is cognizant of the fact that this cannot be done in the immediate future and has expressed willingness to limit the organization's activities to areas of economic, technical, social and cultural cooperation. Some member states, however, have indicated a desire to withdraw from ASPAC under any conditions, and the future of the organization is uncertain. Direct contact between North and South has taken place since August of 1971 when the Korean Red Cross Society in Seoul proposed negotiations with the goal of reunifying families separated by the division and the war. No substantial progress has been made in these exchanges. In May 1972, secret political talks first took place between high-level leaders from the south and north. A joint communique on July 4, 1972, stated that reunification was to be achieved by peaceful means and without outside force or interference. A South-North Coordinating Committee was established; however, as with the Red Cross talks, no tangible results have yet evolved.

In any event, the Republic of Korea is consciously looking for ways to broaden her foreign relations in order to enhance her position in the international community as well as to find new markets for her increasing volume of export commodities. She remains strongly dependent on United

States support, which seems necessary at present to balance North Korea's support from the Soviet Union and Communist China.

Korean economic growth in the past ten years has been considered exemplary among developing nations. The annual growth rate averaged 8.7 percent from 1960–1970, while the value of commodity exports has risen from $41 million in 1961 to $3.2 billion in 1973. In his general introductory essay, Princeton Lyman is positive about the prospects for future growth because of the "great economic, technical and intellectual sophistication in Korea." His essay and Kim's more detailed analysis point up that Korea's economic progress and problems since 1961 are attributable primarily to a highly government-controlled economic system, based largely upon indirect government direction of economic enterprises, rather than upon direct government entrepreneurship. Government policies have included control of bank savings and loan rates in order to encourage investment; favorable treatment of commodity export producing firms; substantial liberalization of import policy, with particular reference to raw materials to be further processed by Korean industry for export; the attracting and absorbing of a substantially enlarged inflow of foreign capital; strict control of currency in circulation and exchange rates with foreign currencies; and achievement of an increasingly favorable international balance of payments.

Jungsae Kim, a long-time analyst of the Korean economy, points out that the country has had reasonable success in experimenting with overall national planning in the general atmosphere of private initiatives. Having begun with stress on light manufactures, Korea is attempting in less than a decade to draw close to the last stage of industrial maturity. Its performance is exemplary of the merits of unbalanced growth with a few modern industries leading in the break-away from the old equilibrium of underdevelopment.

When the country realized at the outset the incapability of agriculture as the mainstay of economic development, it quickly shifted over to the course of an "export-propelled" growth, preceded by a brief interim period of import substitution. On account of the absolute deficiency of physical resources and the limited internal marketability of mass output, there is, however, now emerging a wide-spread apprehension about excessive external dependence of the economy. Exporters confront increasing cartelized pressures in the purchase of raw materials from overseas, and often find themselves extremely vulnerable to the cyclical economic changes and policy-directed alterations of trade flows in the outside world.

On the domestic front the chain of events responsible for the high rate of economic growth is to a large extent attributable to the advent of a forceful political leadership, assisted solely by a well-trained and disciplined civil service with extensive planning and regulatory powers. Its authority derives ultimately from the loyal military which remains on the whole aloof from political engagements, whereas under the pretext of political stability and efficiency there occur detractions from the traditional legislative and judicial functions of government. Further there is a strict disallowance of critical advances by political parties of all persuasions as well as by such organized "liberal" groups as universities and labor unions.

The same basic stance of the government is noticeable in its own ability to manage nearly all aspects and phases of economic activity from the mobilization of domestic saving for industrial investments to the retail sales of final products by resorting to policy incentives and disincentives as the case may be; and stringent price controls, tax drives, and "moral suasion" very effectively check unwarranted profits and other entrepreneurial irregularities and adjust distortions in the distribution of wealth and income, though frequently in defiance of the canons of private property and contractual rights. It is remarkable that there seems to be no special economic interest with which the regime is associated.

It is obvious that, for Korea, foreign policy and economic policy are intricately related—future diplomacy will be based not only upon old issues such as the threat of communism, but also upon the desire to expand markets for Korean commodities.

CHAPTER 7:

The Conduct of Foreign Affairs

YOUNGNOK KOO*

KOREA'S HERITAGE

In the conduct of foreign affairs, Korea has traditionally been handicapped by numerous interacting factors—geographical location, economic weakness, lack of knowledge about foreign nations, lack of technological skill, lack of a coherent ideological foundation in diplomacy, intense factional struggles, and incohesiveness of political groupings in Korea's political system. In present day Korea, many of the above legacies are further aggravated by the division of the nation into two ideologically opposed political systems. Unlike a nation endowed with vastly superior potential for the management of international affairs, Korea has limited capability to influence other nations in international politics. In other words, Korea's power to shape world events to her liking is hampered by the above interacting elements as they relate to the management of Korea's foreign relations.

Geographical Factors. The Korean peninsula is roughly 150 miles wide and 600 miles long with an area of 85,286 square miles. Korea's territory is approximately equal to the size of Minnesota or England-Scotland. On all sides it has natural boundaries: the Yellow Sea on the West, the Eastern Sea (or the Sea of Japan) on the East, and the Korean Strait to the South. The Yalu and Tumen Rivers separate Korea on the North from Manchuria, and, for an eleven-mile stretch,

---

*Youngnok Koo is Associate Professor of Political Science at Seoul National University. His Ph.D. is from the University of Michigan, Ann Arbor.

from the Soviet Union. The main island of Japan is about 120 miles to the southeast, while the Shantung peninsula of China is about an equal distance to the west; Manchuria shares almost all of Korea's northern border except where Korea and the Soviet Union meet. Thus, Korea is surrounded by most of the major powers of the Pacific.

Due to its unique geographical location, Korea occupies an important strategic position with regard to Far Eastern affairs: any control of Korea by one of the powers inevitably affects power relationships of the region. Perhaps this is one of the important reasons that Korea has been described by some as a "springboard for Japanese infiltration into the Asiatic mainland," or by others as a forward base for the invasion of Japan. In view of Korea's geographical configuration, Japan thought of Korea as "a dagger aimed at the heart of Japan"; on the other hand it could be viewed with equally forceful logic as "a hammer ready to strike at the head of China."

In addition to the above, Korea's northeast fronts an important Soviet naval base which constitutes her major outlet to the Pacific, the port of Vladivostok. In essence, Japan has viewed the Korean peninsula as a gangplank for entry to China, while China has regarded Korea as a buffer zone to repel an aggressor from attempts to invade. Russia has traditionally considered relations with Korea essential in the bidding for more southerly port facilities in the Pacific.[1] Indeed, one Korean writer states that the "fundamental fact underlying Korea's tragedy, like that of ancient Palestine or modern Poland, has been its geographical position, the basic cause for the unfortunate events suffered by Korea throughout history."[2]

Historical Factors. The place of Korea in international relations until 1910, the date of Japanese annexation, should be viewed within the context of the regional multipolarity situation among Japan, China, and Russia. The role and policy patterns of Korea may also be assessed according to the action and reaction of the major powers in the Far East. Until recent times, Korea's role in international affairs was characterized by her passive posture rather than one of active role-playing in the management of foreign affairs. With the exception of Korea's relations with China for the purpose of learning and assimilating Chinese culture, Korea rarely took the initiative in foreign relations.[3]

Formal relationships with foreign nations were concluded in the latter part of the nineteenth century: Japan (1876), the United States

(1882), Germany and Great Britain (1883), Italy and Russia (1884), France (1886), and Austria (1892).[4] However, the treaties establishing these relationships were never actively sought on the part of the Kingdom of Korea. These nations rather had *imposed* treaties on a reluctant Korean government. Korea was therefore a rather passive partner in her new-found relations with foreign powers.

The history of Korea has been in part a history of foreign infiltration from all directions. The threat against the physical security of Korea is as timeless as its history: trade, reciprocal fishing rights, imperialism, and communism are terms that have at one time or another been associated with foreign influence or foreign domination. The competition between nations seeking direct control of Korea—Japan, China, Russia—on the one hand, and nations seeking trade interests on the other, has put Korea in an extremely vulnerable international position. Her sovereignty has been denied, compromised, violated and ignored throughout her history, sometimes by one nation but more often by several of her power-pursuing neighbors.

Until the formal opening of Korea on the basis of the nineteenth-century treaties, Korea's foreign policy vacillated between a policy of absolute isolationism and a policy of occasional informal contact with the outside world. In order to understand Korea's position in international relations, it is necessary to assess more closely Korea's traditional relationship with China. The Kingdom of Korea was linked with the loosely structured imperial system of China for many centuries. However, the relationship was primarily cultural and economic rather than political. In other words, the Koreans were independent with respect to their own internal affairs. Under the Confucian system, Korea had failed to develop any concept of a strong, well-knit national government. The concept of power in the management of international relations, as well as the concept of the contractual nature of law as seen in the west, were hardly appreciated by the Koreans.

As a result of the Sino-Japanese war of 1894–1895, China was forced to sign the treaty of Shimonoseki on April 17, 1895. Under the terms of the treaty, China "recognized" Korea's independence. Since Korea's independence did not date from the treaty of Shimonoseki, it could be construed that the treaty was China's renouncement of her influence in Korea. The removal of China's influence meant essentially a renewed struggle between Japan and Russia for the control of Korea. This bipolar struggle for the domination of Korea ended when Japan emerged as the victor in the Russo-Japanese War.

When the Peace of Portsmouth was signed in 1905, Russia specifically recognized Japan's "paramount political, military and economic interest" in Korea, and also acknowledged that Russia would not obstruct whatever measures Japan "might deem it necessary to take there."[5]

As a result of the Russo-Japanese War in August of 1905, Korea was made a protectorate of Japan. By the terms of the Japanese-Korean treaty of November 17, 1905, Japan assumed control of Korea's foreign relations. The Japanese promptly set up the Government-General of Chosen and assumed virtually total control of Korean affairs. Nevertheless, the Emperor of Korea sent his personal representatives to present a protest to the Second Hague Conference (1907) against Japan's imposition of the 1905 treaty, as well as Japan's unwarranted intervention in Korean affairs. This futile effort of protestation became a pretext for the Japanese to force abdication of the Emperor; his son became the new Emperor and was compelled to transfer Korea's sovereignty to the Japanese Empire.[6]

From 1910-1945 Japan was in absolute control of Korea. The Japanese rulers adopted an avowed policy of assimilation through coercive methods, thereby denying the Korean people an opportunity to prepare themselves for eventual independence.

The sudden collapse of the Japanese Empire brought about the hope that Korea would become independent "in due course" as was promised at the Cairo Conference of 1943. However, the division of Korea into two military occupation zones, north and south of the 38th parallel, to receive the surrender of the Japanese forces subsequently resulted in the development of two hostile regimes. The genesis of the division of Korea at the thirty-eighth parallel is a rather complicated story, but the decision was probably made by the Pentagon in Washington to facilitate the surrender of Japanese in Korea.[7]

In the two years from 1945 to 1947 nothing was accomplished toward unifying Korea under a single government of its own choice, and the antagonism between the two occupying powers, the United States and the Soviet Union, increased markedly.

THE FIRST ROUND OF CONFRONTATION

Hardening of the Division. The Founding of the Republic of Korea in the south was the result of the futility of direct negotiation between the two occupying nations. The breakdown of negotiations ultimately meant the division of Korea into two separate political entities along the 38th parallel. The Korean people were thus deprived of the opportunity for independence under a single government.

By 1947 the United States found itself facing three unpleasant alternatives with regard to the future disposition of Korea: (1) the United States could withdraw from South Korea which would mean giving all of Korea to the Soviets; (2) the United States could go to the other extreme and establish a protectorate over South Korea; (3) the United States could aid South Korea economically and militarily to a point where Koreans could accomplish their own goal of a strong, self-sustaining nation-state.[8] Faced with this dilemma, the United States refused to take the responsibility of Korea's future upon itself and decided to lay the whole question of Korean independence before the second regular session of the General Assembly of the United Nations. The General Assembly adopted a resolution proposed by the United States providing for Korean independence. However, North Korea's refusal to let the United Nations Temporary Commission on Korea perform the function of "the right to travel, observe, and consult throughout Korea," led to a total impasse. In 1948 the United Nations recognized the Republic of Korea "as the validly elected, lawful government of Korea in which elections were permitted— the only such lawful government in Korea."[9]

Following the General Assembly resolution of November 14, 1947, urging that member nations and other nations establish their relations with the Republic of Korea, the United States accorded full recognition on January 1, 1949. The same act was soon followed by China, France, the United Kingdom, and the Republic of the Philippines.[10] By June, 1950 the Republic of Korea had entered into formal diplomatic relations with twenty-one nations.[11] However, Korea's efforts to gain membership in the United Nations failed. On January 19, 1949, the Republic of Korea applied for membership. Due to the negative vote of the Soviet Union, no recommendation for admission could be made to the General Assembly by the Security Council. All subsequent efforts to obtain membership in the United Nations were rebuffed by the Soviet Union—the most recent being 1958.

Almost immediately after the establishment of the Republic of Korea, another regime, the "Democratic People's Republic of Korea," was proclaimed in the northern zone under the aegis of the Soviet Union. The creation of the regime in the north was in direct violation of the principles outlined in the November 14, 1947, resolution of the General Assembly. The United Nations Commission on Korea described the regime in the following words:

> The northern regime is the creature of a military occupant and rules by right of a mere transfer of power from that Government. It has never been willing to give its subjects an unfettered opportunity, under the scrutiny of an impartial international agency, to pass upon its claim to rule. The claims to be a "people's" democracy and its expression of concern for the general welfare are falsified by this unwillingness to account for the exercise of power to those against whom it is employed.[12]

North Korea's application for admission to the United Nations was not even considered by the United Nations. As stated earlier, the General Assembly in its resolution of 1948 had already recognized the Republic of Korea as the only lawful government in Korea.

Basic Position of Korean Foreign Policy. The existence of two rival regimes in Korea was the direct result of the antagonism between the two superpowers, the United States and the Soviet Union. Due to the intense cold war political climate in the postwar era, Korea's foreign policy was immensely influenced by the nature of the bipolar ideological struggles. The gradual polarization of power between the Western bloc and the Eastern bloc had a profound impact over Korea's formulation of foreign policy. In fact, the policy of the United States toward Communist countries was reflected in capsule form in Korea's management of foreign affairs.

Syngman Rhee, the first President of the Korean Republic, set the pattern of Korean foreign policy, and the policy revealed his fears and prejudices. In general, Rhee's policies may be classified under three headings: (1) absolute anti-communism in foreign relations; (2) maintenance of friendly relations with free nations, with particular reliance on the United States; (3) active support of the United Nations resolutions on Korean unification. Basic to this policy was the severing of all forms of diplomatic relations with any nation which recognized North Korea. This policy, in effect, amounted to the absolute rejection of the doctrine of "two Koreas" and to open hostility to all Communist nations.[13] In sum, the policy of the rejection of "two Koreas" culminated in what was later known as the so-called Hallstein Doctrine. The doctrine meant the rupturing of diplomatic relations with nations establishing formal diplomatic ties with North Korea. The term, Hallstein, was derived from the name of the late German Chancellor Konrad Adenauer's vice-minister of foreign affairs, and the doctrine was official West German policy from 1954 to 1969.[14]

THE SECOND ROUND OF CONFRONTATION

The Korean Conflict. In perspective, it may be said that the war in Korea was largely due to the power vacuum created by postwar U.S. foreign policy. The United States had expected Nationalist China to play the role of stabilizer in the Far East after the collapse of the Japanese Empire in 1945. The take-over of the Chinese mainland by the Communists in 1949 shattered the very basic frame of American policy in the area: Japan was de-militarized and the American forces in Korea had withdrawn from Korea in 1949. Even under these circumstances, the United States had excluded the Republic of Korea from the American defense perimeter. Since the Republic of Korea was militarily unprepared to launch an attack against North Korea or to be able to defend herself against North Korea's aggression, the situation in Korea was an open invitation for assault by North Korea.[15]

North Korea's full-scale military aggression against the Republic occurred on June 25, 1950. The attack was swift and without warning. The United States, informed of the progress of North Korea's all-out offensive against the Republic of Korea by the U.S. Ambassador, requested an immediate meeting of the Security Council of the United Nations. On June 25 the Security Council found in its resolution that a breach of peace had been committed and ordered the North Korean troops to withdraw; a subsequent resolution of June 27 recommended that members "furnish such assistance to the Republic of Korea as may be necessary to repel the armed attack and to restore international peace and security in the area."[16] The resolutions of the Security Council that condemned North Korea and authorized collective military aid to the Republic of Korea were rendered possible only by the self-imposed absence of the Soviet delegate from the Council table.

Though the Korean National Assembly appealed to the United States Government and the United Nations for effective aid to secure peace, the decision to enforce collective security in Korea was promoted in large part due to President Truman's sense of the gravity and the nature of North Korea's aggression. The initial decision to fight the Korean Conflict was favorably received by the American public: A public opinion survey reported that 81 percent of Americans polled expressed approval.[17] Many who favored action emphasized the illegality of the invasion of the Republic of Korea and the challenge it presented to the authority of the United Nations as expressed in the Charter. In the United Nations itself, support for the Korean action, with the exception of the Soviet bloc, was high. Both domestic and foreign reaction to President Truman's decision to repel aggression in Korea was one of overwhelming approval.[18]

In response to the United Nations call for assistance, sixteen member nations joined the collective security arrangement in Korea to repel the aggression from the north. In actuality, there was a large gap between the symbolic and the substantive aspects of collective security in the Korean case. With the exception of the United States, actions of the other members were largely in symbolic support of the substantial U.S. commitment to the defense of Korea. The gap between the U.S. contribution and that of other nations became larger when the Chinese Communists intervened on October 24, 1950.[19]

It should be noted that the responsibility for directing military operations had been assumed by the United States on its own insistence. General MacArthur and the U.S. Joint Chiefs of Staff are said to have viewed the resolutions of the Security Council as giving necessary authority to cross the 38th parallel after October 6 (the second demand for unconditional surrender). The United States Government also appeared to have thought that the opportunity existed to gain a decisive result, meaning the unification of Korea. The aim of unifying Korea was most clearly debated in an exchange of letters between President Rhee and President Eisenhower in 1953. In opposition to the P'anmunjŏm Peace Negotiations, Rhee stated that he was convinced that the Korean question could not be settled unless the aggressor was punished and Korea unified. In Rhee's view, the principle of collective security stood for the punishment of aggressors, not merely restoration of the status quo.

The position of the United States was clearly stated by Eisenhower in his reply to Rhee: "We do not intend to employ war as an instrument to accomplish the worldwide political settlements."[20] President Rhee contended that the collective security objectives were clearly stated during the first year of the war by both the United States and the United Nations as being "the establishment of a united, independent, and democratic Korea, and the punishment of the aggressor."[21] Rhee blamed the United States for altering its position, and referred to the armistice as an "appeasement." He went on to state that Korea was not interested in the suggested mutual defense pact if the pact was simply offered as an inducement to sign the armistice agreement. Though the Government of the Republic of Korea abided by the terms of the armistice agreement, no one representing the South Korean Government signed the agreement.[22]

In truth, the 1950 war ended as a preventive one. It did not end "as a punitive war but it is hard to maintain that it did not begin as such...."[23]

THE STAGE OF RESTORATION: MUTUAL DEFENSE TREATY

In order to bring about stability in the Korean peninsula, the United States and the Republic of Korea signed a Mutual Defense Treaty on October 1, 1953. There were two major purposes of the pact: (1) prevention of the renewal of Communist aggression in Korea; (2) assurance of America's concern for Korea's security by means of a formal commitment. Under Article III of the treaty, each nation declares that "an armed attack in the Pacific area on either of the Parties in territories now under their respective administrative control, or hereafter recognized by one of the Parties as lawfully brought under the administrative control of the other, would be dangerous to its own peace and safety" and that "it would act to meet the common danger in accordance with its constitutional processes."[24]

The treaty came into force on November 17, 1954. This treaty is considered as a warning to the Communists that the United States would act in case of renewed aggression against the Republic of Korea. Thus the Mutual Defense Treaty became the cornerstone of Korea's security networks along with the pledge of sixteen nations which helped Korea to deter the aggressors. The Sixteen-Nation Declaration affirmed "in the interests of world peace, that if there is a renewal of the armed attack, challenging again the principles of the United Nations, we should again be united and prompt to resist...."[25]

The subsequent Geneva talks on Korean unification were convened from April 26 to June 15, 1954 under the provision of the Korean Armistice Agreement. The failure of the conference was largely due to North Korea's refusal to accept the authority and competence of the United Nations for creation of an independent, unified and democratic Korea under a representative government. To be sure, Koreans were deeply disappointed over the unfinished business concerning their country's unification and the failure of the Geneva talks to bring about any progress on the Korean unification issue. However, the United Nations role in the founding of the Republic of

Korea and its enforcement of collective security during the Korean conflict gave them an exaggerated notion of the United Nations potential for the resolution of the Korean question. A Korean writer described it as one of "faith in the omnipotence of the U.N."[26]

THE PERIOD OF HOPE AND DISILLUSIONMENT

New Trends in Diplomacy. Roughly during the period from 1948 to 1960, the Government of the Republic of Korea took a rather hostile attitude toward the Communist and the non-aligned nations. The Rhee regime was unwilling to make any distinction between the Communist regimes and the non-aligned regimes. However, the Republic of Korea's international position was one of isolation and there was a definite need to modify its policy toward non-aligned nations. Rhee's policy, in short, was characterized by Korea's dependent relationship to the United States, to a limited additional number of nations in the Western bloc and to the United Nations. Though the need to broaden Korea's diplomatic network was felt by many policy makers, no policy adjustment was effected while Rhee was in office.

The toppling of the regime in 1960 stimulated by a student uprising, in effect, ended the rigid, self-isolating foreign policy of the cold-war years. Hŏ Chŏng, head of the caretaker government as well as the new Foreign Minister, held office for a period of three months pending the adoption of constitutional changes and the election of a new National Assembly. Among other reforms, the interim government undertook a comprehensive review of Korea's foreign policy. On April 19, 1960, Hŏ called for a gradual readjustment of Korean policy in international affairs. He took particular note of Korea's attitude toward Japan and non-aligned nations and dramatized the need for re-examination of Korean relations with friendly neutral nations.[27] Thus, the collapse of Rhee government, along with Hŏ's pronouncement of the need to revise Korea's policy, created a new political climate for modification of Korea's management of international relations. Nevertheless, the short lived interim Government implemented no policy change, for Chang Myŏn's Government came into power in August.

In his policy statement of August 27, Prime Minister Chang stated that he would strive for free elections throughout Korea for unification within the framework of the United Nations Charter; he also reiterated Korea's wish to gain membership in the United

Nations. The tone of his speech was interpreted as a renunciation of the so-called "policy of unification by force" as advocated by the past regime of Syngman Rhee. A more comprehensive foreign policy statement was made public by Foreign Minister Chŏng Il-hyŏng. The seven point foreign policy goals outlined by the foreign minister consisted of the following:[28]

(1) In pursuance of the United Nations resolutions concerning the unification of Korea, the unification should be achieved through free elections throughout Korea under the supervision of the United Nations;

(2) Concerted effort should be made to gain admission to the United Nations;

(3) Strengthening of Korean-American relations;

(4) Normalization of Korean-Japanese relations;

(5) Promotion of the unity of free nations;

(6) Expansion of diplomatic activities toward non-aligned nations;

(7) Encouragement of people's diplomacy.

Though these foreign policy goals were not more specifically spelled out, it should be noted that the change in government actually meant a major shift in foreign policy. The shift in policy was partly due to the intricacy of domestic policies as well as the changing state of Korea's international environment. Viewed in terms of domestic politics, it is understandable that the formerly oppressed Minjudang once in power reacted sharply against both the domestic and foreign policies of the Rhee regime. Viewed in terms of international politics, the need for a major shift in Korean foreign policy was long overdue, for Korea could no longer afford to confront uniformly all Communist regimes and non-aligned nations as cold war enemies without enhancing her own isolation in the international community. Too, many Koreans felt that almost sole dependence upon the United States and the United Nations for Korean security was short-sighted and demanded expansion of diplomatic activities to meet the requirement of outside challenges in an ever changing world environment.

Perhaps two important events had particularly profound effects on Korea's policy: (1) an unofficial visit to Korea by Japanese Foreign Minister Zentaro Kosaka on September 6, 1960; (2) an Indonesia-sponsored resolution in the 15th session of the United Nations General Assembly—a resolution inviting both South and North Korea to discuss their problems. The former was related to the Government's willingness to break the deadlock of negotiations of the past and to start anew. The latter forced the Korean Government to reexamine its policy in the United Nations. This change of the General Assembly's handling of the Korean question was made possible by a dramatic increase in Afro-Asian members in the decade immediately past. Many members were simply tired of considering the Korean issue and demanded a new approach. They wanted to hear both sides of the Korean story. Korea's crisis in U. N. diplomacy was resolved by Adlai Stevenson's astute maneuver which provided that North Korea accept the competence and the authority of the United Nations if it were to participate in the Korean debate. The resolution was passed with such a condition; however, North Korea chose not to participate in the debate. To accept the authority of the United Nations would have meant a complete reversal of North Korea's attitude toward the international organization, for North Korea had consistently refused to recognize the Charter of the United Nations.

Unfortunately, Chang's government was unable to implement its policy goals, for it was too short-lived and too weak a government to carry out its ambitious foreign policy programs. The failure of Chang's regime can be attributed to a number of factors. For one, the sudden collapse of the Rhee regime created a power vacuum that was difficult to fill, especially by a faction-ridden opposition party that had never been in power. The people's urge for freedom after twelve years of Rhee's autocratic rule went to extremes in some instances and hardly contributed to a stable political situation. The discredited national police force was unable to maintain any semblance of order. Under these conditions, many impossible demands were made upon the government. Among these demands were the cries of students for national unification; some even sought to achieve unification by meeting with student representatives from North Korea at P'anmunjŏm. Though many students were acting on the basis of a sincere desire for national unity, some advocated outright neutralization of Korea. The latter position was endorsed by the North Korean regime through Radio P'yŏngyang. One Korean writer described the fear of many Koreans in the following words:

> Those who feared communist penetration of the movement could hardly help noticing three things: that it was drawing financial support from leftist elements among Korean residents in Japan, who were in turn backed by the Communist regime in North Korea; that criticism of the United States structured in terms of Communist theory was often incorporated into discussion of unification; and that many of the slogans were surprisingly similar to those used by Radio P'yŏngyang in North Korea and by Communist groups in Japan.[29]

There was a strong fear that the movement might snowball into a movement for national unification "at any price." Thus the maintenance of internal order as well as the demand for "clean" and efficient government appeared to have been the major issues of the day. Considering domestic political conditions in Korea, there is little wonder why Chang's government was unable to carry out foreign policy programs outlined by his foreign minister.

THE PERIOD OF IMPLEMENTATION

The 1961 coup d'etat was successfully executed by dissatisfied army officers. General political conditions as well as Chang's policy to reduce the size of the Korean military establishment and his "refusal" to purge "corrupt" high ranking officials in the military seemed to have triggered the military coup of May 16, 1961. Immediately after the coup, a "Military Revolutionary Committee" was organized and made six "revolutionary pledges" to the people of Korea. Among these six pledges, three dealt with Korea's foreign policy posture. These were:

(1) Positive, uncompromising opposition to Communism is the basis of our policy;

(2) We shall respect and observe the United Nations Charter, and strengthen our relations with the United States and other free world nations;

(3) We shall strengthen our material power and determination to combat Communism, looking forward to the eventual achievement of our unchangeable goal of national unification.[30]

The new military leaders' first task was to express their desire to maintain "the most friendly ties" with the United States: the leaders promised that they will return to their "proper duties of the military" and "hand over the control of the Government to clean and conscientious civilians" after the completion of their mission.[31] Though Washington was displeased with the overthrow of the legally constituted government, it had no choice but to settle with the *fait accompli* in Korea. The problem of recognition of the new regime did not arise since the military leaders were able to persuade titular President Yun Po-sŏn to stay in office to maintain a legal fiction of governmental continuity, even though Premier Chang was being purged.

One of the first diplomatic steps taken by the military government was in the form of efforts to prevent recurrence of the unhappy incidents of the 15th session of the U.N. General Assembly. In July, August, and September of 1961, three large goodwill missions were organized and sent to five different geographical regions. These missions visited some thirty non-aligned nations to promote the understanding of the Korean question in the United Nations. This effort, however, did not prevent the 16th session of the General Assembly from inviting North Korea providing that the regime accept the authority of the United Nations. Again, the North Koreans rejected the resolution of the 16th session of the General Assembly.[32] The moderately successful results of the 1961 goodwill missions led to the organizing of three more missions in 1962, variously tagged as cultural or economic missions. These missions extended invitations to visit Korea to officials of the countries visited, with positive responses from many nations. This so-called "goodwill" diplomacy has been subsequently repeated every year under various names.

The 1963 Presidential and National Assembly elections swept the Democratic Republican Party into power. The leader of the coup, General Park Chung-hee, was elected President, and his Democratic Republican Party won an impressive number of seats in the National Assembly, although the DRP was still seven seats short of a two-thirds majority of 117 seats. Having secured a solid victory over the opposition Civil Rule Party, President Park set out to accomplish three of the earlier foreign policy objectives: (1) Expansion of a diplomatic network *vis a vis* non-aligned nations; (2) Promotion of active economic diplomacy; (3) Normalization of relations between Korea and Japan.

Since President Park and his Democratic Republican Party are still in power at present, it is imperative that we examine his two most important policy commitments in foreign relations.

Normalization of Relations with Japan. Korea and Japan are only six hours apart by boat and less than an hour by modern aircraft. The short distance lends itself naturally to easy political and economic intercourse. However, the relationships between the two nations are delicate and complex. Due to thirty-six years of harsh occupational rule by Japan, Koreans find it difficult to forget the bitter memories of Japan's oppressive behavior during the long years of domination.

A Korean writer described a series of Korean images of the Japanese in the following words:

In the first frame, a Korean sees "The savage and unfeeling

Japanese," who came to Korea at the beginning of the century to plunder. In the second frame, he sees "The punished little criminal," kneeling before the American liberator in unconditional surrender. In the next frame, "The unscrupulous *nouveau riche*," who got rich quick thanks to the war in Korea, where millions of Koreans suffered untold sorrow and misery. And, now in the latest frame, the Korean suddenly encounters "the arrogant Japanese," who refuses to recognize Korea's exclusive right to fish in the Peace Line.[33]

Perhaps the above description may be exaggerated to some extent, but these images are widely shared by many Koreans, though intensity of feeling may differ from person to person. The Koreans' cynical feeling toward the Japanese was nurtured by their own experiences and reinforced by the attitude of the Rhee regime after the liberation. From the Korean standpoint, there are ample reasons to doubt the motives of the Japanese and to some extent much of it is justifiable when viewed from the perspective of Korea's historical context.

The Rhee government was as anti-Japanese as anti-Communist in word and deed. Much of Rhee's anti-Japanese sentiment was understandable, for he spent a major portion of his life in fighting against the Japanese. His own bitter feelings were strongly reflected in Korea's foreign policy toward Japan. The situation was also aggravated by the low and often disparaging Japanese image of the Korean people. During the period of Rhee's control, the relationship between Korea and Japan had deteriorated to the point of no return and Rhee considered Japan as Korea's foremost enemy. Indeed, an American observer states that Rhee's writings and speeches led him to conclude "that the greatest target of his invective was not the Communists but the Japanese."[34]

Politically, there were a number of unresolved problems between the two countries. The outstanding issues that hindered the Korean-Japanese rapprochement were the following:[35] (1) The status of Korean residents in Japan; (2) Problems concerning property claims; (3) Problems concerning the "Rhee Line"; (4) Japanese possession of Korean art treasures; (5) Japan's counter claim to Tokto Island; (6) The Japanese program of repatriation of Korean residents to North Korea.

The first meeting between the two governments regarding the legal status of Korean residents in Japan was made possible through the urging of the Supreme Commander for the Allied Powers. The preliminary talks, which began on October 20, 1951, were suspended in late 1951 without achieving any concrete result. On February 15,

1952, more extensive talks were held though negotiations got nowhere. These over-all talks continued, however, with repeated suspensions until 1965. The seventh round of talks beginning in December of 1964 resulted in agreement for a normalization treaty; a year later the instruments of ratification were exchanged in Seoul. The treaty, in substance, included the following agreements:[36] (1) Invalidation of all old treaties and agreements concluded between the two countries in the past; (2) Recognition of the Government of the Republic of Korea as the only legitimate government in Korea in accordance with the United Nations resolution regarding the establishment of the Republic of Korea; (3) Agreement of mutual cooperation in fishing along the "Rhee Line"; (4) Granting to Korean residents in Japan the right of permanent residence with a number of conditions; (5) Agreement to pay $300,000,000 in compensation over a ten-year period; (6) Agreement by the Japanese to return publicly-owned Korean art treasures.

In reality the issues were not settled by the normalization talks. Although Korea is physically in possession of Tokto Island, Japan's occasional counterclaims continue to make it a touchy political problem. The government of Korea considers it a settled issue while Japan insists that the problem of Tokto is still unresolved. Another issue, which arose in 1958, is the so-called "repatriation" of Korean residents in Japan to North Korea. In the view of the Japanese government, this is repatriation based on moral and humanitarian grounds, whereas the Korean government, still technically in a state of war with Communist-dominated North Korea, regards this as the sending of helpless Koreans to a totalitarian slave camp. Consequently, it is seen as a hostile, immoral, and inhuman act.[37] The Japanese government has yet to terminate this "repatriation" policy and the issue is still an explosive one in the two countries' relations.

For good or ill, the normalization of relations between Korea and Japan was actively sought by the Chang government and was actually accomplished by the Park regime. Therefore, the achievement as well as the responsibility rest with the Democratic Republican regime of President Park. It must be remembered that a large number of Koreans opposed the substance of the treaty and the fate of the Park regime hinged on this issue for many months. The determined government succeeded in ratifying the treaty only after bitter demonstrations and fights on the streets and in the National Assembly.

The Vietnam Decision. The decision of the Korean government to dispatch military forces to war-torn Vietnam came after due consideration in 1964. Partly motivated by America's need for support of friendly nations to preserve South Vietnam's independence from Communist aggression, the Republic of Korea, encouraged by the United States, sent its envoy to Vietnam to discuss matters relating to military assistance. Upon a formal request from the Republic of Vietnam, a mobile army surgical hospital was dispatched in September of 1964. However, this decision was arrived at only after close consultations with the United States. Sending a combat division in 1965 was decided upon by the Korean cabinet after receiving a personal letter of "encouragement" from President Lyndon Johnson. W. Averell Harriman, special presidential envoy, arrived in Seoul for consultations before the actual decision to send a combat division was reached. The details of the discussion concerning the "understanding" reached by the two governments was not made public.

In January and February of 1966, Vice-President Hubert Humphrey came to Korea to arrange for an additional dispatch of Korean troops. In the same month, Premier Nguyen Cao Ky made an official request for additional ROK combat forces, and Korea complied with the request by sending the 26th regiment and the 9th division to Vietnam. The total strength of the Korean forces reached a level of approximately 50,000. In addition to the ROK military forces, 23,319 technicians were sent to Vietnam to engage in various works to assist the war effort. Over a dozen large trucking and construction companies have been engaged in important war projects, the largest being Hanjin, a trucking firm, and Hyundai, a construction company.[38]

Sending ROK forces abroad was a serious foreign policy matter from the standpoint of Korea's national security. When President Park made it clear in his 1966 New Year's message to the National Assembly that one of the objectives of his government's foreign policy was to implement the plan to send combat troops to the Republic of Vietnam, a heated controversy arose as to the advisability of the decision. Opposition members of the Assembly had objected earlier to the dispatching of non-combat units. For many Koreans, the consequences of the decision were too uncertain with regard to Korea's continued security. Would the decision ultimately weaken Korea's defense posture? Would it not antagonize many non-committed nations? The opposition forces were led by former President Yun Po-sŏn who argued that the decision was contrary to the national interest and feared that the removal of combat troops from Korea's front line might possibly invite a renewed North Korean attack.

The opposition party was deeply divided on the issue. In fact, one of the Supreme Commissioners of the main opposition party (Minjŏng Dang-Civil Rule Party), Kim Jun-yŏn, supported the move, stating that "the government decision would be tantamount to repaying a moral obligation this nation owes to the free world." Fearing that the decision might bring diplomatic setbacks and political deadlock with the opposing forces, Kim Chae-sun, a member of the ruling Democratic-Republican Party, commented: "If the government is disposed to send the troops as a gesture to recompense for the U.S. aid given to Korea, I do not see any reason to oppose the decision."[39] Commenting at a press conference of June 9, 1965, President Park stated that the way of man (Ŭi Li) is "to save his drowning friend."[40] His remark was basically an appeal to the Korean national conscience, as the concept of Ŭi Li is deeply ingrained in the Korean conscience as basic to interpersonal relations.

Although the reasons for Korea's dispatch of combat forces were not neatly crystallized in the Korean mind, three justifications for the sending of forces to Vietnam stand out: (1) Repayment of the debt for assistance rendered during the Korean conflict by the United States and other nations; (2) The collapse of the Republic of Vietnam might endanger the security of many Asian nations including Korea;[41] (3) Enhancement of Korea's national prestige, as well as economic and other benefits.[42]

Perhaps President Park's words more accurately represent Korea's position. In his opening address at the Ministerial Meeting for Asian and Pacific Cooperation on June 14, 1966, Park said:

> I, of course, understand that evolution of the Vietnamese situation differs as do opinions of the methods and means to be taken to bring about peace there, even among friendly nations. However, I am firmly convinced that we free peoples have the generosity, the good will and the ability to resolve such differences, and to proceed steadfastly toward our common goals.
>
> I wish to take this opportunity to explain to you our basic position regarding Korea's dispatch of troops to Vietnam. We in Korea endured a terrible war when we were invaded by the Communists. We learned in that war the value of international cooperation to restore peace through collective international action. Therefore, as a matter of right and conscience, we sent a part of our armed forces to repel aggression, and to restore peace. We know—from experience—that the Communists have always withdrawn when faced by the vastly superior strength of the United Free World. Our armed forces were not sent to Vietnam as a belligerent gesture, but rather as an act in defense of

world peace. What we want is not a continuation of the war, but a speedy restoration of peace, with justice and honor for all.[43]

Comparison of the United Nations action in Korea with the collective defense effort of allied nations to Vietnam led to some confusion regarding justification of the Vietnam action. Many Korean writers tend to view the allied nations action in Vietnam as one based upon collective security designed to repel aggression.[44] For public consumption, the term collective security is rather attractive and appealing, but the term has tended to obscure more basic understanding of the nature of Korean involvement in the conflict. This imprecision is likely to produce serious consequences in the future formulation of Korean foreign policy.

Following President Nixon's de-Americanization policy of the Vietnamese conflict, the government of the Republic of Korea reviewed Korea's commitment in Vietnam, including the question of the eventual withdrawal of the Korean military forces in Vietnam. Under an agreement with the South Vietnamese government, approximately 10,000 Korean combat forces were pulled out of South Vietnam in 1972. The withdrawal of the remaining Korean forces was completed following the ceasefire agreement in early 1973.

THE CHANGING NATURE OF KOREA'S FOREIGN RELATIONS

The Many Faces of the Hallstein Doctrine. One of the most notable changes in Korea's diplomatic stance is in the expansion of its diplomatic network. Before the coup of 1961 Korea maintained only 22 embassies and consulates abroad. As of 1973, Korea had expanded its representations abroad to 85.[45] The expansion of diplomatic and consular relations does not necessarily represent Korea's improved international standing, though it is indicative of the sharp break of policy from the time of Syngman Rhee. The biggest inroad is seen in Korea's penetration of non-aligned nations in Africa and other parts of Asia.

Park's more flexible diplomatic posture and his expansion of diplomatic posts have encountered difficulties in Africa. In December of 1964, the Republic of Korea severed its diplomatic relations with Mauritania in retaliation for Mauritania's establishment of formal relations with North Korea. This policy was the first application of the Hallstein doctrine. The second application came in May of 1965 with the Congo (Brazzaville) under similar circumstances.[46] From the view of the Korean government, any simultaneous maintenance of diplomatic relations with the Republic of Korea and Communist North Korea, in effect, constituted acceptance of the theory of "two Koreas," and such policy was in direct contradiction to the Hallstein doctrine.

The wisdom of the rigid application of the Hallstein doctrine was debated by foreign policy decision-makers and scholars alike. Nevertheless, the abandonment of the doctrine was neither seriously considered nor openly advocated in Korea. At present, governmental policy regarding the application of the Hallstein doctrine is flexible and uncertain. On December 1, 1969, the Foreign Ministry spokesman testified before the Committee on Foreign Affairs of the National Assembly that the government would not insist on uniform application of the Hallstein doctrine and that application of the doctrine will be viewed in terms of a "case by case" principle, each situation being viewed in terms of the nation's self-interest.[47] In other words, the government would continue to maintain the doctrine as basic to the nation's foreign policy, though application would be "flexible."

The above policy was hardly a new approach even at the time of the pronouncement. At the time of the National Assembly's Committee on Foreign Affairs hearings, the Republic of Korea maintained consulates-general in two nations even though Communist North Korea also had consular relations. In the United Arab Republic and Indonesia, North Korea maintained embassies, and the Republic of Korea, consulates-general.[48] It had seemed to the South Korean government that the above-cited exceptions to the Hallstein doctrine were not in conflict with a "one Korea" concept. At this time, whether the Government would tolerate the logical next step, that is, both the Republic of Korea and North Korea maintaining embassies in a given country, was open to question. Such a policy would, in effect, have amounted to the discontinuance of the Hallstein principle: abandonment of the denial of the "two Koreas" idea.

In part, the above problem was raised in April, 1972 when the government of Sweden decided to extend formal recognition to North Korea. The Republic of Korea reacted swiftly by recalling the ambassador to Seoul for political consultation purposes, leaving the Korean embassy to the *chargé d'affaires*. The same pattern of action followed in other places.[49] However, the recalling of Korea's ambassador did not resolve the issues. In his "Korea's New Foreign Policy for Peace and Unification" declaration of June 23, 1973, President

Park stated clearly that his government would "not oppose north Korea's participation" in international organizations, provided that it is "conducive to the easing of tension and the furtherance of international cooperation." Furthermore, Park went on to say that "we shall not object to our admittance into the United Nations together with North Korea, if the majority of the member-states of the United Nations so wish, provided that it does not cause hindrance to our unification." These statements were carefully qualified by adding that "I wish to make it clear that matters concerning North Korea in the policies enumerated above are interim measures during the transitional period pending the achievement of our national unification and that the taking of these measures does not signify our recognition of north Korea as a state."[50] In his press briefings, Prime Minister Kim Jong-p'il touched on the same subject when he stated:

> We said that we are not recognizing north Korea as a state. However, we admit that there exists a Communist regime that in fact governs the territory north of the Demarcation Line. In international society, this may lead to the idea of the so-called two Koreas, but for our part, we do not recognize north Korea as a sovereign state, in the pursuit of our long-cherished aspiration for national unification.[51]

The new foreign policy declaration of June 23 brought about a number of changes in Korea's diplomatic front, most significantly the elevation of the status of Korean consulates-general to the status of embassies in Indonesia, the United Arab Republic, and India. In various other places, the Republic of Korea tended to soften its prior stand about the applicability of the Hallstein doctrine. Whether the new doctrine of President Park has replaced the so-called Hallstein doctrine by abandoning it has never been made clear. Officially the Government of the Republic of Korea has not renounced the substance of the Hallstein doctrine. This assertion can be buttressed through the examination of the Prime Minister's statements in the National Assembly to the effect that Korea's position differs from the position taken by West Germany—Korea's position is expressed in a "One Nation, One State, Two Governments" doctrine while the government of West Germany seems to have espoused the doctrine of "One Nation, Two States, Two Governments."[52] The significance of the above distinction has never been clearly explicated and subsequent events tell us only part of the story. On February 15, 1974, the Korean Ambassador to Australia notified the Australians that the Government of the Republic of Korea would sever its diplomatic relations if Australia were to recognize North Korea.[53] Whether the position taken by the Republic of Korea is a bluff to prevent Australia from extending formal recognition to North Korea or a policy applicable to certain countries in certain cases is not known. Regardless of the outcome of the Australia case this seemingly confusing state of Korea's policy will need to be clarified in principle at some future date.

THE MANY PHASES OF THE KOREAN QUESTION IN THE UNITED NATIONS

A modification of the Korean Government's long-standing policy toward the United Nations annual debate of the Korean question was introduced in 1969. For twenty years, the Korean question had been put on the agenda of each regular session of the United Nations General Assembly for "automatic" annual debate. Debates in the past yielded no tangible progress toward achieving Korean unification. In order to avoid tedious debates concerning the Korean question, the Government, in close consultation with the United States, suspended the policy of automatic annual debate and decided to bring up the issue for General Assembly debate only when the need might arise in a given session.[54] In fact, such policy modification by the Republic of Korea did not prevent the Communist nations from bringing up resolutions concerning the "withdrawal of foreign troops" from Korea and the abolition of the United Nations Commission for the Unification and Rehabilitation of Korea (UNCURK). Though the Communist proposals were defeated at the 24th and 25th sessions of the General Assembly,[55] the maneuvering tactics of the Communist nations at the United Nations shed some doubt on the wisdom of the South Korean Policy. On the politically important Communist bloc-sponsored resolution calling for the simultaneous invitation of the Republic of Korea and North Korea to the United Nations debate on Korea, the vote was 40 for, 55 against, and 27 abstentions at the 24th General Assembly session, while at the 25th session the vote tabulation showed 40 for, 54 against, and 25 abstentions.[56]

By 1971 the Government of the Republic of Korea had reason to believe that only a new policy could exclude the risk of a defeat at the 26th United Nations General Assembly. After a series of consultations with the Korean War allies which had supported the Republic of Korea's stand, the Government adopted a new tactic to prevent the Korean question from being taken up at the 26th General Assembly session. The new policy, in effect, meant to postpone the issue for one year and to maintain the status quo. Justifications for the postponement of the Korean question at the United Nations were based upon the South-North Korean Red Cross societies' talks which began in August, 1971.[57] The Red Cross talks were intended to arrange reunion of families and relatives separated between north and south. The new strategy carried the day when the United Nations General Assembly adopted a resolution calling for a postponement of the Korean debate. The same exercise was repeated at the 27th General Assembly session to postpone the Korean debate for still another year.[58]

On May 17, 1973, the World Health Organization, one of the specialized agencies of the United Nations, decided to admit North Korea as a member, brushing aside the plea of the representative of the Republic that the dual representation for Korea might endanger the Korean dialogues and bring about permanent division of Korea. Cognizant of the changes in the world body and recalling President Park's June 23 declaration, the Republic of Korea proposed a dual representation system for Korea and expressed its willingness to acquiesce to the dissolution of UNCURK at the 28th U.N. General Assembly session.

The P'yŏngyang regime's gaining of observer status and its first participation in the Korean debate at the United Nations tended to threaten a big power confrontation in the world forum. Nonetheless, a sudden and dramatic compromise was achieved between South and North Korea through the good offices of United States Secretary of State Henry A. Kissinger after his visit to Peking. Just how this agreement came about to defer a vote on two rival U.N. draft resolutions on Korea has never been clearly explained. The agreement was announced in the midst of the Korean debate by Otto Borch of Denmark, Chairman of the General Assembly's Main Political Committee. The text of the consensus statement on Korea follows:[59]

> After consultations with the cosponsors of the two draft resolutions on the Korean question, the chairman is authorized to announce an agreement that the two draft resolutions on the Korean question will not be put to a vote at the current session of the General Assembly.

The chairman is further authorized to make the following statement:

> It is noted with satisfaction that a joint statement was issued by

north and south Korea on 4 July 1972, which provides for the following three principles on the reunification of Korea: (1) The reunification of the country should be achieved independently, without reliance upon outside force or its interference. (2) The reunification of the country should be achieved by peaceful means, without recourse to the use of arms against the other side. (3) Great national unity should be promoted.

It is the general hope that the north and the south of Korea will be urged to continue their dialogue and realize their many-sided exchanges and cooperation in the above spirit so as to expedite the independent, peaceful reunification of the country.

The General Assembly decides to dissolve immediately the U.N. Commission for the Unification and Rehabilitation of Korea.

The consensus statement was unanimously adopted by the 1973 United Nations General Assembly, thereby ending discussion of the Korean Question without vote. In 1974 the 29th General Assembly session urged continuation of South-North talks and called on the Security council to consider dissolution of the United Nations Command. The vote was 61 for, 43 against, and 31 abstaining. The present position of the Government of the Republic of Korea appears to be that the Korean question should not be used as a means of confrontation and that the issue should be dealt with by the Koreans themselves in their own forums.

The Uncertain Fate of the Asian Pacific Council. In another area of diplomatic endeavor, the government of Korea in 1966 instigated and sponsored the "First Ministerial Meeting for Asian and Pacific Co-operation" in Seoul. This meeting was attended by delegates from nine nations—Australia, China, Japan, Korea, Malaysia, New Zealand, the Philippines, Thailand, Vietnam and an observer from Laos. At the second meeting in Bangkok in 1967, the ministers decided to establish a "Registry of Experts' Services" in Canberra, and a "Cultural and Social Center" in Seoul. Subsequently there were established a "Food and Fertilizer Technology Center" in Taipei and an "Economic Cooperation Center" in Bangkok. ASPAC held its fourth meeting in Tokyo in 1969. On the matter of defining the future role of regional cooperation, members are divided into two groups; one group, led by Korea, sought to define the role of the organization in broad terms, that is, directed to all problems in the political, economic, social and cultural fields; the rival group, led by Japan, wanted to define ASPAC's role in a narrow, more culturally oriented sense. The main difference in these positions is basically political in nature: while making no formal proposal, Korea has tended to consider

ASPAC as a probable foundation on which to build a regional collective defense system, while Japan, Malaysia and other members wanted no part of such a regional alliance system. Even though Korea's position is likely to be supported by Nationalist China and the Republic of Vietnam, Japan and the other members have felt that the ASPAC should be considered as a consultative body for economic and cultural cooperation, not an organization "hostile to any nation or any group of nations."[60]

With Okinawa's reversion to Japan in 1972 and the United States-China rapprochement in gear, the balance of power in Northeast Asia cannot help but undergo a period of drastic alteration. Communist China's threat to the stability of the area is likely to remain as the foremost challenge to some members of ASPAC, as well as to some other nations in the area. Nevertheless, the threat is not perceived in the same way by Japan as by Korea. Differences in perception of the Chinese threat are understandable, for Korea is threatened directly by Communist North Korea which is allied with Communist China.

The internal division of views within ASPAC has compelled Korea to readjust its own view of the organization in line with the majority of other member states including Japan. In his first 1970 press conference, President Park frankly stated that the members of ASPAC are not ready for a collective defense system. However, he hoped that such a system might crystallize in the future from economic, technical, and cultural cooperation among ASPAC member states. In short, the creation of a regional collective defense system is one of the future goals of the Government's foreign policy, though not an immediate objective.[61]

The idea of transforming ASPAC into a regional collective defense arrangement was not exactly in tune with the times. At the Seventh Ministerial Conference of the Asian and Pacific Council which was held in Seoul in 1972, President Park said:

> In enlarging its areas of cooperation and partnership, ASPAC will need to keep its doors wide open to non-member countries.
>
> We cannot afford fondly clinging to fixed ideas and notions which contravene the emerging currents of a new era; nor can we afford to be realistic and practical without possessing our own ideas and beliefs. We need to espouse reason while cherishing our ideals. We must at the same time be men of action dedicated to a lofty cause.
>
> Let more and more countries in the region join our worthy effort, transcending whatever differences they might have in their ideologies or political systems....[62]

The joint communique issued by the 1972 conference outlined the following principles and objectives:[63]
  (a) ASPAC is an organization for regional cooperation pursuing peace and progress in the Asian and Pacific region.
  (b) ASPAC is not a political or military arrangement directed against other nations.
  (c) ASPAC will make endeavours to promote cooperation in the economic, technical, social, cultural and other fields.
  (d) ASPAC is not an exclusive organization; it is open to non-member countries within the region, ready to make a constructive contribution to its objectives and purposes.

The substance of the communique clearly indicated the need of the organization for new directions if the venture is to survive as a viable system of regional cooperation. However, a few member nations at that time came out for the dissolution of the Asian Pacific Council. One of the major reasons for some members' reluctance to participate actively in the organization was the fear of antagonizing the People's Republic of China. Japan, Australia, New Zealand and Malaysia were in the process of extending formal recognition to the Peking Government. Malaysia went a step further by declaring her intention to withdraw from the regional body. Though the Seoul conference designated Bangkok for the next ASPAC ministerial meeting, the conference has yet to materialize. Thus, the future of the Asian Pacific Council is by no means certain at this point.

THE FUTURE OF KOREAN SECURITY AND THE SOUTH-NORTH DIALOGUE

Reduction of United States Forces in Korea. Particularly since the armistice at P'anmunjŏm in 1953, Korea's security policy has been conditioned largely by the containment policy of the United States. By and large, the containment policy was a successful one. It prevented recurrence of the outbreak of open hostilities on the Korean peninsula and provided time for Korea to attain a greater degree of economic self-sufficiency; however, it failed to bring about stable peace and positive progress toward the ultimate goal of unification.

The enunciation of the Nixon Doctrine in 1969 dramatized an apparent hiatus in the perception of Korea's security needs. Many Koreans clung to the notion that tenets of the Nixon Doctrine had no applicability to the Korean situation—until the announcement on July 5, 1970 of the reduction of United States forces in Korea by one army division. A negative response was swift in coming, and angry voices of protest were heard in the Korean National Assembly. On July 15, then Prime Minister Chŏng Il-kwŏn went so far as to state in an interview with an Associated Press reporter that he would resign if the reduction of U.S. forces in Korea were carried out. "If GI's go, I go," he said.[64]

Korea's protest over the reduction of U.S. troops in Korea stems from two primary concerns: firstly, the obvious removal of deterrence and, secondly, its psychological impact on the populace.[65] The Park regime has tried for years to revise Article III of the Mutual Defense Treaty between Korea and the United States. According to that article, the United States is to decide the type of commitment in the case of external attack "in accordance with constitutional processes." Korea has wanted to replace this provision with the so-called "ipso facto" clause of Article V of the NATO Treaty. In fact, such revision of the treaty has been unnecessary, for one U. S. division was positioned along the demilitarized zone through 1970, and that circumstance was probably sufficient for "automatic" American involvement in case of open hostilities in Korea.[66] The net result of Korean Government efforts toward treaty revision has, in effect, been the exact opposite of its wishes: the United States had never seriously considered the treaty revision. In direct opposition to the wishes of the Korean government, the United States carried out limited troop reduction, and in 1971 withdrew all forces positioned along the demilitarized zone.

The Republic of Korea was thus faced with the problem of convincing the North Koreans that the South's defense posture has not been weakened on account of the partial U. S. troop withdrawal and subsequent relocation of the remaining American forces in Korea. In addition, the Korean government has had to convince its own people that the United States commitment to defend Korea stands and that the United States is not in the process of dismantling its Pacific defense system.

The Dialogues. Against the above background and the ethos of the U.S.-Chinese rapprochement came the beginning of new directions in South-North Korean relations. An important development occurred on August 12, 1971 when the Korean Red Cross Society in Seoul proposed to P'yŏngyang that the Red Cross societies of the South and the North begin negotiations to alleviate the plight of families and relatives separated by the division and the War through establishment of the family reunion program. After nearly a year of negotiations between the representatives of South and North Red Cross societies at P'anmunjŏm, they agreed in the early part of August, 1972 on an agenda to be discussed in substantive dialogues. The substantive talks were held alternately in P'yŏngyang and Seoul on seven occasions.[67] These meetings produced no concrete results except reinforcing the conviction that the differences in perceptions and views are so wide that the gaps could not be bridged in the foreseeable future. The Korean dialogues brought about changes in the constitutions of both South and North Korea. The constitutional alterations were said to have been made to facilitate efforts at the dialogues. President Park's position, though not universally accepted, is that temporary suspensions of freedom are justifiable if the Republic of Korea is to have a strong base in negotiating with the Communist North.

From the beginning, the North Korean Red Cross Society came up with a number of unacceptable demands to the South, insisting that '"close friends" be included in the definition of family members and relatives under family reunion program. When this demand was rejected by the representatives from the South, the North Koreans countered with a new demand for freedom of traffic between the two halves as a precondition for the price of continuing the talks.[68] The Republic of Korea came up with a counter proposal by openly proposing the complete opening of the two societies for observation and inspection to anyone wishing to do so. The escalating demands, accusations and counter accusations brought about a stalemate in the Red Cross dialogues which has persisted to the present.

At the political level, secret talks between Lee Hu-rak, former Director of the South Korean Central Intelligence Agency and Kim Yŏng-ju, a younger brother of North Korean Premier Kim Il-sung himself, resulted in a new important channel of communication being established on May 2, 1972. Acting on behalf of ailing Kim Yŏng-ju, Second Deputy Premier Pak Sŏng-ch'ŏl and his party made a visit to Seoul between May 29 and June 1. Pak held meetings with his counterpart Lee Hu-rak and other personalities in the South. The exchange of views between the two antagonists led to a joint communique of July 4, 1972.[69] The communique states that the reunification of the nation was to be achieved through independent Korean efforts without dependence on outside force or interference. It is important to note that in the same communique it was stated that unification was to be accomplished "through peaceful means, and not through the use of force against each other" and that "a great national unity shall be sought above all, transcending differences in ideas, ideologies, and systems." In the same communique, both sides "have agreed to carry out various exchanges in many fields." In order to help abide by these pledges and to "foster an atmosphere of mutual trust between the South and North, the two sides have agreed not to slander or defame each other, not to undertake armed provocations whether on a large or small scale, and to take positive measures to prevent inadvertent military incidents." Furthermore, a South-North Coordinating Committee was established to implement these agreements.

Neither the Red Cross conferences nor the meetings of the South-North Coordinating committee have thus far yielded any tangible outcome. Basically, there have been vast differences in the approaches of the two antagonists. The Republic of Korea has adopted a minimalist approach to unification, i.e., to proceed with a step by step method, beginning with humanitarian issues, as evidenced in their proposal of the family reunion program. If this step is successfully carried out to the parties' mutual satisfaction, there would follow a non-political step entailing economic and cultural exchanges. The last step would involve political conferences dealing with at least partial integration of the two divided sectors if not national unification. North Koreans are highly suspicious of the functional approach, espousing the view that political conferences can relatively quickly resolve all problems that separate the two halves of Korea. The North Korean position is basically the exact opposite of the stand taken by the Republic of Korea.

The diametrically opposed positions of both sides and the subsequent hardening of those views seem to have led to an impasse in the dialogues. The North Koreans have demanded persistently that, as a precondition to reopening the deadlocked dialogues, there must occur an improvement of existing legal and social conditions in the South.[70] Coupled with these political demands came a new wave of propaganda offensives and provocative acts aimed to impute the responsibility of the deadlocked conferences on the South. The efforts of the government of the Republic of Korea to revive the two levels of dialogues have not progressed. Nevertheless, it is probable that continued efforts toward that end may see some success in the foreseeable future.

CONCLUSIONS

The history of modern Korea is a tale of consecutive crises, involving a period of foreign domination (1910-1945); a period of preparation for independence (1945-1948); a period of conflict and self-isolation (1950-1960); a period of internal turmoil and uncertainty (1960-1961); and a period of national self-consciousness (1961-   ).

The establishment of the Republic of Korea in 1945 was the result of the inability of the two occupying powers, the United States and the Soviet Union, to reach agreement on the unification of the Korean peninsula. More accurately, this failure can be attributed to Communist North Korea's refusal to abide by the resolutions of the United Nations concerning unification of Korea. For Korea, the management of foreign affairs became not simply a question of maintaining friendly relations with foreign nations and protecting national interests. South Korea's objectives have been the preservation of her independence and ultimate unification within the framework of the United Nations solutions and rejection of any "two Koreas" solution. Modifications of these policies were effected partly by the South-North Joint Communique of July 4, 1972 and President Park's new foreign policy declaration of June 23, 1973. The substance of those modifications entail the pursuance of unification efforts outside the United Nations framework, i.e., through independent efforts of Koreans themselves as outlined in the above communique and acceptance of a dual representation system in the United Nations while, at the same time, refusing to espouse "two Koreas" doctrine.

South Korea's foreign policy is highly colored by its staunch anti-Communist posture. This policy line has strongly reflected the policy of the United States and her allies during the cold war era. For over a decade, President Syngman Rhee's policy was characterized primarily by its anti-Communist, anti-non-alignment, and anti-Japanese ingredients. Pursuance of such a policy tended to isolate Korea from the non-Communist world and to distort South Korea's assessment of international political developments. Rhee's dictatorial rule made difficult any flexible adjustment of the South Korean policy to external challenges and circumstances. Thus, the projection of a satisfactory outside image remained as one of Korea's major foreign policy problems.

The collapse of Rhee's regime in 1960 ended the policy of self-isolation. However, the short-lived government under Chang Myŏn failed to implement any specific policy changes, though it laid out elaborate new foreign policy goals. The weak and ineffectual Chang government at least recognized the need to modify Korea's posture in international relations, though implementation was impossible given the unstable political climate. The regime actually failed to bring about changes in Korean foreign policy.

The military coup of 1961 was a turning point in Korean foreign policy. The military leaders immediately organized "good will" missions and set out to expand Korea's diplomatic activities abroad. Perhaps one of the outstanding examples of the diplomatic offensives launched by the military regime was in its effort to carry its diplomatic and trade activities to non-aligned Afro-Asian nations. From the elections of 1963 until the present, President Park and his Democratic Republican Party have pursued the same active diplomacy.

Major trends in Korea's foreign policy during the past decade are in the following areas: 1) Normalization and maintenance of amicable relations with Japan; 2) Continuous expansion of diplomatic and trade activities with non-aligned nations; 3) Active pursuance of economic diplomacy with all non-hostile nations; 4) Modification of the Hallstein doctrine as outlined in the June 23 declaration of President Park; 5) Active promotion of regional cooperation; 6) Modification of procedural tactics in United Nations diplomacy, resulting in annual postponement of debate on the Korean question; 7) Unification of Korea through Korean efforts without outside influences.

The enhancement of Korea's image in itself, however, is not a sure guarantee for Korean national security. The problem of Korea's security still remains as the foremost concern of the Korean people. As long as the Soviet Union and Communist China are behind North Korea, the Republic of Korea's security can only be maintained by the active support of the United States. Even so, Koreans are realistic enough to know that neither United States forces in Korea nor the present state of division between South and North will remain indefinitely. As Koreans gain more confidence in security matters, bolstered by rapid economic development, they may be bold enough to come up with more creative and imaginative proposals for national unification. However, at least two major pre-conditions must be fulfilled in the South if the nation is to take bolder approaches for establishing lasting security: 1) Rapid economic self-sufficiency and a continuation of the process toward more "even" distribution of wealth among the population; 2) A more free intellectual environment for creative and imaginative thinking and research. In short, the most urgent task in paving the ground for unification is a rapid building of confidence and a working consensus in the South. Only on such a basis can a more serious effort be made toward dialogue with the North.

FOOTNOTES

1. Chae Kyung Oh (ed.), *A Handbook of Korea* (New York: Pageant Press, Inc., 1957), pp. 28-39; Kenneth G. Clare *et al.*, *Area Handbook for the Republic of Korea* (Washington, D. C.: U. S. Government Printing Office, 1969), pp. 7-12; Gregory Henderson, *Korea: The Politics of the Vortex* (Cambridge: Harvard University Press, 1968), pp. 13-18; Arthur H. Dean, "The Role of the United States in the Far East," *The Annals of the American Academy of Political and Social Sciences*, July, 1954, pp. 49-50.
2. Kyung Cho Chung, *New Korea* (New York: Macmillan, 1962), p. 2.
3. *Ibid.*
4. U.S. Department of State, *The Record on Korean Unification, 1943-1960* (Washington, D.C.: Government Printing Office, 1960), p. 2. Hereinafter cited as *The Record*.
5. Paul H. Clyde, *The Far East* (Englewood Cliffs: Prentice Hall, 1964), p. 382.
6. Cf. Chong-Sik Lee, *The Politics of Korean Nationalism* (Berkeley and Los Angeles: University of California Press, 1965), pp. 70-85.
7. Youngnok Koo, "The Development of United States Policy in the Far East," *Asia*, June, 1969, p. 46.
8. *Aid to Korea*, U.S. 81st Cong., 1st sess., S. Doc., 11299 (1949), pp.12-13.
9. U. N. General Assembly Resolution 195 (III), Dec. 12, 1948. Cf. United Nations, *Official Records of the General Assembly,* Third Session, 1948, Part 1, pp. 961-962; Young-kyo Yoon, "The Problem of the Korean Unification in the General Assembly of the United Nations," *Korean Observer*, October, 1968, p.46.
10. Lawrence K. Rosinger *et al.*, *The State of Asia* (New York: Alfred A. Knopf, 1951), p. 137.
11. Sung-Hon Rhee, "Twenty Years of Korean Diplomacy," *Sedae*, March, 1968, p. 55.
12. *The Record*, op. cit., p. 12.
13. Cf. Yong-Hi Lee, "Challenges to Korea's Diplomacy," *Korean Affairs,* May, 1965, pp. 8-9.
14. U Chae-sŏng, "The Development of Korean Diplomacy and the Hallstein Principle," *Sasangge*, March, 1966, pp. 121-122.
15. Soon Sung Cho, *Korea in World Politics 1940-1950: An Evaluation of American Responsibility* (Berkeley and Los Angeles: University of California Press, 1967), pp. 257-261. Cf. Youngnok Koo, "Strengthening Korea's Policy toward the United States," *Oekyo*, October, 1969, pp.105-108.
16. Leland M. Goodrich, "Korea: Collective Security Measure Against Aggression," *International Conciliation*, October, 1953, pp.131-132.
17. William A. Scott and Stephen B. Whithey, *The United States and the United Nations: The Public View, 1945-1955* (New York: Manhattan Publishing

Company, for the Carnegie Endowment for International Peace, 1958), p. 78.

18. Elmo Roper, *You and Your Leaders: Their Actions and Your Reactions* (New York: William Morrow and Company, 1957), p. 159; Edwin C. Hoyt, "The United States Reaction to the Korean Attack: A Study of the Principles of the United Nations Charter as a Factor in American Policy-Making," *The American Journal of International Law,* January, 1961, pp. 56–58.

19. Cf. Youngnok Koo, "The Passing of Collective Security," in the Second Asian Foreign Service Lectures, held under the joint auspices of the Republic of Korea and the Eastern Regional Organization for Public Administration, *Complete Papers,* Vol. II, Sub. III, IV, and V (Seoul: Foreign Affairs Institute, 1969), pp.3, 6.

20. U. S. Senate, Committee on Foreign Relations, *Hearings on the Mutual Defense Treaty with Korea,* 83rd Cong., 2nd Sess., 1954, p. 52.

21. *Ibid.,* p. 53.

22. *Ibid.,* p. 56.

23. Erich Hula, "Fundamentals of Collective Security," *Social Research,* Spring, 1957, p. 35.

24. U.S. Senate, *op. cit.,* p. 5.

25. UN Doc. S/3079, August 7, 1953; *The Record,* op. cit., p. 132.

26. Cited in Byong-ki Min, "Basic Posture of the Korean Foreign Policy," *Korean Affairs,* May, 1965, p. 3.

27. Foreign Affairs Institute, *Twenty Years of Korean Diplomacy* (Seoul: Foreign Affairs Institute, 1967), p. 123.

28. *Ibid.*

29. John Kie-Chiang Oh, *Korea: Democracy on Trial* (Ithaca: Cornell University Press, 1968), p. 89.

30. Supreme Council for National Reconstruction, *Military Revolution* (Seoul: Supreme Council for National Reconstruction, 1961), p. 1.

31. U.S. Department of State, *American Foreign Policy: Current Documents 1961* (Washington D.C.: Government Printing Office, 1965), p. 974.

32. Sung-Hon Rhee, "Conditions Affecting the Korean Foreign Policy," *Korean Affairs,* May, 1965, p. 48.

33. Pyoung Hoon Kim, "Korea-Japan Rapprochement," *Korean Affairs,* May, 1965, p. 17.

34. Richard C. Allen, *Korea's Syngman Rhee* (Rutland and Tokyo: Charles E. Tuttle Company, 1960), p. 183.

35. James W. Morley, *Japan and Korea: America's Allies in the Pacific* (New York: Walker and Company, 1965), pp. 54–66; Hongkee Karl (ed.), *Korea Flaming High* (Seoul: Office of Public Information, 1956), pp. 42–51; Chung, *op. cit.,* pp. 172–179.

36. See *Sasangge,* August, 1965, pp. 58–73; *Shin Dong-A,* August, 1965, pp. 48–63. For a thorough discussion of the treaty, see Shigeru Oda, "The Normalization of Relations between Japan and the Republic of Korea," *The American Journal of International Law,* January, 1967, pp. 35–56. Cf. Junkyu Park, "Korea and Japan," *The Korean Journal of International Relations,* April, 1968, pp. 47–58.

37. Youngnok Koo, "Pretentious Moral Man and Immoral Policy" (unpublished manuscript, 1959), pp. 1–2. Approximately 90,000 Koreans in Japan have been lured or forced into Japan's "repatriation" scheme. See *The Dong-A Ilbo,* March 12, 1970. Cf. Shannon McCune, "The United States and Korea," in William L. Thorp (ed.), *The United States and the Far East* (Englewood Cliffs: Prentice-Hall, 1962),

p. 91.

38. *The Chungang Ilbo,* December 11, 1969. Cf. Shin Eung-Kyun, "Korea's Diplomacy in Asia," *Koreana Quarterly,* Autumn, 1966, pp. 35-36.

39. *The Korean Republic,* January 20, 1965.

40. Youngnok Koo, "The Misuse of the Concept of National Interest" (unpublished manuscript, 1966), p. 3.

41. Bum Shick Shin (ed.), *Those Who Stop Cannot Win* (Seoul: Hanlim Publishing Company, 1968), p. 226.

42. About 80 percent of the dollar earnings by the Korean forces were sent home. The total amount of earnings up to 1969 was over 1.1 billion dollars. In addition to the above, Korean goods supplied to the ROK troops amounted to over 40 million dollars. The earnings of the Korean civilians amounted to almost 600 million dollars. Cf. *The Chungang Ilbo,* December 11, 1969.

43. The text of the speech is reprinted in the *Koreana Quarterly,* Autumn, 1966, p. 94.

44. Hui-sok Mun, "War in Vietnam and Collective Security in Asia," *Koreana Quarterly,* Autumn, 1966, pp. 25-34. The major differences in the Korean Conflict and the Vietnam situation are discussed in H.G. Nicholas, "Vietnam and the Traditions of American Foreign Policy," *International Affairs,* April, 1968, pp. 189-190. For correct usage of the term, see Arnold Wolfers, "Collective Defense versus Collective Security," in Arnold Wolfers (ed.), *Alliance Policy in the Cold War* (Baltimore: Johns Hopkins Press, 1959), pp. 49-74; Inis L. Claude, Jr., *Power and International Relations* (New York: Random House, 1962), pp. 94-149.

45. Park Chung-hee, "Decade of Confidence and Achievement" (Seoul Ministry of Culture and Information, 1971), p. 7: *The Chungang Ilbo,* June 23, 1973. Cf. Ministry of Foreign Affairs, *The Present State* (1969), pp. 20-21.

46. U, *op. cit.,* pp. 122-123; Shin, *op. cit.,* pp. 41-42; Moon Hyang Choi, "Nine Months in Congo (Brazzaville)," *Oekyo,* November, 1965, pp. 17-52.

47. *The Chungang Ilbo,* December 1, 1969.

48. Cf. Shin, *op. cit.,* p. 41.

49. *The Chungang Ilbo,* June 23, 1973.

50. The full text of President Park's "Korea's New Foreign Policy for Peace and Unification" speech is in the *Koreana Quarterly,* Spring-Summer, 1973, pp. 60-63.

51. The transcript of Prime Minister Kim's press conference is found in the *Koreana Quarterly,* Spring-Summer, 1973, p.72.

52. *The Hankuk Ilbo,* June 27, 1973.

53. *The Hankuk Ilbo,* February 16, 1974.

54. *The Chungang Ilbo,* September 27, 1969; November 26, 1969; *The Dong-A Ilbo,* December 3, 1969.

55. *The Dong-A Ilbo,* December 3, 1969.

56. For an analysis of voting trends, see Youngnok Koo, "Rationales of Korea's Foreign Policy," *Shin Dong-A,* August, 1973, p. 61.

57. United Nations, *Official Records of the General Assembly,* Twenty-Sixth Session, General Committee, 193 meeting, 1971, pp. 72-75.

58. Koo, "Rationales of Korea's Foreign Policy," p. 61.

59. *Korea Newsreview,* December 1, 1973, p. 6.

60. *ASPAC Quarterly of Cultural and Social Affairs,* Summer, 1969, p. 78. Cf. Tong-Won Lee, "ASPAC, A Dynamic for Regional Co-operation," *Koreana*

Quarterly, Winter, 1968-9, pp. 359-367.

61. The complete text of the press conference is found in *The Seoul Shinmun,* January 9, 1970.

62. President Park's address at the Seventh Ministerial Meeting of the Asian and Pacific Council in the *Koreana Quarterly,* Autumn, 1972, p. 77.

63. From the text of the joint communique of the Seventh Ministerial Meeting of the Asian Pacific Council, *Koreana Quarterly,* Autumn, 1972, p. 82.

64. *The Dong-A Ilbo,* July 18, 1970, as quoted in the *Pacific Stars & Stripes,* July 15, 1970.

65. Senator Joseph Tydings (D., Maryland) expressed the opposite view in his speech delivered on the Senate floor entitled "Implementing the Guam Doctrine: The Case for Withdrawing U. S. Troops from Korea," on April 9, 1970 (Seoul: Ministry of Foreign Affairs, 1970) (mimeographed).

66. Youngnok Koo, "Reflections on Korean 'Security Diplomacy'," *Shin Dong-A,* September, 1970, pp. 86-87.

67. Hong Sŭng-myŏn, "Dialogues between the South and the North," *Anbo Yŏngu,* 1972 Annual, pp. 278-293; Joung-Yole Rew, "Korea's New Foreign Policy," *Koreana Quarterly,* Spring-Summer, 1973, pp. 49-59.

68. Rew, *op. cit.,* p. 50.

69. The full text of the South-North Joint Communique is reprinted in the *Koreana Quarterly,* Autumn, 1972, pp. 58-60.

70. Rew, *op. cit.,* p. 52; *The Korea Herald,* February 20, 1974.

CHAPTER 8:

Economic Development in South Korea: A Retrospective View of the 1960's

Princeton LYMAN*

In 1966, it was possible to write that Koreans tended to find foreign—mainly American —observers overly optimistic in predicting imminent economic "breakthroughs" in Korea; while to foreigners, Koreans appeared overly pessimistic, finding two problems getting worse for every one getting better. Today the situation is almost the reverse. It is the Koreans, at least the officials, who exude a supreme confidence in Korean economic capability, founded in good measure on a record of an average 10 percent growth rate since 1964. The foreigners have not become "bearish," but they now tend more to worry about the high level of commercial borrowing, debt problems and other dangers of "overextension."

The period of the middle 1960's thus can now be seen as a period of critical transition. Not only was it an economic transition, but a psychological one. By 1960, economic development was a major political issue in Korea. It was indeed an imperative for any regime that would survive. But by 1960 too, there was a deeply ingrained pessimism about Korea's real prospects: born of the frustrations of partition, the dependence on aid, the disorderliness and corruption of the

---

*Princeton Lyman was Economic Planning Coordinator with the U.S. Agency for International Development in Korea from 1964 to 1967. His Ph.D. is in Political Science from Harvard University. The views in this article are those of the author and not necessarily those of the U.S. Government or any of its agencies. An earlier version of this article was published as "Economic Development in South Korea: Prospects and Problems," *Asian Survey*, Vol. VI, No. 7, July 1966.

growth that had occurred with postwar reconstruction, and finally reenforced—in the aftermath of the 1960 revolution and the 1961 coup—with the period of near absolute economic stagnation in 1962. Recovery was already under way by the end of 1962. Fundamental structural changes were taking place as early as 1963. Impressive growth statistics were catching international attention by 1966. But not really until 1967, and perhaps not really entrenched in the popular mind until the last two years was the feeling in Korea that indeed South Korea could make it: as an independent, highly successful, economic entity. With that transition, a whole new nationalism may have been born in South Korea.

What are the ingredients of this "break-through," and how significant is it really? How much in other words is the recent growth reflective of real and permanent strength in South Korea? And how far has the country gone toward solving the fundamental problems of an "underdeveloped country" rather than having simply achieved growth in a few select categories?

The answers are clearer than a few years ago. Yet there are still some great question marks. If the strengths observed a few years ago appear even more vindicated today, the weaknesses observed then still remain also, only in small part dealt with in the intervening years.

It hardly seems necessary now to demonstrate the depth and degree of economic transformation of the last seven years. The growth figures continue to be impressive and indeed spectacular. But it is useful to review the nature of these changes and on what they are based.

Throughout the period since the end of the Korean War, Korea has known substantial if uneven growth. A large part of the growth, however, was absorbed in the reconstruction and recovery of war damage. Another significant element went into the reestablishment of basic infrastructure that had been lost to South Korea with the division of the country; power, basic industries, minerals. In addition, the economy itself remained largely "insulated," resistant to the pressures for internal modernization: there was a heavy dependence on imports—necessarily financed largely by foreign aid—but little growth in exports; businessmen concentrated on ventures of quick turnover or short-run investment, e. g., trade, land speculation, or industry guaranteed high profit; and the business-financial community as a whole tended to operate, and often depended for its profits, on the basis of frequent and often very rapid inflation. Domestic savings, under these circumstances, remained exceptionally low—in fact were actually negative in every year but one between 1955 and 1962.

These conditions gave the appearance that Korea, despite its progress, was in no ways economically viable and was making little progress in that direction.

In fact, the postwar period saw several elements of the current growth created. Not only the establishment of an independent power supply and similar physical infrastructure, but the creation of a phenomenal educational plant took place in this period. It was one that would raise Korean literacy from 22 percent to over 80 percent in twenty years, multiply the number of high school students thirteenfold in the same period, and the number of college students eighteenfold. The industrial structure rebuilt in the decade after 1953, if seemingly haphazard and ill-planned, proved fortuitous as well. The light industry that was emphasized, dependent on raw materials from abroad and largely free of inefficient domestic industry for its intermediate goods, would in the 1960's become the base for relatively high labor content, low cost of exports of manufactured goods that would give Korea its competitive edge in world markets.

With these assets, however, there was an absence of sound policy direction. Economic policies were influenced by short-range and often ideological considerations, and by the advantages of short-run dependency on aid, i.e., they were featured by over-valued exchange rates, efforts to maximize aid that discouraged both exports and domestic food production, corrupt and politically-motivated allocation of foreign exchange, restrictions on the use of professional talent in the bureaucracy, and a political-psychological resistance to expanding relations with its nearest neighbor and potentially most important investment and trading partner—Japan. It was therefore policy changes that most marked the basic transformation of the 1960's and made for a major departure from the past.

The initial impetus of the present trend was the Government's determination in 1962 to increase Korea's low export earnings. While the export drive was seen in itself at the outset as a measure of self-reliance, it actually proved quite effective as a "lead sector"—challenging the insular character of the economy, introducing it to international standards and pressures, and forcing a reevaluation of some of its basic tenets. The initial export drive met with some success through 1963 with the use of special incentives. The total of goods exported rose from 41 million dollars U.S. in 1961 to 87 million dollars in 1963. But it was impossible to sustain the drive further without a basic exchange reform on the one hand and a means of controlling the periodic inflations in Korea on the other.

In the spring of 1964, therefore, the Government devalued the Won nearly 100 percent and in 1965 a floating exchange rate was put into effect. To control prices, the Government had adopted a stabilization program during 1963, but it had been ineffective with a very sharp rise in prices taking place from the latter part of 1963 to the spring of 1964. In 1964, to protect the effects of devaluation, a more comprehensive program was undertaken, bringing together budget, foreign exchange and credit management under a single overall policy structure. The experience with this program throughout 1964 and 1965 had an important influence on Government policy. It gave the Government the experience and tools for better overall management of the economy, and it pointed up the need beyond stabilization for what were in effect basic reforms in the economic structure. In large part the "stabilization" program became the vehicle for putting more of these reforms into effect.

The stabilization objective itself was largely achieved: prices held steady through the last part of 1964 and rose less in 1965 than in any previous year since the end of the Korean War. But it became obvious at the same time that if the planned export and the overall growth targets were to be met, more fundamental changes were also required and, moreover, in a different direction—i.e., toward less rather than more controls. For Korea, which depended heavily on the processing of imported raw materials, there was a need for a loosening rather than a tightening of trade restrictions on exports. For the industrial sector as a whole, if it were to expand on a competitive basis, there was a need for reorganization of the financial structure with a more rationalized system of industrial credit, one which would, in essence, revitalize the commercial banking sector and strengthen it vis-a-vis the unofficial or "curb" market which in fact was supplying a large share of industrial credit requirements. Related to the latter was a series of steps needed to increase Korea's gross domestic savings as well as to direct those savings into the most constructive channels.

In response to these needs, the Government began in 1965 a program of gradual trade liberalization. By the end of the year, 80 percent of the imports had been placed on the "automatic approval" list, freed of quotas, licenses, export-linking or the other controls which had been part of the Korean trade structure for so long. Also in 1965, studies by both foreign and local experts were undertaken of the whole financial and credit structure. Following upon these in the fall of 1965, a basic interest rate reform was approved by the National Assembly, the first step in a program to revise the relationship between banking, savings, and credit and to restructure the role of the banking sector.

Both trade liberalization and financial reform in turn had repercussions on the Government's original stabilization program. It was still necessary in 1965 and 1966 to maintain a check on prices, the uses of foreign exchange, and the expansion of credit. But it became necessary in the light of these other steps to rely more on indirect than direct controls in the future. Reexamination of tax and customs policy, credit controls, and other aspects of Government economic policy thus became necessary by the latter half of 1965 with the development of more refined tools being prepared for the stabilization program in 1966 and thereafter.

Another major policy departure took place in this period in the arrangement of private commercial loans from abroad. The crux of this policy was in the rapprochement with Japan concluded in 1965, and Japan has been by far the principal source of such credits since then. But the policy itself was initiated in earnest as early as 1962 with several missions despatched to Europe. The flow of commercial credits into Korea not only provided a new source of capital. It helped free Korea from dependence on aid. In 1967, private commercial flows exceeded public capital inflows for the first time and now they represent the principal source of external investment financing. Starting from a virtually zero debt in 1962, Korea had room to expand in this direction. And while debt is now a serious issue, there is no doubt that the emphatic solicitation of commercial loans had two important effects. It provided a more rapid flow of industrial investment capital in this period than could possibly have been obtained through cumbersome public loan procedures. It sped Korea's break from the psychologically debilitating dependence on grant, and even large amounts of concessional loan, funds from the U.S.

The effects of these several basic reforms have been impressive. Exports of goods have risen more than ten times the level of 1961. Whereas in 1961, Korea exported only $41 million dollars of commodities, the Government is now speaking confidently of exceeding two billion dollars in commodity exports in 1973. Surely one of the most spectacular turn-abouts in recent economic history. Domestic savings rose from roughly two percent of the gross national product in 1962 to over 14 percent of GNP in 1968. One of the significant aspects of the Korean financial reforms, moreover, has been the emphasis on private savings which more than doubled in the first year after the interest rate reform, doubled again the next year, and have continued to constitute a major support for investment ever since. The growth of GNP, as noted earlier, was at an average of 10 percent per year from 1963 through 1968. The Second Five Year Plan, issued in 1966, and much technical work within the bureaucracy since then, has laid the basis for well planned investment priorities for the future, including international cooperative arrangements with Taiwan on such key expensive industries as petrochemicals. International lending from the IBRD, as well as from private sources, has been increasing steadily since the mid-1960's, and an international consultative group on Korea has been formed under the IBRD's chairmanship. This marks a significant and likely permanent departure from Korea's long economic role as a "ward" of the U.S.

For a country with very limited natural resources, one of the most densely populated rural sectors in the world, and a low record of previous performance, these achievements seem extraordinary. But Korea has four basic economic strengths which, once set to work by the appropriate policy framework, could contribute to such dynamism and, with continued good leadership, can continue to support high level performance.

The principal strength in the Korean economy is the Korean people. This is not said simply for flattery. The Korean people are well-educated, hard working, and adaptable. The nation's education system must rank among the most developed of the so-called "underprivileged" nations. Literacy stands at about 90 percent, and five percent of the total population has had college training. While there has been heavy emphasis in higher education on liberal arts, there is now increasing emphasis on engineering, business, science and vocational training. The effects of this human asset are noticeable throughout the current economic scene. Korean economic planners are working with the most sophisticated economic models and analytical tools. Korean industrial workers though being trained in this field for the first time, put an oil refinery into operation in one year, well ahead of schedule. Three new fertilizer plants were recently installed in a period of three years without any serious problems— in contrast to many years of problems with Korea's first fertilizer plant in the 1950's. In agriculture, Korean farmers have made a sweeping change in the use of fertilizers and pesticides in just the past few years, adopting in both cases nearly optimum scientific standards. Finally, in the application of economic policies by the Government, a wide range of interlocking steps have been taken with considerable skill: it is no small accomplishment to put into operation in one year (1965) a floating exchange rate certificate system, a trade liberalization program, and a reformation of the credit structure while containing prices and limiting speculation.

The second strength of the Korean economy is in its diversity. Korea is still largely an agricultural economy. But in its industrial development and in its growing trade, it is showing remarkable diversity. Exports include radios, batteries, steel products, and textiles as well as the more traditional items of rice, fish, silk, and minerals. Manufactured goods in fact now represent 75 percent of exports, their value having multiplied 24 times in the last six years. This diversity provides protection against world market price fluctuations that threaten so many of the non-industrialized developing countries relying heavily on one or two main export commodities, and should provide for greater stability in annual export earnings as these increase over the next few years.

A third element of strength is in Korea's comparative advantage with other countries. Korea has an abundant supply of trained or trainable educated labor at comparatively very low cost. This has already proved a competitive advantage even in the processing of high-cost imported raw materials, e.g., in steel products, plywood, rubber goods, etc. In addition, Korea has rather attractive laws for the inducement of private foreign investment. These two factors— when combined with the greater economic and political stability that Korea has experienced in the past few years—should make Korea an ideal place for the manufacture of high labor-content merchandise or labor-intensive components of complex mechanisms. This could be especially true as some countries, like Japan, which have dominated this kind of market, now experience higher wage costs and move increasingly into more complex industrial production.

The fourth element of strength is the basic economic infrastructure that is just emerging now in mature form. Power supply—of which South Korea had virtually none in 1948—caught up with rapidly increasing domestic demand for the first time in the 1960's, and under established investment programs will be able to continue to meet demand in the future. A nuclear power plant, for example, is currently under serious consideration along with numerous planned thermal and hydro installations. Basic industries like cement caught up with demand for the first time in 1964 and began to export. Expanded industrial water supplies have gone into most major cities. Railroads have received substantial investment, and now highways are receiving somewhat overdue attention. In all, the basic sub-structure for industrial growth has now been established with sufficiently well planned provision for further expansion to be able to meet foreseeable future demand.

With these strengths in the economy, there is a place for optimism. All indications are that Korea can continue to grow at a rate of at least seven percent annually for some time to come. Even with a rapidly growing population of around 3 percent, this would mean significant increases in per capita GNP. Korea's exports, moreover, should continue to expand, making the country very soon independent of concessional forms of foreign assistance. Korea should be able to continue to attract foreign capital including much more than before from international institutions, widening both its financial and trade base. Finally, and in the long-run most important, continuing in the direction of current policies, Korea should obtain in the next few years that elusive combination of institutional, psychological, production, and educational factors which results in "self-sustained" or, better, self-generating growth, the only point at which long-run development can really be assured.

To say all this of Korea is to say a great deal, and yet it leaves much unsaid. It describes the very real progress and imminent potential, but it does not describe the distance that is to be covered. For one thing, Korea started in this recent spurt from a very low base, less than $100 per capita GNP in 1960; in 1968, it was still only $135 (1965 prices), less than that of Taiwan, Malaysia, the Philippines and all Latin American countries. By 1974 it had reached approximately $370. For another, while Korea has been fortunate in that basic food (though not nutrition) requirements have been met for several years, and a fairly substantial textile industry provides clothing to the domestic market in quantity, there are still many critical shortages in such basic necessities as housing, health, heating, and clean water supply for which no abundant remedy is in sight. The rural areas particularly have witnessed few of the material changes that have been evident in the cities during the last few years. Moreover, income inequality which has not been a serious issue in Korea heretofore could grow into one as regional differences and class inequalities appear more visible and more onerous, as general expectations rise concomitant to the overall appearance of growth.

These problems are not unfamiliar to any developing country in today's world. But there are certain aspects of these problems which will prove exceptionally difficult to solve in Korea even as the development process moves forward. Some of these, while they may be solved in the very long-run, may actually become worse before they begin to get better. These represent the most critical weaknesses in the Korean economic scene.

One of these is the pressure of rural population on the land. Some 40 percent of rural families in Korea are still reported to own less than a half hectare of land, when a half hectare is considered the minimum to support a family. Several aspects of the Government's development efforts will help in this situation. For example, a widespread land development program in effect since the early 1960's added 25 percent more arable land to the country by 1971. Industry and further development of agricultural processing and of related areas like fishing will help absorb rural workers wholly or part time into new occupations. The Government's vigorous program in family planning will also undoubtedly be a factor. Nevertheless, with all these, the existence of a large percentage of rural families owning less than sufficient land for self-support and not satisfactorily employed elsewhere will continue for some time beyond the capacity of offsetting development elsewhere to absorb them. The regional planning group in Seoul, for example, estimates that with all these programs, and a rapid rate of urbanization, it will still be twenty years before the rural population drops below the figure for 1966.

Korea is fortunate to have carried out a fairly effective land reform program from 1947-1953, so that small farm holdings are not a reflection of gross inequity but of a popular reform. Hence they are not in themselves a source of political unrest. But Korea must make some important decisions on agricultural development in the coming years that could affect this pattern of holdings as well as the share of benefits of small farmers in any new growth. Existing differences between rural and urban areas, and any increasingly sharp cleavages in income distribution within the rural areas are thus potential social and political dangers that compound the economic problems of rural Korea. For the future, a well balanced program of agricultural development, regional dispersal of industry and welfare for the poor is obviously required. But few countries have met such a multi-dimensional requirement effectively.

A second and related critical problem is that of urbanization. Since 1955, cities and towns in Korea have been growing three times as fast as the rural population. There are two aspects of this problem that are serious: urban labor and urban infrastructure. The existence of an abundant supply of low-cost labor is one of Korea's strong points in world competition, but the reverse of this coin is the social and economic cost of unemployment and substantial underemployment that results from an oversupply of labor, skilled as well as unskilled. Statistics on unemployment are not terribly reliable in Korea, but that a serious problem has existed for some time is undeniable. Recent high growth rates have undoubtedly helped, with some estimates being that urban employment has recently been increasing at an average of 8–10 percent per year. There is probably also somewhat less frustration than before among college graduates, of whom for many years it was said that as many as 40 percent could not find satisfactory employment in a reasonable period of time after graduation.

But the labor problem is more complicated than employment alone. As high growth rates continue and the supply of skilled and semi-skilled labor at least comes more in line with demand, there will be new thinking about wages and the share generally that should go to labor. It is doubtful, for example, that labor will be so inarticulate or passive in the 1970's that it would accept a decline in real wages as occurred in the early 1960's. Yet not labor unions, Government policies toward labor and manpower, business attitudes toward labor, nor even the universities in their research and analysis have prepared themselves adequately to help channel the energies of this more dynamic labor force in the next decade. No major political party has devoted itself to this issue. There is thus a shortage of leaders on all fronts of this problem, and a country therefore relatively ill-prepared to meet such changes smoothly.

Urban infrastructure presents enormous problems. Only in recent years has an institutional framework been established to finance middle and lower-middle cost housing on a large scale, and this innovation has not received adequate Government financial backing. Beyond housing lies all the requirements of water, hospitals, transportation, and improved Government services which are related to urban concentration. The magnitude of investment required has not yet been fully calculated nor has it been worked into Korea's otherwise efficient long-range planning. Urban planning in Korea generally has only made significant professional strides in recent years with the impetus of UN and foundation assistance, and is still not meshed with the political decision-making process. Beyond the physical needs, there is the whole question of political organization. Local officials have been centrally appointed in Korea since 1961. Will this system be an effective means for governing a country that will in a few years probably have two-thirds of its population in urban communities (those over 20,000)? Can the present system of nationally elected President and Assembly alone fully reflect and balance all the competing needs of rural and urban areas, especially given the make-up and outlook of today's political parties and the relative absence of diverse private interest groups capable of articulating their needs? Perhaps so; there is after all no magic to decentralized elective government in a country of Korea's size. But the implications of rapid urbanization seem so far to be imperfectly reflected in economic planning and perhaps equally so in political and administrative thinking.

Finally, there is the problem of defense. Korea's armed forces requirement can no longer be seen as a serious detriment to development, even as the cost of these forces is shifted increasingly to the Korean economy from U. S. aid. Like Taiwan, Israel and several other countries with high per capita defense outlays, Korea has experienced above average economic growth. The economic problem in defense is much more in the threat of renewed hostilities or greatly increased insecurity which would reduce confidence, scare away foreign investment, and perhaps encourage repressive government at home. Any one or combination of these would jeopardize the pattern of progress now seen as possible. There are real security dangers, and there is in the continuously tense border situation the danger of exaggerated security threats. South Korea has graduated from the period of the 1950's when fear of North Korea was used as a club against indigenous democracy and a detriment to programs for overall development, without weakening its security. Much obviously depends on its continued ability to remain free from such reactions, in face of constant attempts by the North to make it do precisely the opposite.

These problems place Korean progress more in perspective. There is clearly no easy solution to them. No sudden change in economic policy would remove them. Indeed without the solid underpinning of a dynamic modern economy, now being established for the first time since independence, few of these would have any hope of being solved. At the same time, generalizations about the progress being achieved does not erase their seriousness. And many of them—unlike trade deficits, marketing, and transportation, among others, which Korea must also confront and solve in due course—are directly related to human wants, human predicaments, and human needs in the midst of progress. These qualify in very human and emotional ways the current indices of growth and put a strain on the political and social structure which supports it.

What "solution"—to this dilemma of growing progress and lingering problems—offers itself? Clearly one element is in national will. In the mid-1960's, few Koreans had real confidence in the prospects of South Korea as an independent economic as well as political identity. Today that confidence is relatively widespread. If confidence is retained also in the relative integrity and efficiency of Government, and of the generally decent intentions of the leaders, then there is every evidence in Korean history and culture of a willingness to work hard, look ahead reasonably patiently, and even sacrifice for a more fully beneficial economy at a later stage.

The second element of a solution lies in the peculiar combination of political and economic development that occurred in Korea in the 1960's. As the economy grew, the political restrictions and conflicts of the early 1960's lessened. Rough understanding of student and press rights—and limits—were established. The continued functioning of the Assembly was guaranteed. In all, the constitutional structure for a democratic system, established rather uncertainly in 1963 and preserved rather shakily in 1964 and 1965, has become more sure. In the end, the Korean people's demand for at least a minimum guarantee of democracy—expressed vividly in 1960 and later—had been answered affirmatively. That fact has undeniably given strength and vitality to the economic success and the pyschological uplift in Korea of recent years. If this condition is retained, and adapted successfully to new conditions and new demands in the next few years, then it will almost surely provide constructive outlets for both the inevitable frustrations and the new sources of energy that accompany economic change. Therein lies some of the genius of the last few years' growth in Korea and the hope for successful transition to the next stage of development.

The prospects for South Korea are thus clearly brighter today than at any time in its post-war history, and they continue to improve. The change from the early 1960's is spectacular. There is moreover evidence of great economic, technical and intellectual sophistication in Korea, capable of solving the many difficult problems of development that have confounded many other countries at similar stages. But in some ways, the tasks of modernization—in the broadest sense —are just beginning in South Korea and some of the most serious challenges lie ahead.

CHAPTER 9:

Recent Trends in the Government's Management of the Economy

JUNGSAE KIM*

INTRODUCTION

Korea has been hailed as one of a few successful examples of economic development, and many observers around the world are keenly interested in the principal factors that have been responsible for this astonishing performance. This nation of just over 32 million inhabitants is endowed with few physical resources or accumulation of capital, though it is fortuitously situated in a temperate zone. The per capita Gross National Product nearly quadrupled in the last dozen years, and exports, at the level of approximately 3.3 billion dollars in 1973, are over 80 times those of 1961. It seems all the more remarkable when the fact of the country's territorial division is taken into account. South Korea, occupying only 45 percent of the total area on the Korean peninsula of about 220,000 square kilometers, was known as a farm belt before the advent of industrialization; unless the underlying circumstances change drastically, the South Korean economy is expected to reach full industrial maturity in the next five years. These are grounds strong enough to attract substantial international interest and to serve as useful lessons for other developing countries.

This paper attempts to offer a summary of achievements in some major areas of development policy since the First Five-Year Economic Development Plan came into effect in 1962. Firstly, it presents a brief

---

*Jungsae Kim is Professor of Economics at Sogang University, Seoul. He holds a B.A. degree from Georgetown University, Washington, D.C., and a B.Phil. degree from Oxford University, England.

description of the successive economic plans and their targets, and compares them with the respective records. The second section is an analysis of the official policies designed to facilitate the mobilization of foreign, as well as domestic, economic resources for industrial investment, encompassing the areas of currency and credit, public finance and foreign capital inducement. The third lists a series of measures related to the foreign sector, stressing the steps taken for export promotion, the adjustment of import demand and the stability of the foreign exchange market in view of the predominantly export-based growth. The last makes a short reference to the various disequilibrating phenomena arising out of the rapid economic growth, together with some of the crucial policy issues that may persist in the coming years.

ECONOMIC DEVELOPMENT PLANS

One of the major initial commitments that the revolutionary regime made upon consolidating the new political order in May 1961 was economic reconstruction, culminating in the formulation of the First Five-Year Economic Development Plan for the period between 1962 and 1966. This ambitious plan, the first ever undertaken in the Republic of Korea, was put into effect on a comprehensive scale, though it had been understandably hastily drawn up and though there had been other plans which had never seen the light of day.

Affirming the desirability of building a basis for a self-sustaining economy and presupposing industrialization as the chief vehicle of economic development, the First Plan proposed, for the intermediate period ahead, the following set of strategies: 1) an increase of farm income and the consequent rectification of structural imbalances of the economy by a higher agricultural productivity; 2) the development of power, coal and other sources of energy; 3) the expansion of basic industries and social overhead facilities; 4) the utilization of such idle resources as land and labour; 5) the improvement of the balance of payments by export increases; and 6) the promotion of technological skills.[1] These goals were to be achieved in a setting of "guided capitalism," within the framework of which the rule of private initiatives and entrepreneurial creativity could be harmonized with government intervention or suasion for basic industries and such others as were considered to be outside the sphere of non-governmental participation.

According to the First Plan projection, the Gross National Product was to grow at an average annual rate of 7.1 percent, as against the projected population growth rate of 2.81 percent, or by 40.7 percent by the target year. This would chiefly be propelled by a 51 percent rise in the level of aggregate investment during the five-year period, and as much as 48.8 percent of the total investible resources channeled into basic industries such as power or the social overhead sector. And yet mining and manufacturing was naturally expected to grow by far the fastest of all, i. e., at an average annual rate of 14.8 percent, or nearly to double, so that its proportion of the GNP would rise from 18.2 percent in the base year to 26.1 percent in 1966 while the contributions to the total output by the primary and tertiary sectors would decline from 36.0 percent and 45.7 percent respectively to 34.8 percent and 39.1 percent. The government was to finance 55.6 percent of the total investment spending estimated at 321.5 billion won, 57.9 percent of which would, however, be covered by foreign saving, mainly consisting of long-term development funds provided by international organs or on a government-to-government basis and of commercial loans rather than the U.S. economic aid and farm surplus which had begun to decrease, because domestic saving was initially negligible and its ratio to national income would merely be 13 percent in the end year even if it were to quadruple as envisaged in the plan. Despite the 417.9 percent increase of exports expected in the plan period, there was to be a large imbalance on the visible trade account in the order of 354.7 million dollars in 1966, reflecting a heavy demand for investment goods from overseas. Employment would expand at an average annual rate of 4.71 percent, a contrast to the rate of increase of the labour force itself which was 2.16 percent, so that the unemployment ratio was to fall from 22.3 percent in 1962 to 14.8 percent in 1966, but its feasibility was hardly credible as most of the planned projects were capital-intensive.

The First Plan was subject to criticisms from the outset. There was a sophisticated bias in some responsible quarters toward the promotion of light consumer-goods industries, amenable to small investments and simple technical processes, without sizable inter-industry linkages, and thus capable of prompt productive effects, which, in a developing economy already sensitive to the balance of payments pressures due to the mounting imports of capital goods, could substantially help alleviate its foreign exchange burden. They further held that investments into basic industries were of a long gestation period and would doubtless be accompanied by an over-reliance on imported raw materials. And some questioned the legitimacy of the goal for a self-sufficient food production in a country where the long-run comparative advantage of agriculture was believed to be anything but encouraging.[2] Besides these conceptual divergences, there were ambiguities relating to its technical aspects. Not only was there not any instrument in the First Plan which could link each individual project with the macroeconomic magnitudes, but references to the monetary, fiscal, trade and foreign exchange policies, all having relevance to its implementation, were conspicuously absent.[3]

What is more, practical setbacks confronted it in the first two years of its execution. It was belatedly discovered that the planned investments grossly dependent on capital imports had not been checked against the constraint of debt service and that there was much room for policy improvements in facilitating the timely supply of strategic commodities for major industries. The growth potentials of the economy had apparently been over-estimated. There were difficulties in meeting the investment targets that originated from the failure of private savings and government revenues to increase as expected, and the concomitant fiscal deficits stimulated a high rate of inflation.[4] Furthermore, both years experienced a poor harvest, causing a sudden increase in food imports and so deteriorating the payments imbalance. The currency reform of June 1962, designed to locate hoarded funds for industrial investment, merely ended with a production cut as the credit facilities available to business in the unorganized money market had now been mopped up. These overlapping factors contributed to the growing consciousness among planners of the inevitability of a major revision of the First Plan.

The Revised First Plan for the 1964-6 period, based on the year 1962 and now much more modest in its targets than the original plan, called for a 5 percent average annual growth. Though the relative stress on mining and manufacturing and the generation of power remained, there was to be a large reduction of investment in transport, communications and housing, and such planned projects for an integrated steel mill and machinery industries had to be foregone.[5]

The actual progress during the plan period proved that the pessimistic outlook entertained in the Revised First Plan was without much foundation as the GNP grew much faster than had been predicted even in the original plan. With the rate of population increase just about as great as the one hoped for in the revised plan, it meant in effect higher actual rises in the per capita GNP and private consumption. There occurred a marked transformation in the industrial structure conformable to the aim of industrialization, which was in turn made possible only by the impressive investment record—nearly a three-fold increase in the five years. It must be noted, however, that the proportion of government investment was less than a quarter of the total, rather than one-third as had been planned; such a tendency, implying at least a partial retreat of guided capitalism, confirmed the altered direction of the revised plan: a reduction of the number of government projects and a greater role by the private sector. Behind the buoyant investment activities was domestic saving with a share of 51 percent of the gross investment. Saving was soaring as the price level remained on the whole relatively stable, and the interest rate reform of 1965 and the increasing remittances from overseas added to the people's propensity to save. Singularly outstanding was the tempo of commodity exports, expanding almost 8 times the base-year level whereas imports expanded less than three times; international trade activity, together with the bumper agricultural crops of 1964 and 1966, contributed to the great success of the First Plan.

The Second Five-Year Plan for the period of 1967-71, made public in 1966, was essentially a medium-term plan as a next step toward the attainment of long-run objectives for the 1980's, when the country was expected to have a wholly self-supporting economy capable of an equilibrium in the balance of payments, an independent supply of required investible resources, and full employment. Its main targets did not differ substantially from those of the First Plan, except for its new pronouncement on such heavy industries as chemicals, machinery, and iron and steel, nor were the strategies to achieve them dissimilar so that emphasis continued to be placed on export expansion, capital mobilization, efficient utilization of manpower and financial stabilization.[6]

By 1971 the GNP was to be about 1.5 times the size of 1965, the base year, increasing at an average annual rate of 7 percent, and the per capita national income would increase by 31 percent, provided that the rate of population increase steadily declined to the level of 2 percent by the target year. The industrial structure was to change further away from agriculture, forestry and fishery. The latter three would expand at an even annual rate of 5 percent, while the other sectors would grow at such a rate that 27 percent of the GNP would be attributed to them by 1971. As commodity exports and invisible earnings would amount to 550 million dollars and 169 million dollars respectively by 1971, nearly 75 percent of the imports totalling 962 million dollars could be financed by means other than external aids. The level of aggregate investment would be approximately 240 percent higher, but domestic saving was to be roughly 3.5 times as large, so that, with foreign saving being only 26 percent greater, about 92 percent of investments would be financed out of home resources.

The economic performance of the first two years of the Second Plan demonstrated how it again underrated the growth potentials of the Korean economy, and created an optimistic prospect that the various plan targets would be reached by 1969. Such a bright outlook was due chiefly to the increase of domestic saving resulting from the interest reform, export expansion, rising remittances from Vietnam, private capital imports and the inflow of the claims fund from Japan. On the basis of these changes of pre-plan conditions and assumptions, the Government incorporated an upward revision into the 1969 Overall Resources Budget. The GNP would grow at an annual rate of 10.5 percent rather than 7 percent, and thus nearly double by the end year; the total investment would surpass its original plan figure by 64 percent, its ratio being as large as 25.8 percent while the domestic saving ratio was to increase to 15.7 percent; commodity exports would reach 1 billion dollars and the outflow of invisibles 500 million dollars.[7]

Not only were most of the original plan targets achieved two years earlier than expected, but the revised plan itself proved to be overly conservative and the economy's ability to grow was dramatized in 1969 when it grew at the phenomenal rate of 15.5 percent. But the shining performance could hardly be without some setbacks which appeared inevitable for an economy with a fragile frame and yet seemingly impatient to grow. The price inflation, of a demand-pull kind, was being accelerated; there was a widening external imbalance, or alternatively an increasing saving-investment gap; the emergence of insolvent foreign-invested firms, related to the short-sighted industrial policy and to various symptoms of managerial ineptitude, called for a direct government intervention for liquidation, mergers and financing for rehabilitation; and the relative stagnation of agriculture not merely left the food shortage to be an unresolved issue but fostered the regional income disparity to the extent that it was now a social problem. Toward the end of 1969, the Government began to take note of these maladjustments, and devised a series of restrictive monetary and fiscal policies to dampen the overall level of economic activity as the first corrective step. Thus the last two years of the Second Plan were effectively devoted to solidifying the basis on which the Third Five-Year Plan was to be implemented.

The Third Plan, spanning the period 1972-6, was characterized by an avowed intention to remove such imbalances as had been experienced during the previous two plan periods, and stressed the pursuit of harmony among growth, stability and equilibrium in order that the fruits of development might be equitably distributed among the populace and further the need of a balanced regional development by way of the cultivation of the basins of the four great rivers (i.e., Keum, Yungsan, Nakdong and Han Rivers) and of highway construction.[8] This was obviously an outcome of the reappraisal of the hitherto inordinate bias toward manufacturing industries, and a signal, as well, of a more balanced growth led by exports, but there was scarcely any persuasive explanation of the possible consistency of so great an investment priority for the primary sector with an equally preponderant weight attached to such large-scale industries as petrochemicals, iron and steel, shipbuilding and machinery, which would hold a considerable bulk of 3.5 billion dollars worth of exports planned for the target year in addition to their effects of import substitution and forward linkage, and also with its pledges for welfare measures such as housing, medical care and social security.[9]

During the Third Plan period, which was to elevate the nation to the status of an "upper semi-developed" economy, the GNP was expected to expand at an average annual rate of 8.6 percent, evidently an understatement in comparison with the average rate of the preceding decade which was 9.9 percent; as the population was to increase only at the yearly rate of 1.5 percent after 1973 the per capita income would be 389 dollars, twice its magnitude of the base year 1969.[10]

The first year of the Third Plan was particularly eventful on both political and economic fronts. In July, North and South Koreas jointly announced the opening of a political dialogue, and in the following October the incumbent regime, in a move to strengthen its preparedness and position against its Northern counterpart, introduced a new Constitution effectively restricting the traditional principles of liberal democracy. This so-called October Reform was announced together with a "New Village" Movement intent upon the transformation of local life patterns and outlook through a self-help program by rural inhabitants, as well as a Presidential decree on August 3 providing for the freeze of high-interest curb loans designed to improve the financial viability of business and to assure price stability. These moves provided the momentous occasion for the inducement of a new economic environment and for the presentation of ever more ambitious visions for the 1980's.

In August 1973, the Government made public a "Long-Range Prospect of our National Economy" of a "planning" character, pointing to the basic direction in which the Korean economy would chart itself, to which the Third Plan was to adjust its goals each year. By 1981, it envisaged a per capita income of 1,000 dollars and commodity exports totalling 10 billion dollars, on the basis of a 10.3 percent annual growth, eliminating such structural weaknesses as the intersectoral growth disequilibrium, the high rate of inflation, the external imbalance, and the excessive dependence on overseas financial resources for development on the one hand, and building heavy industries which are bound to have a major share of the manufacturing sector on the other.[11] To help finance the massive investments required, the authorities recently promulgated the Law on Investment Funds, and adopted the national pension scheme, which was, however, criticized as being far from its supposed welfare motives.

But the world-wide oil crisis that began late in the autumn of 1973 has had a severe impact upon Korea in view of the fact that the country is at the last stage of its take-off; it is unfortunate too that this had to occur immediately after a comprehensive long-term plan had been drawn up. The Government is now presumed to be formulating a new plan corresponding to the demands of the changing situation, which is expected at some time in the spring of 1974.

MOBILIZATION OF ECONOMIC RESOURCES

What optimal level of domestic liquidity required for growth to maintain and how to restrain the pace of price inflation have been the interminable concerns of monetary authorities for the last twelve years. In order to mobilize capital funds for the large-scale industrial investments called for in the First Plan which had just been put into effect, to counter the credit and price increases since the previous year's coup and to streamline the currency unit, the military regime carried out in June 1962 a decisive currency reform consisting of its one-tenth denomination along with its change of designation from hwan to won and the simultaneous emergency freeze of most monetary assets.[12] But the measure was self-defeating as there had been found little if any idle speculative funds kept from productive investments on account of the political, economic and social unrest; as the recession resulting from the interruption of flows of working capital and the dislocation of the market mechanism was protracted beyond expectation, by the following month the freeze was practically over. The authorities had intended to block 11.6 billion won, equivalent to nearly one-third of the total money supply, most of which could have been transformed into shares of an Industrial Development Corporation, but the abortive reform merely put the economy into greater confusion and further discredited the value of money.

In the area of traditional monetary policy, one may note the constant resort until 1965 to credit rationing, primarily in the form of loan ceilings and selective allocations of credit based on investment priority schemes and preferential rates of interest: this policy, however, was by no means effective because the preferences became generalized, fewer loans were now subject to credit ceilings, and there were administrative difficulties involved in confirming whether individual credits selectively extended in fact served the purposes for which they were intended.[13]

The interest rate reform of October 1965 was a turning point in the way of shifting over to an indirect monetary control system which would allow for the recovery of an intermediary function of the interest rate in money market. It doubled the hitherto 15-percent time deposit rate, enabling monthly interest payments, but at the same time raised the standard loan rate to 26 percent so that there occurred a negative interest margin. It further provided for the application of a penalty rate of 36.5 percent on outstanding loans in default. Such upward adjustment of the level of interest rates was aimed at prompting the public to save in response to a more attractive real rate, winning curb market funds into the banking system and encouraging business to make fuller use of owned rather than borrowed capital.[14]

The reform was a success, as a substantial part of curb market funds indeed flowed into the ordinary banking channels to cause time and savings deposits to rise by 48 percent in the following quarter and then to accumulate at an annual rate of increase of over 100 percent in subsequent years. And yet it would be erroneous to infer that, in the case of lending, the new high rates were uniformly applicable. There was yet a wide range of preferential rates for import and export financing, for long- and medium-term loans by state-owned financial institutions, and of foreign loans negotiated with government approval or payment guarantees. The real cost of loan funds for firms was mitigated also by the continued increase of prices and by writing off the interest on borrowed funds as a cost in determining corporate profits, so that there continued to be an active demand for loans.[15]

The authorities had not contemplated any prolonged maintenance of the high level of interest rates, nor was the negative margin between the deposit and loan rates considered as unavoidable. Although it served its primary aim of mobilizing domestic capital, it brought great pressures on the interest cost borne by enterprises and the profit position of banks, which therefore had to be supported by the payment of interest on their special deposits required to be maintained with the Bank of Korea and central bank bonds in their portfolios. The disparity between the standard loan rate of commercial banks on the one hand and preferential and foreign loan rates on the other entailed a virtual credit rationing at graduated loan rates which caused potential borrowers to seek ever more preferential treatments. There were, however, arguments against any interest rate reduction on the ground that there was still a buoyant demand for credit in spite of the high level of interest rates, because it would reduce the real rate on account of an inflationary tendency, and because artificially lowered rates would be inimical to an efficient allocation of credit. The increasing insolvency of firms due to high interest rates, the inevitability of preferential supports given to policy-oriented investment projects, the inducement of low-quality bank loans or direct investment from overseas, and the rising interest cost of issues of public bonds and industrial debentures, all justified the five subsequent rate reductions. As a result of the fifth cut in January 1972, time and savings deposits of one-year maturity were entitled to an annual rate of 16.8 percent, and the standard loan rate stood at the level of 19 percent per annum.[16]

The Government moved in 1966 to supplement the financial stabilization program revived in 1963 with the so-called regulation of the "reserve base," a new form of adjustment of money supply ceilings or of control of the total quantity of cash and deposit money.[17] The reserve base itself is the total net assets of the Bank of Korea, i.e. the combination of loans to the government and the public and those on usances a form of short-term credit on imports minus government deposits and balances on the currency stabilization bonds account plus the fertilizer account and net foreign exchange assets; the latter are valent to the total issue of bank notes plus the blocked deposits of commercial banks on their liabilities account. Though of a flexible kind, the reserve base rule, too, has hardly moderated the money supply, which rose at twice the rate of the GNP, a factor attributed to the expanding foreign sector impossible of being appropriately offset by the restraints on fiscal expenditures and loans to the public. The reversion to old-fashioned credit ceilings since the close of 1969 by setting guidelines or using moral suasion explains some persistent underlying impediments to the effective execution of monetary policy.

Pressed between the need, on the one hand, to curb lending for private business in order to check inflation and, on the other, to finance priority investments on preferential terms in such a way as not to create an incentive to credit expansion, the Government conceived of a unique alternative for the relief of cost pressures on business on August 3, 1972: a Presidential decree called for the mandatory rescheduling and conversion of all private non-bank borrowings and short-term bank loans (the latter up to 200 million won) into terms of eight years including a three-year grace period respectively at 16.2 and 8 percent interests; provided for a 2-billion-won government fund for special guarantees and a 50-billion-won Industrial Rationalization Fund; and raised depreciation rates for key industries. It was also an occasion where the Government effected another interest rate cut, i.e. that of the basic bank loan rate from 19 to 15.5 percent and of time deposit rates from 16 to 12 percent; affirmed the fixity of the exchange rate at about 400 won to the dollar and the maximum restraint for the following year's national budget; and committed itself to keeping the annual inflation rate at 3 percent.[18] This policy package already consolidated private non-bank business loans in the amount of 350 billion won—equivalent of about one-fourth of the total official bank lending—into medium-term ones at 16.2 percent interest, and gave not only an immediate, though temporary, assistance to heavily-indebted firms but produced powerful disincentive for private lenders in the future to invest through similar channels. On the other hand, the pledge of a no-more-than-3-percent rate of inflation unduly created an air of incredibility of economic policy in general and of the measure in particular.

It is distinctive of Korea's monetary system that the Government wields a predominant influence on financial institutions in general because the state-owned banks play a significant role; the Government is a major shareholder of the supposedly private banks and the President has an ultimate veto power over any decision on matters of monetary policy by the Committee on Monetary Management made in defiance of views of its chairman, the Minister of Finance.[19] Secondly, most of small savings still flow into unorganized money markets, which thus supply high-interest loans placed outside the sphere of policy to small cities and villages as well as large corporations as operational funds. Thirdly, in addition to the phenomenon of duality of the money market, one cannot overlook the inability to make effective use of traditional monetary control methods that derive from the presence of a large area of policy finance. Lastly, it is worth emphasizing that the rising exports, remittances from abroad, and foreign capital imports have caused a monetary expansion responsible for the latent inflation, which in turn enabled the forced saving, at least partially financing the country's economic development.

The Government has also performed a crucial role in resource mobilization by an energetic tax drive and expenditure outlays in a manner consistent with development. A balanced budget has, since the third year of the First Plan, been characteristic of Korea's fiscal management aimed at optimizing the contribution of the government sector to growth without over-stimulating effective demand, though the issue of national and other public bonds was introduced in 1969 as an additional means of providing for funds required for public investment projects. But as the role of the development budget becomes larger, there is an increasing number of vital questions that the Government should face, namely an optimal allocation of resources between the public and private sectors, the improvement of levying techniques for the minimization of resistance to taxes, the expansion of public saving by restricting current expenditures, the prevention of rigidity of the budgetary structure, and the resource transfers for a regional balance of growth.

The ratio of the total budget to the GNP increased from 14.8 percent in 1964, when the overall cash deficits of the Government had been eliminated, to 23.5 percent in 1972; and the average annual rate of increase of the General Budget for the period between these years was as great as 32.6 percent. Such trend is not critical merely because it may endanger stability. That government expenditures had to be supported by an increasing tax burden biased toward direct taxes strictly within the bounds of a fiscal balance, resulted in widespread resistance to tax obligations. And the share of corporate taxes is now so large and the government initiative in making loans and investments is so predominant that one can hardly dismiss summarily the frequent suggestion that there exists an undue barrier to initiatives of the private sector.

The weight of the local currency counterpart funds generated by U. S. aid which was substantial during the First Plan period, is now negligible, and the ever-expanding government loans and investments, over 60 percent of which are diverted to the social overhead sector and the rest mostly for agriculture and forestry, have been financed out of the rising tax revenues and public loans from abroad, while the declining proportion of defense spending in the total budget, i.e., from 33.1 percent in 1964 to 28 percent in 1973, has also helped keep it in balance.

The internal tax receipts have increased nearly fifteen-fold since 1962, due mainly to the improved tax administration and the modernization of the tax structure through a series of legal amendments. In March 1967, the Office of National Taxation was established as a semi-independent organ with a greater number of tax offices and officers equipped with advanced techniques of assessment and collection. As far as the tax structure is concerned, the first major reform was effected in 1961 to devise an entirely new fiscal basis, upon which the First Plan was to be executed, with such improved features as the abrogation of "presumptive" assessment and the prevention of double levies, higher rates of the indirect taxes on which the future fiscal requirements could not but depend, and lower tax rates on corporate and business incomes to facilitate capital formation.[20]

There began to appear in 1965 effects of the 1961 reform and its subsequent supplementary revisions which prompted the recovery of both price and income elasticities of tax returns and widened the scope of functions of the revenue policy; and with the year's marginal tax revenue ratio of 17.2 percent the Government confidently moved to a flexible development-oriented fiscal policy by promulgating the Law on the Regulation of Tax Deductions and Exemptions for the selective promotion of private capital accumulation and the Law on Assets Revaluation providing for the non-taxability of value differentials accruing from asset revaluation for similar purposes.

The tax reform in 1967, the largest since 1961, was a serious attempt to reorganize the whole tax base so that a great stress would be put on indirect taxation as a means to raise the level of tax revenues, in spite of the popular misconception of direct taxes, hardly a source of equitable generalized taxation, as still the most desirable device of income redistribution. Its highlights were the preferential rate differentiation on the incomes of open corporations, a 6-percent investment allowance for such new industries as had been given a high priority under the Second Plan, the tax for the prohibition of speculation on immovable properties to divert idle funds to industrial investments, tax deductions on housing funds for low-income brackets, and the partial globalization of the existing schedular personal income tax system, allowing for different rates and degrees of progressivity that would, to start with, bind higher echelons with an income exceeding 5 million won, and the legalization of the self-assessment of open corporations.[21] On the whole, direct taxes became more progressive, and the level and coverage of indirect taxes were raised.

There were further adjustments of the tax structure in 1971 to eradicate defects derived from the inequity of tax burdens related to the inclination toward direct taxes, to mark up indirect tax rates so as to encourage domestic capital mobilization, and to simplify the multifarious and complicated tax regulations. The 1971 reform thus widened the scope of globalized income taxes and imposed a 5-percent tax on interest income; abolished the corporate surtax, and liberalized investment and depreciation allowances.[22] But there were criticisms of the heavier indirect levies as being inflationary and some were skeptical of the effect of the tax on interest income which might run counter to the willingness to save.

The over-reliance on indirect taxation, though admittedly a feature of an underdeveloped system of taxation, is expected to last for some time because the people's consciousness of their tax obligations still leaves much to be desired. Also administrative efficiency is less than satisfactory, and there are acute policy considerations for the restraint on consumption and the buildup of strategic industries. Attention must also be drawn to the high rate of tax burden, that is, as high as 12.9 percent in a developing country with a per capita income of less than 400 dollars.

It is a matter of course that a country not endowed with sufficient domestic resources or with accumulated capital has no choice but to rely on considerable foreign savings if it is to follow the path of industrialization. In the decade covered by the two economic development plans—a time when the U. S. grants-in-aid gradually declined and yet there was an increasing demand for foreign raw materials and equipment—Korea showed the remarkable capability of absorbing an enlarged inflow of foreign capital, which had been facilitated by such factors as the normalization of relations between Korea and Japan, the promotional measures of the Government, the country's exceptionally high interest rates, and above all the international confidence in the potentialities of its growing economy.

The Korea-Japan Treaty was concluded in October 1965, stipulating that Japan provide Korea over a ten-year period with medium-term commercial credits worth of 300 million dollars; official grants of another 300 million dollars, and official long-term loans on concessional terms of 200 million dollars.[23] While most of these credits were rapidly committed to development projects, Japan agreed to offer additional credits at each year's ministerial conference of the two Governments. The low interest of foreign commercial loans, less than half of the domestic level following the interest rate reform of

1965, was another attraction amid the heavy demand for funds. And the increasing international confidence demonstrated by the willingness of overseas lenders and investors to provide capital was ascribed to the direct involvement of the interested foreign governments, the still relatively low external debt service ratio of Korea, and the reasonably low wages as far as equity capital was concerned.

Among the most significant measures adopted by the Government for the inducement of foreign capital are its repayment guarantees to commercial loans and the liberal terms offered to equity capital including tax treatment, transfer of profits and capital, and majority capital holding. These features are prominently incorporated into the Foreign Capital Inducement Law promulgated in August 1966, which was in effect a unification of all the existing rules and regulations on the different aspects of capital imports. In summary, the Law provided that the interest and other incomes accruing to the lender from a cash loan or capital goods inducement contract of over three years be not subject to the income or corporation tax and that from a technological inducement contract of over one year exempt fully for 5 years and 50 percent for another three years. But the most attractive incentive was obviously the governmental payment guarantee, though it was supposed only to be available where inducement would be otherwise difficult and intended for priority projects deemed necessary for economic development. It is to be noted that in order to forestall the accumulation of excessive debt burdens the amount of principal and interest to be paid every year under such guarantees was not allowed to exceed nine percent of the total receipts of foreign exchange estimated for the current year.[24]

The rapid increase of foreign capital inflows began to have serious implications for the expansion of imports, the future debt service and the domestic monetary stability toward the end of 1967, when the authorities introduced the "Overall Guidelines for the Rationalization of Foreign Capital Inducement," changing the emphasis in foreign capital inducement from quantity to quality. These guidelines set new criteria for the selection of eligible projects, such as their ultimate profitability and prospective borrowers' financial soundness and ability to raise local funds required in the case of loans guaranteed by commercial banks, the greater restriction on cash loans, the limit of 50 percent of the total private borrowings to those from any one country to diversify the sources of loans, and the preferential consideration of borrowings from members of the International Consultative Group for Korea as well as from international institutions.[25]

By 1969, when there was a great rush of foreign capital imports, it was apparent that these guidelines were not effective enough to restrain the excess, so that a far more stringent device had to be sought. Firstly, the Government initiated annual quantitative ceilings over foreign commercial loans of terms ranging from 3 to 12 years, upon consultation with the International Monetary Fund. Secondly, it prohibited the negotiation of cash loans by individuals or private business to substitute for local funds unless offered by international financial institutions. Thirdly, it continued to encourage such commodity loans as would enable the purchase of equipment and raw materials at favorable terms. Lastly, but most notably, steps were taken to dispose of the so-called insolvent firms that proved incapable of amortization, and no fewer than 16 foreign-invested companies as a result were subjected to auction, bank ownership or management, mergers, or other rationalization measures.[26]

As these ill effects of the concentration on loans appeared and the increase of debt service burdens accelerated, not only did the qualitative aspect of commercial credits begin to be stressed but direct investments or preferably joint ventures, as well as long-term concessional loans on a government-to-government basis, were actively encouraged. Within the broad priority categories, the Law sets no limitation on the proportion of equity of an enterprise to be held by foreign investors; guarantees the remittance of dividends and the repatriation of capital up to 20 percent of the year's total investment beginning two years after its activation; and allows the reinvestment of profits and dividends not exceeding the amount of the original investment, along with the exemption of income, corporation, property, and property acquisition taxes for 5 years and a 50 percent deduction for the following three years.[27]

In March 1970, the Government integrated all foreign investment procedures so that the officials of diverse administrative agencies involved in one stage or another of the process of licensing or approval were to be stationed together at the Economic Planning Board to exercise final authority. Another promotional development during the year was the setup of a committee on the coordination of labour disputes of foreign-invested enterprises which was empowered to settle within 20 days all such disputes referred thereto, occurring in the firms with a foreign equity of more than 100,000 dollars and exporting all of their outputs.[28] Two free export processing zones were established respectively at Masan and Iri, where any resident foreign firms or joint ventures of a domestic equity ratio of less than 50 percent, producing, processing or assembling exportable goods, were to be granted automatic licenses in exporting manufactured goods and importing raw materials, together with other administrative privileges and conveniences.

EXPORT PROMOTION AND EXTERNAL BALANCE

The main policy emphasis on the promotion of exports is by no means difficult to comprehend when one realizes the logic of Korea's economic development, i. e., the sequence of foreign capital imports, the buildup of import-substitution and export industries, the sales of goods overseas, and the fulfillment of debt service obligations. Such a slogan as "export-propelled growth" is hardly far-fetched in view of the rate of export increase in recent years approximately three times as fast as that of GNP growth, the variety of aids to exports, and the long-run target of a 10-billion-dollar export by 1981.

The official means of export promotion up to 1963 included: 1) direct subsidies for some four different categories of selected commodities, each of which was entitled to 10 to 25 won per dollar of export, 2) the premium on marketable rights to import a volume equivalent in value to 100 percent of export income, 3) the allocative priority to, and the preferential interest rate as low as nearly 8 percent for, export credits, the amount of credit per dollar being roughly 110 won by 1963, and 4) the uniform 50 percent tax deduction on all exchange-earning activities including exports. In addition to these various provisions, the Export Promotion Law promulgated in March 1962 limited the eligibility for the use of Korean foreign exchanges to those who exported at least 10,000 dollars worth of goods, and the existing External Trade Law was so revised as to strip any trader failing to sell the legal minimum of his qualification.[29]

As the devaluation of 1964 increased advantages in terms of price for export industries, there were now weaker justifications for the continued release of direct subsidies, which were totally abolished by 1965. The legitimacy of export-import linkages, too, appeared less convincing than before, though a limited number of relatively unprofitable export items was still linked with a few popular importables. While the indirect aids to exports already in effect continued to be potent, there were other devices such as: 1) the differentiated preferential bank credits at unchanged interest rates in contrast to the 26 percent for ordinary commercial loans upon the interest rate reform of 1965, which was tantamount to an interest subsidy; 2) the issuance of domestic letters of credit by exporters which allowed home producers of raw materials accepting them to have the same access as the former to easier credit facilities and tax benefits; and 3) the standby credit arrangements by the central bank to help finance international bids or contracts, to settle export letters of credit issued by the overseas branches of Korean exporting houses, and support other foreign-exchange-earning activities. In 1965, the authorities also introduced a scheme of writing off as a loss a fixed portion of imported raw materials for the manufacture of exports. The Korea Trade Promotion Corporation (KOTRA) expanded its network abroad; more trade missions were dispatched; and the number of trade agreements rose markedly. Since 1965, the Conference on Export Promotion has taken place at the Presidential palace every month; chaired by the President himself, the Conference functioned as the supreme policy-making and coordinating organ for export and related activities.

The Government unified in 1966 all of the current multifarious statutes and regulations into a new International Trade Law, and further transferred most of the procedural work connected with trade from the Ministry of Commerce and Industry to the Bank of Korea and foreign exchange banks. It resorted after 1967 to the more frequent use of export monopoly rights offered to a restricted number of traders who had exported new products or cultivated new markets. Exporters of outstanding achievement were exempt from mortgages against special as well as general customs duties, free from extraordinary tax investigations, and given priority in the allocation of foreign exchanges for marketing activities.[30]

In the realm of imports, however, one can recognize a cyclical fluctuation of restriction and liberalization, in fact a reflection of the precarious balance between the world-wide trend of freer trade and the excess demand inherent in a developing economy. In the first two years of the First Plan, imports were regulated by a half-yearly trade plan which divided all importables into 3 broad classes, i.e., automatically-approvable, restricted and prohibited items, or more precisely by the increase, reduction or cancellation of automatically approvable items depending upon changes in import demand or in foreign exchange reserves, and a distinction was made between those programmed against Korean foreign exchange and aid dollars. The Emergency Law on Special Customs Duty was enacted in July 1961 to divide about 700 selected non-essential goods, the home-currency prices of which had declined by the adoption of a single fixed exchange rate in lieu of the previous system of multiple rates, into 4 categories to which the special duties ranging from 100 to 10 percent were applied according to the degree of non-essentiality.

Beginning in 1963, the authorities tightened the export-import linkage arrangement, whereby only those with a comparable export record were eligible for an import license regardless of whether it involved automatically approvable or restricted items, though it did not affect raw materials for the production of exportables or equipment for development projects. On the other hand, an export bonus scheme was instituted which provided for the allowance of a certain percentage of export earnings to be used for the import of raw materials and machinery for domestic use, in order to prevent any sag of the export drive in an environment in which the production of goods for home consumption was far preferable to that of exportables as long as they required identical raw materials. These measures were replaced, in accordance with an agreement with the IMF following the exchange rate reform of March 1965, by quotas on the restricted items, which in effect provided a much softer form of direct control.

The exchange rate reform certainly initiated a move toward trade liberalization, but was not expected alone to perform the function of adjustment of the import volume. In June 1964, another Emergency Law on Special Customs Duty was promulgated to help restrain import demand by imposing duties on items yielding excess profits and thus to increase tax revenues as well. These duties in fact absorbed 70 to 90 percent of the difference between the total cost of imported commodities, including the general import duty, commodity taxes, handling costs and a permitted mark-up of 30 percent, on the one hand, and the domestic market price on the other.[31]

In the later years of the First Plan, the non-tariff barriers gave way, on the whole, to a greater degree of liberalization. Further measures for freer imports were anticipated in 1967, the first year of the Second Plan, as commodity exports began a fast rise. The inflows of invisibles from Vietnam and West Germany increased, and the import of foreign capital including cash loans grew, so that the exchange reserves ran high. In July of that year, the Government adopted the "negative list system" whereby only those items which were subject to import restriction would be listed. All others then were left eligible for automatic import, with a view to strengthening the competitive power of domestic industries which had been sheltered by high tariff walls, thereby protecting consumer interests, and meeting the obligations required of a trading nation which was now a member of both the IMF and the GATT.[32]

A major revision of the tariff system was made in December 1967 to harmonize it with the negative list system and the progress of industrial development. According to this reform, most items which were of a non-protected kind would be subject to a low uniform rate along with exemptions for raw materials and machinery. The high protective tariffs for the benefit of specially chosen industries would be determined on an individual commodity basis, taking into account the value added domestically, the cost difference between domestic and international products, and the degree of essentiality of goods.[33] But this basic principle was challenged by the pressures of industries concerned, and the new tariff structure turned out to be roughly identical with the old, the average rate in the latter actually being a little higher than that of the former. The tariff reform authorized the Government, among other things, to adjust upward or downward, as the case might be, by as much as 50 percent of the value of imports subject to basic rates in case emergency restrictions or liberalization were deemed necessary and the industrial structure was so changed that there occurred an imbalance of tax rates among different commodities.

Turning to foreign exchanges, it is immediately evident that the overvaluation of the won, due primarily to the upward pressure of prices under the regime of either a fixed or manipulated, though ostensibly fluctuating, exchange rate, was representative of the last decade, in spite of a tightened official control, the export-import linkage to conserve reserves, the inducement of longer-term settlements of payment obligations for the import of raw materials and intermediate products, and the gradual reorientation of the capital import policy toward government loans and direct investments with little or no burden of amortization.

The revolutionary government practically terminated the free exchange of export dollars in June 1961 by announcing the abolition of the circulation of foreign exchange certificates, and pledged to maintain the existing official rate of 130 won to the dollar. There appeared in the market through 1962 and the following year a progressively greater gap between the official and effective rates—in effect a rising premium on the right to import associated with realized exports. The premium rate reached the level of as much as 65 won per dollar in April 1964, and the authorities had to have recourse to a Temporary Special Excess Profit Tax, effective December 1963, of 50 won per aid dollar, thus driving up the effective rate applicable to exports and imports further away from the official level.

In May 1964, the won currency was devalued against the dollar by approximately 50 percent, with a view to stabilizing a new basic rate at the effective level, increasing exports while restraining import demand, and preventing the privileges and corrupt practices originating from its overvaluation. Such multiple exchange rate devices as export subsidies, export-import linking arrangements, and nontariff barriers were either eliminated or relaxed simultaneously.[34] The government then introduced in March 1965 a unitary floating exchange rate system, fully confident of its ability to maintain a stable rate as the import quotas were lifted. The prices on the whole remained relatively stationary and the IMF was already committed to a standby credit of 9,300,000 dollars to serve as a stabilization fund. Under this scheme, a resident recipient of gold or foreign exchange was required to obtain freely transferable exchange certificates valid for 15 days from an authorized dealer or to sell it at the daily buying rate posted by the Bank of Korea, but they were not to be issued against the exchanges out of the PL 480 aid or sold by the UN Command for which the rates posted by the central bank would apply. All exchange payments, except for those by the Government and of less than 50 dollars, would require exchange certificates. The central bank would post buying and selling rates every day on the basis of the weighted average of the market rates of the preceding day, and was to be permitted to intervene in the market to smooth out short-term fluctuations due to seasonal or speculative factors though not so far as to distort underlying market trends or to the extent that the posted rates could be restricted within 2 percent of the average certificate market price of the previous day unless approved by the Minister of Finance.[35]

The initial rate of 270 won per dollar emerged upon the introduction of the new arrangement, and there were subsequent movements around this level until August 1965 when the rate was so rigidly fixed at 271 won against the dollar by the excessive official intervention that it now appeared as if a unitary "fixed" rate had replaced the supposedly flexible one. There were, however, attempts throughout 1967 to revive the self-adjusting mechanism of the floating rate system by widening the spread between buying and selling rates from 0.6 percent to 1.8 percent, extending the period of validity of exchange certificates to 30 days and then to 45 days, and authorizing foreign exchange banks, instead of the Bank of Korea, to post those rates on the basis of their own evaluation of the market.[36] These partial modifications no doubt added to the flexibility of the system, but the government continued to manipulate the exchange rate movement so that it could take place only by small continuous margins.

By October 1969, the rate was 291.90 won to the dollar, merely a 10.6 percent increase since 1965, whereas the money wage rate doubled and the wholesale prices rose on the average by 42.6 percent in the same period. The rapidly expanding exports were made possible by tax and credit concessions that amounted to more than 80 won per dollar, and the resulting effective exchange rate of approximately 370 won per dollar, however, was yet less than acceptable to exporters. In response to the criticism from exporters of the relative stability of the exchange rate despite the rise in domestic prices and wages and also to the recommendation of the upward adjustment by 8 percent by the IBRD Mission in September 1969, the Government decided on November 3, 1969 to raise the existing exchange rate by 4.5 percent to 305.10 won per dollar— the first, though insufficient, devaluation since the exchange reform of 1965.[37] Its constant failure to respond to the changing price level once again compelled the authorities on June 28, 1971 to make another upward adjustment by 12.98 percent to the level of 370 won per dollar. The Government then vowed to stabilize the exchange rate at 400 won per dollar as part of the August 1972 Presidential decree. There was a further 20 percent devaluation on December 7, 1974, with a new rate established at 480 won per dollar.

The tendency of rigidity of the current system emanates from the chronic disequilibrium of the foreign exchange certificate market and the low price elasticities of foreign exchange flows—or more basically from the price and wage increases fully offsetting the changes of productivity of export industries and, further, the prevalence of strong feelings for the inadvisability of flotation on grounds of the high import content of exportables and the foreign exchange denomination of all medium- and long-term foreign loans. The Government, however, does not seem to regard a fixed par value as probable in the near future as it sees no immediate stabilization of the price level nor any considerable improvement of productivity. The best way out of the policy impasse is widely believed to be an increase of the degree of flexibility of exchange rate movements in response to the shifting cost-price relationships, rather than a larger erratic once-over adjustment of gaps between the realized market rate and the effective one under the present arrangement.

IMBALANCES IN THE ECONOMY

The spectacular economic growth of the last twelve years has had to pay its own price in the form of imbalances in different aspects of the economy which still have only a very frail basis. The high rate of GNP growth should not blind one to the fact that the absolute level of national income is presently less than 10 billion dollars, inequitably distributed, that too many ambitious investment projects crowded into the short span of a little over a decade could not but cause a rapid price inflation. In this process numerous mismanaged foreign-invested firms have fallen into insolvency; big business in a limited domestic market has shown distinct monopolistic or oligopolistic tendencies; the industry-biased development has so induced a population concentration in cities that Korea has had to face at a relatively early stage a combination of urbanization, a polluted environment, and land speculation; and agriculture remains a retarded or somewhat ignored industry incapable of producing a self-sufficient food supply, though there has of late been some reappraisal. It should not be overlooked that among economic planners and policy-makers the view is prevalent that it is much too premature to discuss income inequality, despite the widely-held belief that it is now not merely an economic issue but has begun to assume a political dimension, and that any idea of collective bargaining by wage-earners is detrimental to the competitive strength of Korean exports on which economic growth essentially depends. Any serious reference to the environmental problem, though perhaps not a downright taboo, is considered a highly uncomfortable topic to deliberate because the feeling is predominant that industrial investments should not be withheld on that account.

Considering the fact that most modern firms were initially financed by bank credits or foreign loans, one finds that their profitability and ultimate ability to repay are of utmost concern to the Government, which, however, has on its own part failed to devise an industrial policy based on the long-term prospects of demand, financing and comparative advantage. The insolvency or bankruptcy of firms has been due basically to the inefficient utilization of their investible funds, the high cost of output, political pressures on monetary institutions which have forced loans on questionable grounds, and a high interest rate level which created heavy debt service burdens for them. It is notable that in 1972 the Government went so far as to indict a number of so-called "anti-social" industrialists and businessmen who were alleged to have misused borrowed funds while their firms became incapacitated.

Attention has also been focused on the growing Japanese investments in Korea which, though apparently tuned to Korea's development needs, now hold so large a share of the total capital inflow as to arouse considerable resentment among the populace; without these investments, however, the country cannot hope to achieve the kind of economic progress envisaged in the Long-Term Economic Prospects. This is the fundamental dilemma of Korea in her economic relations with Japan.

The Korean economy is of a mixed type in the sense that the Government intervenes widely in an atmosphere essentially of private initiatives, and yet its regulatory powers have tended to expand beyond desirable bounds so that the market mechanism seems to have gradually a less significant role to play. It is more evident than ever that the economy has outgrown the administrative capacity to control nearly every aspect of economic activity; therefore the authorities should begin to contemplate seriously how to divest themselves of some peripheral areas in economic policy making.

CONCLUDING REMARKS

The writer has sketched only some of the highlights of development policy; even in this limited task it is impossible to be wholly successful because the ingredients of such policy are so diverse and complex that any short essay is bound to leave much unanswered. The writer is far from being convinced that the degree of emphasis he has placed on each topic is fully warranted, but few issues in the mutable Korean economic scene lend themselves to any definitive analysis.

One of the fundamental questions of a developing economy is doubtless its ability to mobilize resources. The average annual saving-investment gap ratio, i.e., the investment ratio minus the saving ratio, during the Second Plan period was as large as 11.9 percent; and it would be desirable for the economy to exhibit greater domestic propensity to save and to develop a greater degree of international confidence so as to induce a continued inflow of capital from overseas. In a country long accustomed to an inflationary psychology, savings tend to be transformed easily into speculative funds or to flow into the unorganized money market for high interest bank deposits; also the purchase of securities or insurance policies is susceptible to capital losses. This is the main reason why the Government has constantly pursued an unusually stringent tax policy aimed at involuntary savings and an active foreign capital inducement always subject to official guidance and regulation, though in the case of the latter the recent policy shift from loans to direct investment has created the apprehension of an eventual dependence of Korean industries on foreign investors. There has been criticism of excessive exports resulting in a diminished availability of some basic commodities in the home market. At the same time it seems no longer possible to dismiss the overseas call for greater reciprocity through the removal of various barriers to imports. Compounded by the worldwide oil crisis, which is particularly unfortunate for a Korean economy on the threshold of another leap forward, the tasks of economy policy-making will certainly be more challenging than ever before, particularly in view of such problems as the curbing of inflation, capital imports and amortization, investments in resources abroad, increased exports and, ultimately, trade liberalization.

FOOTNOTES

1. Pak Jung-jae, *Hankuk Kyŏngje Paeknyŏn* (A Hundred Years of the Korean Economy) (Seoul: Korean Productivity Council, 1971), p. 328.
2. Japan Economic Research Council, *Kankoku Keizai no Jitsujo* (Survey of the Korean Economy) (Tokyo: Japan Economic Research Council, 1968), pp. 161–2.
3. Economic Planning Board, "60–nyŏndae Hankuk Kyŏngje ŭi Hwŏeko: Kyŏngje Kaebal Kyehoek" (A Retrospect of the Korean Economy in the 60's: Economic Development Plans), *Kyekan Kyŏngje Chosa,* March 1970, p. 11.
4. Pak, *op. cit.,* p. 330.
5. Federation of Korean Industries, *Hankuk Kyŏngje Yŏngam, 1966* (The Annual of the Korean Economy for 1966) (Seoul: Federation of Korean Industries, 1966), p. II-55.
6. Government of the Republic of Korea, *The Second Five-Year Economic Development Plan* (Seoul: Government of the Republic of Korea, 1966), pp. 33-39.
7. The Bank of Korea, "Jeich'a Kyŏngje Kaebal Okaenyŏn Kyehoek ŭi Sŏngkwa wa Munjejŏm" (The Achievements and Issues of the 2nd Five-Year Economic Development Plan), *Chosa Wŏlbo,* July 1972, pp. 6-7.

8. Government of the Republic of Korea, *The Third Five-Year Economic Development Plan* (Seoul: Government of the Republic of Korea, 1971), pp. 1-3.
9. *Ibid.*
10. *Ibid.*, p. 4.
11. Economic Planning Board, *Major Indicators of the Korean Economy for 1973-81* (Seoul: Economic Planning Board, 1973), p. 4.
12. Japan Economic Research Council, *op. cit.*, pp. 194-9.
13. S. Kanesa-Thasan, "Stabilizing an Economy—the Korean Experience," a paper presented at the Conference on Korean Planning, June 19-21, 1968, sponsored by Intersocietal Studies of Northwestern University at Pheasant Run, St. Charles, Illinois, U.S.A., pp. 11-13.
14. *Ibid.*, pp. 14-15.
15. *Ibid.*, pp. 16-19.
16. The Korea Development Bank, "Kŭmni Inha Chojŏng ŭi Paekyŏng kwa Naeyong" (The Background and Details of the Downward Adjustment of Interest Rates), *Monthly Economic Review*, February 1972, pp. 36-42.
17. T. Miyazaki, "Kankoku no Zaisei Kinyu Jijo" (A Survey of Korea's Public Finance and Monetary System), *The Fiscal and Monetary Situations of Asian Countries*, edited by M. Kimura (Tokyo: Institute of Developing Economies, 1969), p. 39.
18. International Bank for Reconstruction and Development, *The Economic Situation and Prospects of the Republic of Korea* (EAP-33 a) (Washington, D.C.: International Bank for Reconstruction and Development, 1972), pp. 9-13.
19. Miyazaki, *op. cit.*, p. 37.
20. Federation of Korean Industries, *Hankuk Kyŏngje Yŏngam, 1973* (The Annual of the Korean Economy for 1973) (Seoul: Federation of Korean Industries, 1973), pp. 493-4.
21. *Ibid.*, pp. 499-501.
22. *Ibid.*, pp. 502-4.
23. Ministry of Foreign Affairs, *Kankoku Daisanji Gokanen Keikaku Chosadan Hokokusho* (The Report of the Mission on Korea's Third Five-Year Economic Development Plan) (Tokyo: Ministry of Foreign Affairs, 1972), Chapter 3.
24. International Bank for Reconstruction and Development and International Development Association, *Current Economic Situation and Prospects of the Republic of Korea* (EAP-4a), (Washington, D. C.: International Bank for Reconstruction and Development, 1969), Vol. I Main Report, Appendix on External Debt Management, pp. 1-2.
25. *Ibid.*
26. Pak, *op. cit.*, p. 473.
27. International Bank for Reconstruction and Development and International Development Association, *op. cit.*, p. 3.
28. Federation of Korean Industries, *Hankuk Kyŏngje Yŏngam, 1971* (The Annual of the Korean Economy for 1971) (Seoul: Federation of Korean Industries, 1971), p. 111.
29. Korea Traders Association, *Hankuk ŭi Sanŏp mit Muyŏk Chŏngch'aeksa* (Trade and Industrial Policy in Korea) (Seoul: Korea Traders Association, 1971), pp. 71-74.
30. *Ibid.*, pp. 124-9.
31. Federation of Korean Industries, *Hankuk Kyŏngje Yŏngam, 1972* (The

Annual of the Korean Economy for 1972) (Seoul: Federation of Korean Industries, 1972), p. 494.
    32. *Ibid.*, p. 496.
    33. Kanesa-Thasan, *op. cit.*, pp. 28–9.
    34. *Ibid.*, p. 22.
    35. *Ibid.*, p. 24.
    36. The Bank of Korea, *Hankuk ŭi Kukjesuji* (The Korean Balance of Payments) (Seoul: The Bank of Korea, 1970), p. 189.
    37. The Korea Development Bank, "Urinara Hwanyul Pyŏndong Ch'ui wa Hyŏnhwang" (Exchange Rate Changes in Our Country), *Monthly Economic Review*, August, 1971, pp. 27–33.

PART FIVE: **INTERPRETATIONS OF KOREAN POLITICS**

CHAPTER 10: The Authority Structure of Korean Politics
by Bae-ho Hahn

CHAPTER 11: Toward a New Theory of Korean Politics:
A Reexamination of Traditional Factors
by Pyong-choon Hahm

INTRODUCTION TO PART FIVE

One way to approach the political dimension of national development is to examine the authority structure of a particular society. In the ensuing chapter, Bae-ho Hahn has defined "political authority structure" in a general sense as that aspect of a society where political phenomena take place in a certain regularized pattern.

Hahn's analysis is predicated upon the assumption that the political authority structure of Korea is reflective of the wider makeup of Korean society as a whole. He has examined the particular authority structures of traditional Yi dynasty Korea; of the Japanese colonial period; and of the more recent scene. He suggests that the primary distinction to be made is that of an "authoritarian, monarchial and elitist" rule in both of the former periods, and a "more conciliar, representative form" in the latter. The result since World War II has been a mixture of the old and new. While the structures of government were changed, the composition of the power elite in the early post-war years remained essentially the same. The dominant political leadership was part and parcel of the more autocratic infrastructure dating well back into the Japanese colonial days. Those in exile during that time had little administrative experience, and those who had been *petit* officials in the Japanese colonial regime had had little or no real decision-making authority or responsibility. In effect, an autocratic aura pervaded the Rhee regime. There was a progressively authoritarian stance by the Government through the 1950's. The economic situation seemed to require a strong hand, as did the ever-hostile threat from the north. The Korean War was a major contributor to widespread social disintegration and dislocation. These conditions provided justification in the minds of the rulers for a strong and forceful regime, and for an executive-dominated Government.

The most significant change in Korean politics in the years since 1949 has been achievement of a higher degree of formalization and a higher level of differentiation and specialization than in Yi or Japanese-dominated Korea. The emergence of political parties has been most important in this development. Even so, politics in Korea is still largely monopolistic; there are still no significant countervailing groups to offer strong alternatives to the ruling elite, which is inclined to wish to retain its favored position.

Concerning the decade of the 1960's, the Korean political authority structure remained a mixture of traditional patterns and the more recently imposed formal-legalist structural pattern. In the early 1970's, no clear-cut synthesis has yet emerged.

In Pyong-choon Hahm's chapter, guidelines are suggested "toward a new theory of Korean politics." In essence, he cautions us not to attempt to understand Korean values and behavior from the perspective of western culture and value prejudices, but rather to attempt to know the Korean system on its own terms and within the context of its historical development. Hahm criticizes three dominant theories of Korean politics as placing undue emphasis on power and wealth as determinants of national (and human) progress and development. These three with which Hahm differs are those of the mainstream of Japanese scholarship; of K. A. Wittfogel; and of Gregory Henderson. Hahm contends that, in fact, the criteria of power and wealth, upon which the above-mentioned scholars base their analyses, were only two values among many to be found in traditional Korea. And these were not given high priority as national goals. Rather "old Korea was prepared to accept poverty and military weakness as the price for other goals it valued more highly."

In posing an alternative theory, Hahm places great emphasis on traditional Korea's attention to interpersonal relationships—or "overlapping egos." The prime focus of attention for a Yi dynasty citizen was to assure for himself a proper place in his contemporary society and to be assured of visitations, care and attention at his gravesite after his death. In Hahm's words, "Koreans preferred to commit themselves to finite human beings rather than to an absolute and universal entity or concept such as God, Truth, Nation, Justice, Liberty, etc." He also points to the Korean concept of *time* as "indistinct—as much present- oriented as past-or future-oriented." "The Koreans left the concept of time indistinct, leaving eternity to overlap with time." This is in contrast with the dominant western view of time as a continuum, and with a goal or future-orientation for individuals and societies. Hahm also points to the western concept of private property as being alien to traditional Korea. Koreans were expected to earn enough of material possessions to live comfortably but not so much as to appear greedy or miserly. They were expected to, and generally did, share their wealth on a selective basis with others. Exclusivity of property and possessions, basic to western legal precepts, was not a factor in old Korea. Again in Hahm's words, "it is because of the strong goal-achievement orientation inherent in profit maximization that the culture of old Korea came to hold the pursuit of wealth in apprehension and mistrust." Such orientation automatically entails a tendency to separate and isolate egos—a tendency unacceptable to the commonly held values of traditional Korea.

Concerning *power,* Hahm says that "it is power stripped of threat of violence and other forms of severe deprivation to which the Koreans were willing to concede legitimacy." Otherwise, pursuit of power was disruptive

Introduction to Part Five 287

of a stable system of overlapping egos and turned the system into one of enforced subject-object relationships. Power was not discarded, but was to be used in a reasonable and benevolent fashion, always within the context of "humanness."

Hahm's conclusion is basically that contemporary Korea, to be understood properly, must be seen both in the light of traditional values derived from the Yi dynasty period and in terms of the western values superimposed in recent years. Otherwise, the intricacies and complexities of contemporary Korean society are likely to be misunderstood, misinterpreted and/or distorted.

CHAPTER 10:

The Authority Structure of Korean Politics

BAE-HO HAHN*

Like many other developing nations, Korea is in a state of constant social and political flux, perhaps to an extent that no easy discerning of its basic characteristics is possible. However, one may acquire a somewhat clearer perspective of the status of and changes in contemporary Korean society if he adopts a historical view of Korea in terms of three fairly distinct periods in Korean history and three formal authority patterns identifiable with each of the three periods—firstly, a traditional autocratic structure; secondly, a military-dominated Japanese colonial despotism; and, more recently, a constitutional, republican form of government imposed upon Korea at the end of the U.S. military occupation in 1948.

This chapter is divided into two parts. In the first section an analytical description of the traditional Korean structure of political authority and the Japanese colonial rule, which can be regarded in some respects as a continuation of the traditional autocratic system, will be given to provide background for treatment of the contemporary Korean political setting. Some salient features of both the traditional system and the Japanese colonial rule will be pointed out.

In the second part of the chapter, focus will be on the contemporary Korean political system as a "transitional" type characterized

---
*Bae-ho Hahn is Professor of Political Science at Korea University, Seoul. His Ph. D. is from Princeton University.

by a conspicuous disparity between the tradition-rooted social structure and a Western-modelled conciliar authority pattern superimposed in the wake of the termination of U.S. Military rule in 1948. Political processes and changes during the period since 1948 will, therefore, be viewed in terms of dynamic, continuous interactions among various "dissonant" elements in the Korean social setting and in terms of the outcome of interactions of various groups, particularly the political elite and the military.

Before we proceed further, it seems necessary to define the term, *political authority structure*. In general we mean that aspect of a society where political phenomena take place in a certain regularized pattern. In a more technical and specific vein, we are referring to those *aspects of a society that have a recognized responsibility for performing at minimum the functions of social goal attainment by means of legitimate decisions*.[1]

TRADITIONAL KOREA: A CONFUCIAN, CENTRALIZED BUREAUCRATIC STATE

Social Setting. Every political authority structure operates within a social setting. In fact it may even be assumed that a political authority structure would reflect the total social system of which it is a part. A *stable* political system is one where a discrepancy or dissonance between the social structure and political authority structure is at a minimum. Conversely, when political authority structure deviates sharply from social structure the probability that the former will persist is low. With this perspective in mind, we may now examine the salient aspects of traditional Korean political authority patterns.

Traditional Korean society was characterized by two diametrically opposed classes and a number of what Max Weber called *status groups*. Those who stayed at the peak of the social pyramid were *yangban*, the officials and descendants of high-ranking officials who formed a landed aristocracy. As absentee landlords who lived mostly on rent collected in kind from tenant farmers, the *yangban* families resided either in the capital city or major provincial cities. They participated in different capacities in national and local political affairs.

At the lower level of the social hierarchy was the *sang in* class, or commoners, which constituted the majority of the farming population engaged in husbanding land owned either by the central government or *yangban* families. The only channel for upward social mobility open to the members of this class was the Imperial Examination System. In theory, the system was open to all members of the society. In practice, however, only an insignificant number of sons of farmers could succeed in the examination which was administered largely in favor of *yangban.* Even a marriage between *yangban* and commoner did not result in the elevation of the latter's social status.

Besides this clear-cut, sharp division of the social stratification system into two classes, there seems to have existed a number of social groups which can be regarded as *status groups.*[2] One of these was *chung in,* or *intermediary man.* This group was composed of offsprings of marriages between a *yangban* and a commoner. The members of this group were recruited into the Imperial Bureaucracy to fill various clerical and minor roles in the government. The positions held by the members of this group were then inherited by their descendants. Largely because of their inter-class origins this group was held in low esteem both by *yangban* and commoners.

The lowest of all social groups in traditional Korean society was called *ch'ŏn in,* or vile-men. Public and private servants, monks, prostitutes, sorcerers, farm serfs, and butchers belonged to this category. The butchers were regarded as the most inferior, presumably because of their ethnic background. They were either wanderers from another country or war captives. The social status of this group represents an interesting aspect of the traditional Korean social life. They established a separate community in the vicinity of cities and were engaged in hunting, butchery and hide-drying for their living. In a society essentially agrarian, it can easily be seen that such occupations could hardly offer the kind of services demanded in the market. Rather, the life fate of the members of this particular group was determined largely by the negative social estimation of their professions and their ethnic background. Much of Korean historical literature seems to indicate that, at one time, this group was actually a closed caste. Military obligation had been waived for this group, thereby restricting its status distinction by conventions and laws. The descendants of this group were not allowed to enter their names in the national census register. Physical contact with a member of this group was considered to be a stigma which had to be expiated by a religious act.

In such a rigidly stratified and segmented society as traditional Korea, it is easy to see how the ruling *yangban* could perpetuate its dominant position in the hierarchy of social groups largely by means of closing the channels of upward social and political mobility to members of other social groups. Another common method used by the ruling group to maintain its dominant position in society was marriage which was generally considered as an alliance of houses and kinship groups. No doubt, such practices could result in solidifying ties between the members of the ruling group and in rigidifying distinctions between the rulers and the ruled.

As a patrilineal, patriarchal, and patrilocal society, traditional Korea was characterized by all-pervasive and intense personal relationships among the members of kinship units. Seniority in the generational rankings on the family tree determined hierarchical positions of two men who belonged to the same clan. For both *yangban* and commoner, the basic unit of identification was the patriarchically organized kinship group, and the relationship between the members of a kin group was governed to a large extent by both traditionally evolved customs and usages and Confucian principles of morality.

Some Integrative Agents. In view of the high degree of segmentation among different social groups and the great extent of social distance that existed between a sharply dichotomized ruling group and the ruled, one may wonder how such a social system could survive over five hundred years. One explanation might be that the Confucian theory of inequality and its emphasis on harmonious, though hierarchical, human relations provided a congenial basis for legitimizing the dominant position of the highly homogeneous ruling elite of the traditional society. However, whenever the legitimacy of the ruling group was questioned, as has happened on several occasions, the authority of those occupying political roles were vitiated, and rebellions often broke out.

In addition to the presence of a highly homogeneous political elite and the Confucian-derived ethos[3] which provided a significant basis for the integration of traditional Korean society, there was also a highly centralized bureaucratic structure of Chinese origin which operated in a relatively efficient manner. The imported bureaucratic structure seems to have worked far more successfully than its prototype in China largely because of the higher degree of homogeneity in Korea in terms of ethnic composition, language and other cultural elements as well as geographical conditions. Centrally appointed officials of all ranks were entrusted with full authority to rule the localities to which they were assigned, and military troops placed at magistrates' disposal could easily put down rebellions before they could spread too widely. However, in order to guard against the danger of accumulation of power by a magistrate who might turn his troops against the central authority, magistrates were rotated from one area to another on a regular basis.

Coercion alone, however, was not sufficient for maintaining order in such a segmented, immobile society as traditional Korea. Local officials appointed by central authority were not as familiar with local affairs as natives were, and, in order to avoid problems of nepotism, officials were not assigned to their birth places. For this reason, a group of semi-officials known as *ajŏn* were hired by a local governmental unit to assist with details of administrative work. These locally hired administrators who acted as the right-hand men and factotum of the centrally appointed and imported local officials, were from local families whose ancestors had held the same offices in the localities for many generations.[4]

One role of the *ajŏn* was as a skillful negotiator between the local officials and the people, so that whenever the *ajŏn* sensed a sign of rebellion or trouble among the local populace, he warned his superiors of the forthcoming danger and advised them accordingly. When abuse of the local officials became intolerable, the people, joined by the *ajŏn*, turned on the officials and drove them out. Since *ajŏn* were all from local families and had not only their reputations to support but those of their families as well, in times of stress they had to be on the side of the people. Thus, officially they were servants of the Imperial Bureaucracy, but privately they were on the side of the local populace. It was this particular group serving as intermediary between the people and centrally appointed officials that was most responsible for holding the body politic of Korea at the local level together for many centuries. Peace and order in a locality depended very much upon the abilities of the *ajŏn*. If the *ajŏn* were maneuverers and manipulators, it was practically impossible for a bad official to oppress the people; and if the *ajŏn* themselves were bad, their manipulative capabilities made it virtually impossible for a good official to govern. If they were resourceful and masterful in crises, they could effectively check the abuses of centrally-appointed local officials, and in fact could control local affairs in such a way that grievances of the local people could be redressed and a balance between the people and higher officials maintained.

In summary, the social setting in which the traditional Korean authority structure operated was characterized by a simple stratification pattern and a relatively high level of integration between vertically segmented strata. Predominantly ascriptive elements provided the basis of stratification and consequently there was a low rate of social mobility in the society. Kinship and territorial location ties were the most important types of social integrative elements on the basis of which people's thought linked and united. As such, interpersonal relationships tended to be *pervasive* and *intense*. The dominant behavioral orientation of the members of traditional Korean society can be termed *traditional* in that they acted in a particular manner largely because they had acted in the same way in the past. Their orientation to social action and public policy was also characterized by passivity toward authority—they usually adapted themselves to the demands of the bureaucratic administration and central authorities.

Central Authority Structure. Like all rulers of historical bureaucratic societies, the founder of the Yi dynasty was intent on establishment of a unified kingdom based on a centralized bureaucratic structure. Two fundamental goals upon which the polity was established were: (1) maintaining of a friendly relationship with Korea's powerful neighbor, Ming China, on a tribute-paying basis; (2) adoption of Confucianism as an official ideology in place of Buddhism. These two fundamental goals set forth by the founder of the dynasty had a far-reaching impact upon the patterns of development of Yi society. The establishment of a regularized diplomatic relationship with Ming China, a relatively stable empire that ruled China for nearly three hundred years, had eliminated the problem of external threat which plagued the rulers of the previous dynasty, thus giving the Yi rulers a freer hand with their internal problems.

The adoption of Neo-Confucianism as a state religion gave the rulers a few additional advantages. As will be pointed out later, the legalistically oriented doctrines of the Neo-Confucian school had played a significant role in molding the thought patterns of the Yi elite and in legitimizing monarchical rule as a "benevolent and moral system of government." With its heavy emphasis on regulations for the ceremonies of coming of age, marriage, and funerals for the ruling class, and with an elaborate description of the ritual for ancestor worship, Neo-Confucianism served to rationalize the hierarchical distinctions among family members and the members of different social classes.

In Neo-Confucian doctrines, Yi dynasty rulers found a convenient device with which they could accomplish their ultimate goal of maintaining a unified, uninterrupted dynastic rule. Thus, the new ideology was consciously employed by Yi rulers to win the support of the reform-minded young Confucian scholars who had been critical of the Buddhist-dominated Koryo dynasty which had been overthrown by a military coup. The ruling group also made serious efforts to spread Neo-Confucian doctrines by making Confucianism a state religion, by making it a compulsory item in the civil and military examinations, and by building schools to teach the new ideology to the children. These integrative, adaptive, and pattern-maintaining functions of the new ideology were evidently successful in unifying the people, and in rallying and organizing public sentiment in support of the new dynasty.

It is not easy to determine just when the institutionalization process of the centralized bureaucratic state came to its fruition. Korean historians seem to agree in general, however, that a solid dynastic rule came into being during the reigns of Tae-jong (1400–1418), and Se-jong (1418–1450)—that is, roughly two generations after the establishment of the new dynasty in 1392. It was especially during the reign of Tae-jong, an aggressive son of the founder of the dynasty who succeeded to the throne by forcing his elder brother to abdicate, that a firm ground for the bureaucratic state (to a level much more sophisticated than that of the preceding Koryo dynasty) was laid, and major economic and social reforms were initiated.

The political authority structure that became institutionalized during this period bore much resemblance to that of Ming China. It was a structure based on a sharp distinction between the elite and the masses. At the peak of the power pyramid sat the absolute monarch who, if he were competent and assertive enough, could exercise unbound power over his subjects. In administering the affairs of the state he was assisted by a hierarchy of national and local officials. A rather complicated system of bureaucracy, modelled after that of China, directed the daily business of government from the Capital down to the provinces. A group of three highest-ranking officials, known as *ŭijungbu,* was the major central governmental unit for assisting the monarch with important decisions. These decisions were then carried out by the officials of six administrative boards named after the Chinese prototypes—Civil Office, Revenue, War, Ceremony, Punishment, and Public Works. Intermediate in rank between the *ŭijungbu* and the six administrative boards were the *ŭikŏmbu,* correctional tribunals which took charge of the disciplines of officials, and the *hansŏngbu,* which had charge of all municipal affairs in the capital city.

All public officials were classified according to nine degrees of rank. Each degree was, in turn, divided into two categories, primary and secondary. Officials were also classified according to the location of their offices. Those who were sent to provinces were called *external* officials and those in the Capital, *internal.* The external officials took charge of local administration in eight provinces. Each province was headed by a governor whose immediate staff consisted of a number of military and civil officials who formed a miniature cabinet at the local level.

Public officials were recruited through the Imperial Examination. However, there were officials who were sons of relatives of distinguished officials and as such entitled to certain privileges, though they were barred from certain high positions such as the Civil Office Board, which was responsible for personnel matters. Public officials were also divided into two major categories—military and civilian. The military officials were called *sŏban*, or "western section," and the civilian, *dongban* or "eastern section." Together, they formed the ruling class, *yangban*, meaning literally double, or two, sections. The term was originally a courtesy title used for the sons and grandsons of high-ranking officials, but was gradually extended to embrace all persons related to the royal family and persons whose ancestors had held important offices in the Imperial Bureaucracy.

The political process in Yi Korea might be said to have been the result of interactions between successive kings and members of royal families on the one hand, and members of Imperial Bureaucracy and the *yangban* class on the other.[5] Struggle for control over the throne and for a greater degree of influence in the King's court was waged between these factions. Consequently, there were frequent purges within the ruling class; some were initiated by an incumbent faction against threatening individuals or factions, and others were launched by the descendants of the victimized in reprisal. Undoubtedly, alliance of politics and Neo-Confucian scholarship with its rigid ideological orientation and its relentless persecution of any deviation or opposition made royal struggles and conflicts quite intense and sanguinary.

In this connection, it seems important to note the dynamic relationship between power and issues involved in the factional feuds characteristic of the period. Although the more immediate cause of a conflict between competing political groups involved some ludicrous arguments concerning questions of rules related to ancestral worship or funerals, it was always linked ultimately to the question of succession to the throne. In summary, the rulers of Yi Korea were quite successful in perpetuating their political authority structure in spite of several devastating and humiliating calamities visited upon them by Japanese and Mongolian invasions in the 16th and 17th centuries. They could do so largely by maintaining a fairly efficient centralized bureaucratic system through which material and human resources necessary for the continuance of the dynasty were easily mobilized and placed at the disposal of the ruling class. The traditional political structure could also maintain its stability because of Confucian doctrine, the precepts of which were the essential basis of legitimacy for the regime. Confucian principles also created an ethos at the mass level, thereby engendering widespread acquiescence among the general populace.

The Yi dynasty rulers were also aided in maintaining their power by a rigidly defined social structure which made their control easier and simpler. By closing the channels of political participation to those other than the homogeneous *yangban,* but by demanding either acquiescence or apathy from the peasants that made up the bulk of the populace, the ruling class of Yi Korea could maintain its uninterrupted rule for more than five hundred years.

JAPANESE COLONIAL RULE

Although the Japanese colonial rule lasted only 36 years—a relatively short period as contrasted with the centuries of traditional rule—its impact upon Korean society was far-reaching and left a lasting imprint. At the same time, the political change implanted by Japan was rooted in an authority pattern quite similar to that of the Yi dynasty. Therefore, the Japanese colonial rulers faced no serious difficulty in terms of disparity between the authority pattern they introduced and the social milieu that already existed in Korea at the time of "annexation" in 1910. Hierarchically organized communal and kinship groups and a highly centralized bureaucratic structure inherited from the ruling class of the Yi dynasty provided a solid basis upon which the colonial rule could be entrenched. At the same time, the Japanese made some serious efforts to understand the traditional bases of Korean society through extensive historical and ethnographic research into such matters as Korean class delineations, clan structure, and social customs in order to make the colonial rule more effective.

The primary aim of the Japanese colonial rulers was to turn Korea into a colony that could supply both agricultural resources and industrial raw materials for the Japanese economy. Therefore, two major policies pursued by the colonial administration were, firstly, development and mobilization of such resources and, secondly, political indoctrination of Koreans through a formal educational system. Bureaucracy and the educational system became two basic policy instruments for the colonial rulers. The Imperial Bureaucracy of Old Korea was replaced with a more objective and western-oriented bureaucracy staffed by legally trained Japanese civil servants. Through a civil service examination system patterned after the western model, a limited number of Koreans trained in the Japanese legal system were recruited to fill minor posts in the colonial bureaucracy. Also, a limited number of Koreans who formerly held high-ranking posts in the Imperial Bureaucracy were made peers by the Japanese and appointed to the House of Councilors, an all Korean body organized by the Governor-General to advise on administrative problems. Former top-level Yi bureaucrats also were accorded important posts in the Chosen Trust Company—a Japanese version of the East India Company. The Korean ruling class under the Japanese colonial system was thus composed of Korean members of the colonial bureaucracy and former officials who had switched their allegiances to the new master.

Colonial control by Japan appears to have passed through several stages, each of which was significant in the establishment of certain social and economic institutions. In the first phase, 1910–1920, the Japanese created the administrative machinery of control mentioned above and thereby set the pattern of colonial subjugation. In the second decade, 1920–1930, they established a new form of social and economic exploitation by forging an alliance between themselves and Korean aristocratic and middle-class groups. In the third phase, 1930–1940, as the Japanese military stepped up their adventures in Manchuria and mainland China, construction of an industrial complex in Korea was intensified to feed the growing war machine.[6]

In all these phases of colonial rule, the Japanese relied heavily on the strength of the nationally organized police network and the military forces deployed in major cities of the colony. Naked power was freely exercised in the process of pursuing the colonial goals. For example, economic exploitation was pursued through the Chosen Trust Company which carried out an extensive land survey during the 1910–1918 period. It made possible the establishment of a system of land ownership for the Japanese based upon negotiable private property. A large amount of Korean government-owned land was confiscated by the colonial government and a significant number of small farm owners were forced to sell their land to the Company and to migrate to Manchuria where they established a Korean community which was later to become a seedbed for the anti-Japanese guerrilla movement. Eventually, the Company took over nearly all the large farms in Korea and employed Koreans as tenant farmers.

The other goal pursued by the colonial rulers, though less successfully, was an "assimilation policy." A system of compulsory attendance at the Japanese-established Shinto Shrines was enforced rigidly for Korean students enrolled in both elementary and secondary schools. The Korean language was proscribed by the Japanese rulers, and elaborate lessons in loyalty of individuals to the State and to the Japanese Emperor were conducted in Korean schools. The policy of forcing Koreans to adopt Japanese family names was established during the second phase of colonial rule. In short, the educational system was used by the Japanese as the primary vehicle for the political socialization of Korean youth toward Japanese perspectives. However, largely because of influence in the home, Korean youths were not so easily molded into what the Japanese considered the proper ideological pattern required of loyal subjects of the Japanese Empire.

In spite of many rigorous administrative reforms introduced by the colonial rulers, no parliamentary practices were introduced, although Korean advisory councils at various levels were eventually established to legitimate Japanese policies. The members of the councils were appointed by the Governor-General of the colonial administration and were expected to serve merely as "rubber stamps" for the colonial administration. They never initiated legislation nor adopted any significant policy for implementation by the colonial administration.

Since political parties were illegal, Korean political activities, including those by groups in exile, were conspiratorial and clandestine. Typical responses of Koreans to Japanese rule ranged from collaboration and cooperation to subversion and revolutionary violence. On the one hand, a significant number of Koreans joined the Japanese colonial rulers in carrying out suppressive policies. For instance, of about 23,000 policemen under the colonial administration, some 9,000, or nearly 40 percent, were Koreans, mostly low-ranking.[7] In addition, at the lower clerical level in the colonial bureaucracy, the Koreans occupied approximately two-thirds of the lower positions.

On the other hand, several political groups were organized by Koreans at home and in exile following the *Sam Il* Independence Movement of 1919, but none of them could gain a solid footing among the populace largely due to rigorous Japanese surveillance. A Korean provisional government was established at Shanghai, China, in the aftermath of the *Sam Il* Movement and served at least as a symbol of Korean hopes for independence throughout the colonial occupation. A Korean Communist Party was formed in Seoul in 1925 but disappeared after three years as the result of internal frictions as well as persecution by the Japanese police. A combined nationalist-communist coalition modelled after the Chinese Kuomintang and constructed partly upon Comintern advice was organized in 1927 under the name of *Sin Gan Hoe* but by 1931 had disappeared. However, domestic Korean Communism seems to have maintained a fragmented, quasi-incarcerated underground existence throughout the Japanese reign.

It can be concluded that the experiences of Koreans under Japanese rule left two lingering imprints upon the political and administrative cultures of Korea. One Korean scholar in public administration has described them in the following terms:

> One was the psychological impact upon the Korean participants of the colonial administration and the other was the attitude of the Korean people in general toward the government. The psychological impact was a distorted form of what some social scientists call *need aggression*. They were conditioned to both hate and imitate the colonial masters....This imprint explains to a large extent the very aggressive attitude which these officials manifested toward their fellow-countrymen after the end of the colonial rule. [Second was the impact upon Koreans' attitude toward government.] As the colonial rule could never be legitimate in the eyes of the indigenous population, it was more patriotic for them to break or evade the laws and taxes rather than to abide by them.[8]

Furthermore, the Yi legacy of intensive factionalism within all Korean independence movements made its impact felt upon the structure of political competition that came to exist at the close of the Japanese rule and that has continued until the present. To make clear the basic nature of political competition in post-liberation Korea it is necessary to digress briefly to examine the nature of the pre-liberation political movements at home and abroad. They may be characterized in the following terms: (1) integrating ideology; (2) socio-psychological texture of the movements; and (3) major carriers of the movements.[9]

As mentioned earlier, there was a polarization of Korean political leaders in the wake of the *Sam Il* Independence Movement around two loosely defined issue clusters: revolutionary communism and more conservative nationalism. The conservative nationalist movements at home and in exile tended to adhere to the ideas of "preservation of Korean culture and nationality in the face of the Japanese attempt to assimilate Koreans as an integral part of their political system." Also, they upheld the idea of *kaehwa* (enlightenment or awakening) espoused by such prominent nationalist leaders as Sŏ Jae-p'il around the turn of the last century. But such a loosely defined ideology could hardly serve as an effective integrating force in the nationalist movements. Although the domestic Korean communist movements were guided by somewhat more explicit doctrines and revolutionary strategies, they too suffered from frequent dissensions and secessions.

In Korea as elsewhere, it can be said that any political movement tends to be shaped to a large extent by the characteristic quality of socio-psychological interrelations among members of the movement. The attitudes and motivations of the members provide a basis for development of a peculiar socio-psychological texture for a particular political movement. Motivations of individual members may vary to a great extent, but it may be assumed that certain types of motivations or combinations of types will predominate in any given political movement. One can distinguish three prototypes of such texture patterns. We may refer to them as (1) sect-like fellowship or spiritual community of followers; (2) charismatic following; and, finally, (3) rational association. In Korea's pre-independence period the first two were predominant.

By virtue of their revolutionary character and ideologically-oriented commitments on the part of their members, the Korean pre-independence communist movements tended to be small and militant in a manner similar to a fervent religious sect. Controversy within these movements generally was inclined to take the form of disagreement among members over the interpretation of a dogma to which they adhered; it often led to secession and schism. Where there was a charismatic following, which seemed to have been the predominant texture pattern in the conservative nationalist movement, it was the sense of attachment to a personal leader which motivated the members to join and remain in the movement. Generally speaking, a movement based upon personal loyalty to a single leader may have varying degrees of reliability. Since, in such a movement, common goals usually are not dogmatically or permanently established but rather are subject to change through orders from the leader, the movement is often fraught with constant internal friction and dissension. This was certainly the case with regard to conservative nationalist groups in Korea through the World War II period.

The nature of pre-independence Korean political movements might also be viewed in terms of the predominant character of those individuals and groups who served as the major carriers of the movements. It seems that the chances of an idea's becoming part of the integrating ideology for a particular movement depends upon its ability to appeal to certain social strata and groups. In general, both the Korean nationalist and communist movements managed to absorb a considerable number of intellectuals who were mostly the products of Japanese universities. However, the dominant leadership in both movements belonged unmistakably to those who represented two sharply distinguishable social backgrounds. For instance, those who might be categorized as representatives of status groups and religious organizations within Korean society tended to occupy major leadership roles in the conservative nationalist movements, whereas the leadership in the communist movements was characterized by a strong emphasis on the part of the leaders in identifying themselves with the laboring classes. Needless to say, all these legacies of the Japanese colonial rule were bound to play a crucial part in shaping post-liberation Korean politics.

CONTEMPORARY KOREAN AUTHORITY STRUCTURE: A POLITY IN TRANSITION

Various approaches could be taken by political scientists to describe and analyze the salient features of a political authority structure. At the outset, it should be emphasized that any attempt to describe such a transitional polity as Korea's is likely to leave some aspects unaccounted for and other features overlooked. Also, a conceptual framework employed for such purposes has to be anything but *static* because, by definition, a transitional political authority has a structure which cannot long exist without substantial change or modification. A transitional polity, therefore, is inherently dynamic in that it is undergoing constant transformation and change. In the ensuing discussion we shall treat some of the dynamics of the contemporary Korean authority structure in terms of legitimacy; functions; types of goals pursued; and decision-making.

Legitimacy. Every political system needs legitimacy. *Belief that the structure, procedures, acts, decisions, policies, officials, or leaders of government possess the quality of "rightness," propriety, or moral goodness and should be accepted because of this quality* is what we mean by legitimacy. Types or forms of legitimacy acquired by the leaders of a political system vary depending on the manner in which the people concede legitimacy to their rulers in various times and places. As Max Weber's famous typology of legitimacy suggests, people may concede legitimacy to their rulers on an emotional basis, on calculation of expedience, or because they conceded it in the past in the same way. Legitimacy may also be claimed and granted on the basis of acceptance of the leader who makes the claim. Such a state of legitimacy may be called "personal and status legitimacy."

In generating loyalty and commitment of the people to his rule, Syngman Rhee exploited his image as the leader of the independence movement during the Japanese occupation and as the "heroic" leader during the Korean War period. As an invaluable symbol of Korea's fight against both the Japanese and the Communists, Rhee came close to being an indispensable man in the crisis-ridden young republic. But he brought with him out of long years of exile several characteristics which limited his capacity for developing the political institutions and leadership urgently required for the republic's future. He had little administrative experience before he assumed power. To him, problems of contemporary life, such as economic problems, did not matter ultimately; instead of viewing the many practical problems of government as items to be solved through systematically developed policies, he tended to deal with them summarily in accordance with his limited preconceptions. Since he thought that he alone could head the newly established republic, it followed that his administrators must be drawn primarily from among those who had worked for him during his 33 years of exile and who were absolutely loyal to him personally. On the whole the criterion of extreme personal devotion, rather than that of specialized knowledge and experience, was followed in appointments.

Another of Rhee's traits was his strong belief in himself. This belief made it impossible for him to conceive of any Korean independence and rehabilitation movement after the war without Syngman Rhee at its center. As a result, he not only conducted a one-man government, so far as he could control his subordinates, but he also did little to develop able leaders at the higher levels of government. With the chief executive himself inexperienced and often actually unaware of what his subordinates were doing, operations of the government necessarily became in many respects both arbitrary and inefficient.

In brief, a combination of the following elements seems to have affected the legitimacy pattern of the Rhee regime: A mixed feeling of revivalism and aspiration for the future as being the dominant orientation of the ruling elite; the image of Rhee as "hero" and "national father," which had substantial appeal to the peasants who gave him their unqualified support; the maintenance of the *status quo* as being the *substantive* concern of the ruling elite; and finally the frequent rationalizations of politics through affective and conventional procedures on the part of the ruling elite in order to legitimize the authority and decisions of Rhee.

In examining the legitimacy aspect of a political system, it seems important to focus on the degree of legitimacy rather than the types or forms that legitimacy may take. We have noted that heroism, affectivity, and aspirations for the future—possibly the future of a unified Korea—were the underlying characteristics of legitimacy claimed and conceded to the Rhee regime. We may also inquire into the extent or degree of legitimacy of the Rhee regime as seen by the populace in general. Such an inquiry should include both *extensiveness* and *intensiveness* of legitimacy. By *intensiveness* is meant the ratio between voluntary compliance, coercive compliance and non-compliance. Although some degree of coercion is employed by every political system, the extent to which it relies on coercion varies from one political system to another. By *extensiveness* is meant the extent to which legitimacy results in the commitment of the members of the system to a polity. Commitment implies compliance or voluntary submission of an individual to an authority structure even at the sacrifice of his personal values. On the other hand, alienation means a tendency not to comply with the authority even at the risk of sacrifice. To the degree that a large portion of the members of a political system are committed to the polity, there is less need for such a polity to rely on coercion. Such a system might be said to have been endowed with an extensive legitimacy.

It is not easy to make any definite statement regarding the degree of legitimacy acquired by the authority structure of the Rhee regime. In the early phase of the regime, there seemed to have been fairly extensive support for Syngman Rhee but it began to slowly dissipate as his administration proved inadequate to deal with the many urgent tasks facing the nation. The people expected the new regime to engage in more equitable distribution of land, wealth, opportunity, and honor. The large number of refugees from North Korea expected the new state to defend them from internal and external threats. Despite these numerous demands placed upon the feeble authority structure, there were few administrative actions to cope with the mounting expectations of the people. This governmental inaction bred a lack of confidence in government as a vested institution, and reconfirmed in the minds of the people their deeply rooted suspicion of all government and the underlying belief that officials generally are moved more by a desire for private gain than by any desire for the well-being of the public. This attitude induced a withholding of genuine commitment to the regime and of reliance on the established political order. Under the circumstances, the people were compelled to resort to any means at their disposal in order to satisfy their immediate needs. Tax collection lagged, and laws and ordinances were easily ignored and violated.

As the legitimacy of the Rhee regime progressively weakened, the degree of reliance on coercion by the ruling elite increased in direct proportion. Force and fraud came to be used more outrightly as electoral devices by the ruling elite in order to maintain its dominant position. More intensified conflicts resulted between the ruling and opposition forces, as reflected in frequent confrontations between the members of the two groups in the national legislature. Increasingly suppressive measures adopted by the ruling elite against the press and the academic community then resulted in the alienation of the intellectuals who became openly critical of Rhee and his "dictatorial" style of governance.

The downfall of Rhee occasioned by the tragic climax of April 19, 1960, ushered in a new phase of post-war Korean politics. The military take-over of the government in May, 1961, brought further changes in the form of legitimacy which had been established under the Rhee regime. In a society which has traditionally looked to famous names such as Syngman Rhee, An Ch'ang-ho and Kim Ku, both Premier Chang Myŏn and President Park Chung-hee represented a situation which had little precedent in Korean political experience. The new regime of Chang Myŏn, for all its good intentions, had neither the authority of Rhee's nor any solid basis of legitimacy—the popular revolution had been largely the doing of students, while political leaders of the Chang regime differed little ideologically from those associated with Rhee. In spite of Chang Myŏn's dedicated efforts to establish a government of laws rather than men, his regime was overthrown by a military coup after he had been in office only nine months.

It is a strong tendency for any regime which comes into possession of political power through naked force to attempt to find ways to legitimate its authority. In fact, throughout the period of military rule, the revolutionary leaders of the military junta were faced with the question of legitimacy. They were also faced with opposition both domestically and from the United States. Various steps were taken to alleviate tensions with the United States and to seek general support abroad and at home. Another step taken by the military junta to enlist more widespread support was the promise to restore civil rule. The sixth of the revolutionary pledges promulgated on the day of the military *coup* had been a vague commitment to transfer governmental authority back to civilians "as soon as revolutionary tasks had been fulfilled."

The question of whether to extend military rule or to arrange for transfer of power to civilians became one of the major issues which generated disintegrative forces within the military junta itself. After substantial infighting, the ruling group split into two opposing camps, and the leader of the military junta, General Park Chung-hee, decided to perpetuate the military rule by running as the presidential candidate of the new Democratic-Republican party in the 1963 election. He won in 1963 by only about 150,000 votes, and was re-elected in 1967 by a substantial margin. In 1971, his margin of victory was 904,928 votes in his successful race for a third term.

The prestige and popularity of President Park over the last several years has been greatly enhanced by his initiating some bold programs in the economic sphere. Some impressive economic strides have been made under his leadership and some degree of political stability has been achieved, but only at the cost of alienating the more politically conscious segments of the population from the normal channels of political participation. The regime has also succeeded in establishing a highly developed mechanism of control over potential or manifested elements of threat toward the party in power. It remains to be seen, however, whether the present political authority structure will eventually succeed in establishing more enduring, legally-based forms of legitimacy that will result in more voluntary compliance of the masses toward the regime.

FUNCTIONS OF THE POLITICAL AUTHORITY STRUCTURE

The extent to which political authority structure performs functions for a society varies from one political system to another. The functional scope of a political system can be distinguished on various bases. It can be distinguished on the basis of multiplicity of social functions performed by the system on behalf of the total society—that is, *many* versus *few* functions. It can also be distinguished on the basis of functional significance, e.g., the extent to which functions performed by authority structure are shared by other structures in the society. For instance, in a traditional political system it might be said that everything is controlled by the central authority structure, whereas in a modern political system there will be a high degree of differentiation between those functions which are considered strictly political and those that are not. In general, it might be posited that the functional scope of a political system varies according to the degree of specialization and differentiation in the society.

We have seen in our brief review of some salient features of the traditional authority structures of Yi Korea that the level of specialization and differentiation in that society was kept low and that there was an absence of sharp distinctions between political, economic and social functions. The level of specialization was minimal in that there was virtually no sharing of certain functions between the authority structure and other structures in the society. Congeries of autonomous groups existed in the form of kinship groupings and a few guild-like trade organizations, but functions performed by the imperial bureaucracy were never shared by these independent and autonomous groups.

The establishment of a Western-modelled bureaucratic system under the Japanese rule did not bring any substantial change in this aspect of Korean life. The Japanese retained the centralized bureaucratic structure of the Yi dynasty with no sharing of responsibility for various functions between central and local structures. The overriding concern of the Japanese colonial rulers was to insure through a highly developed bureaucracy the possibility of rapidly mobilizing a sufficient amount of economic resources and to make certain that their colonial goals and policies were implemented successfully. This necessitated a concentration of both integrative and adaptive functions in the hands of a few high-ranking officials in the colonial bureaucracy.

The new government established in 1948 inherited this "monopolistic" tradition but without competent, well-trained civil servants because of the summary withdrawal of all Japanese officials. Those Koreans of colonial bureaucratic backgrounds (mostly low-ranking officials) who were elevated to higher ranks after the Liberation imitated the Japanese by jealously guarding the "tradition" they inherited from their former masters. Thus, the central bureaucracy came to be dominated by men with comparatively limited education, most of whom were former clerks who shared a strict, legalistic outlook toward major socio-economic and technological problems of the new era.

Even three years of cataclysmic war (1950–1953) failed to effect any drastic change in the basic nature of the Korean bureaucracy.

However, increasing pressures of official business occasioned by the war had resulted in boosting the status of the former colonial servants who now filled the top positions in government as well as in the political party which had been created hurriedly by President Rhee to circumscribe the growing strength of opposition forces in the National assembly in 1951. It was also during the mid–1950's that a close pattern of collusion developed between former civil servants coopted into the ruling party and their subordinates who remained in the bureaucracy. The latter were to serve the leadership elite as the controlled instruments of their political interests. In other words, the bureaucracy was deliberately used by the ruling group to foster its private interests. The bureaucrats, in turn, took advantage of the monopolistic function of the central government to accumulate wealth and to enhance their own positions in the government.

Prior to 1960, Korean society was already experiencing violent social and political changes, but these changes were accompanied by a political leadership which was ill-equipped, in orientation and capacity, to respond to them. A greater level of social differentiation as an outcome of the universal education system was achieved by 1960 with the phenomenal growth of the university population that made up one of the most explosive sources of discontent toward the immobile regime. There was also a noticeable advancement in the process of urbanization as a result of a large scale movement of population during the war, not to mention the movement south of some five million refugees from North Korea who had settled at various provincial cities and in the Seoul and Pusan areas. These urban segments of the population had reached a considerable level of politicization as they became increasingly exposed to mass communication media which reported of corruption and fraud within the ruling elite and in the bureaucracy.

The Rhee regime was evidently unable to adjust itself in the face of these sweeping transformations. No effective reform program was undertaken by the regime to cope with the situation by increasing its administrative capacity or by expanding its scope of functions to meet the challenge. The bureaucracy remained essentially a mechanism of control which served only the interests of the ruling elite and which catered to the corrupt taste of a few businessmen who accumulated illicit fortunes by providing a portion of their wealth to the ruling party in the form of bribery or kick-backs.

Upon assuming political power in 1960, the ruling elite of the new Democratic regime under Chang made conscious efforts to respond to the mounting problems in the political environment. Describing some important changes made in the central bureaucracy following the demise of the Rhee regime, Professor Lee Han-been noted the following:

> To a large extent the external barrier of the bureaucracy was levelled and the internal discrimination against the university graduates in matters of work assignments and promotion was eliminated. Bureaucracy's intercourse with the intellectual community began and the latter's influence began to be felt upon the bureaucracy.... At the senior civil service levels, some bold promotions of younger officials with fresh outlook were made, breaking across rigid barriers of old bureaucracy.... Just waiting to be tapped for such bureaucratic breakthroughs were a number of ambitious young officials who had joined the bureaucracy either through the High Civil Service Examination or after returning from many years of specialized training in foreign countries.[10]

He further remarked that the most explicit approach of the bureaucracy to the university community was a special program of recruiting 2,000 fresh graduates of universities through an open competitive examination which was administered in the early part of 1961. Upon passing this examination, the recruits were to go through a short training course designed to give a developmental orientation and a three-month work experience at the sites of major public works projects. The new regime had also initiated a fairly comprehensive five-year economic plan, but its implementation was interrupted by the military coup.[11]

The military junta took up the task of economic development where the ousted Democratic regime left off by initiating its first five-year economic plan in 1962 and a second in 1967. With the establishment of the Economic Planning Board, a separate governmental organization fully entrusted with the planning and the implementation of the economic development plan, the major emphasis of the bureaucracy shifted drastically from a control and coordination focus to a goal-attainment function. This emphasis was matched with the creation of a multiplicity of agencies and a rapid expansion of governmental employees assigned to these agencies.

What this implies is that, largely due to the heavy emphasis placed on a goal-attainment function of the political authority structure under the present regime under President Park Chung-hee, the government has come to assume a far greater responsibility and more important general social role than any of the two previous regimes. There has also been a tendency for the present political authority structure to carry out its economic plan in cooperation with private industrialists who in turn expect the government to provide them with necessary financial and administrative support. This situation conceivably could lead to a greater sharing in the execution of national goals by the governmental and non-governmental structures. A persistent and deeply rooted problem, however, is that of corruption in the ranks of the government and the ruling political party, particularly that related to collusion with private business enterprise. In fact, many observers of the domestic political scene make the point of stressing that the rapid expansion of the functional scope of governmental authority has tended to induce corruption at a far greater scale and in an even more pervasive manner than ever before.

Types of Goals Pursued. Another dimension closely identified with a political authority structure is that of goals pursued by a given political system. In our discussion of the traditional political authority structure in Korea, we have touched briefly on the characteristic types of goals espoused by the ruling elite of the Yi dynasty. In terms of a typology suggested by S.N. Eisenstadt in his *The Political Systems of Empires,* the types of goals pursued by the Yi elite come close to what he called the "executively oriented" type in that their major emphasis was on the perpetuation of the polity and its rulers, as well as on the maintenance of the status quo of the political system.[13]

There were no deliberate efforts on the part of the Yi elite to seek territorial expansion and to maintain a strategic position in international diplomacy. Nor were the Yi leaders oriented to economic development and advancement, either of particular social groups or of the population as a whole. Their goals were typically internal-oriented in the sense that they were primarily concerned with maximization of security and minimization of external threats.

The Rhee regime might be said to have inherited the same goal orientation as that of the Yi ruling elite. The ruling elite of the Rhee regime seems to have shared the "executively oriented" goals with their ancestors as best epitomized in the catch-phrase often reiterated by the regime, "internal stability and anti-communism." Because of the rigid anti-communist posture of Syngman Rhee, Korea, in post-war international politics, became almost completely isolated from other Asian countries. At the same time she drew close to the United States to such an extent that many non-committed nations tended to view Korea in terms of a vassal status vis-a-vis the United States. Needless to say, such a close relationship resulted from the existence of a communist North Korea which launched a wide-scale armed invasion of the south in 1950 and which, since the 1953 armistice, has sought to infiltrate the Republic of Korea by sending armed agents to build bases for guerrilla activities in the south.

Because of the unfortunate experiences of the 1950–1953 war, there has arisen deep popular resentment against communism in South Korea, and one side-effect of this sentiment has been popular suspicion about socialism in general. Many Koreans find it difficult to distinguish socialists from communists with the result that the former are often confused with and persecuted for communists. This state of affairs has tended to inhibit the emergence of a non-communist, socialist political movement in the Republic of Korea. It goes without saying that the conservative ruling elite of the Rhee regime could and did take advantage of this frame of mind, using "suspicion-of-communist-affiliation" as a pretext to destroy its political enemies within the Republic. The military suppression of socialists in the very early sixties after their momentary return to activity during the Chang regime was apparently rooted in the same fear of collusion with communist North Korea on the part of these South Korean socialists.

This state of affairs has left Korea without a viable socialist alternative to what are predominantly conservative politics. The maintenance of the status quo and the perpetuation of the Rhee rule were the underlying themes in the goal orientations of the ruling elite of the Rhee regime. And basically the new ruling elite of the Democratic regime in 1961 differed little ideologically from those associated with Rhee, although it demonstrated considerable sensitivity toward the goal-attainment aspect of the political system and exhibited a greater degree of tolerance toward socialist opposition groups.

Since the military take-over of the government in 1961, there have been increasing signs of a shift in the general goal orientations of the ruling elite toward greater emphasis on economic strength and expansion. Economic advancement and development are seen by the present ruling elite as the fundamental means of improving the polity. The decision to dispatch a Korean military contingent to South Vietnam in 1966 was undoubtedly based on the expectation of economic gains to be derived from direct involvement in the Vietnamese War. But it seems not far fetched to view the decision also in the light of a desire to improve Korea's status in relation to the United States and to secure a strategic position in inter-Asian diplomacy. The creation of a Korean-initiated regional cooperative body in cultural, social and technical affairs, the Asian Pacific Council, might be seen in the light of the more externally-oriented goals of the present regime. The conclusion of the normalization treaty with Japan in 1965 might be considered as another indication of more externally-directed goal orientations, though the motivations for concluding the treaty were governed chiefly by an immediate concern with economic development at home.

Decision-Making. The decision-making structure of any political system can be examined in terms of the extent to which political roles and institutions are differentiated from other roles and institutions; the extent to which they are concentrated or dispersed; the extent to which roles and institutions are formalized; and, finally, the extent to which they are either autonomous or dependent. If we examine the structure of decision-making in the traditional Korean political authority structure on the basis of these analytical dimensions, it seems that the decision making structure of traditional Korean society was characterized by a high degree of formalization, in that highly specified rights and duties governed the relationships among members of the imperial bureaucracy. Explicit rules and explicitly delimited competences generally guided the recruitment process and decision-making behavior of the officials of Yi dynasty until the reign of Sŏnjo (1567–1608) who frequently resorted to irregular recruitment practices including the holding of the imperial examinations in disregard of fixed schedules. Further erosion of the Bureaucracy was brought about by selling of offices and statuses. Due to the decline of the economic power of the ruling elite occasioned by the invasion of the Japanese in 1592, open selling of titles and bureaucratic offices came to prevail, which in turn led to a disintegration of the existing social status system. Needless to say, a large number of less qualified officials were produced during the reign of Sŏnjo.

The traditional authority structure was also characterized by a highly centralized decision-making structure: political roles were heavily concentrated in a relatively small, limited segment of the population—the officials and the members of the *yangban* class—who were recruited into the bureaucratic system. Later, through the practice of purchase of status, some rich commoners were adopted into the ruling group. Nevertheless, every major political decision was made at the center by a relatively small group of officials in the King's court, and the decision was implemented by officials at lower echelons of the Imperial Bureaucracy. Both in the process of arriving at a major political decision and in implementing the decision, the officials never acknowledged the need for explicit institutions for bringing together the interests of the government and those of the common people. It was assumed that the government had a monopoly of all the relevant wisdom necessary for a just and successful rule. As such, the autonomy of the ruling elite in the decision-making realm was almost absolute.

In sharp contrast to societies in the west where the aristocracy, joined by other groups and social strata, fought for their interests within the framework of existing political institutions, the basic attitude of various social groups and strata in traditional Yi Korea was "passivity" toward the ruling elite. The relationship between rulers and ruled was never conceived of in terms of reciprocity and interdependence. Rather the rulers assumed complete autonomy in official decision-making. As a result the political roles and institutions of Yi Korea at the level of the masses of the peasants remained undefined and obscure, in contrast to the more explicitly defined roles of the ruling strata.

This does not imply, however, that the life of the peasants was significantly distinguishable internally from those of the more politically active strata. Nor does it mean that the political institutions of Yi Korea achieved a level of differentiation and specialization that enabled the ruling elite to penetrate into the whole of society for the purpose of obtaining an integrated political and social structure, as some modern totalitarian polities have sought to accomplish. Rather it would be more reasonable and accurate to assume that the two levels maintained their autonomous lives in a disjunctive fashion, each being loosely tied to the other on the basis of an overall ethos shared by both segments of the population.

The foregoing observations on traditional Korean patterns of decision-making are meant to throw some light on the present structure of decision-making, as well as to point up some significant changes under the three post-World War II South Korean regimes. Although a monolithic, centralized governmental structure has been retained to a large extent, a greater degree of formalization and a higher level of differentiation and specialization seem to have been achieved since the establishment of the Republic of Korea in 1949. One single factor which has contributed most to this development has been the emergence of political parties, a phenomenon observed in most newly emerging and developing nations since the Second World War.

However, as our brief review of the authority structure of Yi Korea suggests, the highly centralized structure of decision-making under the traditional system was not germane to the emergence of political parties and interest groups. Furthermore, the tradition of monopolistic politics, established under the Yi dynasty and reinforced by the Japanese colonial rule, has tended to hinder the development of parties capable of significantly influencing policies of the government. As Lucian Pye aptly points out, the emergence of competitive party systems depends upon at least a minimum separation of the political sphere from the social and economic spheres of life.[13] Unless there is some separation between the dynamics of politics and the ordering of social and economic life, then it is likely that any shift in the political realm could become a major threat to the security of all with basic social and economic interests. This kind of situation is simply not conducive to the development of active interest groups which are divorced from the immediate stakes of political controversy and which can pursue their interests independently of the political realm. Only when such groups are developed can they act as a countervailing power against the instincts of the ruling elite, the members of which are naturally inclined to keep the political process as monopolistic as possible.

SUMMARY AND IMPLICATIONS

The general framework of analysis employed in this study of the Korean political authority structure was predicated upon the assumption that, as a sub-structure of Korean society, it invariably has reflected the dominant characteristics of the total make-up of Korean society. We are, therefore, concerned chiefly with the nature of relations between the Korean political authority structure and the large social setting within which it operates—conditions under which the present political authority structure could endure or change over time as well as conditions for effective functioning of the authority structure.

In order to gain some insights into the nature of change in the Korean authority structure over an extended period of time, we have placed the contemporary authority structure within the historical context of the traditional Korean and the Japanese systems of political authority. For brevity, it might be suggested simply that the difference between the contemporary authority structure and the two aforementioned structures lies in a drastic shift in the form of the authority pattern from an authoritarian, monarchical and elitist rule to a more conciliar, representative form. The latter was superimposed at the close of the Japanese colonial rule and represented an attempt to engineer changes in a traditional society in order to effect a transition to a popular democratic form of government. Also, those who undertook the task of political engineering tried to accomplish their objective without making any significant change in the power-elite structure that existed at the time.

Consequently, those who filled the major positions in the newly instituted authority structure were hardly equipped to initiate innovative programs for effecting drastic change in the existing social setting or to make necessary inroads for building solid infrastructures for an effective representative rule. The task can be viewed as an enormous one, requiring unselfish devotion and commitment on the part of the ruling elite to the principles of popular democracy; the members of the ruling elite, however, were generally lacking in such qualities since most of them had been either associates or followers of Syngman Rhee since the days of his exile. As such, they either had had no administrative experience or had been *petit* officials in the Japanese colonial bureaucracy. Furthermore, the ruling elite in the early phase of the Rhee regime was under attack from two directions. Internally, economic depression and armed rebellions instigated by local communists posed a threat to the infant regime. Externally, it was threatened by the increasingly hostile communist regime in the north. Thus, even before the attack from the communist North began in 1950, the political authority structure of the Rhee regime was compelled to adapt itself to the situation by reverting to a style of rule more familiar both to the ruling elite and the ruled—that of autocracy.

The tensions and discrepancies between the formal rules governing the office of the President and actual behavior of its occupant, Syngman Rhee, became more pronounced as Rhee began to act in an increasingly authoritarian manner and to manifest his determination to perpetuate his rule. By 1952, a virtual one-man rule by Rhee was established and by the time he had rammed through another constitutional amendment Rhee's authoritarian position became complete. The decision-making power was concentrated exclusively in the office of the President and a small number of oligarchical groups who were loyal and responsible to the President. Cabinet members were appointed and removed at the President's whim and the bureaucracy became increasingly ruler-dominated. The gap between the ruling elite and the masses became hopelessly widened in spite of the presence of the Liberal Party which functioned more as a mechanism of control than as a structure for communication, policy-making, and popular participation in politics.

The Rhee regime lasted for twelve years without serious interruption, partly because of its adaptability and partly because an extensive degree of legitimacy was conceded by the populace to the personalistic authority of Syngman Rhee. The period was also characterized by a slow rate of social change, particularly with regard to differentiation and specialization of roles and institutions within Korean society. However, the pace toward differentiation and specialization of social roles and, concurrently, erosion of the tradition-bound social setting had been accelerated during the three years of the Korean war. By 1960, therefore, two politically significant groups had emerged from two institutions which the ruling elite of the Rhee regime had helped to establish and foster, namely, the military and the universities. Not only did the Rhee regime exacerbate the gap between the elite and the masses, a situation which it exploited for immediate political gains, but it also accelerated the divisions and antagonisms both at the elite and mass levels by alienating a significant number of intellectuals from normal channels of political participation.

We may conclude that the injection of a formal-legal structure into the post-war Korean political system was largely irrelevant to the then existing conditions of Korean society. The structure simply adapted itself to the prevalent conditions by reverting to a more traditional style of rule. However, as time passed, inconsistencies became more evident between the essentially traditional authority pattern and the changing face of the Korean social setting. Korean society had experienced a cataclysmic change during the three years of war and was also undergoing rapid urbanization and educational development—factors which resulted in an increasing level of politicization of the urban segment of the population. The explosive student uprising in 1960 was, in many respects, an event rooted in the social disintegration that swept the country following the Korean War.

The military take-over of the government in 1961 represented a drastic break away from the then existing formal-legal structure which had provided only an ineffectual framework of government for the Rhee regime and to some extent for the short-lived Democratic regime. It also represented an attempt to effect basic change in the established power-elite structure which had remained substantially unchanged despite the 1960 Student uprising. Most of the military revolutionaries had come from a social stratum traditionally held in low esteem. Many were sons of peasants and merchants. Very few represented the more prestigious strata of Korean society, such as that of the large landowners.

Like all revolutionary regimes, the Korean military revolutionaries were confronted with the problem of institutionalization of the revolutionary regime. It was in attempting to solve this problem that disintegrative forces came to affect the core-members of the military junta, with a resultant sharp division of the members into two opposing camps. The military government also made many abortive attempts at drastic political engineering. Foremost in these attempts was the imposing of restrictive measures in the economic sphere in the hope of curtailing excessive consumption habits of the populace. However, the masses ignored or evaded such measures, which were eventually repealed as hopeless causes. Also, forceful measures to weed out corruption in the government were imposed at the initial phase of the military rule, but these too failed.

It would be highly presumptuous to make any definite statement at this juncture about the future pattern of Korean political authority. No clear pattern arose during the 1960's out of the rule of the military-dominated Democratic Republican Party which publicly pledged on the day of the military coup that it would work to establish a "new system of government, whatever the form it may take." Such a major innovative task requires a great sense of dedication, of commitment by the members of the Korean political elite, because, after all, they make up the group in Korean society equipped with the power, influence, and capacity necessary to effect significant and progressive changes.

FOOTNOTES

1. Recently, many political scientists have been increasingly concerned with the problem of defining and delimiting the scope of their subject matter. In his inquiry into the state of political science, David Easton concluded that political scientists share one problem in common and that problem he defined as that of "the authoritative allocation of values for a society." He called that aspect of a society which performs the function of authoritative allocation of values a "political system." Applying Easton's definition to his comparative analysis of the politics of the developing nations, Gabriel Almond noted three attributes of a "system" which included the following: (1) comprehensiveness, (2) interdependence, and (3) existence of boundaries.

While it is possible for a political system to have a certain "pattern" or "order," this does not mean the same thing as Almond's concept of "political system." It seems highly unlikely that change of political structure will be followed by changes within the system. Furthermore, the notions of comprehensiveness and interdependence—that is, that all parts tend to work together to maintain the system—is only a tendency and not determined by empirical investigation. It is these considerations which prompt us to use the term *political authority structure* rather than the notion of *system* to refer to that aspect of a society where political phenomena take place in a certain regularized pattern.

2. For distinctions between this group and the concept of class, see Max Weber, "Class, Status, Party," in Reinhard Bendix and Seymour Martin Lipset (eds.), *Class, Status and Power* (Chicago: The Free Press, 1953), pp. 63–75.

3. The term is used as a synonym of the term culture. Many sociologists have defined culture as the central element of a society which assures its unity, existence, and self-regulation. This element is closely related to legitimacy in a political system since belief in moral goodness or rightness of the leaders of government can flow from this element. In his study of communist China, Franz Schurmann argues that Confucianism which provided ethos in traditional China was substituted by ideology under the communist rule. Franz Schurmann, *Ideology and Organization in Communist China* (Berkeley: University of California Press, 1966), pp. 5–15.

4. A detailed description of the role of *achŏn* in local governmental setting appears in Homer Hulbert, *The Passing of Korea* (New York, 1906). See also, Hahm Pyong-choon, *The Korean Political Tradition and Law* (Seoul: The Royal Asiatic Society, Hollym Publishing Company, 1967), pp. 66–67.

5. Some historians in Korea take a broader perspective of the political process of Yi Korea by regarding the peasants or even serfs as major forces in traditional political life. It is questionable, however, whether such groups really had a great impact upon the outcome of normal political processes during the dynastic rule. Rather, the more persistent and politically relevant groups which exercised significant influences over the decision-making structure within the political system were the officials in the Imperial Bureaucracy and *yangban* in the capital or in the rural areas.

6. For an elaborate description of the nature of the Japanese colonial rule in Korea, see Andrew J. Grajdanzev, *Modern Korea* (New York: John Day, 1944), pp. 105–115.

7. These figures were cited in Gregory Henderson, *Korea: The Politics of the Vortex* (Cambridge: Harvard University Press, 1968), p.142.

8. Lee Han-been, "Bureaucracy and Politics," draft chapter in Chong-Sik Lee et al. (eds.), *Politics and Society in Korea*, p. 5 (mimeographed).

9. Rudolf Heberle, *Social Movements* (New York: Appleton-Century-Crofts, Inc., 1951), pp. 12–16.

10. Lee Han-been, op. cit., p. 19.

11. *Ibid.*, p. 20.

12. If one defines ideology simply as a set of ideas prevalent in a community, Confucianism can be regarded as an ideology. Carl Friedrich and Z.K. Brzezinski regard it essentially as action-related "systems" of ideas concerning practical means of how to change and reform a society, based upon a more or less elaborate criticism of what is wrong with the existing or antecedent society. Ideologies defined in this sense are recent phenomena or products of the age of parties and mass political

movements. Carl Friedrich and Z.K. Brzezinski, *Totalitarian Dictatorship and Autocracy* (New York: Frederick A. Praeger, 1966), pp. 88–89.

13. Eisentadt does not distinguish goals from value orientations prevalent in a political system. He developed, however, a typology of goals and value orientations on the basis of dominant emphasis manifested in specific goals of the centralized bureaucratic states. For instance, some systems would pursue purely political-collective goals with emphasis on conquest and territorial expansion, while others might seek collective-executive goals with emphasis on the economic strength and collective expansion of the polity *per se*. Still others would place an emphasis on the mere perpetuation of the polity and the rulers, and on the maintenance of the political *status quo*. The goals pursued by the Yi ruling elite would come close to the last category. See S. N. Eisenstadt, *The Political Systems of Empires* (New York: Free Press, 1963), pp. 238–239.

CHAPTER 11:

Toward A New Theory of Korean Politics: A Reexamination of Traditional Factors

Pyong-choon HAHM*

The term theory usually signifies "attempts to 'explain' phenomena, especially when that is done in general and abstract terms."[1] The emphasis here is upon the words "explain" and "general and abstract terms." Therefore, any theory of Korean politics must be an attempt to explain Korean politics in general and abstract terms. Further, if this theory is to be "scientific," it has not only to be a product of scientific method but has also to offer a "causal" explanation. It is true that no scientist would demand perfect causality in every theory. It is nonetheless agreed among most scientists, however, that the best explanation is causal. Thus, the importance of prediction is evident; the greater the accuracy of prediction, the better the explanation and the theory which offers it. But there is another requirement: explanation must be formulated in general and abstract terms in order for it to be a theory. "Inductively reached factual generalizations" are an important component of scientific methodology. In addition, an explanation has to be more than *ad hoc* in character and episodic in its scope of reference to be considered a theory.

What is offered in this chapter is not *the* theory of Korean politics. It merely attempts to present a perspective for theorizing about Korean politics. It does *not* pretend to be a scientific theory. There

---
*Pyong-choon Hahm is Ambassador of the Republic of Korea to the United States. He was formerly Special Assistant to the President for political affairs and Professor of Law at Yonsei University in Seoul. He holds the Juris Doctor degree from Harvard University, Cambridge, Massachusetts.

must be more observation, description, measurement, generalization, hypothesis, and so forth about Korean politics before one can attempt to construct a theory of Korean politics. But many references will be made throughout the chapter to the problems encountered in formulating a scientific theory about Korean politics. Several theories of Korean politics have already been made available to us. In the first part of this paper, a general review of them will be attempted. In the second part, the shortcomings and inadequacies of those theories will be pointed out. And then, a perspective or approach that will be necessary in formulating a more effective theory of Korean politics will be delineated.

CURRENT THEORIES

There is only one book that is currently in print that attempts to formulate a comprehensive theory of Korean politics.[2] But other theories have been formulated by other scholars, though less articulately and sweepingly. First attempts at modern forms of theory-making with reference to Korea were made by Japanese historians and colonial policy-makers. Inasmuch as Korean politics had remained different from the more "advanced and developed" political systems of the modern age, the difference had to be explained somehow. The most readily available explanation was found in the backwardness or primitiveness of the Korean political culture. The underlying assumption was that the Korean polity somehow failed to progress beyond a primitive stage of development. Terms such as fossilization and stagnation were most often used to explain the phenomenon. There were many causes for such a fossilization. The innate immorality and phlegmatic mentality of the Korean people were the favorite of Japanese observers. A nation that had failed to wage even a single victorious war all through its four-thousand-year history must have appeared to the Japanese to have epitomized spiritual impotence. The fact that Korea was always a victim of foreign invasions and military conquests seems to have prompted the Japanese to conclude that there must have been some flaws in the Korean character that prevented Koreans from militarily organizing and disciplining themselves in order to at least defend their country against foreign enemies.

There were other causes for stagnation. The factionalism and the thorough-going corruption of the ruling elites of Yi dynasty Korea were the most prominent among them. The fierce factional struggles among upper strata groupings are said to have sapped most of the intellectual and moral vigor out of these contentious elites. The resulting spiritual malaise is supposed to have manifested itself in pervasive corruption among the literati-bureaucrat stratum of society. The ruling elites are described to have plundered the masses mercilessly. The masses who were constantly driven to desperation and destitution were simply too enervated to be productive materially or culturally.

Other causes somewhat related to the preceding were the Confucian political ideology that entailed the installation of the literati as the ruling elites rather than the military caste, consequent lack of constant preparation for war which might have encouraged development of capitalism, and excessive centralization of government. Many observers of the Korean scene, especially Japanese, have tended to equate the Confucian elites (such as those who ruled the Yi Korea) with moral effeminacy and political decadence in contrast to the military castes of Japan and the Occident which, as political rulers of those civilizations, imparted moral vitality and political progress to their polities. Unlike the military, the literati tended to depreciate the importance of robust power, be it military, physical or political. The literati were liable to deprecate aggressiveness which possessed the propensity to upset the delicate social equilibrium. What they did not realize, it is argued, was that without aggressiveness a nation loses impetus and motivation towards excellence and conquest. Such a polity was bound to become effete. It failed to develop a dynamic and viable concept of masculine vigor. No notion of gallantry or chivalry ever developed in Korea. The Korean literati of the past who downgraded the military branch of the bureaucracy to a subordinate status was consequently marked by cowardice, duplicity, rapacity and hypocrisy. They lacked a sense of fair-play, courage or sportsmanship. In its factional struggle for power, the literati's behavior can be characterized as devious, sinister and treacherous.

As the traditional elites of Korea were more concerned about ethics in politics than about power, they lacked any strong aversion to "chaos." As Adolf Berle would reiterate,[3] power never rests until it succeeds in imposing order upon chaos. One can hardly think of military power without order, nor can economic power emerge amid chaos. It was this lack of drive towards achievement of goals and want of regimentation and discipline required for such achievement that disturbed the foreign observers of the Korean scene. Of course, it mattered little to these observers that the kind of chaos they were terrified of was not necessarily chaos for the Koreans, or that the type of order they were hungering for could be something less than desirable for the Koreans. To the foreigners chaos meant absence of rationality, and order implied a condition in which prediction of future behavior was forthcoming with varying degrees of mathematical certainty.

Nothing is more strongly detested by economic rationality than uncertainty. In their common dislike of chaos and uncertainty, economic rationality and military rationality share a great deal in common. For the military, hierarchical order, effective discipline and rational organization are indispensable for winning a victory. In order to achieve a goal, the military must mobilize all the resources in a rational and orderly manner. As Machiavelli once pointed out, the strength of war does not lie in men alone; it requires "iron, money, and bread" also. In other words, military power without the support of industrial (economic) power is simply unreal. The military must foster and nurture economic development. Max Weber has pointed out to us that without constant preparation for war, capitalistic development is hard to come by.[4] This means that the pacifist methods of the Yi Dynasty elites deprived Korea of the need for constant competition in armament, which in turn resulted in a lack of economic development. By having "a chilling effect on martial ardor"[5] of the Korean people, the Confucian political ideology (which was the official ideology of Yi Dynasty) succeeded in both emasculating and impoverishing Korea.

The absence of manorial feudalism in Korean history also indicated to some Japanese historians the backwardness as well as the profound defect in traditional Korean politics. The fact that Korea has had a centralized government for the past thirteen centuries in contrast to Japan which came to have feudalism prior to its emergence as a modern, westernized polity was taken as a proof of political fossilization. According to this view, Korea failed to progress beyond the literati civilization which had reached its apogee in Japan in the tenth and eleventh centuries and which was subsequently replaced by feudalism there. The indication was that Korea's political development was arrested at the stage where Japan had been nearly a millennium ago. Inasmuch as modern Occidental nation-states have all emerged out of feudalism, Japan has progressed in conformity with "the law of historical development" whereas Korea clearly has not.

Furthermore, the absence of feudalism has also meant the absence of a military ruling caste in Korea's history as a nation-state. The lack of military tradition resulted in the lack of such fine cultural institutions as bushido (the moral code of chivalry in feudal Japan), chivalry, and economic development, as we have already seen in the above. Even in their religions, the Japanese possessed a definite orientation toward universalism, goal-attainment, and achievement (in contradistinction to ascription).[6] But it was the kind of centralized government and public administration that Korea had in the past that manifested most glaringly certain built-in disadvantages as compared to manorial feudalism. It has been pointed out that the bureaucrats appointed by the central government of the Yi kings neither possessed familiarity with the province which they were sent out to administer, nor harbored any sense of affective involvement with the jurisdiction and its inhabitants. When a provincial magistrate was appointed, it was for a term of two years or less. As a rule, the central government deliberately avoided sending a bureaucrat to his home province for fear that he would not be an effective representative of the central government. It was a conscious policy of the central government to prevent the growth of a provincial power center that could effectively challenge the central power. If a magistrate was permitted to stay in one jurisdiction for a long period of time, there might develop a close affective tie between the province and the magistrate. The magistrate would develop greater loyalty for his provincial constituency than for the interests of the central government. He would come to develop a base for personal power. The longer a magistrate stayed in one jurisdiction, the more reluctant he became to leave it for another post.

Another rationale was that a short tour deprived a magistrate of having enough time to develop a taste for corruption before he was compelled to settle official accounts as a preliminary to transferring his mandate to a successor. The idea was that no lichen could grow on a rock that was constantly moved about. It was thought that the people would feel little need to bribe and otherwise corrupt a magistrate if they realized that he was to have power over them for only a couple of years. Unfortunately, for many observers, the centralized government, the above-mentioned advantages notwithstanding, was inferior to manorial feudalism as a technique of public administration. Whereas the lord of a manor would rise or fall with the prosperity or impoverishment of his fief, no bureaucrat would find such identity of interest with the jurisdiction with which he was entrusted for only two years. While the former would do his utmost to nurture material prosperity and cherish the inhabitants out of necessity to maintain the industrial and military strength of his fief, the latter would only view his jurisdiction as an object of exploitation out of which he had to suck as much personal fortune as his short tenure permitted him to do. Since a feudal fief was transmitted from one generation to the next, staying in one family so long as the male line of descent was maintained, the lord not only gained familiarity with his jurisdiction but was also compelled to familiarize himself with his fief in order for him to maintain his military viability. A close emotional tie was bound to develop between the lord and his people over many decades, as well as a sense of community of interest. In short, a feudal lord was prevented from exploiting his fief as mercilessly and thoroughly as a Yi dynasty bureaucrat by his need to base his military existence upon the material prosperity and emotional loyalty of his people. Thus, the kind of civilian supremacy that prevailed throughout the Yi dynasty is again made out to be a cause for bureaucratic corruption and popular impoverishment that are supposed to have plagued the old Korea. The manorial feudalism of Japan was said to be clearly an improvement upon the centralized literati government of Yi Korea; the former was an enlightened precursor of modern political civilization while the latter was an epitome of backward misgovernment.

In theorizing about the politics of old Korea, the label of "Oriental despotism" has often been used. The followers of Karl Marx have used "Oriental feudalism" (or "Asiatic System") as a convenient conceptual category in writing their version of Korean political history. Their difficulty was that they could not find "feudalism" in Korea, but they could not deviate from their "law of historical development" by making an exception in the case of Korea. "Oriental despotism," popularized by Wittfogel,[7] seems to be derived from the same kind of need to construct a grand theory with a universal validity. It is not appropriate to recapitulate the full extent of Wittfogel's view here. It is sufficient merely to point out that the Yi dynasty political system has been considered fully explicable in terms of "Oriental despotism." It is true that Korea has lacked the kind of great rivers that would unequivocally validate his "hydraulic theory." But it cannot be denied that Korea certainly has had an "hydraulic agriculture" whose principal product was rice. Therefore, old Korea clearly falls into the category of Wittfogel's "hydraulic society." Moreover, the political institutions of Yi Korea, for example, had all the trappings of "total power." There were no constitutional checks. No private interest was permitted to organize itself for political participation. Even property rights were never legally recognized or protected ("hydraulic property"). The people had no rights as against the rulers. The rulers had no constitutional duties toward the people. Even religious authority was attached to the state in keeping, it seems, with his argument that "agrarian despotism always keeps the dominant religion integrated in its power system."[8] Little individual freedom was in evidence in old Korea.

When we come to the absence of genuinely "autonomous secondary organizations," Wittfogel takes us right into Gregory Henderson's theory of the vortex. Henderson, like Wittfogel, emphasizes a continuous high degree of political centralization, imposed on a geographically small and ethnically and culturally homogeneous polity, resulting in "a powerful, upward-sucking force active throughout the culture."[9] Although Henderson does not explicitly subscribe to Wittfogel's "Oriental Despotism," he more or less arrives at the same conclusions. Henderson states that the "vortex" has an overpoweringly "atomizing" tendency which undermines all forms of integrative groups such as "social classes, political parties, and other intermediary groups." Further, the vortex also hinders "such developments as definition of function, legal boundaries, formal procedures, and specialization."

As to the vortex that destroys "intermediary organizations," Wittfogel would heartily concur by saying: "As manager of hydraulic and other mammoth constructions, the hydraulic state prevents the nongovernmental forces of society from crystalizing into independent bodies strong enough to counterbalance and control the political machines."[10] Henderson's "mass society" with its "atomized entities, related to each other chiefly through their relations to state power— a society whose elite and masses confront each other directly.... a society characterized by amorphousness or isolation in social relations,"[11] is hardly distinguishable from Wittfogel's "total loneliness" and "total alienation" under conditions of "total power." This is especially true when Henderson talks about Syngman Rhee's manipulation of "the atomized mass society" and quotes William Kornhauser as saying: "Deliberate atomization is a technique of total domination."[12] Surely, when Henderson says: "Men sold friends, honor, and nation for power, yet stood always on the edge of the abyss. The psychology of this plight explains much of their erratic and cruel behavior,"[13] he is clearly talking about the same thing as Wittfogel's total loneliness and alienation.

As Wittfogel finds little evidence of class struggle in an oriental despotism, so does Henderson with respect to Korea. In the case of hydraulic society "total power" paralyzed class struggle because it would not tolerate any political mass action as a means of settling social conflicts. "Agrarian despotism" was "suspicious of all rallies of socially dissatisfied persons."[14] In the case of Korea "the vortex" so atomized the society as to prevent Korea's social classes from acquiring real boundaries and cohesion. But Henderson's view on the extent of social mobility differs from that of Wittfogel. While Henderson considers the mobility in Korea to have been much more pervasive and extensive as the result of the overpowering "updraft," Wittfogel maintains that vertical mobility in hydraulic society resulted from manipulation from above and was therefore "passive." Also, Wittfogel states that the masters of hydraulic society "formed one of the most class-conscious groups in the history of mankind."[15] But Henderson finds that Korea's social classes vanished "almost without trace into the vast classless Korean mass," without leaving any accent or behavioral characteristics that can mark off various class origins and backgrounds.[16]

But Korea's tendency to "avoid definition" did not signify social equality for Henderson. On the contrary, he finds "involved inequality" and "deeply ingrained obedience."[17] When he stresses the consolidation of religion, ethics, education and politics in the hands of government, thereby knotting the Korean society into "an obedient whole," we more than get a glimpse of Wittfogel's "total submission" and "total obedience." Wittfogel eloquently points out how "disciplinary education" prepares the populace for "total obedience." Similarly, Henderson observes that "the government—an encompassing control mechanism built into the home, extending to clan, academy (sŏwŏn), or family—organized administration and education so that no large groups could exercise rights and responsibilities except in the prescribed way."[18] As for Wittfogel's thesis concerning the absorption or religious authority by the hydraulic state, Henderson gives us the Korean parallel in the form of Yi Dynasty political system which stripped state support from Buddhism, allowing "no institutions outside central government in which moral or religious power could, with any degree of independence, inhere in such a way as to check central power."[19]

Both Wittfogel and Henderson emphasize underdevelopment of judicial institutions, lack of constitutional checks on government, nebulous legal boundaries, ill-protected property rights, and economic underdevelopment—all resulting from overpowering concentration of political power in the extremely centralized government. Absence of feudal heritage is considered significant—in the sense that such absence has been detrimental to democracy, political development and civil liberties—by both writers. The only difference is to be found in the different causes with which the two writers attempt to explain the extreme concentration of political power in the state. Wittfogel adduces the decision of the irrigation farming community to pursue the advantages of this type of agriculture on a major scale, involving a large supply of water and utilizing mass labor under a coordination and directing authority, as the cause for Oriental despotism.[20] On the other hand, Henderson places more emphasis on the smallness of Korea's geographical scale, cultural homogeneity, political unity in the face of foreign invasions, and "exceptional historical continuity" as the causes for inducing "enormous centralization of politics, administration, values, and even emotion" in Korea.[21]

In the foregoing we have surveyed various theories which have attempted to explain Korean politics in general terms. One common feature shared by all these theories is the assumption or the conclusion that something had gone wrong with Korean politics. What went wrong with Korean politics took many forms: underdevelopment, backwardness, stagnation, despotism, authoritarianism, autocracy, centralization, lack of individual freedoms, absence of constitutional checks, incohesiveness, disunity, inchoate formal procedures, weak private property rights, a feeble military establishment, economic underdevelopment, low-level industrialization, nepotism, corruption, moral bankruptcy, submissiveness, and so on. Another assumption is that whatever is wrong with Korean politics at present is due to bad influences from the past. A part of this assumption is the admission that democracy is not functioning very effectively at present in Korea. In other words, the assumption is that, if Korea had a "good" political tradition, it would be enjoying effective democracy right now. Thus, all the theories unanimously agree in their negative evaluation of the Korean political tradition and its contribution to the present-day situation.

IMPLICATIONS AND PRESUPPOSITIONS

With regard to factual elements in the above-mentioned theories, there can be little doubt as to their general accuracy. For example, no one can deny that Korea lacked manorial feudalism and had a highly centralized government; it was militarily weak; it failed to enjoy a high level of industrialization; it certainly did not possess an independent and sophisticated judiciary; no struggle for individual freedoms was evident; property rights were not well defined. But facts that are chosen by a theorist as important or significant are not mere data without the benefit of a theory. Observational data become facts when they are chosen in the light of a theory. Therefore, one theorist would consider the "fact" that there was much factional struggle among the ruling elites of Yi Korea as the "important" or even "primary" cause for Korea's backward or stagnant political heritage, while another would consider the "fact" of extreme cultural homogeneity as the primary cause for excessive centralization of political power and consequent incohesion and underdevelopment.

In other words, the "significance" or "importance" of data is as crucial to theory-making as is the "factual accuracy" with which the data is processed. Why should a theorist deem the pervasive poverty of old Korea significant enough to merit a serious explanation while the same theorist does not consider, for example, the low incidence of violent crimes in old Korea as equally significant? In this day and age when world peace is said to be one of the highest goals of mankind, why should a theorist take the fact of old Korea's political and military weakness which had subjected her to a continuing series of humiliating defeats at the hands of foreign aggressors to be important enough to merit a systematic explanation whereas the same theorist refuses to assign similar importance to the fact that old Korea had been a highly centralized nation-state which had never waged a war upon her neighboring peoples for over a millennium? What renders the possession or the lack of possession of power and wealth of such crucial significance to these theorists?

One almost gets a feeling that there is a kind of conspiracy or obsession on the part of almost all of the theorists to establish power and wealth as the two values with which to evaluate every culture or civilization. If a civilization is highly industrialized and militarily powerful, such a civilization is to be accorded an ultimate accolade of being a "highly developed, advanced, progressive, enlightened, dynamic and civilized" civilization. On the other hand, if a nation is both poor and militarily weak—and the two conditions usually go hand in hand—such a nation is said to be "underdeveloped, backward, primitive, stagnant and uncivilized." Thus, power and wealth are to be the ultimate measures of human civilization and even life itself.

It may be argued by these theorists that there are good reasons for such a seeming obsession with power and wealth and that one cannot think of any polity that has not posited these two values as its ultimate goals. Further, inasmuch as power and wealth are goals "universally" pursued by every polity, the capacity to achieve these two goals does serve as a most realistic standard by which every polity may be judged for its performance. It should be pointed out here, however, that in old Korea power and wealth were just two values among many and they were not even the most desired as the national goals. Indeed, they were values to be wary of and even distrusted. If a theorist were to persist in his unwarranted assumption that old Korea, just as any other polity, had pursued power and wealth as its two most important goals and yet owing to some deficiency failed to succeed in its pursuit, he would only be transforming his assumption into a cultural bias. It seems best for him to abandon his urge to treat old Korea as one instance of a "universal" phenomenon, provided of course that there is such a thing.

Many a theorist has evidenced a tendency to assume a kind of universal uniformity in basic human motivation. If one civilization has maintained certain values as the *summum bonum* of communal life, it is only natural for a man who has gone through most of his socialization process in such a civilization to assume that other communities have done the same. At this stage of human history when there is an overwhelming impetus toward a form of world-wide cultural unity, a man who has gone through a process of formal education anywhere is scarcely immune from such an assumption. This is especially true if he has been at all exposed to any scholarly discipline which styles itself a "science" with its urge for generalization and universal validity. Of course, a true scientist never ceases to reexamine his basic assumptions and will be the first to caution against any blind faith in the proposition that the truth has to be not only uniquely single but also eternal as well as universal. Nevertheless, one encounters only too often those who would prefer to take refuge in the assumption of uniformity in human phenomena in the name of scientific validity. Such persons are apt to convert the process of intersubjective validation into a kind of majority rule. But such a majority rule, based as it is on another prevalent cultural prejudice found in some cultures, is liable to become a form of cultural imperialism in today's context. Majority rule—a mechanism by which numerical superiority or "quantity" is transformed into validity or "quality"—is, after all, itself a manifestation of the cult of power.

Classification is frequently said to be the beginning of systematic human cogitation. When classification is further refined, it becomes measurement. The importance and indispensability of either of these two forms of cerebration can hardly be gainsaid. It is for the purpose of classification that dichotomization is employed in theory-makings of various kinds. Thus, we have a long series of dichotomies employed in the literatures dealing with the subject of the Korean polity, past and present: developed *vs.* underdeveloped, advanced *vs.* backward, primitive *vs.* civilized, weak *vs.* powerful, dynamic *vs.* stagnant, heterogeneous *vs.* homogeneous, centralized *vs.* decentralized, despotic *vs.* democratic, rational *vs.* emotional. The usefulness of the foregoing examples of dichotomous classification in any theorymaking can hardly be denied. But the danger of injecting normative ambiguities into any orderly reasoning is equally clear. It is in the very nature of dichotomous classification that the classifier's own normative judgment determines the choice of either one of the dichotomous choices. No matter how careful the classifier may be in his use of a dichotomy and however solidly his use may be grounded upon a large amount of detailed empirical investigation, he cannot avoid normative ambiguities entirely. Normative judgment is an integral part of every dichotomous classification.

Normative ambiguities cannot be entirely avoided even if we resort to measurement. Although more refined forms of measurements enable us to avoid cruder varieties of simplistic black and white judgments, normative evaluation cannot be entirely dispensed with. Moreover, a measurement presupposes a scale whose termini invariably stand for some sort of dichotomous classificatory categories. Instead of simply designating a polity to be underdeveloped, it is now said to have the value of 2 on a development-scale of 10, for instance. It is true that few scientists would have the temerity to rank all the political units of the world on a universal scale. A true scientist would confine his scaling to measuring a phenomenon which is on a much lower level of generality. But it should be noted here that we do in fact have such a universal scale with which to rank all the nation-states of today in the form of gross national product (GNP). It may very well be that many would protest that GNP is only an economic scale and that only a "vulgar" scientist would use it for non-economic measurements. It is not difficult, however, for us to realize that we have few other indicators or scales with as much effectiveness and wide acceptance even in political science as GNP.

Underlying every dichotomous classification and scalar measurement is a hidden premise that there is a kind of natural law of development which governs all human cultural life. Such a law of development is often assumed to be unilinear, having one beginning and one end, and universal in its applicability. Without the aid of such a grand presupposition, it is difficult to see how anyone can feel confident enough to talk about "development" or "progress" in any field of social science. Unless two cultures can be placed on a unilinear scale of development, one culture can hardly be said to be more advanced than the other in terms of any valid comparison. Aside from such progression-oriented dichotomies as development *vs.* underdevelopment and primitive *vs.* civilized, even such dichotomies as homogeneous *vs.* heterogeneous, despotic *vs.* democratic and rational *vs.* emotional have the connotation of a unilinear progression of human history. In a world where democracy is made out to be almost a fulfillment of the highest of human aspirations, despotism, dictatorship, absolutism, or totalitarianism is usually associated with political underdevelopment and backwardness. Similarly, democracy is so often associated with pluralism that homogeneity is liable to be connected with political underdevelopment. Heterogeneity and diversity are, therefore, usually treated as indicative of development. In view of the cult of rationality prevailing throughout the world today, anything that has a propensity to vitiate rationality is again tied to a lower level of civilization. Emotionalism even in an individual is treated as coterminous with psychological immaturity. In the case of a culture emotionalism is synonymous with primitiveness.

The notion that human history has to have a primordial beginning and has to move or progress from that beginning toward a grand finale has held a peculiar fascination for some minds. Inasmuch as man himself has always had a beginning and an end, it was perhaps easy for him to project a similar *modus vivendi* upon history. A major ramification growing out of such a view of history is the compulsion to place all the cultures of man upon a single line of developmental continuum and classify them according to the "stage" or "level" on which each culture finds itself placed. No culture is allowed to get off this continuum and remain unclassified, that is, neither "developed" nor "underdeveloped" but simply remain itself. A culture must either be highly developed, relatively well developed, at a "take-off" stage, emerging, beginning to develop, still backward, hopelessly backward, primitive, barbaric, prehistoric, neolithic, paleolithic, or something.

Furthermore, there is a strong conviction that a transition from weakness to power is to be a development or progress while the reverse is to be a decline, decay or deterioration. A culture that remains weak through many centuries, like old Korea, naturally gets classified as stagnant, fossilized, arrested or even condemned. Similarly, a culture that becomes increasingly wealthy is described as developing, if not already highly developed, whereas a culture whose wealth is diminishing is described as either decaying or regressing. A culture that has never managed to become affluent is of course classified as underdeveloped, backward or stagnant. Thus, almost every classificatory category could be translated into a position on the unilinear continuum of historical development.

But the matter does not end there. The urge to equate development or progress with goodness, and backwardness or underdevelopment with evil is simply too pervasive to be ignored lightly. Given the dichotomy of development *vs.* decline or progress *vs.* decay, few can resist the temptation of pairing development or progress with good, and decline or decay with evil. Since power and wealth are also equated with development and progress, they are also made synonymous with good, while weakness and poverty are equated with evil. Despite the fact that few theorists with any sophistication at all would risk such a bald judgment on good and evil with regard to a political entity, there can be little doubt that such a normative judgment is inherent in any discussion of political and cultural "development."

It is with the above-mentioned classificatory categories and presuppositions that most of the theorists have approached the subject of Korean political history and culture. In view of the fact that what was most significant about Korean politics was its underdevelopment in the sense that the Korean polity, in spite of its long history of highly centralized and distinct existence as a political entity, remained weak and poor, students of Korean politics mostly focused their attention upon what was, or went, "wrong" with Korea. It mattered little (or perhaps more accurately, it scarcely occurred to them) that power and wealth were not desirable goals to be pursued in the Korean polity of the past, and this sort of heritage from the past still exerts a considerable amount of influence upon the Korean politics of today. Without a clear understanding of the heritage transmitted from the past it is not possible for any student of Korean politics to formulate a theory about the Korean politics of today with any degree of validity. A student of Korean politics must be prepared to abandon some of his familiar classificatory categories and premises and attempt to grasp the patterns of value priorities and political desiderata that were prevailing in old Korea. In short, he is simply requested to free himself of his cultural biases.

Having striven for many centuries to create cultural homogeneity, there can be little doubt that Korea is distinguished by its cultural homogeneity. Similarly, it cannot factually be more accurate to state that old Korea was weak and poor. Old Korea was prepared to accept poverty and military weakness as the price to be paid for other goals it valued more highly. Now, it is one thing to state that old Korea lacked, for instance, a clearly defined institution of private property, but it is another to regard such a lack as an indication of political underdevelopment. Going a step further, a theorist may well propose a remedy by recommending the establishment of a highly rationalized institution of private property. He might even counsel the adoption of an European institution of private property as a model for Korea. There is no question but that such a policy recommendation is made in all good faith and with good intentions. But such a recommendation is too often based upon an assumption that the elites of old Korea did in fact endeavor to secure the well defined institution of private property (or that had they known its advantages, they would have made efforts to secure it) and that due to inadequacy of the system or a lack of "political genius" on their part, they failed to develop the institution. Such an assumption, however, overlooks the fact that the elites of old Korea did not regard the development of a highly sophisticated institution of private property as compatible with a desirable political order such as they envisaged for themselves. They were not unaware of the advantages to be derived from a well-defined system of private property, but they were also keenly conscious of the threats it posed to the political order they preferred. Unless a theorist is fully cognizant of the reasons why the elites of old Korea refrained from establishing a rationalized system of private property, no theoretical explanation or policy recommendation with respect to private property can hope to be cogent or effective.

REEXAMINATION AND EXPLICATIONS

In attempting to gain a clearer understanding of the Korean politics of the past, we will mainly focus our attention on the Korean politics of the Yi Dynasty period. Of course, the Yi period covers only the most recent five centuries and cannot be said to be representative at all of Korean political history in its entirety. But the fact that the Yi epoch lies closest to us temporally also means that it has the greatest influence upon the present. Therefore, it would not be entirely meaningless if we studied the Yi era with a view toward constructing a theory which would afford us a more effective explanation of the Korean politics of today as well as of tomorrow. We shall first examine some of the reasons why power and wealth which have had overpowering appeal to other political cultures earned only suspicion and distrust from the Yi elites. And then, we shall survey some of the values other than power and wealth that occupied the most desired positions in the Yi pattern of value priorities. On this basis we should be in a much more tenable position to attempt a coherent explanation of Korean politics.

Apart from an "instinct" of an individual human being, no human community can survive without some material needed for minimum subsistence; nor can it maintain an ordered existence without some mechanism through which coercive sanctions may be applied to the behavior of its members. The material needed for survival ranges from food of all kinds to clothing, shelter (including fuel for cooking and heating), tools and even medicine. Luxuries, amenities, conveniences and other forms of surpluses are not included in the material needed for subsistence. As for the coercive sanction needed for orderly community living, it can take both physical and psychological as well as positive and negative forms. Of course, the foregoing dichotomies are by no means clear-cut; in most cases a coercive sanction is both physical and psychological. Praise, which is a positive sanction, for example, is reinforced by the availability of negative sanctions against contravening behavior. In any event, a community has to be prepared to employ coercive sanctions in order to secure the observance of behavioral norms deemed indispensable for its orderly maintenance.

The Yi polity was no exception; it endeavored to ensure the minimum of adequate subsistence to the people, on the one hand, and possessed a set of coercive sanctions to preserve the preferred order of community living, on the other. It is with that portion of wealth which was in the form of surpluses beyond and above what was required for subsistence that the Yi polity experienced uneasiness. As far as adequate subsistence was concerned, wealth was not only desirable and valuable but also something to be earnestly pursued. But as soon as wealth was to be accumulated for the purposes other than subsistence or generosity, it immediately became an object of suspicion and distrust. Though rarely articulated, the reason for the suspicion and distrust was that such a surplus was thought to have the propensity to destroy the basic decency in the man who accumulated it. To paraphrase the common Korea parlance, surplus wealth was liable to cause its possessor to "lose his humanness."

Lacking in the Korean culture was the sanctification of the human urge to dominate Nature. Koreans did not possess a spiritual heritage which commanded them to conquer and exploit the Material World for their use and enjoyment. The material environment for Koreans was not merely an object, separate and distinct from their egos, which was to be "placed at their feet," but was something with which their egos overlapped and interlocked. They were an integral part of Nature and it was an integral part of them. Man could not live without the Material World, and the universe without man was nothing. Man took from Nature, or rather Nature gave to him, what he needed for his life. Man did not have dominion over Nature, nor did it dominate him. The fact that he did not challenge and conquer the forces of Nature did not have to mean that he abjectly surrendered to them. Absence of aggressive bellicosity against his environment did not need to be synonymous with passive submission.

Nor did the interlocking or overlapping of Nature with man signify the complete merging of the two into one single undifferentiated whole. A portion of each overlapped with the other, leaving the remainder different and even distinct. But, because of the overlapping portions, the difference and the distinction contained within them less of conflict and less of "dialectical tension" in Korea than the similar relational properties would indicate in the Occident. The acknowledgement of my ego's overlapping with Nature renders it a "subject" like me rather than an object to be cognized as separate and distinct from me. The "dialectical" relationship did not need to be a struggle or "anti." In short, there was no legitimation of unlimited domination of the Material World in the form of unlimited wealth.

The real threat to "humanness" came, however, from the change in the interpersonal dynamics which the possession of surplus wealth usually coerced upon its possessor. The problem was miserliness which was thought to be unavoidably concomitant with the accumulation of any amount of surplus wealth. Given the fact that the quality deemed desirable in a possessor of wealth in the Korean culture was unlimited generosity, miserliness could not but become an object of aversion and distaste. It should be noted here, however, that for Koreans generosity was not a matter of goodness or love in the abstract. It was humanness itself. On the other hand, unlimited generosity could hardly be anything but antithetical to accumulation of wealth. For achieving the latter, man must first of all learn to limit his impulse of generosity in order for him to accumulate any amount of wealth. Secondly, he must learn to draw a boundary line between what is his and what is not his. Thirdly, he must separate his ego from other egos. Fourthly, he must orient his whole life toward the achievement of a goal, i.e., maximization of profit.

In addition to the loss of humanness entailed by miserliness, the separation and isolation of one's ego from other egos contributed further to the impairment of interpersonal decency for the possessor of wealth. Now, for the Koreans, what bestowed ultimate meaning to life lay in a man's ability to forge sturdy overlapping patterns of egos with as many human beings as possible. No supreme, jealously unique, omnipotent, universal, and "historical" Creator-God was ever posited by the Koreans. Consequently, the Koreans did not seek the ultimate meaning of life in their relationship with a God. If there were a salvation for them, it was to be found in man's relationship with other human beings, not with god. Even "salvation" was to be human and this-worldly for the Koreans rather than divine and other-worldly.

It is in this context that we are examining the Korean concept of interpersonal decency. The type of inter-ego relationship deemed desirable by the Koreans was first of all the dilution or the erasure of ego boundaries. It was not enough that two egos merely came close enough for the two boundaries to come into contact with each other. The mutual drawing-closer should be carried out further so that a portion of each ego may overlap or interlock with the other. To be sure, such an overlapping is not possible with just any ego; and there is a limit to the number of egos with which one's ego can overlap. There will always be strangers, egos with which one's ego remains separate and isolated. The Koreans feel most uncomfortable in a situation when they are put into close contact with other egos with whom their egos remain unoverlapped. A great part of their childhood socialization process is taken up by a learning process in which they master the procedures, etiquettes and rules by which they determine with what egos they may overlap and how.

It is with one's immediate family members that a Korean child first learns the essentials of inter-ego dynamics. Because of the blood relationship and affective involvement dating from prenatal period, a child usually has little difficulty in learning the dynamics. The intense affective commitment on the part of its ancestors functions as a potent support and reinforcement for the child's learning experience. A child that fails to develop successfully an adequate inter-ego dynamics with his immediate family members may well be said to have failed in acquiring basic humanness itself. It is for this reason that the Korean culture attributes such a high valuation upon a man's loyalty and commitment to his own family. There is a strong predilection on the part of the Korean culture for a family which is knit closely together by warm affection and fidelity. This type of partiality for a successful childhood socialization manifests itself in Korean preoccupation with a man's family background in determining his worth as a human being, that is, his humanness. A man who came from a discordant family was most likely to have lacked an adequate opportunity to master the proper inter-ego dynamics. This concern for a man's family background—which a sociologist might term as ascriptive orientation in contradistinction to achievement orientation—was not so much an interest in finding out his family's history with regard to such items of "success" as honor, wealth, or influence but a desire to determine the degree of humanness he had acquired in his own family situation.

It is customary for the Koreans to insist that the kind of intrafamily devotion which serves as the indispensable foundation upon which interpersonal decency is to be constructed is "natural" to man in the sense that even the beasts are capable of it. Therefore, a man who is not capable of a high degree of affectionate commitment to his immediate family is said to be inferior to even beasts. The underlying assumption is that no conscious effort or special aptitude is required for acquiring and maintaining affection and loyalty toward one's own family members. It is in this cultural milieu that filial piety must be comprehended. Just as maternal love and paternal devotion toward a child were "natural," so it was with filial affection. Filial piety was never to be a unilateral obligation (if such a "legalistic" term could be used in the family setting) on the part of a descendant without parental affection reciprocating it. The image of a stern Korean father who wields absolute power over his son who abjectly obeys his father in trembling fear conveys only a small part of the real picture. Such a picture is simply too legalistic and Roman.

For an Occidental man of the twentieth century, the talk of paternal devotion to a male child may smack of Victorian hypocrisy. Even the notion of maternal love for a male child may produce a feeling of uneasiness. It is submitted here, however, that whatever validity it might have had in an Occidental culture, the Freudian paradigm of parent-child relationship should be, at least, modified before it is made applicable to the Korean context. In view of the fact that filial piety and ancestor worship involve a father-son relationship— although it should be made clear that filial piety and ancestor worship are as much directed to mother as to father—Oedipal complex may appear to be indispensable in any discussion of these topics. A possible relevance of the Oedipal pattern in the Korean family setting is a question weighty and complicated enough to merit a separate and fuller treatment elsewhere. Here, only those factors that seem to have some bearing upon future consideration of the subject will be enumerated.

First of all, the Korean culture has lacked the image of a Father-God figure who is given to anger and punishment in the face of disobedience on the part of children-people. Second, Koreans have lacked the concept of tragedy that might have afforded a room for an Oedipal drama. Third, the high valuation of deep and close interpersonal commitment to the point of overlapping one's ego with other egos has rendered pitching of one's ego against another ego reprehensible to Koreans. Conflict or struggle has never enjoyed that aura of power, progressive energy, dynamism and development in the Korean culture. No dialectical predilection was attached to inter-ego conflict as a means for "resolution" or synthesis of any kind. Fourth, a son held a "religious" significance in the culture of old Korea. To put it somewhat extremely, the father's "salvation" lay in his son, not in his God, in old Korea. As old Koreans used to say, filial piety was in fact a parental piety toward children and ancestor worship meant son-worship in practice. The Korean father's devotion to his son made it very difficult for the latter to develop an Oedipal complex.

Not possessing the concept of salvation which would enable a man to "return" to the bosom of the Creator after death and there lead a life that is utterly divorced from human life on this earth, a Korean had to provide for his after-life somehow. Unlike a Christian who believed that blood and marriage relationships formed on this earth would have no significance in Heaven, Koreans firmly believed that the same relationships would persevere throughout eternity, if there was an eternity. Such a belief naturally prompted Koreans to attach a crucial importance to their family relationships—much more so, certainly, than an Occidental. If a man were to "live" on this earth after death, he needed someone, some human being, to look after him. He needed someone who cared for him enough to look, after his death, for a sunny, dry, peaceful and comfortable "home," sheltered from the chilly north wind and commanding a beautiful view. Moreover, he would be most miserable if he were to have no one to visit him at his posthumous resting place once in a while. He would be most gratified if he could have his beloved son keep him company at his grave-side at least during the initial mourning period of two years (as the sons indeed did in old Korea).

Given the popular belief that the most wretchedly miserable condition of after-life was to lead a lonely existence without the comforting love and care of one's own flesh and blood, not many fathers could afford to regard their own sons with less than affectionate devotion. Added to this was the pattern of overlapping egos between father and son and the notion that a part of each was contained in the other. A man without a son was a most miserable man; a man almost gave anything to obtain a son of his own. It is within this kind of mental and emotional framework that the son is eagerly awaited by the father. Few sons were ever greeted with jealousy at their births; most sons were welcomed with gleeful joy by all the family. Inasmuch as extended family with three or four generations living within the same household was the rule, the grandparents or the great grandparents who of course had more reason to worry about their impending after-life than young parents usually lavished boundless affection and devotion upon a male descendant.

Furthermore, the value of a son went beyond his status as an affectionate caretaker of his father's and mother's after-life. It was his function also to care for and comfort his father's ancestors. Thus, it was also the father's duty toward his own ancestors that he ought to do everything in his power to see to it that his son would receive all the paternal love and affection necessary in order for the youngster to grow up to add luster to the names of the ancestors. A man's ancestors would be simply overjoyed if, for example, his son could finally get himself elected to be enshrined with Confucius as one of a handful of scholar-sages to be so honored in Korean history. This was certainly the highest honor attainable by the very few "elites of the elites" of old Korea. A man who failed to secure a decent son not only failed himself but his ancestors also.

The prevailing pattern of child-rearing practice in Korea observable even today should be of some value as a pithy aid to our understanding of the Korean father-son relationship. As a suckling, a child was given to the full and continuous physical possession of its mother. The Korean mother usually carried her child tightly strapped on her back while she had to move around and work. The child slept during the night in its mother's arms, often holding her breasts in its hands. The whole culture considered the child's monopoly of physical possession by its mother only natural. Such monopoly often continued beyond weaning if the child had no younger sibling. The father, therefore, was relegated to the status of snatching whatever physical access to his wife that was possible without daring to lay an open claim that was in any way superior to that of his child. No open competition between the father and the son for the physical possession of the mother was ever possible. The sleeping arrangement was such that the children were given the priority in sleeping with the mother. But most fathers were simply too happy and proud to have a son to begrudge his son of depriving him of untrammelled access to his wife. Knowing that his male child carried a part of him within it, the father was only too glad to see his child secure in the uninterrupted contact with its mother who had presented him with a son.

In a different culture even the kind of deep commitment the Korean father made to his son would very well be considered unhealthy in the sense that it would jeopardize the wholesome growth of the child's ego. Furthermore, the kind of close physical contact and emotional involvement between the Korean mother and the son would be little short of being scandalous. The unabashed affirmation of maternal love pervasive throughout the Korean culture would strike a non-Korean observer as crass sentimentalism, if not a symptom of underlying psychopathology. But Koreans have experienced little difficulty in enjoying profound interpersonal commitment and devotion without implicating sex, be it heterosexual or homosexual. Korean males enjoy close and enduring friendship with other males without being hung up on the question of homosexuality. The same is true with Korean females. Maternal love for the son has been so much taken for granted that it will be the mother who has scruples about her love and devotion to her male child who will be branded "unnatural." The Koreans have managed to apotheosize intense interpersonal commitment as the basic component of humanness without glorifying sex as the single most effective human faculty with which to construct and maintain lasting interpersonal commitments. As for the concept of wholesome personality premised upon autonomous and self-sufficient ego, the Koreans would have declared offhand that such an ego would seem to be most lonesome and that the personality based on it sadly deficient in humanheartedness. Clearly, the Koreans of old Korea would have shown little enthusiasm for individualism, rugged or otherwise.

It is as an index of basic humanness that filial piety was burdened with a crucial importance in the ethical system of old Korea. It was made into an embodiment of highest virtue. In spite of the Korean penchant for turning filial piety into an end in itself, however, the rationale for the spectacular homage paid to it lay in the conviction that a man incapable of filial piety (which was "natural" or even "animal" for Koreans) was doubly incompetent to maintain interpersonal decency with non-family members of the community. The Koreans considered it to be a height of illogic even to admit the possibility of an unfilial person being virtuous and a filial person being incapable of interpersonal decency. Thus, the first and the foremost qualification for a successful bureaucratic career was filial piety. The Yi statute contained many provisions for turning government officials away from their bureaucratic duties in order for them to minister to an aging parent for an indefinite period of time. The death and the consequent two-year mourning automatically suspended a bureaucrat's career or tour of duty for the duration of the mourning. Only an extreme national emergency could bring a military officer out of his mourning by a special royal command and dispensation. Unlike in Japan, the loyalty to the king or the nation was never given a clear-cut precedence over filial piety.

Korean history is replete with frustrated young men of the *yangban*[22] class who were being continuously thwarted from climbing the ladder of bureaucratic success by a recurrent series of mourning periods. In the case of a young man adopted into another branch of his clan, it was not unusual to have four parents (two by birth and another two by adoption) die at regular intervals so as to keep a man from extricating himself from intermittent mournings long enough even to take the state examination. This seeming irrationality which resolutely sacrificed administrative efficiency for the sake of familial affection has prompted many an Occidental observer of the Korean scene to characterize the Korean culture as lacking a "goal-orientation." Inasmuch as ancestor worship which, for Koreans, was a posthumous continuation of filial piety and intrafamily affection looking backward to the dead, the Korean culture has also been described as "past-oriented" rather than "future-oriented." The fact that Koreans preferred to commit themselves to finite human beings rather than to an absolute and universal entity or concept such as God, Truth, Nation, Justice, Liberty, etc., has earned for their culture a categorization as being "particularistic" rather than "universalistic."

Reverence for the dead ancestors, in spite of seeming primacy attached to its supernatural aspects, has had no particular affinity with either the past or the future. It has operated in a different temporal dimension. As the Koreans refused to separate and detach their egos from Nature or other egos, so they declined to sever the past from the present and the present from the future. The future overlapped and interlocked with the past; the new overlapped with the old. The past already contained a portion of the future within itself; the future had a part of the past within itself. Similarly, life always contained a share of death within itself and death was not completely devoid of life. Since the dead ancestor retained a portion of the descendant and the living descendant possessed a part of the dead ascendant, it was not possible for the descendant to detach himself sharply from the dead ancestor simply because the latter was "dead." *Inter vivos* inter-ego affection naturally survived death. Filial piety simply continued in another form after the parents' death.

This is certainly a strange notion of death for an Occidental observer. Death did not mark the beginning of a totally different existence which was qualitatively different in an entirely separate dimension from life. The Koreans believed that the dead retained all human senses and desires. A corpse was not something to be dissected, a piece of inert matter. Although the Koreans fully realized the difference between life and death and the fact that a dead body eventually turned into dust, they refused to perceive death as a sharp and severe line of demarcation beyond which life had little concern. For the Koreans ancestor worship was as much a matter of "present-orientation" as it was a past- or a future-orientation. The Korean concept of time was not *unilinear* or *uni-directional;* nor was it circular, repeating itself. The past was certainly different from the future; the two never could merge into one. The Koreans left the concept of time indistinct, leaving eternity to overlap with time.

As long as the achievement of humanness was posited as the goal, the Koreans were as strongly oriented toward goal-achievement as any other people. It was when the goal was something other than interpersonal decency as the faculty of maintaining a durable pattern of overlapping egos that they refused to regiment themselves in achieving the goal. If a man could not achieve humanness with regard to a particular person, he was thought to be certainly unable to achieve humanness universally. To be sure, the Koreans were so involved in accomplishing humanness with concrete individuals that they were never able to accomplish anything universalistically. Still, they refused to distinguish private ethics from public philosophy; they rejected the separateness of familial loyalty from patriotism. To be more realistic, however, it should be pointed out that the kind of articulate thought pattern implied by the foregoing statements would be foreign to the people of old Korea. Such conceptual categories as particularistic-orientation or public philosophy would not have even occurred to them, let alone been the ingredients of their thoughts.

Nevertheless, if the people of old Korea had been confronted with the necessity of sacrificing a couple of million human lives, with thousands of children being permanently crippled by malnutrition, for the sake of preserving federalism in the face of tribalism, they would not have admitted such a necessity but would have shrunk back from it. If a bloody war had had to be waged in order for the Truth to march on in glory, they would rather have left the Truth to be stranded in ignominy than to see countless human lives destroyed in the march. If the adequate defense of the fatherland had required the ultimate destruction of humanness in the governmental process, the elites of old Korea would have preferred to "appease" the potential aggressor. Despite their realization that the path to military greatness and economic might lay in "enriching the nation for a strong army" as the Legalists of China had advocated a couple of millennia before, they were willing to sacrifice the attainment of such a goal if it meant the impairment of the humanness of the government,

It may very well be that a non-Korean student of Korean culture would interpret the pattern of value priorities described in the above as indicative of cowardice, moral bankruptcy, spiritual degeneracy, cultural stagnation, political decay, defeatism, fatalism, primitive animism, infantile emotionalism, irrational and immature escapism, and so on. A list of similar evaluations can be continued *ad infinitum*. It is not for us, however, to render a final judgment as to the validity or the invalidity of all or any of the above-cited evaluations, except to point out the advisability of holding such assessments in abeyance during the process of theory-construction.

Now it is because of the strong goal-achievement orientation inherent in profit maximization that the culture of old Korea came to hold the pursuit of wealth in apprehension and mistrust. The first tendency easily noticeable in a specialist in wealth is the desire to separate his ego from other egos. He tends to dull his sense of intimate involvement even with his close kin in order to isolate his material possessions clearly enough for him to identify them as his property. The ability to distinguish clearly what is his and what is not is the cardinal virtue for a specialist in wealth. He must check his impulse for generosity even toward his own parents and siblings. The isolation of ego of course marked the beginning of the destruction of interpersonal decency for Koreans. As such, pursuit of wealth invariably entailed an impairment of humanness. Moreover, it appeared that as a man's wealth increased so did his miserliness.

Such marks of "homo oeconomicus" as efficiency, rationality, cost-consciousness and idealization of productivity all signified the hardening of the heart, if not the dehumanization process itself. It is the readiness and the willingness of the pursuer of wealth to steel himself against any feelings and emotions which are only human and decent that Koreans experienced revulsion against what seemed to them to be the coldly calculating and ruthlessly economical mentality of the accumulator of wealth. Koreans witnessed too many instances of father and son suing each other in the court of law as soon as money became involved. In other words, money was the malignant agent that subverted the affection and humanness of father and son— so much so that they had to fight each other. Being a sharp hand at figures meant cold-heartedness to Koreans; being thoroughly economical meant ruthlessness. Economic efficiency was prone to thrive by feeding on the carcasses of affection and interpersonal involvement. Economic rationality was simply not compatible with interpersonal decency as far as the Koreans were concerned.

It is true that such an evaluation of economic rationality is short-sighted and overly preoccupied with the here and now. From the future-oriented perspective the short-sightedness of Koreans would appear to be immature and primitive. It is certainly economically devastating, as their history amply demonstrates. By stigmatizing any form of substantial saving the Koreans found themselves condemned to perpetual poverty. But they were willing to pay the price. To them material deprivation was less dear a price to pay than dehumanization. The Koreans fully realized that nothing precious in life came free. They were prepared to pay the price of poverty for humanness in life. They could find meaning in life without wealth but not without humanness. If wealth and humanness proved to be incompatible with each other, they elected to forgo the former.

It is in this pattern of value priorities that the elites of old Korea took pride in their personal poverty. Poverty was always ethically "clean" to them. The polity devised a specific respect category of "cleanly poor officials" by which it bestowed substantial positive recognition to those elites who lived up to the polity's ideal. Of course, not all the elites were always able to practice what they preached. But the dominant myth never waivered in its affirmation of clean poverty as the desirable condition to be expected from the elites. Those elites who waxed rich could never entirely escape the lingering suspicion of ethical filth, that is, loss of humanness. And of course, this was not merely a matter of "private" ethics; the same thing was true with the entire polity. Since the elites deemed the preoccupation with the matter of national wealth in elite discussions of state affairs indecent, pursuit of national wealth tended to be lukewarm at best. The elites felt that excessive pursuit of national wealth was liable to destroy the humanness of the system, as happened in the case of the Ch'in dynasty (221-206 B.C.) which had first unified China under the guidance of a Legalist ideology.

Given the prestige attached to poverty, economic subsistence for the masses was much more bearable than under another pattern of priorities. Poverty did not need to be equated with ignorance, sloth, or immorality. Poverty was not something to be ashamed of. Wealth was not necessarily a badge of high social status because there were many elites who were poor. Poor elites were in fact in a worse financial condition than peasants, especially if they could not pass the state examination and obtain bureaucratic appointments; they were quite reluctant to jeopardize their status by appearing to be incapable of preserving humanness in the midst of poverty. In practical terms they were not free to pursue a trade or earn a living. Contrary to the common misconception of today that the elites of old Korea despised manual labor, craft, and other productive skills, they in practice respected and honored physical work so long as it bolstered rather than impaired humanness. If agricultural labor had been an object of their contempt, they would not have thought it proper or even mandatory to have the king perform the ceremony of rice transplantation in the spring. It is only when such a labor or skill is performed for material gain, i.e., when it became a means for specializing in wealth, that it became something demeaning. Many a *yangban* cultivated manual skills, but they kept them a hobby, not a means for material gain.

In old Korea commerce was the least esteemed function in the wealth process. The reason was that commerce was based upon an essentially profiteering motive and was considered little productive of added social benefit to the nation. In other words, it entailed the greatest amount of danger of dehumanization against those who were engaged in it. Manufacturing was more esteemed than commerce because it involved honest labor of adding new values to a commodity. But agriculture was the most honorable function because no haggling was possible with Nature. Agriculture permitted, more than any other function in the wealth process, wholesome humanness. One can never cheat the soil; nor did the earth ever take unconscionable advantage of a farmer. Agriculture was consequently thought to be the mainstay of human life.

It is a peculiar property of power and wealth that they have invariably been closely associated through human history. It seems one cannot be pursued without the other. In the modern cliche of "military-industrial complex" and the Legalist slogan of "rich nation for strong army," power and wealth are coupled together. It seems one can easily convert power into wealth by waging a war of imperialism and colonialism. As for converting wealth into power, we know that wealth *is* power. Military power without industrial power is a contradiction in terms. It is hardly necessary to cite the examples of Biafra in 1969, or Japan in World War II, to demonstrate the indispensability of wealth for power. Having decided wealth to be odious, the people of old Korea could hardly be expected to esteem power. Power was suspect, too, for the same reason as wealth; it was injurious to humanness.

Power involves negative sanctions, severe deprivations.[23] It also involves other persons; power is never exercised in a vacuum and, therefore, is a form of interpersonal relation. More specifically, power involves an exercise of influence upon other human beings with the threat of sanctions. In extreme cases, the constraint employed against another human being will be violence. But even in "peaceful" cases, the threat of severe deprivations, such as disgrace, is implied when we are talking about power. When power is adopted as the primary value by an individual, he endeavors to maximize his power. As with other values, especially wealth, desire for power is said to be limitless.

In the context of the political culture of old Korea, the indispensability of negative sanctions prompted the Koreans to fear and mistrust power. Power had the propensity to force its pursuer to separate and isolate his own ego from other egos as a preliminary to "producing intended effects upon" them. What he sought was not humanness in interpersonal relations but influence upon others with the threat of severe deprivations. If there ever was a negation of humanness in interpersonal relations, it was to be found in violence and other negative sanctions. Power turned egos that ought to overlap and interlock with each other into a dichotomous relationship of subject and object. To the people of old Korea, power corrupted interpersonal decency.

In pursuing power, man operated according to "the postulate of maximization." He calculated. He steeled himself against emotions and feelings. He became future-oriented. He could not be always generous. He preferred to uphold an abstract and general norm in interpersonal relations rather than affection or particular equities involved. In the power arena even the intrafamilial affections were not immune from killing each other. Even a father was known to kill his son who posed a threat to his throne. Such species of affection as friendship and loyalty were often too frail to withstand the drive for power. Power rendered a man who desired it as ruthless and "shameless." In short, power was thought to be incompatible with humanness.

But it should not be thought that the Koreans regarded power as unnecessary for maintaining their polity. They realized fully that power was necessary and even indispensable in their political life. Just as wealth possessed two conflicting properties, so did power. Power, as a form of influence exercised by a large amount of humanness possessed by a man through the bridge of overlapping egos, was not only indispensable for insuring the normal operation of Nature's rhythm, but was decent and precious also as a faculty of increasing humanness in other human beings. It is power stripped of threat of violence and other forms of severe deprivation to which the Koreans were willing to concede legitimacy. Even severe emotional or psychological deprivations were reprehensible to them. So long as power functioned as a faculty which operated to produce the desired effect upon another person by causing that person to opt voluntarily for the desired effect in an atmosphere completely free from any expectation of severe deprivation, power was legitimate and acceptable to the Koreans. The question whether the concept of power thus defined is intellectually tenable or not, of course, remains. What was mightier than the sword to the Koreans was not the pen but humanness. It is for this reason that the Koreans were said to have believed in the myth that the ideal government was rule by virtuous example. But they were realistic enough to realize that even power so "humanized" had the inherent propensity to eventually dehumanize its exerciser. Power inexorably changed man's personality as if casting a spell. It corrupted man as if a disease. Exactly as wealth invariably damaged its pursuer's interpersonal decency, so did power. For this reason, power was especially taboo in familial context; so was it in any non-statal situation. Consequently, the Koreans made an exception in the case of affairs of state such as royal succession, royal marriage, royal ancestor worship, and prosecution of treason where power in all of its dehumanized coldbloodedness was grudgingly allowed legitimacy.

It was only when power in its human and decent form failed to secure humanness that law as synonymous with punitive sanctions was called into operation. Inasmuch as penal sanctions were extremely hateful constraints applicable only against biological entities devoid of humanness, such sanctions were extremely inhuman. The humanization of penal sanctions would have been a contradiction in terms because such sanctions were inhuman by definition and, if humanization was to be admitted at all, such sanctions ought to be dispensed with by recognizing the offender's humanness. If a man committed an assault upon his parent, he was no longer human. As such, he deserved inhuman treatment. If his humanness was to be admitted at all, severe deprivations should not be applicable to him. The only penal reform acceptable to the Koreans of the past was that of applying no penal sanctions at all. The only humane treatment of offenders was to recognize the offenders' humanness and dispense with punishment. The Koreans experienced little difficulty in entirely absolving a man's most glaring criminal guilt if he himself or his relatives exhibited an overwhelming sign of humanness.[24]

In view of their strong aversion to violence, the military man who was a specialist in violence found himself discriminated against by the polity. Even that aspect of military which was concerned with national defense was hardly free from pervasive antipathy. This kind of attitude was diplomatically suicidal. But Koreans were prepared to appease aggressors or accept military defeat if the price for military viability of the nation was the dehumanization of the governmental process. Thus, military weakness became chronic. From the perspective of a culture that practiced the cult of power, the Korean culture embodied everything that was contemptible, despicable, effete, stagnant, degenerate and sick. From the standpoint of a person who was accustomed to identifying strength with goodness and weakness with evil, the Korean culture symbolized all that was evil and barbaric in the Oriental way of life.

Even more "dysfunctional" from the modern political perspective was the incapacity of the elites of old Korea to extract themselves from the two horns of a dilemma which postulated two mutually irreconcilable imperatives—on the one hand, the power arena ought to have been occupied exclusively by those who possessed enough personal humanness to preserve humanness; on the other hand, however, the reluctance of those who possessed requisite humanness to participate in the power arena resulted in delivering the arena into the hands of those who had little humanness to check their cupidity for power. According to the myth, those elites who gave the appearance of desiring power were by definition "shameless." Any elite who at all wanted to preserve his humanness or at least the appearance of possessing humanness had to exhibit utmost reluctance to assume power. But it was also the myth that power ought to have been assumed by those who had the most humanness. In the ensuing confusion, power was assumed by those who shamelessly pursued power and who, under the myth, were least qualified to assume power.

It was in a sense inevitable that there developed a division of the elites into the bureaucrats and the literati. The former made it their goal of life to strive constantly, generation after generation, to secure participation in the national arena. The latter stayed away from the arena and devoted themselves to scholarship, taking pride in the fact that they kept themselves undefiled by power and refusing the bureaucratic honors proffered them periodically. They considered themselves truly superior to bureaucrats in terms of greater humanness. As such, they regarded it their duty to criticize those in the power arena by submitting memorials to the king in which they remonstrated the monarch for all that was contrary to humanness. But such tactics could not fail to earn the intense animosity of the power specialists. Yi dynasty history contains many instances when such anti-literati hostilities exploded into bloody purges in the form of treason prosecutions which decimated the ranks of the literati and momentarily silenced the most strident of the critics.

These sanguinary purges have often been confused by the students of Korean political history with factionalism among the literati. On the part of the literati, factionalism performed the function of an agency for exploring those institutional practices that best fostered the greatest possible magnitude of humanness in the community process of civilized life. Factionalism also served as a means by which the decisions and behavior of the participants in the power arena could be held in check by the literati who themselves chose to remain outside the scene of the struggle. Although the elites had every reason to criticize themselves for their factionalism, there can be little doubt that their factional divisions contributed to the preservation of humanness in the power process by restraining the excessive concentration and abuse of power. If we survey Yi political history, the community process, as had been originally constituted by the founders of the dynasty in conformity with their preferences, retained vitality throughout the factional period. During this period there was adherence to the original constitutional requirement that the monarch could under no circumstances have oral communication with a member of the bureaucracy without the silent participation-observation of a "history official" who made a verbatim record of the exchange.[25]

But, having been seriously mauled by two devastating foreign invasions (the Japanese invasion of 1592-1598 and the Manchu invasion of 1636-1637), the Yi dynasty, in its last centuries, saw the power process slowly become the trophy of rapacious royal in-laws. Factionalism, which was losing vitality, in the meantime became a pawn for the royal in-laws and other power specialists in their power manipulations. Factionalism, which had originally been the province of the literati, now became indistinguishable from the overall contest for power. It became merely a convenient means for the power specialists to manipulate the literati. The literati began to purge other literati; they were no longer able to transcend their factional divisions and unify themselves in opposition to the power specialists. As soon as the viability of factionalism started to ebb, there was no way of stemming the tide of corruption and dehumanization of the power process. The "history official" became increasingly dispensable. The power process, which lacked any institutional mechanism whereby power could be checked and balanced, and premised as it was upon the myth that it was to be operated by those who possessed humanness and disdained power, became an object of unbridled voracity.

VESTIGES AND MODERN RAMIFICATIONS

It is for the purpose of enabling ourselves to be more effective in understanding or even explaining the present community and power processes of Korea that we have spent a great deal of time in studying the past myths and practices. It is not a difficult task for anyone who has some understanding of Korean history to see the reason why the adversary system, for instance, does not, and will not, function too well in Korea. One who knows anything at all about the Korean value structure will find it relatively easy to anticipate that "contract" will have little importance even in business relationships among Koreans and to comprehend the Korean psychology which renders a request to sign a contract offensive to most Koreans. Those who are familiar with Korean political history will grasp the limited usefulness of attempting to gain an insight into today's politics of Korea by running elaborate statistical analyses of popular voting behaviors, parliamentary roll call votes, outcomes of various majority decisions in a formal setting, etc. The Korean obsession with unanimity in almost every decisional situation becomes much more comprehensible if we have some understanding of the Korean mentality.

Even the style of political participation has been different in

Korea. It is not because of their authoritarian mentality that the Koreans fail to appreciate the importance of "loyal" political opposition, but because of their pervasive habit of disrelishing every form of tension, strain, conflict, challenge, confrontation, opposition, adversity, counterbalance, aggressiveness, combativeness, acquisitiveness, determination to win a personal victory, "willingness to fight for one's legal right," and so forth. There is no inclination to establish an equilibrium by depositing power in the hands of the rulers and then constructing a "countervailing" force to oppose it. Koreans would rather demand that the rulers check themselves against greed and make efforts to discover what the demands of the populace are in order to have such demands reflected in their decisions. It must be here granted that it is difficult for an average human being to check his own greed and be solicitous enough for others' needs. But as far as the Yi dynasty Koreans were concerned no ordinary human had any business becoming a ruler. They were not disposed to give power to an ordinary man and then check him through institutionalized means; rather they wished to give power to a superior man whose humanness was big enough to check his own rapacity and forget about any institutionalized controls.

It is for this reason that the Koreans were quick to show deference to a man of high bureaucratic rank, not so much for the reason that they respected the power he happened to hold but for the humanness he was supposed to possess. The elite status by definition signified a great humanness; and if an elite displayed lack of humanness, the Koreans could be devastatingly rebellious and anarchically disrespectful of authority. To them, the essence of authority was not power but ample humanness. Such a way of thinking as this was not a mere matter of idealism but a matter that went to the root of the fundamental meaning of life itself. As such, it was an intensely realistic and pragmatic matter for the Koreans.

This is not to say, however, that the old value structure has survived intact to this day. Very far from it. The new value structure which is in many ways diametrically opposed to the old indigenous one has been imported wholesale into modern Korea. The old and the new have successfully distorted each other, thereby introducing confusion and complexities into the modern Korean political scene. In terms of myth, defined here as a pattern of authoritative symbols, the modern elites have made an articulate choice to abandon the old as the hateful culprit that was responsible for today's political impotence and economic underdevelopment. The old myth is even made to shoulder the blame for the crassest forms of mammonism, commercialism, rapacity and corruption that seem to be afflicting contemporary community process. Despite the fact that it is the new myth rather than the old which is saturated with a cult of power and wealth, the old myth rather than the new is held guilty for the contemporary "shameless" struggle for power and avidity for wealth. Even the ineluctable disorientation in the wake of the devastation of the old value structure is exonerated in favor of condemning the old structure.

In the Occident where power and wealth were allowed legitimacy, an elaborate body of "rules of the game" was devised to contain human rapacity within some reasonable bounds. The Korean culture, having disallowed any such legitimacy to power and wealth, devised no such rules, only striving to suppress behaviors openly specialized in power and wealth. To take the game of boxing as an illustration, if a fist fight between two men were evil, a culture would attempt to ban it rather than devise a set of rules for the fighters to observe under pain of defeat. It is only when a culture decides that boxing is a manly sport that it carefully works out the rules for the participants to observe and evaluate the performances.

According to the rules applicable to the power and wealth situations in the Occident, one who is in possession of power and wealth is expected to act in a "responsible" manner usually in the form of abiding by his conscience, a sense of fair-play, a sense of mission, and a spirit of service. But this is not all. In the modern industrialized Occident, the normative preference for dialectical tension, countervailing force, loyal opposition, check and balance, pluralism, competition among variety of interests, and even an adversary system as a means of conflict resolution, has contrived an institutional means for constraining the power and wealth specialists to be more "accountable" and circumspect in their observance of the rules of game. If we remember that the contemporary Korean polity neither has become accustomed to the imported "rules of games" nor has succeeded in "internalizing" the modern, "democratic" normative preferences, we can very well expect an unmitigated "jungle" in the power arena and wealth market. Whatever constraints are available upon the modern behaviors of the participants in the arena and market are still the vestiges of the discredited and moribund myth from the past.

But these surviving vestiges only contribute to confusion and contradiction by operating in an alien milieu. Instead of divorcing humanness from power and authority, they only weaken the resolve of the polity to set up an institutional mechanism by which a countervailing power could operate. The vestiges of the old perspective toward wealth are prompting the contemporary Koreans to swing between the two extremes of either belittling the specialization in wealth or idolizing it as the quintessence of modernity. The wonder is not that the contemporary community process of Korea allows a relatively low level of dignified human life, but that it allows any human dignity at all. Poverty which inflicted only physical pain in the past under the myth which attributed positive significance to material privation now is psychologically painful also under the myth which makes poverty as something shameful as a mark of failure and underdevelopment. As power becomes increasingly detached from humanness and comes to be justified by achievement, efficiency, productivity, national glory, strength of the national currency, etc., the edge of power feels sharper especially when it is not tempered by countervailing forces. Under these circumustances, the worst mistake students of Korean politics can make is to read into the past what they see in the contemporary community process of Korea. The past community process of Korea must be understood in its own right.

FOOTNOTES

1. Arnold Brecht, *Political Theory* (Princeton, N.J.: Princeton University Press, 1959), p. 14.
2. Gregory Henderson, *Korea: The Politics of the Vortex* (Cambridge, Mass.: Harvard University Press, 1968).
3. Adolf A. Berle, *Power* (New York: Harcourt, Brace & World, 1969).
4. The following passage bears quotation:
   > Just as capitalism lacked a judiciary independent of substantive individualization and arbitrariness, so it lacked political prerequisites. To be sure, the feud was not lacking.... Since the pacification of the world empire, however, there has been no rational warfare, and what is more important, no armed peace during which several competing autonomous states constantly prepare for war. Capitalist phenomena thus conditioned through war loans and commission for war purposes did not appear.

   Max Weber, *The Religion of China,* transl. H.H. Gerth (Glencoe, Illinois: Free Press, 1951), p. 103.
5. Arthur F. Wright, *Buddhism in Chinese History* (New York: Atheneum, 1965), p. 74.
6. Robert N. Bellah, *Tokugawa Religion* (Glencoe, Illinois: Free Press, 1957).

7. K.A. Wittfogel, *Oriental Despotism* (New Haven, Conn.: Yale University Press, 1957).
8. *Ibid.* p. 96.
9. Henderson, *op. cit.*, p. 193.
10. Wittfogel, *op. cit.*, p. 49.
11. Henderson, *op. cit.*, p. 4.
12. *Ibid.*, p. 62.
13. *Ibid.*, p. 210.
14. Wittfogel, *op. cit.*, p. 328.
15. *Ibid.*, p. 320.
16. Henderson, *op. cit.*, p. 55. Henderson also says: "Class or clan characteristics, a sense of community, pride, and loyalty could not solidify" (p. 46).
17. *Ibid.*, pp. 24–25.
18. *Ibid.*, p. 25. Of course, when we talk about total loneliness or total obedience, we are reminded of Hannah Arendt's similar observation about totalitarianism. Hannah Arendt, *The Origins of Totalitarianism* (Cleveland: The World Publishing Company [Meridian Book], 1958), pp. 437–479.
19. *Ibid.*, p. 24.
20. Wittfogel, *op. cit.*, pp. 11–21.
21. Henderson, *op. cit.*, pp. 13–35.
22. *Yangban* literally means the two branches, civilian and military, of bureaucracy. However, it became a term designating that social stratum from which the members of the bureaucracy were to be recruited. The membership in the class was determined by birth with rare exceptions. The loss of membership was much easier, however. The literati who, though born into the class, refused to follow the bureaucratic career could nonetheless retain the status for himself as well as for his descendants by maintaining a certain level of scholarship. *Yangban* is usually translated into literati-bureaucrat or scholar-official and is regarded as a Korean equivalent of Chinese mandarin.
23. Harold D. Lasswell & Abraham Kaplan, *Power and Society* (New Haven: Yale University Press, 1950), pp. 74–102.
24. In this connection the readers are referred to a story narrated in Pyong-choon Hahm, "The Decision Process in Korea," *Comparative Judicial Behavior*, G. Schubert & D. Danelski, eds. (New York: Oxford University Press, 1969), pp. 19–47; and 32–34.
25. The "history official" was put on duty 24 hours a day on a rotation basis in the palace. The record he kept remained secret even from the king and later furnished the raw data from which the official history was compiled for each monarch's reign after his demise. This practice operated as a powerful check upon the royal power as well as on the power of the bureaucracy. Although the practice did not fully open the power arena to contemporary public scrutiny, it did render the transactions amenable to careful scrutiny by historians and posterity.

TEXT OF THE CONSTITUTION OF THE REPUBLIC OF KOREA*

PREAMBLE

We, the people of Korea, possessing a glorious tradition and history from time immemorial, imbued with the sublime spirit of independence as manifested in the March 1st Movement, and with the ideals of the April 19th Righteous Uprising and the May 16th Revolution, now being engaged in the establishment of a new democratic Republic which consolidates further the basic, free, democratic order on the foundation of the historic mission of the peaceful unification of the fatherland, having determined:

To afford equal opportunities to every person;

To provide for the fullest development of the capacity of each individual in all fields of political, economic, social and cultural life;

To help each person discharge his duties and responsibilities;

To promote the welfare of the people domestically, and to strive to maintain permanent world peace internationally, and thereby to ensure the security, liberty and happiness of ourselves and our posterity eternally.

Do hereby amend, through national referendum, the Constitution, ordained and established on the Twelfth Day of July in the year of Nineteen Hundred and Forty Eight A.D., and amended on the Twenty Sixth Day of December in the year of Nineteen Hundred and Sixty Two A.D.

Dec. 27, 1972

*English translation by Korean Overseas Information Service.

CHAPTER I
GENERAL PROVISIONS

Article 1. (1) The Republic of Korea shall be a democratic Republic.

(2) The sovereignty of the Republic of Korea shall reside in the people, and the people shall exercise sovereignty either through their representatives or by means of national referendum.

Article 2. The citizenship of the Republic of Korea shall be determined by law.

Article 3. The territory of the Republic of Korea shall consist of the Korean Peninsula and its adjacent islands.

Article 4. The Republic of Korea shall endeavor to maintain international peace and renounce all aggressive wars.

Article 5. (1) Treaties duly concluded and promulgated in accordance with this Constitution and the generally recognized rules of international law shall have the same effect as domestic laws of the Republic of Korea.

(2) The status of aliens shall be guaranteed in accordance with international law and treaties.

Article 6. (1) All public officials shall be servants of the entire people, and shall be responsible to the people.

(2) The status and political impartiality of public officials shall be guaranteed in accordance with the provisions of law.

Article 7. (1) The establishment of political parties shall be free, and the plural party system shall be guaranteed.

(2) Organization and activities of political parties shall be democratic, and embody necessary organizational arrangements to enable the people to participate in the formation of political will.

(3) Political parties shall enjoy the protection of the State in accordance with the provisions of law. However, if the purposes or activities of a political party are contrary to the basic democratic order, or endanger the existence of the State, the Government may bring an action against it in the Constitution Committee for its dissolution, and the political party shall be dissolved in accordance with the decision of the Constitution Committee.

CHAPTER II
RIGHTS AND DUTIES OF CITIZENS

Article 8. All citizens shall be assured dignity and value of human beings, and it shall be the duty of the State to guarantee such fundamental rights of the people to the utmost.

Article 9. (1) All citizens shall be equal before law, and there shall be no discrimination in political, economic, social, or cultural life on account of sex, religion or social status.

(2) No privileged caste shall be recognized, nor ever be established in any form.

(3) The awarding of decorations or distinctions of honor in any form shall be effective only for recipients, and no privileged status shall be created thereby.

Article 10. (1) All citizens shall enjoy personal liberty. No person shall be arrested, detained, seized, searched, interrogated, punished, subjected to involuntary labor, or placed under probationary supervision except as provided by law.

(2) No citizen shall be tortured nor be compelled to testify against himself in criminal cases.

(3) Warrants issued by a judge upon request of a prosecutor shall be presented in case of arrest, detention, search or seizure. However, in case a criminal is apprehended flagrante delicto, or in case where there is danger that a criminal may escape or destroy evidence, the investigating authorities may request an ex post facto warrant.

(4) All persons who are arrested or detained shall have the right to prompt assistance of counsel. When a criminal defendant is unable to secure a counsel by his own efforts, the State shall assign the same for the defendant as provided by law.

Article 11. (1) No citizen shall be prosecuted for an act which does not constitute a crime under the law effective at the time it was committed, nor shall he be placed in double jeopardy.

(2) No restrictions shall be imposed upon the political rights of any citizen, nor shall any person be deprived of property rights by means of retroactive legislation.

Article 12. No citizen shall be subject to restriction of freedom of residence or moving, except as provided by law.

Article 13. No citizen shall be subject to restriction of freedom of choice of occupation, except as provided by law.

Article 14. All citizens shall be free from trespass of their place of abode except as provided by law. In case of search and seizure in the residence, a warrant issued by a judge upon request of a prosecutor shall be presented.

Article 15. Privacy of correspondence of all citizens shall not be invaded except as provided by law.

Article 16. (1) All citizens shall enjoy freedom of religion.

(2) No state religion shall be recognized, and religion and politics shall be separated.

Article 17. All citizens shall enjoy freedom of conscience.

Article 18. No citizen shall be subject to restriction of freedom of speech and press, or freedom of assembly and association, except as provided by law.

Article 19. (1) All citizens shall enjoy freedom of learning and of art.

(2) The rights of authors, inventors and artists shall be protected by law.

Article 20. (1) The right of property of all citizens shall be guaranteed. Contents and limitations thereof shall be determined by law.

(2) The exercise of property rights shall conform to public welfare.

(3) Expropriation, use of restriction of private property for public necessity, and the standards and method of compensation thereof shall be determined by law.

Article 21. All citizens who have attained to the age of twenty and over shall have the right to vote, in accordance with the provisions of law.

Article 22. All citizens shall have the right to hold public office in accordance with the provisions of law.

Article 23. (1) All citizens shall have the right to petition in writing to any State agency in accordance with the provisions of law.

(2) The State agency shall be obliged to examine such petitions.

Article 24. (1) All citizens shall have the right to be tried in conformity with the law by judges as qualified under the Constitution and law.

(2) Citizens who are not on active military service or employees of the military forces shall not be court-martialled except in case of espionage in military affairs or in case of crimes committed in regard to sentinel, sentry-posts, supply of harmful food, and prisoners of war as defined by law; and except when an extraordinary martial law has been declared, or except when the President has taken an emergency measure concerning the power of the Courts.

(3) All citizens shall have the right to a speedy trial. The accused shall have the right to public trial without delay in the absence of justifiable reason.

Article 25. In case the accused under detention is acquitted, he shall be entitled to a claim against the State for compensation in accordance with the provisions of law.

Article 26. (1) In case a person has sustained damages by unlawful acts of public officials done in the course of their official duties, he may claim against the State of public agency in accordance with the provisions of law; however, the public officials concerned shall not be immune from liabilities.

(2) In case a person on active military service or employee of the military forces, a police official or others as defined by law, sustains damages in connection with the performance of official duties such as combat action, drill and so forth, he shall not be entitled to a claim against the State or public agency on the ground of unlawful acts of public officials done in the course of official duties, except for com-

pensation as provided by law.

Article 27. (1) All citizens shall have the right to receive an equal education corresponding to their abilities.

(2) All citizens who have children to support shall be responsible at least for their elementary education and other education as provided by law

(3) Compulsory education shall be free.

(4) Independence and political impartiality of education shall be guaranteed.

(5) Fundamental matters pertaining to the educational system and its operation shall be determined by law.

Article 28. (1) All citizens shall have the right to work. The State shall endeavor to promote the employment of workers through social and economic means.

(2) All citizens shall have the duty to work. The contents and conditions of the duty to work shall be determined by law in conformity with democratic principles.

(3) Standards of working conditions shall be determined by law.

(4) Special protection shall be accorded to working women and children.

Article 29. (1) The right to association, collective bargaining and collective action of workers shall be guaranteed within the scope defined by law.

(2) The right to association, collective bargaining, and collective action shall not be granted to workers who are public officials, except for those authorized by the provisions of law.

(3) The right to collective action of public officials and workers engaged in State, local autonomous governments, state-run enterprises, public utilities or enterprises which have a serious impact on the national economy may be either restricted or denied in accordance with the provisions of law.

Article 30. (1) All citizens shall be entitled to a decent human life.

(2) The State shall endeavor to promote social security.

(3) Citizens who are incapable of earning a livelihood shall be protected by the State in accordance with the provisions of law.

Article 31. All citizens shall be protected by the State for purity of marriage and health.

Article 32. (1) Freedoms and rights of citizens shall not be neglected on the grounds that they are not enumerated in the Constitution.

(2) Laws which restrict freedoms or rights of citizens shall be enacted only when necessary for the maintenance of national security, order or public welfare.

Article 33. All citizens shall have the duty to pay taxes in accordance with the provisions of law.

Article 34. All citizens shall have the duty of national defense in accordance with the provisions of law.

CHAPTER III
THE NATIONAL CONFERENCE FOR UNIFICATION

Article 35. The National Conference for Unification, being a national organization based on the collective will of the people as a whole to pursue peaceful unification of the fatherland, shall be the depository of national sovereignty, entrusted with the sacred mission of the unification of the fatherland.

Article 36. (1) The National Conference for Unification shall be composed of delegates elected through direct popular elections.

(2) The number of delegates to the National Conference for Unification shall be determined by law within the range of no less than two thousand and no more than five thousand persons.

(3) The President shall be the Chairman of the National Conference for Unification.

(4) Matters pertaining to the election of the delegates to the National Conference for Unification shall be provided by law.

Article 37. (1) Any person who is capable of faithfully carrying out the sovereign will of the people for the sake of peaceful unification of the fatherland, who is eligible to run for the National Assembly, and who has attained to the age of thirty years or over as of the election date, shall be eligible to be elected a delegate of the National Conference for Unification.

(2) Matters pertaining to eligibility of those who may be elected delegates of the National Conference for Unification shall be determined by law.

(3) No delegate of the National Conference for Unification may affiliate himself with a political party, or concurrently hold a membership in the National Assembly or other public offices as determined by law.

(4) The terms of office of the delegates of the National Conference for Unification shall be six years.

Article 38. (1) The President, in determining or changing important policies on unification, may refer them for deliberation to the National Conference for Unification when deemed necessary for attaining the consensus of the people.

(2) A policy on unification approved by the majority of the total delegates to the National Conference for Unification under the provisions of Paragraph (1) shall be regarded as the collective will of the people as a whole.

Article 39. (1) The National Conference for Unification shall elect the President through secret ballot, without debate.

(2) The election of the President shall require the concurrence of the majority of the total delegates to the National Conference for Unification.

(3) In case no person receives the required number of votes as prescribed in Paragraph (2), a second ballot shall be conducted to elect the President. In case no

person receives the required number of votes as prescribed in Paragraph (2) on the second ballot, the final ballot shall be conducted between two persons receiving the largest and second largest number of votes if no two persons have received the same largest number of votes; and to all those persons receiving the largest number of votes if two or more persons have received the same largest number of votes; and the person receiving the largest number of votes thereupon shall be elected the President.

Article 40. (1) The National Conference for Unification shall elect one-third of the total number of the members of the National Assembly.

(2) The President shall recommend in a group the candidates for the members in the National Assembly as prescribed in Paragraph (1). Concurrence or objection to the election of the candidates on the slate shall be put to a vote and their election shall be determined with the quorum of majority of the total number of delegates to the National Conference for Unification, and concurrence of majority of the delegates present.

(3) In case no concurrence is obtained as prescribed in Paragraph (2), the President shall again prepare another slate with all or part of the candidates changed and submit the same to the National Conference for Unification, requesting their election, until their election is determined.

(4) The President, in recommending candidates as prescribed in Paragraph (2), shall submit a reserve list of candidates with the order fixed within the range of one-fifth of the total number of members of the National Assembly to be elected by the National Conference for Unification. The reserve candidates, if they receive the approval prescribed in Paragraph (2), shall take over the vacated memberships in the National Assembly in the order of names entered in the list.

Article 41. (1) The National Conference for Unification shall make the final decision on any draft amendments to the Constitution proposed and passed by the National Assembly.

(2) The decision prescribed in Paragraph (1) shall require the concurrence of more than one half of the total number of delegates.

Article 42. Organization, operation and other matters pertaining to the National Conference for Unification shall be determined by law.

CHAPTER IV
THE PRESIDENT

Article 43. (1) The President shall be the head of the State, and represent the State vis-a-vis foreign states.

(2) The President shall have the responsibility and duty to safeguard the independence, territorial integrity, and continuity of the State, and the Constitution.

(3) The President shall have the duty to pursue sincerely the peaceful unification of the fatherland.

(4) The executive power shall be vested in the Executive Branch headed by the President.

Article 44. Citizens who are qualified to be elected to the National Assembly and who shall have resided continuously in the country for five years or more as of the date of the presidential election, and have attained to the age of forty years or over, shall be eligible to be elected President. In this case, the period during which a person is dispatched overseas on official duty shall be deemed as a period of domestic residence.

Article 45. (1) At the expiration of the term of office of the President, the National Conference for Unification shall elect a successor at least thirty days before the term of the incumbent President expires.

(2) In case of vacancy in the office of the President, the National Conference for Unification shall elect a successor within three months. However, if the remaining term of office of the President is less than one year, a successor shall not be elected.

(3) In case of vacancy in the office of the President, the term of a successor shall be the remaining term of his predecessor.

Article 46. The President, before he takes office, shall take the following oath: "I do solemnly swear before the people that, by observing the Constitution, defending the State, endeavoring to promote freedom and welfare of the people and pursuing the peaceful unification of the fatherland, I will faithfully execute the office of the President."

Article 47. The term of office of the President shall be six years.

Article 48. In case of vacancy in the office of the President or of his inability to discharge the powers and duties, the Prime Minister and the members of the State Council in the order of priority as determined by law shall act as the President.

Article 49. The President may submit important policies of State to a national referendum in case he deems it necessary.

Article 50. The President shall conclude and ratify treaties; accredit, receive or dispatch diplomatic envoys; declare war and conclude peace.

Article 51. (1) The President shall be Commander in Chief of the National

Armed Forces in accordance with the provisions of the Constitution and law.

(2) The organization and formation of the National Armed Forces shall be provided by law.

Article 52. The President may issue presidential decrees concerning matters which are within the scope specifically delegated by law and which are deemed necessary to enforce the law.

Article 53. (1) In time of natural calamity or a grave financial or economic crisis, and in case the national security or the public safety and order is seriously threatened or anticipated to be threatened, thereby making it necessary to take speedy measures, the President shall have power to take necessary emergency measures in the whole range of the State affairs, including internal affairs, foreign affairs, national defense, economic, financial and judicial affairs.

(2) In case of Paragraph (1), when the President deems it necessary he shall have the power to take emergency measures which temporarily suspend the freedom and rights of the people prescribed in this Constitution, and to enforce emergency measures with regard to the powers of the Executive and the Judiciary.

(3) The President shall notify the National Assembly without delay of such an emergency measure taken according to Paragraphs (1) and (2).

(4) The emergency measures set forth in Paragraphs (1) and (2) shall not be subject to judicial review.

(5) When the cause for the emergency measures ceases to exist, the President shall terminate these measures without delay.

(6) The National Assembly may recommend to the President to lift the emergency measures with the concurrence of a majority of the total members of the National Assembly, and the President shall comply with this recommendation unless there are any special circumstances and reasons.

Article 54. (1) The President may, in time of war, armed conflict, or similar national emergency, when there is a military necessity, or a necessity to maintain the public safety and order by mobilization of the military forces, declare martial law in accordance with the provisions of law.

(2) The martial law shall be subdivided into an extraordinary martial law and a precautionary martial law.

(3) Under the extraordinary martial law, special measures may be taken, as provided by law, with regard to the warrant system, freedom of speech, press, assembly and association, or with regard to the powers of the Executive or the Judiciary.

(4) The President shall immediately notify the National Assembly of the declaration of martial law.

(5) The President shall lift the declared martial law when the National Assembly so requests, with the concurrence of more than one half of the members of the National Assembly.

Article 55. The President shall appoint public officials in accordance with the provisions of the Constitution and law.

Article 56. (1) The President may grant amnesty, commutation and rehabilitation in accordance with the provisions of law.

(2) The President shall receive the consent of the National Assembly in granting a general amnesty.

(3) Matters pertaining to amnesty, commutation, and rehabilitation shall be determined by law.

Article 57. The President shall award decorations and other honors in accordance with the provisions of law.

Article 58. The President may attend and address the National Assembly or express his views by written message.

Article 59. (1) The President may dissolve the National Assembly.

(2) In case the National Assembly is dissolved, a general election for members of the National Assembly shall be conducted within thirty to sixty days from the date of dissolution.

Article 60. The acts of the President performed in accordance with law shall be executed by written document, and all such documents shall be countersigned by the Prime Minister and the members of the State Council concerned. The same shall apply to military affairs.

Article 61. The President shall not hold concurrently the offices of Prime Minister, a member of the State Council, the head of any Executive Ministry, or other public of private posts, as prescribed by law.

Article 62. The President shall not be charged with criminal offence during his tenure of office except for insurrection or treason.

CHAPTER V
THE EXECUTIVE

Section 1. The Prime Minister and the Members of the State Council

Article 63. (1) The Prime Minister shall be appointed by the President with the consent of the National Assembly.

(2) The Prime Minister shall assist the President and shall supervise, under order of the President, the Executive Ministries in their administration.

(3) No member of the military shall be appointed Prime Minister unless he is retired from active service.

Article 64. (1) The members of the State Council shall be appointed by the President on the recommendation of the Prime Minister.

(2) The members of the State Council shall assist the President with regard to State affairs, and as constituents of the State Council, shall deliberate on State affairs.

(3) The Prime Minister may recommend to the President the removal of a member of the State Council from office.

(4) No member of the military shall be appointed a member of the State Council unless he is retired from active service.

Section 2. The State Council

Article 65. (1) The State Council shall deliberate on important policies that fall within the power of the Executive.

(2) The State Council shall be composed of the President, the Prime Minister, and members of the State Council, whose number shall be no more than twenty-five and no less than fifteen.

(3) The President shall be the chairman of the State Council, and the Prime Minister shall be the vice-chairman.

Article 66. The following matters shall be referred to the State Council for deliberation:

1) Basic plans on State affairs, and general policies of the Executive;
2) Declaration of war, conclusion of peace and other important matters pertaining to foreign policy;
3) Draft amendments to the Constitution, proposals for national referendum, proposed treaties, legislative bills, and proposed presidential decrees;
4) Budgets, closing of accounts, basic plan on disposal of State properties, contracts creating financial obligation of the State, and other important

financial matters;
5) Emergency measures of the President, and declaration and termination of martial law;
6) Important military affairs;
7) Dissolution of the National Assembly;
8) Requests for convening an extraordinary session of the National Assembly;
9) Awarding of honors;
10) Granting of amnesty, commutation and rehabilitation;
11) Matters regarding the determination of jurisdiction between Executive Ministries;
12) Basic plans concerning delegation or allocation of powers within the Executive;
13) Evaluation and analysis of the administration of State affairs;
14) Formulation and coordination of important policies of each Executive Ministry;
15) Action for the dissolution of a political party;
16) Examination of petitions pertaining to executive policies submitted or referred to the Executive;
17) Appointment of the Prosecutor General, the presidents of the National Universities, Ambassadors, the Chief of Staff of each armed service, Marine Corps Commandant and such other public officials and the managers of important State-operated enterprises as designated by law;
18) Other matters presented by the President, the Prime Minister or a member of State Council.

Article 67. (1) The National Security Council shall be established to advise the President on the formulation of foreign, military and domestic policies related to the national security prior to deliberation of the State Council.

(2) The meetings of the National Security Council shall be presided over by the President.

(3) The organization, scope of function, and other matters pertaining to the National Security Council shall be determined by law.

Section 3. The Executive Ministries

Article 68. Heads of Executive Ministries shall be appointed by the President from members of the State Council on the recommendation of the Prime Minister.

Article 69. The Prime Minister or the head of each Executive Ministry may, under the delegation of powers by law or presidential decree, or ex officio, issue ordinances of the Prime Minister or the Executive Ministry concerning matters that are within their jurisdiction.

Article 70. The establishment, organization and the scope of functions of each Ministry shall be determined by law.

Section 4. The Board of Audit and Inspection

Article 71. The Board of Audit and Inspection shall be established under the President to inspect the closing of accounts of revenues and expenditures, the accounts of the State and other organizations as determined by law, and to inspect the administrative functions of the executive agencies and public officials.

Article 72. (1) The Board of Audit and Inspection shall be composed of no less than five and no more than eleven members, including the Chairman.

(2) The Chairman of the Board shall be appointed by the President with the consent of the National Assembly. The term of the Chairman shall be four years.

(3) In case of vacancy in the office of the Chairman, the term of a successor shall be the remaining period of the predecessor.

(4) The members of the Board shall be appointed by the President on the recommendation of the Chairman for a period of four years.

Article 73. The Board of Audit and Inspection shall inspect the closing of accounts of revenues and expenditures every year, and report the results to the President and the National Assembly in the following year.

Article 74. The organization of the Board, the scope of its functions, the qualifications of the members of the Board, the range of the public officials subject to inspection and other necessary matters shall be determined by law.

CHAPTER VI
THE NATIONAL ASSEMBLY

Article 75. The legislative power shall be vested in the National Assembly.

Article 76. (1) The National Assembly shall be composed of members elected by universal, equal, direct and secret ballot by the citizens and the members elected by the National Conference for Unification.

(2) The number of members of the National Assembly shall be determined by law.

(3) Matters pertaining to the election of members of the National Assembly shall be determined by law.

Article 77. The term of office of the members of the National Assembly shall be six years. However, the term of office of the members of the National Assembly elected by the National Conference for Unification shall be three years.

Article 78. No members of the National Assembly shall concurrently hold any other office, public or private, as prescribed by law.

Article 79. (1) During the sessions of the National Assembly, no member of the National Assembly shall be arrested or detained without the consent of the National Assembly except in case of flagrante delicto.

(2) In case of apprehension or detention of a member prior to the opening of the session, such member shall be released during the session upon the request of the National Assembly, except in case of flagrante delicto.

Article 80. No members of the National Assembly shall be held responsible outside the National Assembly for opinions officially expressed or votes cast in the Assembly.

Article 81. The members of the National Assembly shall not abuse their positions and privileges.

Article 82. (1) A regular session of the National Assembly shall be convened once every year in accordance with the provisions of law, and special sessions of the National Assembly shall be convened upon the request of the President or one-third or more of the total members.

(2) The period of regular session shall not exceed ninety days and the same of special sessions, thirty days.

(3) The National Assembly shall not convene for more than 150 days annually, including regular and special sessions. However, the days of any special session convened upon the request of the President shall not be included in this count.

(4) If the President requests the convening of a special session, the period of the session and the reasons for the request shall be clearly specified.

(5) During a special session of the National Assembly convened upon the

request of the President, only bills submitted by the Executive shall be treated, and the National Assembly shall hold its sessions only within the length of the period requested by the President.

Article 83. The National Assembly shall elect one Speaker and two Vice Speakers.

Article 84. Unless otherwise provided in the Constitution or in law, the attendance of a majority of the members, and concurrence of a majority of the members present, shall be necessary for decisions of the National Assembly. In case of a tie vote, the matter shall be regarded as rejected by the National Assembly.

Article 85. (1) Sessions of the National Assembly shall be open to the public. However, they may not be open when so decided by a majority of the members present, or when the Speaker deems it necessary to do so for the sake of national security.

(2) Contents of sessions which are not open to the public shall not be publicized.

Article 86. (1) Bills and other subjects submitted to the National Assembly for deliberation shall not be abandoned on the ground that they are not acted upon during the session. However, it shall be otherwise in case the term of the members of the National Assembly not elected by the National Conference for Unification has expired, or in case the National Assembly is dissolved.

Article 87. Bills may be introduced by members of the National Assembly or by the Executive.

Article 88. (1) Each bill passed by the National Assembly shall be sent to the Executive and the President shall promulgate it within fifteen days.

(2) In case of objection to the bill, the President may, within the period referred to in the preceding paragraph, return it to the National Assembly with written explanation of his objection, and request its reconsideration. The President may do the same during adjournment of the National Assembly.

(3) The President may not request the National Assembly to reconsider the bill in part, or with proposed amendments.

(4) In case there is a request for reconsideration of a bill, the National Assembly shall reconsider it, and if the National Assembly repasses the bill in the original form with the attendance of more than one half of the total members, and with concurrence of two-thirds or more of the members present, it shall become law.

(5) If the President does not promulgate the bill, or does nor request the National Assembly to reconsider it as provided within the period referred to in Paragraph (1), it shall become law.

(6) The President shall without delay promulgate the law as determined in accordance with the foregoing Paragraphs (4) and (5). If the President does not promulgate a law within five days after it has become law under the foregoing Paragraph (5), or after it has been returned to the Executive under Paragraph (4), the

Speaker shall promulgate it.

(7) A law shall take effect twenty days after the date of promulgation unless otherwise provided.

Article 89. (1) The National Assembly shall deliberate and decide upon the national budget.

(2) The Executive shall formulate the budget bill for each fiscal year and submit it to the National Assembly within ninety days before the beginning of a fiscal year. The National Assembly shall decide upon it within thirty days before the beginning of the fiscal year.

(3) If the budget bill is not passed within the period referred to in the foregoing Paragraph (2), the Executive may, within the limit of revenues and in conformity with the budget for the previous fiscal year, disburse the following expenditures until the budget is passed by the National Assembly:

1. The emoluments of public officials and basic expenditures for administration.
2. Maintenance costs for agencies and institutions established by the Constitution or law and the obligatory expenditures provided by law.
3. Expenditures for continuing projects previously approved in the budget.

Article 90. (1) In case it shall be necessary to make continuing disbursements for a period longer than one fiscal year, the Executive shall determine the length of the period for such continuing disbursements. The continuing disbursements shall be approved by the National Assembly.

(2) The establishment of a reserve fund for unforeseen expenditures not provided for in the budget, or for any disbursement in excess of the budget, shall be approved by the National Assembly in advance. The disbursement of the reserve fund shall be approved during the next session of the National Assembly.

Article 91. When it is necessary to amend the budget due to circumstances arisen after the passage of the budget, the Executive may formulate a supplementary or revised budget bill and submit it to the National Assembly.

Article 92. The National Assembly shall, without the consent of the Executive, neither increase the sum of any item of expenditure nor create any new items in the budget submitted by the Executive.

Article 93. When the Executive plans to issue national bonds or to make contracts which may create other financial obligation of the State outside the budget, these matters shall be passed in advance by the National Assembly.

Article 94. Items and rates of all taxes shall be determined by law.

Article 95. (1) The National Assembly shall have the right to consent to the ratification of pacts pertaining to mutual assistance or mutual security, conventions concerning international organizations, treaties of commerce, fishery, or peace, treaties which will burden the State or people with a financial obligation, treaties concerning the status of alien forces in the territory, or treaties related to legislative matters.

(2) The National Assembly shall also have the right to consent to the declaration of war, the dispatch of armed forces to foreign states, or the stationing of alien forces in the territory of the Republic of Korea.

Article 96. (1) The Prime Minister, the members of State Council and Representatives of the Executive may attend meetings of the National Assembly or its committees and report on the state of administration, or deliver opinions and answer questions.

(2) When requested by the National Assembly or its committees, the Prime Minister, the State Council members and Representatives of the Executive shall appear at any meeting of the National Assembly and answer questions. If the Prime Minister or State Council members are requested to appear the Prime Minister or State Council members may have State Council members or Representatives of the Executive appear in any meeting of the National Assembly and answer questions.

Article 97. (1) The National Assembly may individually pass a motion for the removal of the Prime Minister or a State Council member from office.

(2) A motion for removal set forth in Paragraph (1) shall be introduced by one-third or more of the total members of the National Assembly, and shall be passed with the concurrence of a majority of the total members of the National Assembly.

(3) When a motion referred to in Paragraph (2) is passed the President shall remove the Prime Minister or the State Council member concerned from office. However, when a motion for the removal of the Prime Minister is passed, the President shall remove en masse the Prime Minister and all members of the State Council from office.

Article 98. (1) The National Assembly may establish the rules of its proceeding and internal regulations, provided that they are not in conflict with law.

(2) The National Assembly may review the qualifications of its members and take disciplinary action against its members.

(3) The concurrence of two-thirds or more of the total members of the National Assembly shall be required for expulsion of any member.

(4) No action shall be brought to court with regard to decisions under Paragraphs (2) and (3).

Article 99. (1) In case the President, the Prime Minister, or the State Council, Heads of Executive Ministers, members of the Constitution Committee, Judges, members of the Central Election Management Committee, members of the Board of Audit and Inspection, and other public officials designated by law have violated the Constitution or other laws in the performance of official duties, the National Assembly shall have power to pass motions for their impeachment.

(2) A motion for impeachment, under the foregoing Paragraph (1), shall be proposed by one-third or more of the total members of the National Assembly, and shall require the concurrence of a majority of the total members of the National Assembly to pass it. However, if a motion for impeachment against the President shall be proposed by a majority of the total members of the National Assembly, the concurrence of two-thirds or more of the total members of the National Assembly shall be required to pass it.

(3) Any person against whom impeachment has been instituted shall be suspended from exercising his power until the impeachment has been decided.

(4) The decision on impeachment shall not cause any other action than expulsion from public office. However, it shall not exempt the impeached person from civil or criminal liability.

CHAPTER VII
THE COURTS

Article 100. (1) The judicial power shall be vested in courts composed of judges.

(2) The courts shall be composed of the Supreme Court, which is the highest court of the State, and other courts at specified levels.

(3) The qualifications for judges shall be determined by law.

Article 101. (1) Divisions may be established in the Supreme Court.

(2) The number of judges of the Supreme Court shall be sixteen or less.

(3) The organization of the Supreme Court and lower courts shall be determined by law.

Article 102. The judges shall judge independently according to their conscience and in conformity with the Constitution and law.

Article 103. (1) The Chief Justice of the Supreme Court shall be appointed by the President with the consent of the National Assembly.

(2) Justices of the Supreme Court shall be appointed by the President on the recommendation of the Chief Justice.

(3) The term of office of the Chief Justice shall be six years.

(4) The term of office of judges other than the Chief Justice shall be ten years.

(5) Judges may be reappointed in accordance with the provisions of law.

(6) Judges shall retire from office when they reach an age as determined by law.

Article 104. (1) No judge shall be removed from office, nor shall he be suspended from office, have his salary reduced or suffer from any other unfavorable treatment, except by impeachment, criminal punishment, or disciplinary action.

(2) In the event a judge is unable to discharge his official duties because of mental or physical deficiencies, he may be removed from office in accordance with the provisions of law.

Article 105. (1) When the constitutionality of a law is a prerequisite to a trial, the Court shall request a decision of the Constitution Committee, and shall judge according to the decision thereof.

(2) The Supreme Court shall have the power to make a final review of the constitutionality or legality of administrative decrees, regulations or dispositions, when such constitutionality or legality is a prerequisite to a trial.

Article 106. The Supreme Court may establish, within the scope of law, procedures pertaining to judicial proceedings and internal rules and regulations on administrative matters of the courts.

Article 107. Trials and decisions of the courts shall be open to the public; however, trials may be closed to the public by court decision when there is a danger that such trials may disturb the national security or public safety and order, or be harmful to public morals.

Article 108. (1) Courts-martial may be established as special courts to exercise jurisdiction over military trials.

(2) The Supreme Court shall have the final appellate jurisdiction over courts-martial.

(3) Military trials under an extraordinary martial law may be limited to the original jurisdiction only in case of crimes of soldiers and employees of the military, in case of espionage on military affairs, and crimes as defined by law in regard to sentinels, sentry-post, supply of harmful food, and prisoners of war.

CHAPTER VIII
THE CONSTITUTION COMMITTEE

Article 109. (1) The Constitution Committee shall judge the following matters:
1. The constitutionality of a law upon the request of the Court.
2. Impeachment.
3. Dissolution of a political party.

(2) The Constitution Committee shall be composed of nine members appointed by the President.

(3) Among the members referred to in Paragraph (2), three shall be appointed from persons elected by the National Assembly, and three shall be appointed from persons nominated by the Chief Justice.

(4) The Chairman of the Constitution Committee shall appoint its members.

Article 110. (1) The term of the members of the Constitution Committee shall be six years.

(2) The members of the Constitution Committee shall not join any political party, nor shall they participate in political activities.

(3) No member of the Constitution Committee shall be expelled from office except by impeachment or criminal punishment.

(4) The qualifications for the members of the Constitution Committee shall be determined by law.

Article 111. (1) When the Constitution Committee makes a decision on the unconstitutionality of a law, impeachment, or dissolution of a political party, the concurrence of six members or more shall be required.

(2) The organization, operation and other necessary matters of the Constitution shall be determined by law.

CHAPTER IX
ELECTION MANAGEMENT

Article 112. (1) Election Management Committees shall be established for the purpose of fair management of elections and national referendums and dealing with affairs concerning political parties.

(2) The Central Election Management Committee shall be composed of nine members appointed by the President.

(3) Among the members referred to in Paragraph (2), three shall be appointed from persons elected by the National Assembly, and three from persons nominated by the Chief Justice.

(4) The Chairman of the Committee shall be appointed by the President from among its members.

(5) The term of the members of the Committee shall be five years.

(6) The members of the Committee shall not join political parties, nor shall they participate in political activities.

(7) No members of the Committee shall be expelled from office except by impeachment or criminal punishment.

(8) The Central Election Management Committee may, within the limit of laws and decrees, establish regulations pertaining to the management of elections, national referendums, and matters concerning political parties.

(9) The organization, the scope of function and other necessary matters of the Election Management Committees of each level shall be determined by law.

Article 113. (1) Election campaigns shall be conducted under the management of the Election Management Committees of each level within the limit set by law. Equal opportunity shall be quaranteed.

(2) The expenditures for elections shall not be borne by political parties or candidates, except as otherwise provided in the law.

CHAPTER X
LOCAL SELF-GOVERNMENT

Article 114. (1) Local self-government shall deal with matters pertaining to the welfare of local residents, manage properties, and may establish, within the limit of laws and decrees, rules and regulations regarding local autonomy.

(2) The type of local self-government shall be determined by law.

Article 115. (1) A local self-government shall have a local council.

(2) The organization, powers and election of the members of the local councils, election procedures for the heads of local self-government bodies, and other matters pertaining to the rganization and operation of the bodies shall be determined by law.

CHAPTER XI
THE ECONOMY

Article 116. (1) The economic order of the Republic of Korea shall be board on the principle whereunder freedom and cerative ideas of the individual in economic affairs are respected.

(2) The State shall regulate and coordinate economic affairs within the limits necessary for the realization of social justice and for the balanced development of the national economy to fulfill the basic living requirements of all citizens.

Article 117. (1) Licenses to exploit, develop or utilize mines and all other important underground resources, marine resources, water power, and natural powers available for economic use may be granted for limited periods of time in accordance with the provisions of law.

(2) The land and natural resources shall be protected by the State, and the State shall establish a plan for their balanced development and utilization.

Article 118. Tenant farming shall be prohibited in accordance with the provisions of law.

Article 119. The State may impose restrictions or obligations necessary for the efficient utlization, development and preservation of farming land, forest and other land in accordance with the provisions of law.

Article 120. (1) The State shall establish a plan for the development of farming and fishing villages on the basis of self-help of the farmers and fishermen, and shall strive for the balanced development of regional communities.

(2) Organizations founded on the spirit of self-help among farmers, fishermen, and businessmen engaged in shall and medium industry shall be encouraged.

Article 121. The State shall encourage foreign trade, and may regulate and coordinate it.

Article 122. Private enterprises shall not be nationalized or transferred to public ownership, nor shall their management be controlled or administered by the State, except in cases determined by law to meet urgent necessities of national defense or national economy.

Article 123. (1) The development of the national economy and science and technology necessary for such development shall be promoted and enhanced.

(2) The President may establish an advisory body for the purpose of promoting and enhancing economic skills and scientific technology.

CHAPTER XII
AMENDMENTS TO THE CONSTITUTION

Article 124. (1) A motion to amend the Constitution shall be proposed either by the President or by a majority of the total members of the National Assembly.

(2) Amendments to the Constitution proposed by the President shall be determined by national referendum, and amendments to the Constitution proposed by members of the National Assembly shall be determined by the vote of the National Conference for Unification, after being passed by the National Assembly.

(3) When an amendment to the Constitution has been finally approved, the President shall promulgate the amendment immediately.

Article 125. (1) Proposed amendments to the Constitution introduced in the National Assembly shall be announced to the public for twenty days or more, and the National Assembly shall decide upon the proposed amendments within sixty days from public announcement.

(2) Proposed amendments to the Constitution by the National Assembly shall require the concurrence of two-thirds or more of the total members of the National Assembly.

(3) When the proposed amendment to the Constitution has received the affirmative action referred to in Paragraph (2), it shall be referred to the National Conference for Unification without delay; and the amendment to the Constitution shall be finally determined by its vote. The proposed amendment to the Constitution referred to the National Conference for Unification shall be voted on within twenty days from its receipt.

Article 126. (1) A proposed amendment to the Constitution by hte President shall be announced to the public for a period of twenty days or more, and shall be submitted to a national referendum within sixty days from its public announcement.

(2) The amendment to the Constitution submitted to a national referendum shall be determined by more than one half of all votes cast by more than one half of voters eligible to vote for election of members of the National Assembly.

SUPPLEMENTARY RULES

Article 1. This Constitution shall come into force on the date of its promulgation. However, enactment of laws necessary for the enforcement of this Constitution, and the preparation for election of the President, delegates to the National Conference for Unification, and members of the National Assembly under this Constitution and other matters pertaining to the enforcement of this Constitution may be made prior to the promulgation of this Constitution.

Article 2. (1) The term of office of the first President elected by the National Conference for Unification under this Constitution shall start from the promulgation date of this Constitution.

(2) The terms of office of the delegates to the National Conference for Unification elected for the first time under this Constitution shall start from the date of its initial convening and shall expire on June 30, 1978.

Article 3. The first election of members of the National Assembly under this Constitution shall be held within six months from the enforcement date of this Constitution.

Article 4. The authority of the National Assembly exercised by the Extraordinary State Council from October 17, 1972 to the date of the first convening of the National Assembly under this Constitution shall be regarded as having been exercised in accordance with this Constitution at the time of promulgating this Constitution, and by the National Assembly formed under this Constitution.

Article 5. The public officials and directorial officers of enterprises appointed by the government at the time of enforcement of this Constitution shall be regarded as having been appointed under this Constitution; provided, however, that public officials whose appointment methods and whose appointing authorities are changed under this Constitution shall perform their duties until their successors are appointed. In this case, the terms of office of predecessors shall last until the day before the appointment date of their successors.

Article 6. (1) Laws, decrees and treaties in force at the time of promulgation of this Constitution shall retain their validity unless they contradict the provisions of this Constitution.

(2) Presidential decrees, state council decrees, and cabinet decrees in force at the time of the promulgation of this Constitution shall be regarded as presidential decrees under this Constitution.

Article 7. Laws and decrees passed by the Extraordinary State Council, trials, budgetary measures and other actions taken thereunder, shall retain their validity, and neither court actions nor any type of objection may be raised against them by reason of this Constitution or otherwise.

Article 8. Agencies performing duties belonging to the authorities of agencies to be newly established under this Constitution at the time of the promulgation of this Constitution shall continue to fulfill these duties until new agencies are set up under this Constitution.

Article 9. Neither court actions nor objections may be raised against the Special Declaration issued by the President and the extraordinary measures taken thereunder from October 17, 1972 to the promulgation date of this Constitution.

Article 10. Local councils under this Constitution shall not be formed until the unification of the fatherland shall have been achieved.

Article 11. (1) The Extraordinary Law Concerning the Punishment of Specific Crimes, the Law Concerning the Punishment of Persons Involved in Illicit Elections, the Political Activities Purification Law and the Illicit Fortunes Disposition Law and laws related thereto shall retain their validity, and no objection may be raised against them.

(2) The Political Activities Purification Law and the Illicit Fortunes Disposition Law and laws related thereto may neither be amended nor abrogated.

SELECTED BIBLIOGRAPHY OF BOOKS IN ENGLISH ON SOUTH KOREAN POLITICS

Allen, Richard C., *Syngman Rhee: An Unauthorized Portrait*. Tokyo: Tuttle, 1960. (An accurate picture of Rhee's activities from 1945–1960. The first five chapters give background material on Korean history and the development of the Korean revolutionary tradition.)

Area Handbook for the Republic of Korea. Washington: U.S. Government Printing Office, 1969. (A good descriptive introduction to Korea with a useful bibliography.)

Asiatic Research Center, Korea University, *Bibliography of Korean Studies: A Bibliographical Guide to Korean Publications on Korean Studies Appearing From 1945 to 1958,* Vol. I. Seoul: Asiatic Research Center, 1965. Volume II, also published in 1965, covers the period from 1959–1962. (English translation of bibliography of Korean language materials.)

Baldwin, Frank, ed., *Without Parallel: the American-Korean Relationship Since 1945*. New York: Pantheon, 1973. (A series of interesting essays written from a revisionist bias.)

Bartz, Patricia, *South Korea*. Oxford: Oxford University Press, 1972. (A well organized and carefully prepared descriptive geography of South Korea.)

Bemis, Samuel Flagg, editor, *The American Secretaries of State and Their Diplomacy,* Volumes 7–17. New York: Pageant Book Co., 1958. (An excellent portrayal of the policies of Secretaries of State up to 1913 and the reasons for their actions or non-actions in Asia, including Korea. Especially significant are the American misinterpretations, deliberate or not, of the Chinese-Korean relationship.)

Berger, Carl, *Korea Knot: A Military Political History*. Philadelphia: University of Pennsylvania Press, 1957. (An introductory treatment).

Brown, Arthur J., *The Mastery of the Far East*. London: G. Bell and Sons Ltd., 1919. (The story of Korea's transformation and Japan's rise to supremacy in the orient.)

Caldwell, John C., *The Korea Story*. New York: Regnery, 1952. (Helpful background material on Korean politics and government.)

Cameron, Meribeth E., *China, Japan and the Powers*. New York: Ronald Press, 1960. (A history of international relations in modern East Asia).

Chien, Frederick Foo, *The Opening of Korea: A Study of Chinese Diplomacy, 1876–1885*. Hamden, Connecticut: Shoe String Press, Inc., 1967. (Originally written as a doctoral dissertation at Yale University. The title is misleading because Dr. Chien not only isolates the events connected with and conducive to the opening of Korea and is obviously mainly interested in Chinese diplomatic strategy, but he also treats numerous diplomatic activities of other nations involved at that time. There are many heretofore unknown incidents included. The author has also prepared an annotated bibliography.)

Cho, Soon-Song, *Korea in World Politics, 1940–1950*. Berkeley: University of California Press, 1967. (An evaluation of American responsibility.)

Chung, Kyung Cho, *Korea: The Third Republic*. New York: Macmillan, 1971. (In part I Chung presents Korean government origins, briefly touching on all aspects of history, from 2333 B. C. to the period after the military coup of 1961 through 1963. He treats in depth efforts to implement the Constitution as amended in 1962 and 1969; the functions of various branches of government; foreign relations; national security; development of democracy; and the need and desire for unification. Although rather emotionally presented, this work can be a useful tool for gaining insight into the workings of the Korean Third Republic.)

Clyde, Paul H., *The Far East*. New York: Prentice-Hall, 1971. (Informative treatment of the western impact on Asia and responses of eastern nations, including Korea.)

Cole, David C. and Lyman, Princeton N., *Korean Development: The Interplay of Politics and Economics*. Cambridge, Massachusetts: Harvard University Press, 1971. (An informed and readable survey of political and economic developments in South Korea with emphasis on the 1960's. Part I is a survey of political events; Part II, an analysis of the government's role in Korea's economic growth; Part III, a concluding evaluation of the government's role in the economy. Underlying the analysis is a sense of regret that the startlingly fast development of Korea's economy could not have been accompanied by a greater degree of liberalization in the political processes. This book should be required reading for understanding the various factors behind Korea's spectacular economic growth during the 1960's.)

Conroy, Hilary, *The Japanese Seizure of Korea, 1868–1910*. Philadelphia: University of Pennsylvania Press, 1960. (Useful background material. Based on Japanese sources.)

Fairbank, John King; Reischauer, Edwin O.; and Craig, Albert M., *East Asia: Tradition and Transformation*. Tokyo: Houghton Mifflin Co., 1973. (Updated and condensed contents of *East Asia: The Great Tradition*, 1960, and *East Asia: The Modern Transformation*, 1965. This book's treatment of Korea has sometimes been criticized as having a Japanese bias.)

Goodrich, Leland Matthew, *Korea: A Study of U.S. Policy in the United Nations*. New York: Council on Foreign Relations, 1956. (A thorough study which, however, gives little attention to internal developments in Korea.)

Hahm, Pyong-choon, *The Korean Political Tradition and Law*. Seoul: Royal Asiatic Society-Hollym Corporation, 1967. (A series of essays in which the author makes the basic point that the Korean legal superstructure, essentially European in character, is only tenuously related to Korean social and cultural realities. He contends that "the notion that a process of law, *due* or otherwise, is essential for the protection of life, liberty and property is simply not *Oriental*".)

Han, Sung Joo, *The Failure of Democracy in South Korea*. Berkeley: University of California Press, 1974. (Analysis of the collapse in 1961 of Chang Myŏn's Government and its subsequent effect on Korean politics.)

Henderson, Gregory, *Korea: The Politics of the Vortex*. Cambridge, Massachusetts: Harvard University Press, 1968. (A highly provocative work which treats Korean political history as the story of a greatly centralized and homogenous polity.)

Hong, Yi-Sup, *Korea's Self-Identity*. Seoul: Yonsei University Press, 1973. (Collection of essays by the author attempting to interpret ideas, movements and schools of thought which influenced the beginnings of modern Korea in the 18th century. He concludes with a treatment of the "characteristics of Korean nationalism".)

Hong, Sung Chick, *The Intellectual and Modernization: A Study of Korean Attitudes*. Seoul: Social Research Institute, Korea University, 1967. (Chapter five is a perceptive treatment of political development, with particular reference to intellectuals' attitudes about democracy and individual freedom.)

Hulbert, Homer B., *The Passing of Korea*. Seoul: Yonsei University Press, 1969. (A treatment of the Japanese takeover of Korea in the late 19th century. Originally published in 1906.)

Institute of East Asiatic Studies, *Korean Studies Guide*. Berkeley: University of California Press, 1954. (Bibliography of works in English, French and German. A supplement of Russian-language works was added in 1958.)

Jo, Yung-Hwan, editor, *Korea's Response to the West*. Kalamazoo, Michigan: Korea Research Publications, Inc., 1970. (A collection of essays on the subject by Korean and American scholars.)

Kim, C. I. Eugene, and Chee, Ch'angbok, editors, *Aspects of Social Change in Korea*. Kalamazoo, Michigan: Korea Research Publications, Inc., 1968. (A collection of essays on the subject by Korean and American scholars.)

Kim, C. I. Eugene, and Kim, Han Kyo, *Korea and the Politics of Imperialism: 1876-1910*. Berkeley: University of California Press, 1967. (The most comprehensive English language study yet of the subject during this period.)

Kim, Kwan-Bong, *Korea-Japan Crisis and the Instability of the Korean Political System*. New York: Praeger, 1971. (Description of Korean politics in the early 1960's, with particular focus on the question of normalization of diplomatic relations with Japan.)

Kim, Se-Jin, *Politics of Military Revolution in Korea*. Chapel Hill: University of North Carolina Press, 1971. (A well organized survey of military participation in recent Korean politics and a useful base for further and more detailed research on the subject.)

Kim, Se-Jin and, Cho Chang H., editors, *Government and Politics of Korea*. Silver Springs, Maryland: Research Institute on Korean Affairs, 1972. (A collection of essays on the subject, some of which contain perceptive and helpful interpretations. Includes a selected bibliography.)

Kim, Young C., *Major Powers and Korea*. Silver Springs, Maryland: Research Institute on Korean Affairs, 1973. (Papers delivered at a symposium in April 1972 on "The Major Powers in the Far East and Korea." Contents include essays on the policies of the Soviet Union, China, the United States, Japan, and North Korea toward the Republic of Korea, as well as one paper on South Korean policy toward North Korea. A concluding chapter by Young Whan Kihl delineates Korea's response to major power rapprochement.)

Korean Legal Center, *Laws of the Republic of Korea*. Seoul: Korean Legal Center, 1974. (A compilation through May 1974 including constitutional laws; administration laws; laws on judiciary;

civil codes; commercial codes; criminal codes; educational and social codes; economic codes, and tax codes.)
Lee, Chong Sik, *Politics of Korean Nationalism*. Berkeley: University of California Press, 1964. (A valuable historical treatment of the development of nationalism in Korea from 1894 on.)
Lee, Han-Been, *Korea: Time, Change and Administration* Honolulu: East-West Center Press, 1968. (A theoretical treatment of administration and bureaucracy as applied to developmental problems.)
Lee, Man-Gap and Barringer, Herbert, editors, *A City in Transition: Urbanization in Taegu, Korea*. Seoul: Hollym Corporation, 1971. (Prepared by the International Liaison Committee for Research on Korea and the Society for International Development. Contains chapters on urban administration and politics by Eugene C.I. Kim, In Joon Hwang and Edward Reynolds Wright.)
Linebarger, Paul M.,A.; Djang, Chu; and Burks, Ardath, *Far Eastern Governments and Politics*. New York: D. Van Nostrand Co., 1956. (An excellent base for understanding Chinese political concepts down to the 20th century and the effect that they had on Korean politics at various periods in history.)
McCune, George M.; and Grey, Arthur L., Jr., *Korea Today*. Cambridge, Massachusetts: Harvard University Press, 1950. (Extensive treatment of political events during the period 1945-1948. Also summarizes the history and economy of old Korea, as well as Korea as a Japanese colony).
McCune, George M., and Harrison, John A., editors, *Korean-American Relations: Documents Pertaining to the Far Eastern Diplomacy of the United States. Volume I, The Initial Period, 1883-1886*. Berkeley: University of California Press, 1951. (Documents pertaining to the East Asian diplomacy of the United States with an introduction by the editors. For the companion volume on later years, see Palmer, below.)
McKenzie, Frederick A., *The Tragedy of Korea*. Seoul: Yonsei University Press, 1969. (Reprinted from 1908 London edition) (Description of Japanese aggression before and after the signing of the Treaty of Protectorate and the struggle for restoration of Korean independence.)
McKenzie, Frederick A., *Korea's Fight for Freedom*. Seoul: Yonsei University Press, 1969. (Reprinted from 1920 London edition) (A chronology of the Japanese takeover of Korea and the early years of colonial rule. This book is essentially an impassioned plea for Korean independence. This and *The Tragedy of Korea*

provide informative, though admittedly biased, background material for understanding the modern period.)

McNelly, Theodore, editor, *Sources in Modern East Asian History and Politics.* New York: Appleton, 1967. (Especially deals with politics and government in Vietnam and Korea.)

Meade, E. Grant, *American Military Government in Korea.* New York: King's Crown Press, 1951. (The organization, techniques and functioning of the military from October 1945-October 1946 seen through its operation in the strategic South Korean province of Cholla Nam-do.)

Morley, James W., *Japan and Korea: America's Allies in the Pacific.* New York: Walker and Cox, 1964. (Useful as a basic introduction.)

Murphy, Jay, *Legal Profession in Korea.* Dobbs Ferry, New York: Oceana Publications, 1967. (An explication of the role of the legal profession in Korean society. Sponsored by the Korea Law Research Institute of Seoul National University.)

Nahm, Andrew C., editor, *Korea Under Japanese Colonial Rule.* Kalamazoo, Michigan: Western Michigan University Press, 1973. (Essays on the policies and techniques of Japanese colonialism. Sponsored by the Center for Korean Studies at Western Michigan University.)

Nelson, Frederick M., *Korea and the Old Orders of Eastern Asia.* Baton Rouge: Louisiana State University Press, 1946. (An attempt to clarify the Confucian, pre-western international system which shaped East Asian affairs before the coming of the West. Reviews Korea's legal status among other Asian nations to 1914.)

Oh, John Kie-Chiang, *Korea: Democracy on Trial.* Ithaca, New York: Cornell University Press, 1968. (Role of the United States in South Korea's attempts at democratization.)

Oliver, Robert T., *Syngman Rhee: The Man Behind the Myth.* New York: Dodd, 1954. (A sympathetic biography.)

Paige, Glenn D., *The Korean Decision, June 24–30, 1950.* New York: The Free Press, 1968. (A well-researched chronological account of the decision to enter United Nations troops into the Korean War.)

Palmer, Spencer J., *Korean-American Relations: Documents Pertaining to the Far Eastern Diplomacy of the United States. Volume II, The Period of Growing Influence, 1887–1895.* Berkeley: University of California Press, 1963. (Documents on the subject with an introduction by the editor. Also see McCune and Harrison, above, for the companion volume on earlier years.)

Pihl, Marshall R., editor, *Listening to Korea*. New York: Praeger, 1973. (Contents cover a variety of subjects, including some political commentaries.)

Reeve, W.D., *The Republic of Korea: A Political and Economic Study*. Oxford, England: Oxford University Press, 1963. (Deals with the history and development of Korea from independence to 1963. Tedious reading but highly informative.)

Shinn, Rinn-Sup and others, *Area Handbook for North Korea*. Washington: U.S. Government Printing Office, 1969. (Especially pertinent is the 38-page bibliography on Korea, north and south. This book compliments the *Area Handbook for the Republic of Korea*, listed above.)

Shulman, Frank J., *Japan and Korea: An Annotated Bibliography*. Ann Arbor, Michigan: University of Michigan Press, 1972. (Ph.D. dissertations in western languages written from 1877-1969.)

Sunoo, Harold H.W., *Korea: A Political History in Modern Times*. Columbia, Missouri: Korean-American Cultural Foundation; and Seoul: Konkuk University Press, 1971. (A historical synopsis followed by a detailed description of the period from the opening of Korea to liberation in 1945.)

Tewksbury, Donald G., *Source Materials on Korean Politics and Ideologies*. New York: Institute of Pacific Relations, 1950. (A selection of documents and basic source materials ranging from the "Korean reply to Japanese post-restoration proposal" in 1871 to the U.S. "White Paper" on the Korean crisis in 1950. Includes 82 documents, few of which particularly are related to "politics and ideologies," as such.)

U.S. Department of State, *A Historical Summary of United States-Korean Relations*. Washington: U.S. Government Printing Office, Department of State Publication 7446, Far Eastern Series 115, 1962. (This short volume includes a chronology of important developments from 1834-1962, with concentration on the period following World War II.)

U.S. Department of State, *The Record of Korean Unification: 1943-1960*. Washington: U.S. Government Printing Office, Department of State Publication 7084, Far Eastern Series 101, 1960. (A narrative summary with principal documents including those related to agreements of World War II; U.S.-Soviet negotiations on Korean unification from 1945-1947; early U.N. efforts at unification from 1947-1950; U.S. relations with the Republic of Korea,

1948–1950; the Korean War, 1950–1953; U.S.-Korean policy in the post-armistice period; the Korean phase of the Geneva Conference, April-June 1954; the Korean unification issue, 1954–1960.)

Vinacke, Harold, *A History of the Far East in Modern Times.* New York: Appleton-Century-Crofts, Inc., 1959. (Especially good treatment of Korea's role in the Russo-Japanese War. Covers the period to 1958.)

Weems, Benjamin, *Reform, Rebellion and the Heavenly Way.* Tucson: University of Arizona Press, 1964. (A detailed chronological description of Ch'ondogyo [*Religion of the Heavenly Way*] and its significance in the development of Korean Nationalism. Describes the part that this political-religious organization played in internal politics and the international relations of Korea from 1860 to 1950. Includes treatment of the Dong-hak Rebellion of 1894.)

INDEX

Acheson, Dean 20
Achŏn, 67
Almond, Gabriel A., 33
American Military Government: student activism during, 120-21; system of education under, 107
April 19 Revolution. *See* Student Revolution of April 1960
Asian Pacific Council (ASPAC), 204, 230-32, 311-12

Basic Law of 1961, 183
Berle, Adolf, 323
Buddhism: as declared religion of bureaucrats, 73; as one of foreign influences on education, 112
Bureaucracy: authority patterns in, 74-77; Chinese influence on, 15-16; general description of, 47, 80-83; policy formulation, 77-83; relation to National Assembly, 79-80; relation to political parties, 80-81; relation to press, 80; size, 72; social background of members, 73-74; structure of, 71-72; under Japanese regime, 17-18

Cairo Conference of 1943, 210
Central Election Management Committee, 97, 98
Central Intelligence Agency of the Republic of Korea (CIA): 186, 187, 188
Chae, Myŏng-sin, 191
Chang, To-yŏng, 181
Chang Myŏn Government: foreign policy, 216-19; general description, 25-29, 49, 63; relation to intellectuals, 119; relation to military, 171-74; relation to police, 170-71; relations with United Nations, 216-18; student activism during, 107-8, 124-26
Cheju rebellion, 163
Chiang Kai-shek, 99
China, 15-16, 109, 203, 209
Cho, Bong-am, 88, 89, 94, 169
Cho, Byong-ok, 88, 89, 169
Cho, Suk-choon, 47, 71
Ch'oe, Chu-chong, 185
Ch'oe, In-kyu, 94
Ch'oe, Yŏng-hŭi, 172
Ch'ŏn in, 291
Chŏng, Il-hyong, 217
Chŏng, Il-kwŏn, 233
Chosen, 210. *See also* Japan
Chosun Ilbo, 25
Citizens' Apartments, 5

Civil Rule Party (Minjŏng Dang), 183, 220, 224
Clark, Mark, 165, 166
Communist China. *See* People's Republic of China
Confucianism: influence on education, 107, 112–13, 146; influence on government and politics, 112; influence on student values, 146, 147; relation to the bureaucracy, 73, 74, 292–97; relationship to traditional society in general, 6, 292
Constituent Assembly of 1948, 19
Constitution: of 1948, 20, 21, 22, 49; of 1972, 261, 50–63, 357–83 (text)
Constitutional Amendments: of 1952 and 1954, 22; of 1958, 63; of 1960, 27, 53; of 1969, 108; of 1971 and 1972, 49–50
Communist China. *See* People's Republic of China
Court Organization Act of 1895, 57
Court Organization Act of 1948, 57
Court Reorganization Law of 1907, 57

Democracy, *Koreanized,* 32, 48, 101
Democratic Party, 24, 25–29. *See also* Chang Myŏn Government
Democratic People's Republic of Korea, 211
Democratic Republican Party, 30–32, 47, 86, 97–98, 101, 143, 182, 187. *See also* Park Government and New Democratic Party

Economic Development Council (EDC), 82
Economic Development Plans, 256–62
Economic Planning Board, 309
Eighth Graduation Class of Korea Military Academy, 173, 185
Eisenhower, Dwight D., 165, 214
Election practices, 92–99
Emergency Law on Special Customs Duty of 1961, 272–73
Emergency Measures of 1974, 32
Ewha Womans University, 132
Exports, 30–31, 245, 271–76

Geneva talks on Korean unification, 215–16
Green, Marshall, 180

Hahm, Pyong-choon, 5
Hallstein Doctrine, 203–4, 225–27
Harriman, Averell, 223
Henderson, Gregory, 27, 327–29
Hŏ, Chŏng, 25, 170, 171, 216
Hong, Sung Chick, 145
Hulbert, Homer B., 67

Index

IBRD (International Bank for Reconstruction and Development) Mission of 1969, 276
Intellectuals: role of in contemporary Korean society, 118-20
Interest groups, 23, 80
International Monetary Fund (IMF), 270, 273, 275
Iri, 270

Japan: colonial regime, 17-19, 210, 297-302; influence on education, 112-13; normalization treaty, 128, 247, 268; student attitudes toward, 109
Japan-Republic of Korea Relations. *See* Japan; Park Government; Rhee Government
Judiciary, 57-62. *See also* Constitution
June 10, 1926, Movement, 113

Kennedy, John F., 183
Kim, Ch'ang-yong, 168
Kim, Chong-p'il, 110, 173, 182, 186-88, 227
Kim, Chŏng-yŏl, 161, 170
Kim, Hong-il, 100
Kim, Hyŏng-uk, 188
Kim, Jun-yŏn, 224
Kim, Ku, 169
Kim, Kyu-t'aek, 95, 185
Kim, Tae-jung, 86, 89, 91, 99, 100
Kim, Tong-ha, 173, 185, 187
Kim, Yŏng-ju, 234
Kim, Young-sam, 100
Kim, Yun-hŭn, 185
Kim, Yun-kŭn, 187
Korean Democratic Party (KDP), 90-91
Korean National Youth Movement (KNY), 157-59
Korean question (in the United Nations), 216-19, 228-30
Korean War, 19-20, 110, 164, 166, 167, 213, 246
Korea Trade Promotion Corporation (KOTRA), 272
Korea University, 130, 131, 132
Kornhauser, William, 327
Kwangju Uprising of 1929, 113

Lee, Han-been, 185, 309
Lee, Hu-rak, 188, 234
Li, 6
Liberal Party, 24, 25, 27, 28, 53, 85, 91, 168, 169
Literacy rate, 118, 245, 248
Local Autonomy Law of 1949, 63

Local government, 63-68

MacArthur, Douglas, 214
McCune, George M., 17-18
Macgruder, Carter B., 180
March First Movement. (1919), 113
Martial Law: 1952, 22; 1960, 24, 123; 1972, 50
Masan, 122, 270
Military English Language Institute, 156
Military establishment: commitment in Vietnam, 191; history, 29-30, 154-69; professional personnel 192-93; rise to power, 109-10, 188-89
Military Junta. *See* Supreme Command for National Reconstruction
Military Revolution of 1961: ideology, 174-79; leadership of, 184-88. *See also* Supreme Command for National Reconstruction
Ministerial Meeting for Asian and Pacific Cooperation, 224. *See also* Asian Pacific Council
Mus, Paul, 6

National Assembly, 52-56. *See also* Constitution
National Conference for Unification, 50, 100
NATO Treaty, 233
Neo-Confucianism, 294-96
New Democratic Party (NDP): comparison with DRP, 91; finances, 98; formation, 28, 47; schism, 100; slogans, 86
New Village (*Saemaul*) Movement, 261
Nixon Doctrine, 225, 232
Normalization treaty between Korea and Japan, 1965, 127-28, 247, 268, 312
North Korea: provocations against Republic of Korea, 191-92; repatriation of overseas Koreans, 221-22; Soviet Russian support, 19-20; United Nations policy on, 226-28. *See also* Democratic People's Republic of Korea; Hallstein Doctrine; Korean War

October 1972 Revitalizing (*Yushin*) Reforms, 32, 50, 100
Oh, Byung-hun, 96

Pak, Im-hang, 185
P'anmunjŏm Armistice Agreement, 214-15
Park Government: land reform program of, 251; military role of in Vietnam, 191, 223-24; monetary policies of, 262-71; United Nations policy of, 219-20, 228-30. *See also* Constitution; Democratic Republican Party; Japan
Peace Preservation Corps of the Committee of Preparation for Korean Independence, 154-55
People's Republic of China, 231, 232

Index

Political culture: and political parties, 87; and voting behavior, 95–99
Political parties, 48, 85–92, 99–101. *See also* Democratic Republican Party, Election practices, New Democratic Party, Park Government, Rhee Government
Political Purification Law of 1961, 181
Portsmouth, Treaty of, 210
Powell, G. Bingham, 33
Pusan, 22, 53, 63

Republic of Korea: diplomatic recognition by United Nations and other countries, 211; founding of, 49, 90, 210
Republic of Korea War College, 186
Reunification. *See* Korean question (in the United Nations)
Revitalizing Reforms. *See* October 1972 Revitalizing (*Yushin*) Reforms
Rhee Government: educational system, 107; legitimacy of, 302–5; and the military, 159–68; political system, 11, 20–25, 90–91; relations with Japan, 220–23; student activism during, 121–26; and the United Nations, 27–28, 211–16
Rhee Line, 221–22
Ridgway, Matthew, 165
ROTC program, 134
Russo-Japanese War, 210

Sam Il Independence Movement. *See* March First Movement
Second Hague Conference of 1907, 210
Seoul, 4, 24, 63, 66, 127, 156
Seoul National University, 130, 132, 138, 139, 140
Seoul-Pusan expressway, 4
Seoul Shinmun, 24
Shils, Edward A., 101
Shimonoseki, treaty of, 209
Shin, Ik-hŭi, 89, 90, 94, 169
Sino-Japanese War, 209
Sŏ, Jae-p'il, 301
SOFA agreement (status of forces agreement with the United States), 128
Sŏk, Chŏng-sŏn, 173
Song, Yo-ch'an, 170, 181, 187
South-North Coordinating Committee, 204, 235
South-North joint communiqué, 234–35
South-North Korea Red Cross Talks, 204, 229, 233–35
Soviet Union, 13, 19–20, 212, 236–37
S.S. *Pueblo*, 192
Status of forces agreement with the United States, 128
Stevenson, Adlai, 218

Student Defense Corps, 121–22
Student demonstrations, 49, 108, 120–30
Student Revolution of April 1960, 11, 24, 25, 122–24, 169–70, 174, 178
Supreme Command for National Reconstruction: functions, 53; ideology, 29, 174–79; membership, 184–88

Taegu, 5, 7–8, 53, 63, 66
Tokto Island, 221–22
Truman, Harry S., 214

Ui Li, 224
UNCURK, 27, 28, 204, 228–30. *See also* United Nations Commission on Korea
Unification. *See* Korean question (in the United Nations)
United Nations Charter, 216, 218, 219
United Nations Commission on Korea, 211–12. *See also* UNCURK
United Nations General Assembly, 19, 27, 160, 211, 217, 220, 228–30
United Nations Security Council, 211, 213–14
United States: influence on Korean educational system, 107, 114; Korea Policy in 1948, 19, 211; military aid to South Korea, 20; opening of relations, 208–9; and Rhee Government, 24; status of forces agreement with Korea, 128. *See also* Park Government; Rhee Government
United States Armed Forces in Korea. *See* USAFIK
United States Military Advisory Group to the Republic of Korea (KMAG), 160–61
United States-Republic of Korea Mutual Defense Treaty, 167, 215–16, 233
United States-Republic of Korea Mutual Security Pact. *See* United States-Republic of Korea Mutual Defence Treaty
Urban Planning, 252–53
USAFIK (United States Armed Forces in Korea), 154, 155, 160

Weber, Max, 290, 303, 324
Weimar Constitution, 19
Wittfogel, K.A., 326–29
World Health Organization, 229

Yangban, 15, 290
Yi, Ch'ŏlsŏng, 100
Yi Chong-chan, 167
Yi, Chu-il, 185
Yi, Hyŏng-kŭn, 156
Yi, Ki-bung, 91, 169
Yi, Pŏm-sŏk, 157, 162
Yi, Si-yŏng, 88

Yi Dynasty: political authority structure, 294–97; political culture, 17, 348–55; political system, 14–17; social classes, 290–94
Yonsei University, 131, 132
Yoon, Chon-ju, 96
Yosu mutiny, 163
Yu, Chin-san, 100
Yu, Wŏn-sik, 187
Yujŏnghoe, 100
Yun, Po-sŏn, 25, 89, 180, 219, 223